CHARITY APPEALS

The Complete Guide to Success

Marion Allford

JM DENT
in association with
The Institute of Fundraising Managers

First published in the UK in 1993 by
J M DENT & SONS LTD
The Orion Publishing Group
Orion House
5 Upper St Martin's Lane
London WC2H 9EA
in association with
The Institute of Charity Fundraising Managers

ISBN 0460 861220 (hardcover)
ISBN 0460 861913 (paperback)

Printed in Great Britain by
Butler & Tanner Ltd,
Frome & London.

All those connected with this book would like to thank
the photographers and copyright owners who kindly
contributed their photographs for this publication.

ALL NET ROYALTIES HAVE BEEN DONATED TO GREAT
ORMOND STREET CHILDREN'S HOSPITAL FUND
(Registered Charity 235825)

To my mother

CONTENTS

Foreword by HRH The Prince of Wales... ix
Preface by The Rt. Hon. The Lord Prior P.C. xi
Business in the Community xiii
Acknowledgements... xiv
The Author xvi
Author's Note: How to use this book xvii

PART I: INTRODUCTION 1

 1 Introduction.. 3
 2 The Story of the Wishing Well Appeal... 6

PART II: PREPARATION 19

 3 Overview 21
 4 Project Research... 27
 5 Appeal Research... 41
 6 Leadership 51
 7 Appeal Strategy 67
 8 Marketing Strategy and Initial Documents 77
 9 Organization, Legal and Fiscal Aspects 88
10 Administration and Personnel 103

PART III: THE PRIVATE APPEAL 125

11 Overview 127
12 Marketing 131
13 Major Donors 136
14 The Business Appeal... 148
15 Administration and Personnel 158

PART IV: THE PUBLIC APPEAL 163

16 Overview 165
17 Marketing 169
18 Planning the Publicity Campaign 176
19 Advertising 191
20 Regional Groups 200
21 National Organizations 210
22 International Appeals 219
23 Trading 228
24 Commercial Partnerships 236
25 Managing Special Events 252
26 Risks and Rewards of Special Events 269
27 Publishing 283
28 Company Giving 290
29 Other Fund-raising Methods 300
30 Administration 312
31 Finale – Announcing the Achievement 321

PART V: SMALLER AND LOCAL APPEALS 329

32 How They Differ from the Large-Scale Appeal 331
33 Case Histories 345

PART VI: AFTERMATH 363

34 Reviewing Results and Future Planning 365
35 Epilogue 379

PART VII: APPENDICES 383

1   Organization Chart (Wishing Well Appeal) 385
2(a) Usual Methods of Giving 386
 (b) Tax Efficient Giving Examples 388
3   Gifts Guide and Gift Opportunities 390
4(a) Fund-raising Techniques – The Private Appeal 392
 (b) Fund-raising Techniques – The Public Appeal 393
5   A Sample Calendar for a £10m Target 395
6   Special Events Budget Sheet 397
7   Tax Implications of Special Events 399
8   The Charities Act 1992 406
9   Bibliography 419
10   Useful Addresses 423

Index 427

FOREWORD BY
HRH THE PRINCE OF WALES

KENSINGTON PALACE

As Patrons of the Wishing Well Appeal for Great Ormond Street Children's Hospital, my wife and I saw how successful a well planned charity appeal can be - particularly when the cause is so important and so close to many people's hearts. But major appeals don't just happen. An immense amount of hard work, careful research and detailed planning is required, together with creative marketing and a business-like approach from all concerned.

The Wishing Well Appeal was an outstanding success and I am delighted that the Director, Marion Allford, has found time to write a book based on her fundraising methods and experiences, and been able to publish it through the commitment and generosity of a number of sponsors. I am sure that this book will be a great asset to anyone setting out to raise funds for charity, and to the voluntary sector as a whole.

PREFACE

The Wishing Well Appeal was one of the most successful appeals ever launched in the United Kingdom. For all of us who took part, it was an emotional and very exceptional experience. We shall remember it with pride and affection. The quiet dignity of the children, the anxiety so stoically borne by parents and the skill and dedication of the staff ensured it could not have been otherwise. At the Press Conference called to announce the achievement of the target, I commented that helping to secure the future of the Hospital was perhaps the most rewarding experience of my public life.

You will not be surprised if I record here my pleasure that Marion Allford has written this book – a manual of advice for all fund-raisers, whether they are responsible for large capital appeals or smaller local versions. It incorporates detailed examples from a number of appeals, particularly the Wishing Well Appeal, but also other recent campaigns. Readers will gain a fascinating insight into the machinery of a large appeal. Others who were involved, in either a professional or voluntary role, will be reminded of the exhilaration and tension of a very productive period of their lives.

The voluntary sector as a whole will gain great benefit from this book. Its advice underlines the need for strategic planning and the use of professionals and illustrates methods for every type and size of appeal. It took a long time for professional fund-raisers to become accepted – the Victorian overtones of the word 'charity' meant that remuneration for helping a charity was perceived as somehow not in the British tradition. I am glad to say that this viewpoint is no longer valid – every charity simply deserves to have the best help, professional or voluntary, although great care and attention must be paid to the control of expenses, whether incurred by professionals or volunteers. Nothing does more harm than an appeal perceived to be extravagantly run.

Not every appeal requires professional full-time staff, but they benefit from professionalism in their methods. Where professionals and volunteers do mix, the opportunities for innovative and collaborative work seem to me greater than in any other form of enterprise. This book shows the reader how to make the best of all available resources.

As one of the voluntary sector's leading professionals, Marion Allford has raised funds and found donors to contribute to the costs of producing this book. She has not only shared her knowledge and extensive experience of capital appeals for the benefit of fellow fund-raisers, she has also given half of the time she has spent writing the book as her own voluntary contribution. In addition, she has requested that all the book's royalties should be paid to Great Ormond Street Children's Hospital in return for the use of the Wishing Well Appeal case history. In fact, with her wealth of fund-raising knowledge and the amount of time involved, Marion has undoubtedly been the major benefactor in making this book possible. Marion has, once again, shown those qualities of perseverance and flair, together with commitment to her cause, which have made her such an exceptional professional fund-raiser.

The Rt. Hon. Lord Prior P.C.

BUSINESS *in the* COMMUNITY

This book has been written with the support and financial assistance of Business in the Community and the encouragement of its President HRH The Prince of Wales.

Business in the Community (BITC) is the leading authority on the promotion of corporate community involvement. Its mission is to make community involvement a natural part of successful business practice and to increase the quality and extent of business involvement in the community.

BITC is an independent, not-for-profit organization, financed by contributions from over 400 member companies with special project funding from both the public and private sectors. Supported by a network of 11 regional offices, BITC's staff work closely with member companies to:

- promote business partnerships with local and central government, the voluntary sector and trade unions;
- collect and share examples of good practice;
- provide expert advice on developing and communicating community involvement programmes;
- achieve practical action by matching business resources with community needs;
- conduct a year-round programme of events to stimulate debate and develop new approaches in addressing community involvement issues.

This book contributes to the sharing of 'good practice' which will help to increase the understanding of partnerships between those in the private, public and voluntary sectors.

In addition to Business in the Community, a number of companies and charities have contributed to the costs of production.

ACKNOWLEDGEMENTS

I believe the best answers to any problem come from a collection of minds, correctly focused, rather than from one individual. My own knowledge and experience of appeals is as a general manager, pulling together advice and skills from a variety of specialists: lawyers, accountants, marketeers, business people and information technologists, as well as fund-raisers. So I have found myself using some of the same methods in producing this book. It has been very much a team effort, bringing together contributors of funds and of time.

My first thanks must go to Business in the Community, the not-for-profit organization which initially encouraged me to write this book and acted as the umbrella to this charitable endeavour.

But there would have been no book without financial backing. Sincere thanks are due to those who had faith in this project, recognized its value for the voluntary sector as a whole and helped to meet the costs. They are:

ITV Telethon – Telethon Training Initiative
Automotive and Financial Group Limited
BT, formerly British Telecommunications
Lex Service
Midland Bank
United Biscuits (U.K.)
Tesco
Servite Houses Charitable Trust
Earl Cadogan's Charity Trust
Charities Aid Foundation

I owe special gratitude to Alan Kilkenny, who assisted in innumerable ways.

The in-house team were: William Kay, who was invaluable in helping me to write and edit the book; Isobel Read, Sally Russell and Diana Payne, the secretaries who supported me so well during the writing process.

Particular thanks are due to my two key volunteers. These were Ken Connelly, who carried out some drafting and much of the research – I greatly valued his wise counsel and support throughout – and Jacqueline Page, who researched and managed the project during the latter stage. I owe them both a great deal for the considerable time and dedication they gave.

Due acknowledgement must go to the wide variety of experts and friends who have been consulted or helped this project in other ways. There are many more than can be mentioned here, but I would specifically like to thank:

Commander Richard Aylard, RN	Jules Kosky
Peter Bagnall	Charles Lubar
Tony Baxter	Roger Mitty
Bridget Cluley	Joyce Norden
Stuart Defries	Doreen Osborne
Nicholas DeLuca	Phil Rusted
Dr. Henry Drucker	Philip Sadler
John Farrell	John Salmon
Sue Holliday	Alison Stewart
Godfrey Jackson	Andrew Thomas
Peter Jenkins	Sir Anthony Tippet
Jane Kaufmann	James Tysoe
Melinda Kilkenny	Paddy Vincent
Dennis Kingshott	Jane Waldegrave
	David Williams

Special thanks go to the following, who looked over the book from the viewpoint of their respective special knowledge of the law, finance and general fund-raising:

Jonathan Burchfield and his colleagues in the Charity Group at Solicitors, Turner Kenneth Brown;

Pesh Framjee, partner in charge of the Charity Unit at Chartered Accountants, BDO Binder Hamlyn;

Giles Pegram, Appeals Director of the NSPCC, for sharing with me and the reader his wide experience of sophisticated fund-raising;

Stephen Lee, Director of the Institute of Charity Fundraising Managers, for advice, generally, but specifically on the implications for fund-raising of the new Charities Act 1992.

Although this book would not have been possible without the generous assistance of all these people, responsibility for error is entirely my own.

Marion Allford
London SW4
March 1993

THE AUTHOR

Marion Allford is a fund-raising consultant, specializing in charity appeals. From 1985 to 1989, as Director of the Wishing Well Appeal for the redevelopment of Great Ormond Street Children's Hospital, she developed the appeal strategy, managed its implementation, set up and ran the appeal office. The target, which rose from £30 to £42 million during the appeal, was achieved a year ahead of schedule. Eventually £54 million was raised from the public and £30 million from government.

A background in public relations and marketing ensured that Marion Allford was eminently well equipped for the world of fund-raising. She first moved into the charity field in 1973, when she started working for a development agency in Geneva. Since then, she has run and advised appeals for a variety of charities, including Help the Aged, The Guinness Trust and the Charing Cross Medical Research Centre.

Marion Allford is an honorary adviser to Great Ormond Street Children's Hospital, the Institute of Child Health and the Abbeyfield Development Trust. She is a Fellow and founder member of the Institute of Charity Fundraising Managers and a member of the Institute of Public Relations. This book brings together her expert knowledge of the charity field.

AUTHOR'S NOTE

This volume is primarily intended as a handbook for those contemplating a one-off capital appeal. I have written it in response to many requests from people in the charity field who have asked me to distil the lessons I learned from the Great Ormond Street Hospital Wishing Well Appeal and other fund-raising projects with which I have been involved.

The book is divided into seven parts – including one on smaller appeals – in the hope that, while keeping to a broadly chronological order, the material is easily accessible to readers who want to see what is said on any specific aspect of an appeal which interests them. Thus, it is not necessary to read right through the book, although I believe that doing so once will help by showing how all the elements fit together.

This publication flags up areas of especial relevance to a one-off appeal and therefore radically condenses many subjects which have warranted a book in their own right – hence the extensive Bibliography in Part VII. This Part also includes a list of useful contacts where additional help and information may be obtained.

Fund-raisers are concerned about the effects of the new Charities Act 1992 and are keen to know how it will work in practice. As a result this book includes, in Part VII, a special paper about the Act – as it affects those concerned with a one-off, capital appeal – split between legal, financial and fund-raising considerations.

Many readers will be women – we do, after all, play as much a part in the voluntary sector as men. However, in general references, I have utilized masculine pronouns and terms such as 'chairman' merely because it is editorially convenient to do so.

This book is intended to assist the many thousands of people who have a desire to do something worthwhile for an especially deserving group or cause within their community. The purpose is to provide an 'easy-read' so that it can be used both by the experienced fund-raiser – with a need to learn about the one-off capital appeal – and the less experienced volunteer who has taken on the task of running a local appeal. Organizing an appeal is an exciting task, as I can readily vouch, and immensely rewarding, but it can also be one of the most complex, perplexing and frustrating projects you will undertake. This book cannot promise to help you overcome all the problems you will encounter, but I hope that, by sharing a few of them, it will give you some ideas – and at least the comfort that you are by no means alone!

My aim has been to give a comprehensive overview of all that is encompassed when setting up and running a one-off capital appeal. Many legal and tax issues are raised but no attempt has been made to give precise advice applicable to any particular case. Such advice should be obtained from the appropriate experts. It is also important to remind the reader that laws and fiscal regulations constantly change. Therefore it is crucial to ensure that you receive up-to-date information from your advisers before committing yourself in any way.

I should add that this book is all about taking a professional approach to running a one off appeal. But what do I mean by the word professional? It seems to be a word which causes great misunderstandings and confusion. Perhaps this is not surprising when you check your dictionary and see that it lists eight different definitions. In essence, however, in today's usage of the word it has three main meanings:

- Payment for services
- Membership of a professional body
- High standards of skill and expertise

As far as the Charities Act 1992 is concerned, the term Professional Fund-raiser refers to the paid variety but the Act singles out independent or freelance fund-raisers. It excludes all fund-raisers who are charity employees; this is more than strange because all are paid and most strive to be 'professional' in their approach and are proud of it.

'Professional' will continue to be used for all three of the above meanings. I just want to clarify that where I refer to 'professional advice' I am alluding to expertise which has nothing to do with whether the individual is paid or a volunteer, just that he has a wide knowledge of the subject. By 'professional approach', once again, I do not mean remuneration; rather, I am referring to someone's commitment to be efficient, effective, conscientious and thoroughly dedicated to achieving the highest standards.

With charity appeals, volunteers are often highly-skilled professionals in their own disciplines or may be amateur fund-raisers who operate in a most proficient and effective way. I believe it is important to make this clear as the whole purpose of this book is to encourage all fund-raisers to do the best they can for their cause – in other words to aspire to the highest professional standards.

Marion Allford
London SW4
March 1993

Part I

INTRODUCTION

Chapter 1

INTRODUCTION

Mention the Wishing Well Appeal to many people in Britain, even now, and there is an immediate response. 'Ah yes,' people say, 'that was the charity that raised all that money for Great Ormond Street Hospital, wasn't it?' At a time when the public is constantly besieged by appeals, which themselves form only a small part of the flood of events flowing daily through our newspapers and televisions, it is remarkable that the Wishing Well Appeal name still evokes such a powerful reaction. The professional analyst might counter that it is no more than one ought to expect after all the publicity generated by the Appeal. But this response, I believe, begs the question of why there was so much coverage of this 14-month campaign.

It did not just happen because a team of marketing experts decreed it should, much though we appreciated the contribution from our marketing team. We could not have done it without the determined and dedicated effort of very many people: Royal Patrons, trustees, volunteers and Hospital and Appeal staff. But they could not have done what they did without the knowledge that they were campaigning on behalf of what is arguably the most vulnerable single category of people in our community. The Wishing Well Appeal produced so much publicity because it was appealing on behalf of a cause that tugs forcefully at nearly everyone's heartstrings – sick children.

I am only too well aware – having been involved with a wide range of different types of appeal – that few causes can rival this. Naturally, that made some aspects of our job easier. We did not have to spend as much time as might otherwise have been necessary explaining why we needed the £84 million which we eventually raised (including interest earned and statutory funds). However, it made other aspects of our task considerably more difficult. It was essential to prevent any publicity leakage during the prolonged initial private phase of the Appeal to ensure that we had the opportunity to obtain maximum revenue from substantial donors. Then, once the publicity floodgates were opened, people were so eager to come and help that preventing the Appeal from getting out of hand was a constant problem. Even so, we were able to close the Appeal nearly a year earlier than we had intended. That left many people with fund-raising events planned for which they were able to choose an alternative cause if they wished.

No one-off appeal is easy to manage, whether your target is thousands or millions of pounds. Charity is such an emotive subject that it can easily go wrong, for reasons which seem random or even unfair at the time. Nevertheless, problems can be avoided if you have the benefit of experience.

Charity is big business and, despite recent recessions, it is still growing. Brilliantly successful media appeals, such as Band Aid, Children in Need, ITV Telethon and Comic Relief have helped to establish the concept of a caring society. They have enlarged the constituency of donors by drawing in that large young section of the population which had not been approached before, at least not in such a direct manner. At the same time companies, appalled by the social unrest of the early 1980s, have seen that it makes excellent business sense for them, too, to present a more caring face. Large companies in Britain and in the United States have instigated a wide range of charitable projects, as well as community programmes of urban renewal, training for jobs in inner cities, education/business partnerships, help for the homeless and so on. They have done this in a variety of ways – through sponsorship, secondment, training, purchasing policies, customer involvement, employee fund-raising and straightforward giving. From the management's point of view an idealistic partnership of stakeholders in the community is created, comprising customers, employees, suppliers, shareholders and the community at large – which works to the benefit of them all. Also, employee volunteering is part of a wider movement to encourage people to contribute their skills to voluntary organizations – on a regular or a one-off, project-by-project basis.

THE ONE-OFF APPEAL

I have chosen to focus on one highly specialized aspect of charitable activity. There is a great difference between the organization and management of an ongoing fund-raising operation and that of a one-off appeal. The ongoing campaign has the luxury of plenty of time to establish its public image, to construct long-term relationships and to develop activities that benefit from regular repetition. They can also have capital appeals. None of these benefits is available to the organizer of the one-off appeal, at least not to anything like the same extent. Time is at a premium if momentum is to be generated and maintained. Long-term donations, such as legacies, can form only a small part of the revenue an appeal expects to raise. At root, people – rich or poor, spending their own pocket money or a multi-million pound budget – have to be persuaded to hand over money. There are many ways to achieve this, as I will explain later, but, in the end, they all rely on inspiring would-be donors to feel that they must do something about the cause you are propagating. That in itself heightens and sharpens the decision-making process. Ideas, initiatives, plans, arrangements, networking and meetings are the stock-in-trade of the one-off appeal. Certainly, these elements should be brought to bear on an ongoing charity's development strategy, but a short-term appeal's sense of urgency is that much greater because time is so much scarcer and the room for mistakes so much less.

Apart from an increased availability of skilled managers, launching an appeal during a recession is not something to do lightly. Although the Wishing Well Appeal closed before the recession really hit the business world, our public appeal was launched a week after 'Black Monday', when the London stock market crashed on the 19 October, 1987. For those who have launched such an appeal during this time, it is worth noting that the same fund-raising principles apply. I am thinking particularly of two recent successes – the Royal Marsden Hospital Cancer Appeal for £25 million, and The Sick Kids Appeal on behalf of the Royal Hospital for Sick Children, Edinburgh, for £11 million. Both used the strategy and methods described in this book and both received considerable advice and guidance from the Wishing Well Appeal team – as they generously acknowledge. (Further information on these appeals is given in Chapter 34.)

The Wishing Well Appeal raised money for the redevelopment of Great Ormond Street Children's Hospital and was essentially a building appeal. Many appeals are; it is the natural way to raise a capital sum relatively quickly. However, it is by no means the only type of cause suitable for a one-off appeal. The principles can easily be adapted to any other type of appeal: to fund a pool of nurses for home visits, to raise money for chairs at a medical institution or university, or even to pay for an expensive piece of equipment. All are equally worthy. All can be achieved through an appeal. The issues discussed in this book are applicable to them all.

Having received a successful response to an appeal, a charity can benefit the whole community if it takes the trouble to share the knowledge it has gained. Great Ormond Street Children's Hospital is doing just that by making its archives available to me and the readers of this book. It is regrettable that there are not more detailed case histories available to would-be appeal organizers. However, a step towards remedying this has been taken by the magazine *Professional Fundraising*, which is introducing a scheme of awards to be given, on the basis of case histories submitted to a panel of judges, to campaigns which have been particularly successful or innovative.

I hope my experience – with the Wishing Well and other appeals – will help the growing band of dedicated people with responsibilities within appeals, as well as those visionaries whose desire for a better world is the inspiration that generates appeals in the first place.

Chapter 2

THE STORY OF THE WISHING WELL APPEAL

On Tuesday, 27 October, 1987, HRH The Prince of Wales, via a specially set up satellite link from his home in Gloucestershire, told a gathering of journalists at Great Ormond Street Children's Hospital in central London:

> *Great Ormond Street offers a symbol of hope to many children and their parents who know that miracles can be and are performed there daily. But the whole future of this wonderful hospital is in jeopardy because of extremely outdated and inadequate buildings and facilities. In fact, it is amazing that the doctors and nurses still manage to perform so well, working as they do in such stressful and difficult conditions. This cannot continue.*

It was a firm and confident beginning, setting the tone for what was to prove a record-breaking fund-raising campaign. It was to generate £84 million, including government funding, and reveal what a deep seam of goodwill there is among British people when they are asked to contribute towards something as important as children's health.

The following morning, every national newspaper reported the launch, including the personal message from His Royal Highness. It was later calculated that news of the Appeal's progress appeared in a newspaper or other publication on nearly every day for the rest of the Appeal. It was the fund-raising event of 1988. Thousands of people gave up their time to persuade thousands of others to contribute everything from pocket money to what most of us would count as considerable fortunes.

On Thursday, 29 June, 1989 – 611 days after the public appeal had begun – Jonathan Dimbleby, the television presenter, took the floor. He was not addressing a press conference, but guests attending a reception following the Appeal's Service of Thanksgiving at Westminster Abbey, which was graciously attended by the Prince and Princess of Wales. These guests included people involved with the Hospital and supporters from Britain and abroad who had worked to make the Appeal such a success. He spoke personally and movingly.

> *I'm going to talk as a parent, I hope on behalf of a great many parents, about what it is to be a Great Ormond Street parent. To express some of their feelings and some of*

their gratitude, because I have shared with them and with my wife that curious mixture of alarm and dismay, combined with relief on being told your child is being referred to Great Ormond Street. Your precious child, needing to go to what is known to be the most famous children's hospital in the world. Dismayed because you are under no illusion — it's serious, it's very serious and the case needs the very best care that is possible. And then the relief: the relief that your child will have the very best care that there is. So you arrive, your child at that stage probably, sometimes frequently, too young to know what is going on but over the years they discover and they know the hospital and you're embraced by the nurses, by the orderlies, by the doctors, by the specialists. You're embraced by their expertise and by their compassion, and you place your trust in them.

In that brief statement, Jonathan Dimbleby encapsulated the feelings that parents have had since they began bringing their children to Great Ormond Street in 1852. He struck at the heart of the reason for the Appeal's enormous success: it is an ordeal that no parent wants to undergo and, therefore, everyone wants the best for the 80,000 cases that are handled there each year. Each one involves a child in need.

THE HISTORY OF THE HOSPITAL

Like many other acts of philanthropy in the 19th century, the origins of Great Ormond Street lie in the determination of one person, driven by a sense of futility and injustice. In this case it was Dr. Charles West. Brought up in Amersham, Buckinghamshire, he left school and became an apothecary's apprentice. In 1839 he was attached to the Royal University Infirmary for Children in Waterloo Road, London. He was sufficiently interested in the plight of his charges to visit them at home, a practice that was not unprecedented but still rare. He was so incensed by what he saw that he became determined to found a children's hospital where he could ensure that the highest standards of care were observed and that those standards would be continually raised by fresh scientific discoveries.

Early days

There had been previous attempts to care for children. It could hardly be otherwise in the face of a mortality rate which hit 74 per cent of under-fives at the height of London's gin-drinking fever in the mid-18th century. Christ's Hospital School had been built in 1552, originally with children in mind. In 1686 Sir Thomas Rowe established a 'Colledg of Infants' to take care of parish children under the patronage of the Middlesex Sessions, rather than boarding them out with nurses.

Workhouses spread after an Act of Parliament of 1772 allowed small parishes to combine and build 'Union Workhouses' for the 'unemployed and indigent' poor. At a time when mothers sometimes stripped their children and sold their clothes to buy gin – to quieten the children and get themselves drunk – the workhouses did nothing to safeguard children's health. One observer noted in 1768: *The parish infant poor's mortality may be called 80 or 90, or if you please, upon those received under 12 months old, 99 per cent.*

A short walk to the north of Great Ormond Street is Coram's Fields, the site of the Foundling Hospital. Thomas Coram, a sea captain, was so moved by the sight of abandoned infants that he undertook an appeal for funds to build a hospital which would take newborn infants and care for them until they were old enough to be apprenticed. The hospital became a haven for stray children. He opened under government charter in 1745 and effected an improvement in the survival rate, although it remained shocking. Of 1,384 children admitted in the Foundling Hospital's first 11 years, only 724 died, according to Jonas Hanway, one of the governors. From 1756 to 1760 the government paid for all children brought to its doors to be admitted. The hospital was besieged. Out of 14,934 children admitted in that period, only 4,400 survived long enough to be apprenticed. The scheme ended amid accusations that it encouraged immorality and irresponsibility towards children. Parliament continued to pay for those who had already been accepted by the hospital, but it gradually became a private charity once more.

Nevertheless, Coram's philanthropy raised the consciousness of influential people of the plight of poor children. In 1750 Dr. Cadogan wrote *An Essay on the Nursing and Management of Children*, which ran to 20 editions before the decade was out. The Foundling Hospital adopted his principles of loose clothing and simple diet, and in 1754 Cadogan became the Foundling's physician.

Not far to the south of Great Ormond Street, in Red Lion Square, the dispensary movement 'for the Relief of the Infant Poor' began. The idea was to create centres where the poor could obtain advice and free medicine. Adding to Cadogan's work, the dispensaries helped both the poor and the medical profession to get to grips with problems of hygiene and disease. Doctors, in turn, passed on their discoveries to those in local and national government.

In the mid-19th century, the French scientist Louis Pasteur made discoveries about the nature of micro-organisms, which led to new developments in the treatment and prevention of disease. Unfortunately, this initially worked against the interests of children as most hospitals excluded them on the grounds that their presence might increase the risk of infection. In 1843, only 26 out of 2,363 patients in London's hospitals were children under the age of ten. These first years are now recognized as the most critical period of anyone's life from the point of view of health. Yet in 1850, an appalling 21,000 children died in London, more than 40 per cent of the capital's total death toll. This scandal was to inspire Dr. Charles West to found Great Ormond Street Hospital for Sick Children.

Great Ormond Street Hospital

West had studied medicine in Paris in 1836. There, he visited L'Hôpital des Enfants Malades, which had been converted in 1802 from an orphanage to the first true children's hospital in Europe. However, the level of complacency about children's health in London was so great that it took West more than ten years to find the right support and to raise the funds necessary to start a children's hospital. He faced opposition from local doctors who saw his scheme as taking income away from them. Luckily, he had befriended the influential Dr. (later Sir) Henry Bence Jones, who persuaded a galaxy of wealthy and intellectual figures to form the hospital's first provisional committee. Public attitudes to the plight of poor children had become more sympathetic, partly through the popularity of the stories of Charles Dickens, particularly *Oliver Twist*, and the committee raised the £249 conversion cost and £200 annual rent to convert 49 Great Ormond Street in Bloomsbury, the former house of Dr. Mead, Physician to Queen Anne.

It was a propitious choice. Apart from the proximity of Red Lion Square and Coram's Fields, Great Ormond Street leads into Queen Square which became – and still is – the centre for several hospitals and medical institutions. It was also surrounded by a catchment area of slums and alleyways, breeding grounds for disease. A small out-patient department and a humble 20 cots formed the Hospital for Sick Children when it opened on 14 February, 1852. Three days passed before the first young patient stepped over the threshold.

West and his colleagues were not content simply to treat those who came their way; they were also aware of the possible implications of their venture for public health policy. They laid down three objectives:

- To provide for the reception, maintenance and medical treatment of the children of the poor during sickness and to furnish their parents with advice.
- To promote the advancement of medical science generally, with reference to the diseases of children, and particularly to provide more efficient instruction to students in this discipline.
- To spread greater understanding of the management of infants and children during illness among all classes of the community, by employing it as a school for educating and training women in the special duties of children's nursing.

It is a tribute to West's foresight that all three of these aims have been fulfilled, and continue to be so with the help of the Institute of Child Health and the School of Nursing, all on the same island site as the Hospital.

Royal Patrons and prominent supporters

Other traditions were established early. After only a few years, the royal, the prominent and the famous were anxious to associate themselves with the Hospital. Queen Victoria donated £100 a few months after the Hospital opened and became the first Patron, the great philanthropist Lord Shaftesbury was its President, and Charles Dickens was an enthusiastic fund-raiser. Children feature strongly in his novels. In his periodical *Household Words*, he wrote: *Of all the coffins that are made in London, more than one in every three is made for a little child.* He then called attention to Great Ormond Street, which had opened just six weeks earlier. The money required to buy the adjoining house, number 48, was forthcoming only after an appeal made by Dickens as the host of a Festival Dinner in 1858. His eloquent speech raised £3,000, which became a long-lasting fund-raising record. He raised still more money by giving readings of his famous story *A Christmas Carol*.

In 1870 the Prince of Wales launched an appeal for funds to finance the building of Great Ormond Street's Garden Hospital, which was to hold 120 beds and a chapel. Two years later, the Princess of Wales laid the foundation stone for the extension, and in 1878 the School for the Training of Paediatric Nurses began. Throughout Britain, the British Empire and North America, specialist children's hospitals were being founded with the help of doctors and nurses either trained at Great Ormond Street or stimulated by its example.

The Hospital's tradition of literary supporters reached a new peak in 1929 when J. M. Barrie decided to turn over to Great Ormond Street the royalties from his chil-

Children Calling

Mr. Punch. "It's getting taller every day, but we need more help from kind friends to finish it."

When fund-raising, it helps to involve prominent personalities. Eminent names – such as Charles Dickens, JM Barrie and even Mr Punch – were recruited to assist in previous Great Ormond Street redevelopment appeals.

dren's entertainment *Peter Pan*. The royalties have continued to flow unabated since Barrie's death in 1937. They were due to stop in 1988, when the copyright would have expired, but Lord Callaghan, the former Prime Minister, successfully promoted a change in the law to perpetuate them.

Other prominent personalities came forward with help when the Hospital embarked on major reconstruction in the 1930s. Authors J. B. Priestley, John Masefield and Vita Sackville-West wrote in support of the fund-raising effort, and in October 1938, King George VI and Queen Elizabeth opened the newly completed main Hospital block.

World War II and after

During the war Great Ormond Street became a casualty clearing station while centres for the care of sick children were organized at Hemel Hempstead and Watford in Hertfordshire, and Haywards Heath, Sussex. The Hospital still received emergency cases.

The war stopped all building at the Hospital. In September 1940 a bomb penetrated the two upper floors of the Surgical Wing, badly damaging it. Fortunately, no one was injured. Another bomb fell in nearby Guilford Street and shattered the water main, flooding the basement and boiler room of the Hospital to a depth of nearly five metres. The engineer on duty, with great bravery, stayed in the rising water and shut down the boilers, preventing much greater damage. He was awarded the George Medal.

The Hospital was very fortunate that Lord Southwood had become Chairman of the Board in 1939. Thanks to his dedication and energy, plus his organizational and financial skills, the Hospital was led with vision, courage – and financial success. In 1948, two years after his death, the Southwood Fund amounted to well over £1 million.

Following the creation of the National Health Service in 1948, the Hospital was designated a postgraduate teaching hospital. Management was transferred to a board of governors, who were to be appointed by the Ministry of Health. The Ministry underwrote running costs, while the board retained endowments.

Princess Mary, the Princess Royal, who had trained in nursing at the Hospital and worked there during the war, named the main block The Southwood Building in 1946. In 1952, the Hospital's centenary year, she laid the foundation stone for the new out-patients' building. A new building for the School of Nursing followed in 1960, and another for the Institute of Child Health was opened in Guilford Street five years later. The historical circle was completed in 1969 when the Institute opened its Wolfson Centre in Coram's Fields, on part of the site of the old Foundling Hospital. The Centre works with the Institute to assess children's disabilities.

A year earlier, the Queen Elizabeth Hospital for Children in Hackney Road, East London, and its associated hospitals were transferred to the control of the Board of Governors of the Hospital for Sick Children. Apart from adding 272 beds to the total, the Queen Elizabeth group also included a casualty department. This provided an access to hospital care which has continued to be of importance to the local community. The Queen Elizabeth Hospital complements the work at the Great Ormond Street Hospital so that together they can deal with the whole range of children's illnesses and disabilities. Nurses train in both Hospitals, which provide an unequalled base for experience in all children's conditions.

THE APPEAL

Great Ormond Street was a pioneer of the concept of total family care, encouraging parents to live in the Hospital with their children. This increased the strain on already outdated and inadequate buildings, so in 1983, the Board of Governors and Special Trustees began to discuss an Appeal. Straitened finances had caused the Governors to consider selling Tadworth, the Hospital's convalescent home near Leatherhead, Surrey. This provoked strong opposition and local people joined parents of Great Ormond Street patients and staff to form the Tadworth Action Group. Eventually, Tadworth Court became an independent charitable trust with a grant from the government.

Against this background in October 1987, Jonathan Dimbleby unveiled the logo of the child's face smiling through a tear. Then he introduced the media to some of the key figures at Great Ormond Street: Caroline Bond, Chairman of the Hospital's Board of Governors, Professor Martin Barratt, Professor of Paediatric Nephrology at the Institute of Child Health, Betty Barchard, the Hospital's Chief Nursing Officer, and Sir Anthony Tippet, the General Manager. They were followed by Jim Prior, Chairman of the Wishing Well Appeal, who became Lord Prior of Brampton that same month, whose role in the Appeal was supported by five panels, dealing with Commerce and Industry, the City, Overseas, Marketing, and Special Events. These panels all played an important part in approaching major donors.

Even before the launch, the 12-strong Appeal staff were being helped by more than 50 volunteers, each donating two or three days a week. They were being trained for the onslaught that would follow the launch, to answer telephones and dispatch thousands of 'thank you' letters from a converted basement of the Appeal Office at 49 Great Ormond Street. For the first three months, however, all the letters were opened by Midland Bank – who banked and acknowledged the donations as part of their contribution to the Appeal.

The Armed Forces, Police, Fire Service, Scout and Guide Movements, Women's Institutes, Youth Clubs, Rotary Club, Lions Club International and many other organizations were approached with requests to adopt the Appeal as their charity of the year. The Federation of Army Wives was one that did so, raising £26,000. So did the WRNS. The Metropolitan Police raised £300,000, including £25,000 from their fingerprint department, and £20,000 from the Met's golfers. The London Fire Brigade rattled the collection bucket to such effect that they poured £150,000 into the Appeal.

To reinforce the nationwide coverage of the Appeal, parents of former patients (with their consultants' agreement) received a letter telling them about it and giving them an address and telephone number to use if they wanted to get involved. More than 90 volunteers were asked if they would be Regional Chairmen, to direct and coordinate the efforts of individuals and groups all over the U.K. They were responsible for counties and London boroughs.

Two days after the official launch, the Variety Club of Great Britain unwrapped their initiative with a huge fanfare at the London Zoo. Debenhams and Allders stores gave £1 for every bear sold during the forthcoming Christmas period. Allders' Jingle Bear raised £100,000 that first Christmas. A year later Jingle Bear was joined by a glove puppet version; the two raised a total of £250,000.

Within five weeks, in December 1987, the total reached £10.7 million, including the £9.5 million already pledged before the launch. The initial publicity produced a flood of money through the post: one day the Midland Bank received more than 2,000 letters.

Boy George, Hazel O'Connor, Grace Kennedy and many other stars recorded a song, *The Wishing Well*, which climbed into the charts.

The *Sun* newspaper launched a 'Dash for Cash' project, which raised nearly £400,000. Readers telephoned the paper every day for a week to hear a Wishing Well message and answer a question posed by an actor impersonating a well-known personality. They opened the campaign with a two-page feature and kept the Appeal in front of readers week by week for the next six months with stories of how people were raising money.

On 3 December, the Princess of Wales visited the Hospital, handing the children presents donated by the Variety Club of Great Britain. Meanwhile Jimmy Tarbuck, the television personality, played Father Christmas on a sleigh drawn by white ponies. It gave newspapers the perfect photo opportunity – of which they took full advantage.

At the end of December, once the Christmas festivities were over, the BBC transmitted a moving documentary, *A Fighting Chance*. This did an enormous amount to focus public attention on the Appeal by conveying the joyful and caring atmosphere at Great Ormond Street, as well as the sadness. It was skilfully presented by Martyn Lewis. So moved and committed was the producer, Terence O'Reilly, that he arranged to put the Appeal's name and address on screen at the end. The telephones were jammed before the credits had stopped rolling. On a quieter level, the ITV series *The Bill* discreetly kept the Wishing Well logo in front of people's eyes by continually featuring it on posters and collecting boxes appearing in the background.

By the start of 1988, the touch paper was burning. Sales promotion companies were coming to the Wishing Well office asking to be involved. Wendy Wools, which has had a long association with James Barrie and even has a Peter Pan brand, made a small donation for every knitting wool band returned.

A televised Royal Gala in Southampton was organized by TVS, the independent television franchise holder at that time for the south of England. The Prince of Wales attended, and it featured such stars as Alfred Marks, Robert Hardy, Leslie Crowther, Paul Nicholas and Bonnie Langford. The chairman of the Gala was Isobel Gatward, whose husband, James, headed TVS and was co-chairman of the Appeal's Special Events Panel.

February produced £2 million. The United Biscuits Penguin Swimathon was held in pools all over London. It was started by the Princess of Wales at the Queen Mother Sports Centre near Victoria Station. The 5,500 swimmers raised £689,000, putting the event in the *Guinness Book of Records* as the most financially successful sponsored swim.

In May, the Appeal received publicity it would have preferred not to have happened. Prince Harry, younger son of the Prince and Princess of Wales, was rushed into Great Ormond Street for an emergency hernia operation. Nevertheless, it

The involvement of the entertainment industry always helps an appeal to 'hit the headlines'. Boy George, Grace Kennedy and Hazel O'Connor were among the top rock and pop stars who responded to MBS Record's call for volunteers to help make a record for the children of Great Ormond Street. More than 150 musical volunteers gathered at a West End Studio to record the song which was called 'The Wishing Well'. The result was an instant success in the music charts as well as in fund-raising terms – it raised £100,000 for the Appeal.

resulted in more valuable acres of newsprint. Like thousands of other mothers, the Princess stayed overnight to be near her son's bedside.

In June 1988, Boris Becker, Pat Cash, Henri Leconte and Stefan Edberg were among tennis stars to play an exhibition match in front of a black-tie audience at the David Lloyd Slazenger Racquet Centre at Hounslow, Middlesex. The event was sponsored by Fosters Lager. The Princess of Wales attended, as well as stars such as Cliff Richard and David Frost. A Michael Jackson concert, shared with the Prince's Trust, added £100,000 and gave the star the excuse to visit the Hospital. After much pleading, for he is notoriously reluctant to be photographed off-stage, he agreed to allow one photographer within range as he toured. The resulting picture hit every front page.

Athletes Sebastian Coe and Steve Cram raced round the Great Court of Trinity College, Cambridge, in a re-enactment of the famous scene from the film *Chariots of Fire*. Coe won. So did the Appeal; it gained £50,000.

In July 1988 the Appeal had to make an agonizing decision – to increase the target sum. Some £20 million had been contributed, but the organizers were confronted by irrefutable estimates showing that the cost of clearing the way for and building the new five-storey block would be £72 million rather than the £50 million originally thought. The government increased its contribution from £20 million to £30 million, but that still left an additional £22 million to be found.

Appeal Chairman Jim Prior admitted: *It is wonderful that fund-raising is going so well, but it is disappointing that we have had to raise our target. We always recognized that certain elements of the costings were provisional, but the increase in building costs in the south-east has outpaced even the significant allowance we made for building inflation.*

Nevertheless, the fund-raising effort had gathered such momentum that the money continued to flow in. Jim Prior issued a rallying call at the Mansion House in September: *It's one hell of a chunk still to raise, so I beseech you please to keep running, keep swimming and cycling, keep slimming, keep shaving your heads and keep fund-raising for the Wishing Well Appeal so we can ensure a secure future for this world-famous children's hospital.*

Commercial sponsorship played a valuable part in raising money and keeping the Appeal in the public eye. Hula Hoops and Skips snacks, Comfort Fabric Softener, Volvo, W. H. Smith, Mars and many others launched promotional campaigns that involved donations to the Appeal. The Appeal's teardrop logo appeared on 40 million Mars bars as well as innumerable sweatshirts, T-shirts, mugs and greetings cards. Jim Prior was so keen to do his bit by consuming as many Mars bars as possible that he then raised more money by taking part in a sponsored slim called the Fat Cats' Diet!

Support from children was overwhelming. A 10-year-old girl organized a sponsored bike ride. Eight-year-old Sarah Older, suffering from muscular atrophy, rode her pony, Oliver, from her home in Hampshire to London. A 16-year-old ex-patient cycled 200 miles. Matthew Norman, aged 11, had a sponsored kick at Ipswich Town Football Club. Nicola Street, aged 10, from Croydon in Surrey, ran 15 miles in four and a half hours. Jo Penny, 14, from Dunstable, Bedfordshire, had a sponsored dressing session; she put on 125 items of clothing, including 14 pairs of knickers. A little girl sent her 12p pocket money in an unstamped envelope. It was simply addressed 'To Great Ormond' and signed 'Love Sarah XX'. Lora and

Despite appeal organizers' entreaties for caution, some of the most ambitious charity supporters do deeds that are desperate, daring and downright dangerous, to raise funds. Above, grandmother Jessica Stone celebrated her 80th birthday by freefall parachuting from 12,500 feet, raising £1,500 for the Appeal. Just as intrepid were a group of Great Ormond Street nurses (below) who kidnapped Lord Prior off his plane at Heathrow and held him to ransom in aid of the Appeal.

Amy Clemance and Alex and Daniel Whyke of West Hoathly, Sussex, held a 150-minute sponsored silence.

It was not just a children's appeal. Everyone seemed to want to join in – including a librarian at the *Financial Times* who stood astride the wings of a Tiger Moth for a flight I bet she will not forget in a hurry! Another sponsor who took to the air celebrated her 80th birthday with a free-fall parachute jump. Some were carried away by their own enthusiasm, such as the man who streaked in front of the Queen at Epsom race course on Derby Day. He was fined, but he also raised money for the Wishing Well. The magistrate said, *There are other means of raising money for charity without breaking the criminal law.* The streaker wrote to the Queen to apologize.

Less controversially, but more welcome, was the contribution of a father whose child had been saved by the Hospital. He organized a vintage car auction at Brocket Hall in Hertfordshire, featuring 11 cars and held by Christie's. This parent, who wished to remain anonymous, donated two Lamborghinis for the televised sale, which raised a total of £561,759.

The International Appeal was launched in April 1988, six months after the U.K. Public Appeal began. Once again, the Prince and Princess of Wales got the momentum going with a reception at Kensington Palace. Diplomats' spouses and the directors of companies with activities abroad gave valuable support.

In December 1988 the Appeal received £130,000 from the Royal Premiere of the film *Willow* at the Empire Cinema, Leicester Square, matched by receipts from the final night of Cliff Richard's 30th Anniversary Concert Tour at the Hammersmith Odeon. That month the Appeal reached £30 million – its original target – after counting pledges (money raised but not yet received) and forthcoming events. To keep faith with the public, we announced that this meant the Appeal would reach its new £42 million target much earlier than anticipated.

On 11 January, 1989, we declared that the target had been struck, thanks to major fund-raising events in December, and an overwhelming response by the public over the Christmas period. Cash received totalled £34.6 million, and we had covenants of £1.1 million, and £6.7 million in pledges. Jim Prior said: *From today, no new fund-raising initiatives will be instigated by the Wishing Well Appeal office and the Appeal will wind down its activities. However, many of our regional supporters have already planned events for the coming months and we very much hope that they will continue with them. We hope funds raised from planned events can be shared with local hospitals or with another charity, if that is the wish of the organizers.*

The money kept rolling in until a staggering £54 million (excluding government funds) had been received. Typical was the magazine *Woman's Realm*, which in April presented the Appeal with £110,091 after a year of competitions, a Fun Run, a celebrity draw and a series of stories about children who had been treated at the Hospital.

We succeeded, said Lord Prior, *by making it a highly professional appeal. By making known our commitment to build the best children's hospital, on time and to exacting specifications. Only by setting out specific targets in this way could we convince people that we were serious and that this was an appeal worth supporting.*

The formal finale to the Wishing Well Appeal was the Service of Thanksgiving at Westminster Abbey on 29 June, 1989. It was attended by the Prince and Princess of Wales and as many of those involved with the Appeal as we could fit into the

Abbey. After a campaign that had lasted four years as far as I was concerned, the real impact of the Appeal was brought home to me – and, I believe, to Sir Anthony too – halfway through the service, when we were singing the hymn which begins *Immortal, Invisible, God only wise*. As the procession of nurses and children came into view, Sir Anthony and I stopped singing. Lumps in our throats had caught us both unawares.

Part II

PREPARATION

Chapter 3

OVERVIEW

Planning a major capital appeal is a complex project. Even professional fund-raisers, who are involved in several such campaigns during their careers, should approach each new one with great care. For the appeal trustees and the governing board of the organization that needs the money, it may be a unique experience. It is, therefore, extremely important that they take as much advice as possible at the earliest stage. There is a tremendous premium on getting it right first time.

The three key elements for any appeal are the cause, the strategy and the leadership. The cause must lead everything, while strategy and leadership will vary according to the cause. That was the bedrock of the Wishing Well Appeal. Children's health is a subject of universal concern and Great Ormond Street Hospital is known throughout the world for its ability to treat sick children – given the resources. It is a centre of excellence for paediatric medicine and for training doctors and nurses from all over the world. It is linked to the Institute of Child Health which, through research, teaching and clinical work, develops new methods of treating children. These facts gave us the confidence to spread the net wide.

Conversely, an appeal such as the Campaign for Oxford on behalf of the University, although international, cannot expect to raise funds from everyone, partly because some see it as elitist. The appeal for a scanner for a local hospital should be marketed only in the hospital's catchment area (apart from national funds specifically earmarked for that type of project). If the cause has wide appeal, then the scope of communications will be correspondingly comprehensive. If the charity is little known and its area of activity obscure, the marketing methods will have to be more carefully refined.

Many people concerned with an appeal will take the cause as a fixed element but, like anything else, it is capable of being fine-tuned in order to maximize the response from donors. It is wrong to be inflexible. Those involved at the appeal's inception should ensure that they select the most propitious elements of their cause as their primary theme. These considerations are inevitably tied up with the whole question of marketing the appeal in the most effective manner.

The second critical element is the correct strategy. Everyone seems to think that he knows how to raise funds, yet basic mistakes are often made because some fundamental rules of fundraising are not immediately apparent. Giles Pegram, past Chairman of the Institute of Charity Fundraising Managers and Appeals Director of the National Society for the Prevention of Cruelty to Children (NSPCC), had this to say at a seminar we organized at Great Ormond Street to share experiences with other charities:

> *It still amazes me that sometimes people can be recruited into organizations to run large fund-raising departments, with no experience or knowledge of the business of fund-raising. It would be unthinkable for somebody to be appointed headmaster of a school who has never taught before, and fund-raising is very much like any other profession in that respect. There is a body of knowledge, there are right and wrong ways of doing things.*

This is undoubtedly correct for a large fund-raising department, but, as there are insufficient top fund-raisers to go round, smaller appeals often have to recruit from outside the fund-raising profession. In such cases, a marketing background is best, backed by suitable fund-raising advisers to get the correct strategy.

STRATEGY

Evolving the right strategy is a process that should begin even before an appeal director is appointed. The strategy must be comprehensive in order to avoid unforeseen problems and flexible so that if a problem occurs, it can be confronted and overcome rather than simply ignored. It is essential to recruit the right person for the task in hand. That, in turn, implies that the governors or trustees have some general outline of strategy by which they can set criteria for choosing the individual who will, in effect, be the chief executive of the appeal. The evolution of strategy will then be carried on by that chief executive and the appeal chairman in a continuous development as leaders emerge and begin to make their contributions. In 1985 I was appointed Director of what became the Wishing Well Appeal. A key part of my role was to draw up the overall strategy for the approval of the Executive Committee. This took much research, thought and advice from many quarters. Finally, the strategy document I drew up in August 1986 was accepted. It was, of course, refined further in the following months as the Appeal approached its public phase.

The master strategy should pull together all the strands and give dates when specific targets should be reached. It also coordinates the roles of the many independent activities in an appeal and shows how they all fit together. The strategy we used was not unique; we employed the classic principles of fund-raising. However, by recruiting leading voluntary experts from every field, especially in marketing, we were able to produce a freshness of design and a flair in the publicity for the Appeal. The credit belongs to so many that no one person should be singled out, but no team can succeed unless there is a clear plan and the right leadership. This is the final element which can lead to the success or failure of an appeal.

LEADERSHIP

Undoubtedly the very public leadership of such well-known parents as the Prince and Princess of Wales, in their role as Patrons, played a crucial part in ensuring that the Wishing Well Appeal was taken to the hearts of the British people and beyond. However, the pivotal person in terms of management is the appeal chairman. He can make all the difference between success and failure, however well the other two factors – cause and strategy – have been handled. The appeal chairman makes it happen. He is the leader who recruits top names and ensures that they give and that they ask others to do likewise. He finds suitable chairmen for the panels, each of which adopts a particular objective and target. If the chairman's stature or determination is not sufficient, the appeal has little chance. If he is not respected, how can he recruit a top-level team to serve under him? The Trustees of the Wishing Well Appeal made a very wise choice in approaching Jim Prior. Not only was he the Chairman of one of Britain's top companies – General Electric Company – he is also a popular ex-Cabinet Minister with a national public profile. Add to these attributes his enormous circle of friends and contacts and his down-to-earth, approachable style, and it is difficult to see how we could have done better.

In day-to-day terms, the right appeal director or chief executive can make a big difference to the efficient running of an appeal. In exceptional circumstances, he can do much to make up for a less than ideal chairman – although that certainly was not needed in the Wishing Well Appeal! If there is not a good administrator at the heart of the appeal office, ensuring that all helpers work together in a coordinated fashion, chaos reigns. The director has to be an effective leader, capable of dealing tactfully with personnel problems, but also able to talk on equal terms with the chairman, trustees, governors, committee members and panelists who lead the appeal and make the vital requests for funds.

PHASES OF AN APPEAL

Appeals can usually be split into three main phases: planning, the private appeal and the public appeal. The planning phase involves progressing very different activities simultaneously. On the operational side, the project will develop as decisions are made, costings refined and specifications prepared. At the same time, the appeal will be researching potential sources of funds, investigating the feasibility of raising the necessary money, drawing up a strategy and identifying suitable leaders to involve in the private and public phases.

The private appeal ensures that potential donors are approached personally in advance of the public launch. The public appeal should be launched once the campaign looks like being a success. Sometimes the public phase of the appeal is expected to raise serious money – as in the case of the Wishing Well Appeal. On other occasions, it is more of a public relations exercise to ensure that the project becomes well known and fits into its local community. This was so with the Charing Cross Medical Research Centre Appeal. After raising most of the £4 million needed from national sources during a private phase, it went public in December 1983, leaving the remainder to be raised by an appeal to the local community. The local appeal was successfully chaired by Sir Clifford Chetwood, then

Chairman of George Wimpey, the largest employer in the area. Depending on the type of cause, it may be decided that the charity does not appeal to the general public and therefore does not warrant a public appeal at all.

The relationship between a charity and its ongoing supporters should be considered both before and during each phase of the appeal. Careful thought should be given to how the frequently intense publicity of a one-off appeal will fit into and lead on to the ongoing support required by a charity. Too often, voluntary bodies forget the need to say 'thank you' and to keep in touch with supporters to let them know how their money is being spent. Handled correctly, these supporters will be with the charity for a lifetime.

All these phases are covered in more detail later.

SEED MONEY AND ADMINISTRATIVE COSTS

Finding the seed money to pay salaries and start-up costs before funds start to flow in is a problem at the start of a capital appeal. Even before that, a charity may wish to commission detailed fund-raising advice from consultants. That has to be paid for. Established charities tend to look to long-term supporters for these early funds so that the project can get off the ground and the preliminary report on the appeal can be produced. If it is a totally new project, without any long-term supporters, discreet calls must be made to likely sympathizers. It is easier to find initial backers if you are armed with preliminary documents and research. The project then seems to have the makings of success because it is being undertaken on a business-like basis.

Many reluctant donors excuse themselves from giving on the grounds that charities spend too much on administration. However, it is a false economy to restrict administrative costs too much. It takes money to raise money – as in business. To quote the Charity Commissioners' 1989 Annual Report:

> The cost of administering charities is a matter which arouses strong feelings and varied opinions. It is sometimes assumed that people who work for charity should do it for nothing, or, at most, for a pittance. Donors often express a wish that their money should go exclusively to the objects and beneficiaries, and none towards the cost of administration. Charities have on occasion colluded with such attitudes, advertising that no part of any contribution from the public will be spent on administration, and some claiming even lower administrative costs in a competitive downward spiral. Such attitudes, however, imply that administration is a bad thing, and that the ideal administrative cost is nil. If carried into actual practice, such an attitude can only lead to badly administered charities and to inefficiency and abuse.
>
> Effective and efficient administration cannot be bought on the cheap. It is a critical prerequisite to the corporate achievement of any purpose. Good administration is all the more desirable where charity is concerned – carrying, as it does, the goodwill of individual donors into the public domain. The critical task is, therefore, not simply to reduce administrative costs as an end in itself (which might also reduce the charity's capacity to pursue its objects successfully), but to identify what level of administration is necessary in each case and to ensure that the strength of a lean and efficient administration is wholly devoted to the objects of the charity in question.
>
> No attempt to identify a level of administrative costs applicable to all charities ever

succeeded. Charities vary too much. This does not mean that excessively high admin-
istrative costs cannot be identified in any particular case. This is a matter of concern
to us, particularly since undue expenditure on administration may well be a
symptom of positive abuse calling for corrective action on our part. While a small
charity relying on voluntary effort may not even have to pay for the postage, tele-
phone and petrol of its honorary officers (although it should always be ready to do so),
any medium-sized or large charity needs accountable and efficient administration.
Such charities then face a crucial question: since they cannot address their objects, let
alone achieve them, without sound administration, how can they persuade the public
that money spent on administration is money well spent?

Although many charities have high standards of management such standards are
not universally adopted and in many instances the standard is capable of improve-
ment. Considerable effort is now being made – and with increasing momentum – to
raise those standards.

The one-off capital appeal can achieve a cost-to-income ratio of around ten per
cent, shared equally between fund-raising and administration, if the policy is to
look for the maximum number of gifts in kind to cut costs. It has the advantage of
being able to obtain very large gifts. Because we sought maximum support in
terms of gifts in kind (offices, equipment, seconded staff, sponsored advertisements, etc.), the combined fund-raising and administrative costs of the Wishing
Well Appeal were only four per cent of our £42 million target. As we eventually
raised over £54 million (plus £30 million from the government), the percentage of
costs fell even further.

Charities' administrative costs can vary considerably. It could be said that all
funds raised by the Samaritans are spent on administration (providing support
and advice in the form of people, training and motivating advisers). An ongoing
charity's costs for fund-raising and administration will be at least double those for
a capital appeal, depending on the type of charity, i.e. whether it runs its own projects or raises money to fund other organizations. As a bonus, the seed money and
the administrative costs, but not the fund-raising costs of the Wishing Well
Appeal, were funded by the Special Trustees of the Hospital, which was a helpful
point to be able to make in fund-raising literature. This practice is attractive to
some donors and I believe it is acceptable – with two provisos.

- It is important to stress that the essential overhead costs have already been paid
  for. Otherwise you will reinforce and perpetuate the myth that charities should
  be run on a shoestring.
- This ploy must not be used to cover up the fact that administrative costs have
  been unacceptably high. Full details of such costs should be spelled out in your
  accounts, whether or not they have been sponsored.

'Administration' legitimately means different things to different charities and their
accounts reflect this. For this reason, the accounts of all charities should indicate
what is meant by 'administration'.

STEERING GROUP

Little money will be generated without one or more supporters of the charity devoting a great deal of time to ensuring that the desired project gets off the ground. These people usually form a steering group or study group to pull all the necessary strands together: to prove the need, to make a convincing case for an appeal and to find top leadership to take on the responsibility of raising the funds. (The steering group's function is covered in more detail in Chapter 6.)

CONCLUSION

Once it was over, many people asked me what I felt was the key to the Wishing Well Appeal's success. It was a combination of factors that included an emotive cause backed by creative marketing and strong leadership. However, somewhere at the top of the list was the recognition that we had had to allow enough time to prepare. Proper preparation will ensure that you really know your cause, the project you will be funding, how important it is to whom and – through all this – the correct fund-raising strategy. When you first start an appeal, there are few promises you can make about the likelihood of success. Once you have thoroughly researched the subject and chosen your appeal leader, the probable outcome begins to take shape. I was fortunate to have a chairman who gave me the time I needed, even though the time lag made several people doubt whether we knew what we were doing. This period is so important that I always advise delaying your planned launch date, if possible, until all the crucial goals have been achieved.

To underline the need to take time to prepare adequately, I quote Giles Pegram of the NSPCC:

> With our centenary appeal, we spent over two years from recruiting a chairman of the appeal to the real start of the private phase. This time was essential to get the right leadership in place and the right infrastructure. During this time, there was a constant pressure to accept second-rate people into leadership positions and to accept small cheques. Holding our nerve was a key factor of our success, and failure to do so is a reason why so many ambitious appeals fail.

Chapter 4

PROJECT RESEARCH

This chapter is about collecting all the relevant facts – which often prompt decisions that should have been made earlier – to prove the need for the project and make the case for an appeal. Facts about the charity and the appeal are packaged in three ways.

- The Business Plan. This is the master plan for all those tasked with the charity's management.

- The BROADSWORD mnemonic. This checklist covers all the facts which need to be collected, or decisions made before embarking on an appeal.

- The Preliminary Report. This presents the BROADSWORD facts in a form suitable for the potential leadership for the appeal. It makes the case for the appeal.

The Business Plan is the responsibility of the charity's trustees. The BROADSWORD checklist and Preliminary Report are compiled under the direction of the specially formed steering group (see Chapter 6).

PRELIMINARY RESEARCH

It is surprising how many charities bring in fund-raisers before they have a clear idea of why the funds are needed and how the money will be spent. Time and time again, I discover that an organization has not thought through exactly what it intends to do about a particular need, how much money is required to accomplish what, and why certain decisions have been made.

I learned my lesson when I was taken on by a charity to raise money for a building project. The first questions I asked covered the need for the project and the breakdown of costs. I also asked to become a member of the committee developing the project. The firm response was that this would be a waste of my time. I should just concern myself with raising the money – they would decide how to spend it.

This was not a very encouraging start. I had to explain that I could not approach important potential donors until I fully understood the problem and had convincing answers to the questions such donors would almost certainly ask. Otherwise, I would appear incompetent and that would reflect badly on the charity. I had to persuade my new colleagues that fund-raising is an integral part of developing, preparing and packaging the project.

It is both interesting and revealing to know the background to a decision. For example in the case of an extra-care home, it is useful to know why certain residents are housed and others are excluded; or, in Great Ormond Street's case, why we were building on an already congested site and why some highly desirable facilities had to be omitted from the final building plans.

To have a detailed scheme for spending the money before starting to raise it may seem like putting the cart before the horse, but it is essential to pinpoint and approach potential major donors first – and they need to be put fully into the picture.

In fact, before contacting any hoped-for sources of funds, the appeal needs to have a distinguished and impressive appeal chairman in place. Candidates for that post will also want to know as much as possible before they will consider a close association with the project. A detailed 'shopping list' is essential for the organizers to calculate how much they need to ask of any donors. Paradoxically, far fewer questions are asked during the public phase of the appeal, by which time those involved with the project have made detailed decisions and should have all the answers off by heart!

> It is worth practising your presentation of the facts to make sure that you have thought of every important angle and have satisfactory answers to all the questions donors may ask. Ask a friendly businessman to be your 'guinea pig' when the project is beginning to take shape. He should ask questions about the validity of the proposed scheme and comment on your presentation style; there is always room for improvement.

Typical questions donors ask

- Does the charity know where it is going?
- What is the problem the appeal is designed to overcome?
- Is an appeal the right solution?
- Are the organizers capable of doing a good job? Who is associated with them, who will vouch for their ability?
- Do they have good staff or consultants?
- Do the figures make sense? Have they really thought them through?
- Have they made allowances for inflation?
- Are the running costs assured, or at least realistic, so that the scheme does not eventually become a white elephant?
- Will they get planning permission for a building scheme?
- Do they know how to raise funds?
- What sort of support do they have already?

- Is the government contributing? Has the appeal claimed all possible government support? Are donors expected to do the government's job?
- What will I get for my money?

Business Plan

You cannot expect people to back an appeal unless they can examine a comprehensive plan which demonstrates convincingly that the management has a clear idea of where the organization is heading. I usually advise charities to produce a Business Plan for the next three to five years – perhaps with the help of a management consultant – before they look at ways of raising additional funds.

A company usually produces a Business Plan when it is asking a bank or other financial institution for funds. Similarly, a charity should be working to a plan all the time to keep a check on aims and progress, regardless of whether it is contemplating an appeal. It is an extremely effective way to monitor the health, reputation and achievements of any organization. I would go so far as to say that it is an impertinence to seek major donors if the charity has not already drawn up a plan for several years ahead.

A particular project may well be needed by the community, but that is not enough. The charity aiming to set up and run that project must be able to prove two things: that the project is necessary and that it is the best body to take on the task. Otherwise, sponsors and supporters may decide to realize their aims through another organization.

Compiling the plan

A Business Plan describes the key features of the charity in some detail. This does not mean that it must be an inordinately long document, but the act of composing and agreeing a detailed description is both instructive and constructive. The plan consists of a formal description of the organization with financial projections, so that everyone concerned can immediately understand what the charity is trying to do and can assess it. It is an ongoing master plan, which underlines the overall aims of the charity and specific targets, with deadlines, costs and progress made. The Business Plan should be reviewed annually to ensure that all involved do not lose sight of the objectives.

It is unlikely that the appeal will wish to publish the plan in its entirety, especially if, when they compile it, the organizers are being completely frank with themselves! The Business Plan should ideally be produced jointly by those respon-

---

Benefits of a Business Plan

- a self-teaching aid
- a basis for the Preliminary Report and so a means of selling the appeal to possible backers
- helping to avoid the most obvious mistakes and pinpointing serious weaknesses
- a focus on the 'shopping list' and the charity's needs over the next few years to see whether it is possible to raise all the money to carry out those plans.

sible for running the charity – honorary and paid officers. It is for the eyes of those in the organization and, possibly, for highly motivated major supporters and financial backers.

It describes the charity's leaders – who they are, their backgrounds and where they think they are going. This may point to a need which they would like to satisfy, which can be achieved only through an appeal. The detailed justification should be provided in a separate publication – the Preliminary Report – which is then used to recruit key players in a one-off appeal. When they are compiling the Preliminary Report, appeal organizers may find that it has the spin-off benefit of focusing ideas more sharply, giving a deeper insight into the objectives of the umbrella charity and, therefore, into what the appeal is trying to do in that broader context.

Organizing the plan

To compile the Business Plan for your charity, collect every piece of relevant information and collate it under the following headings:

1. Title cover
2. Contents list
3. Report Summary
4. Market conditions for fund-raising
5. The charity's history, mission and objectives
6. Analysis of 'competitors'
7. Current and future programmes, and progress
8. Current accounts, financial forecasts and milestones
9. The need for an appeal
10. Management
11. SWOT:
     Strengths
     Weaknesses
     Opportunities
     Threats
12. Conclusions
13. Appendices

Guidelines for writing the plan

Be clear and concise
Put yourself in the donor's position
Assume ignorance
Avoid jargon and clichés
Keep the Summary to a single A4 page
Keep other chapters to a maximum five A4 pages
Present the information logically
Cite sources to support assumptions and assertions
Do not attempt to disguise difficulties and weaknesses
Clarify the aspirations of the charity itself, of which the appeal is only a minor part.

If the appeal is set up to raise money to form a charity which does not already exist, it is still necessary to produce a Business Plan. This demonstrates how the charity intends to operate if it receives the necessary funds.

BROADSWORD

To help charities assemble the necessary facts for an appeal's Preliminary Report I have devised the mnemonic BROADSWORD. It is a checklist to highlight questions that must be answered, indicating areas for further detailed research.

B **Background.** What is the origin and history of the charity?

R **Role.** What is the charity's current national and international role?

O **Others.** Are other charities operating in the same field? Are they competitors providing the same service or do they differ significantly? Do you liaise with them and how do you intend to avoid duplication?

A **Aims.** If your charity already exists, do you have a five-year plan or Business Plan? You should make its annual report and accounts available to potential donors.

D **Distinguished supporters.** Listing your best supporters encourages more recruits. A letter of commendation from the appropriate government department is very useful, especially if it can confirm its own contribution to the project.

S **Snag.** Explain the problem which the appeal is designed to overcome. In the case of Great Ormond Street Hospital, the facilities were inadequate and run-down.

W **Way out.** Outline the solution. There was a redevelopment plan for Great Ormond Street for which the Appeal would find the money.

O **Operational expertise.** Make sure you have the right team to handle the project. The members should be suitably qualified, whether social workers, project managers or fund-raisers.

R **Revenue.** Capital costs and running costs must be detailed separately. Some charities set out to raise capital sums without assuring revenue. Potential donors are particularly sensitive on this point.

D **Delivery of funds.** How the money will be raised.

The delivery of funds section will increase as the fund-raising strategy becomes more defined. The strategy should be developed only after the main appeal leaders have been recruited. However, a donor will want to know that experienced, professional advice will be called upon to produce a comprehensive strategy and that qualified staff will be recruited to deal with this crucial aspect.

THE PRELIMINARY REPORT

Many of the names that will make a major impact on the appeal will come from the business world. They will take the leading roles in the appeal's management, lending credibility because of their proven ability to raise and deploy funds in their businesses. They will want details of what the appeal is intended to achieve. Most will consider their most precious possession to be their reputation; they will want to be assured that they are linking themselves to a success.

Tugging at the heartstrings is not enough to persuade such people to commit themselves. The case should be contained in the Preliminary Report, which should demonstrate that the appeal has reviewed the facts in a thorough and professional manner. As it is intended for external consumption, it should not include sensitive information.

The Preliminary Report is a selling document in which the organizers are entitled to present the appeal as convincingly as possible. Although it may be shown to potential key donors, its most crucial function is to persuade people to join the top leadership. It is used after the supporter most likely to influence their decision has made a verbal presentation. The Preliminary Report is used regularly until the people required for the initial structure have been recruited. It is then replaced by a strategy document and the appeal brochure.

The Report should be updated as decisions are made and as information – such as the appeal's progress, new recruits and lead gifts secured – becomes available. In this way, initial backers can be presented with an accurate and complete picture of the appeal's supporters and achievements. At this stage, as it is important that this Report is 'owned' by the growing appeal committee, it is advisable to call it a draft document. You can then seek the advice of the key people you will be bringing into the appeal structure to refine the document again and again. In this way, the appeal committee ends up 'owning' the targets, methods, timetable, etc.

Practical presentation

It is a good idea to store the Preliminary Report on a word processor or personal computer so that it is easily updated. The published version should look attractive and smart, but be inexpensive to produce, as it is a working document. The Preliminary Report is the embryo of the appeal brochure. This should not be produced until later, however, when the relevant facts have been collected and the most senior and prestigious voluntary fund-raisers have been recruited. Their names must be printed in the brochure. Think about it: how many people read the introduction to the brochure and turn to the 'names page' to see who they know?

Topics for the Preliminary Report

1. Introduction by a key supporter
2. Background to the appeal, including the charity's history and current work
3. The problem to be met by the appeal
4. The solution: action which the appeal will finance
5. Costs and target
6. Known contributions
7. Project management: who
8. Organization of fund-raising responsibility: who
9. Potential sources of funds
10. Strategy: how (to raise the funds)
11. Timetable: when

12. Gift opportunities: shopping list, naming rooms, funding specific items
13. Publicity
14. Conclusion
15. Appendices
    - sketch of proposed new work
    - architect's plans
    - staff/honorary structures
    - breakdown of costings

(Potential sources of funds (9) will be discussed in Chapter 5. Strategy (10), Timetable (11), and Publicity (13) will be discussed in Chapter 7.)

1. Introduction by key supporter

A well-known figure should put the story in a nutshell for those who do not have time to read the entire report. It is often undertaken by the chairman of the steering group. It should be positive and well-written, so that people feel they are being asked to become involved in an exciting project.

2. Background to the appeal

This should give a complete picture, explaining how the charity reached its present point, leading up to the conception of the appeal. It is also an opportunity for the report's authors to engage in a little useful introspection. At this stage of preparation, the charity should find out what sort of reputation it has with supporters, competitors and organizations with which it collaborates. Commercial companies do not launch a new product until they feel they have got it right; the same applies to a charity appeal. Problems, weaknesses and other negative aspects of the project and the charity that will be operating it should be identified and overcome before appealing for funds. These may range from an inefficient telephone service to a refusal of planning permission by the local authority. In other words, how do others see you? If your charity's image is not as good as it should be, this is not the time to launch an appeal.

3. The problem/challenge to be met by the appeal

To make the case for an appeal you must point to the particular problem to be solved, or the challenge to be met. Collect as much data as possible to underline the difficulties being endured. This may mean highlighting the plight of individuals, but take care not to demean the very people that the charity exists to serve.

Great Ormond Street's problem was straightforward. The Hospital had just received government funding for a new cardiac block, so would not have qualified for further major government funding for up to ten years. By that time, the very inadequate facilities for patients and staff would have jeopardized the Hospital's performance and standing. This was expanded into a truly mammoth list of obstacles to proper care:

• The operating theatres were too small and lacked modern facilities

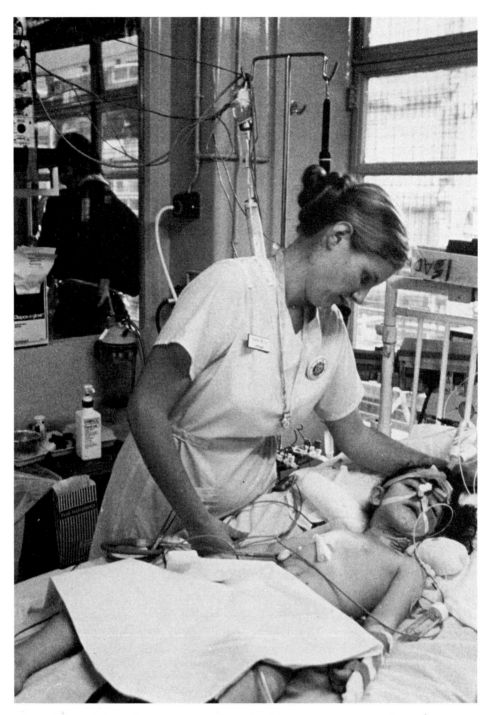

Never let the fun and excitement of fund-raising events detract from the cause. Remember that fund-raising is merely the enabler. If your cause is emotive, it should be portrayed as such, but with sensitivity. As far as the Wishing Well Appeal was concerned, the above photograph showed what the Appeal was all about – very sick children in cramped, outdated wards. (Photograph: Keith Waldegrave)

- There were no recovery rooms
- Accommodation for parents was very limited and much of it was too far from the wards
- Intensive care units were cramped and unsuitable
- Overspill into the corridors clogged them with equipment, visitors and toys
- All of this reduced staff morale, making the problem even worse.

4. The solution

All problems have possible solutions. A one-off capital appeal is only one potential answer to a problem. It must be constructed to fund a specific provision that has been costed in detail. Just throwing money at the difficulty is not satisfactory. Once the problem or challenge has been explained, a careful plan must be compiled to:

- expound the proposed provision in detail
- explain how it would alleviate the problem
- detail how it is to be developed and managed
- indicate the development programme
- break down the capital and revenue costs and the cash flow.

Great Ormond Street had already developed its solution before I became involved. They had worked out that there was enough space on the congested site for a new building, calculated the basics of what it should include and even produced the initial design concept and plans of the new building. That is the minimum needed by a fund-raiser before speaking to potential supporters if a building is in question. The solution also had to demonstrate that the Hospital had the right management team to see the development through on time and to budget. Donors wanted to be assured of this because of the horrors of inflation in building costs.

Our policy was to invite people to visit the Hospital before they were asked to contribute in a major way. The route that tours should take and the people visitors should meet were carefully considered to give potential donors a balanced view of the Hospital's strengths and the appalling conditions in which specialists and nurses had to work. There was nearly a disastrous accident when a piece of equipment fell through a staircase in the old building, leaving a gaping hole. Once we had recovered from the shock, we decided to look on the bright side: it was a dramatic illustration to convince wavering donors that we really did need their gifts!

5. Costs and target

Charities often look to fund-raisers for a particular sum of money without first drawing up accurate costings to justify their target. No major donor will back a project that has not been carefully costed. There should be a detailed breakdown of each item, including the price of equipment, and cash flow analysis to demonstrate when the money will be needed to keep the spending programme on time.

It is important to list goods and services which might be the subject of gifts in kind. These include furniture, equipment and advertising space. Different approaches are needed to attract gifts in kind for fund-raising support and for the project itself. Specific items, such as the appeal brochure, can be reserved for individual donors. A plaque in the office recording that a company has contributed all the lighting and heating, for example will be seen by many other donors as they come to discuss the appeal. Charities should ensure that corporate donors realize that if a gift is forthcoming on the basis of a promise of a certain benefit, then that constitutes a commercial return to the company and hence attracts VAT. The precise wording of plaques, for example, should therefore be very carefully controlled.

It is also wise to decide what can be omitted if the appeal does not reach its full target – and what extra facilities can be justified if the appeal exceeds expectations. Both can be embarrassing if the appeal has not planned for such eventualities. The appeal literature must specify what will happen if either of these circumstances occurs. For example, if the target is not met as the literature stipulates, the money must be returned to the donors net of the cost of finding them – the money is not owned by the appeal but held in trust to achieve the objective of the appeal. Often, therefore, the literature will include a caveat allowing the trustees to make changes to the development programme if circumstances so dictate. The Charities Act 1992 has simplified the procedures necessary before the Charity Commissioners can direct a 'Cy-pres' application of the funds but careful wording of the appeal literature will avoid this necessity (see Appendix 8). Cy-pres is an ancient doctrine which has evolved in English law to ensure that, if a gift is clearly for charitable purposes only, it will not be allowed to fail because the precise object to be benefited, or the means of application of the gift, is uncertain.

> A detailed cost breakdown will justify the chosen target for your appeal. Establishing the final target will still require some fine-tuning to match your cost and funding expectations.

Agreement should be reached with the relevant government department before you approach outsiders. If such a department makes a commitment, ask it to take responsibility for funding the less attractive items. At Great Ormond Street, we decided that the new boilerhouse, while extremely important, would not be particularly appealing to donors, so the government agreed to cover the cost. Afterwards, I wondered if we had been right. To our surprise, the Hospital archives revealed that the old boilerhouse had been bought in 1909 with the proceeds of a three-day fair at Olympia, of which the Prince and Princess of Wales were Presidents.

When I joined Great Ormond Street, the Appeal Trustees, formed to carry out the independent appeal, had been advised by fund-raising consultants not to attempt a target of more than £20 million. The Hospital was trying to scale down its needs to fit that figure, but after research into both the building need and the fund-raising potential, together with previously unforeseen government input, the budget for the building was set at £48 million. During these initial stages, our Chairman successfully negotiated with the Department of Health to provide half the capital costs of the building if we raised the other half. We elected to pay for items in the second half of the building programme in order to have sufficient time to raise the money. This meant that we had to bear a far greater burden of inflation; in cash terms, we were raising more than half. We also set out to raise £2 million to fund two chairs for the Institute of Child Health. This raised the appeal target to £50 million (including government input). We knew that the government contribution was vital to answer any criticism that we were doing the government's job by funding a National Health Service hospital. The Hospital had no option but to do something about its own needs. So determined were our early supporters that they made large pledges conditional on that state support.

6. Known contributions

The Preliminary Report should be positive in telling potential supporters about those who have already joined the party. When it is updated, include known contributions to the project in the most positive light. This is an indication to those considering involvement that the project and appeal are being taken seriously by their peers and, therefore, that the appeal is likely to be successful.

7. Project management

It is not enough for a charity to say that it wants to undertake a project. It will not receive the necessary backing unless it can prove that it is the right organization for the task. The proposed scheme has to fit in with the charity's objectives and, most important, there must be suitably qualified people to run the resulting development.

Great Ormond Street Hospital has long had a reputation as a centre of excellence for childcare, but it still had to recruit a first-rate team to plan, cost, build and equip the new building to budget and on time. The Hospital's Board of Governors appointed specialist medical planners and architects with a wealth of experience in hospital building. They were supported by a team which included quantity surveyors, engineers and project managers. The Hospital then took on its own project director, with a proven capability for a complex undertaking, to deal with this vital area and to ensure that it did not impede the smooth running of the service provided by the Hospital.

8. Organization of the responsibility for fund-raising

Fund-raising management is as important as project management. The two go hand in hand. I once interviewed a leading industrialist who was considering the role of an appeal chairman. When he was told that it was difficult to find a one-off appeal director with exactly the right qualifications to guide strategy, he decided against involvement. Anyone becoming involved in an appeal must take account of this. The correct fund-raising strategy and resource must be available, and the charity must be prepared to pay for the right expertise. An effective and efficient appeal office is needed to support the efforts of the chairman and his executive committee.

Points 9, 10 and 11 are discussed in Chapters 5 and 7.

12. *Gift opportunities*

The management of many charities often prefers to receive gifts that are not allocated to any specific item or area. These can then be used to fund whatever is the charity's top priority when the money is available. Such gifts can also be used to pay for overheads, a difficult proposition to put to donors. However, if the appeal is related to specific items, far greater amounts can be raised. It may also be possible to add a figure to the target to boost general funds. So the appeal for specifics can be used as a vehicle for raising the general level of income to the charity – it is the natural result of a heightened profile.

Donors of substantial sums expect to be taken into the confidence of the appeal organizers just as much as if they were being asked to invest in a business venture. They need to feel that their support will make a substantial contribution towards the well-being of the community. Commercial organizations also want to feel that being seen to be involved will be a real benefit to them. However, costing the areas that can be named is not easy. Simply stating the real cost of each item is unsatisfactory, as some are more attractive than others. The reception area is most visible of all – the boiler room hardly at all.

The best plan is to work out the Big Gifts schedule first, outlining what large sums might be expected and in what numbers. (This is explained further in Chapter 13.) Then match this with the areas available for naming. These lists can be modified to take account of actual costs and the potential popularity of each area. (See Appendix 3.)

We did this at Great Ormond Street. It was complicated, but we were marketing the choices in a way that we hoped our donors would find understandable and acceptable. A more modest approach, used in fund-raising for the St. Mary Abbots Geriatric Day Hospital in Kensington, West London, was to total the cost of decorating, furnishing and equipping particular rooms. We offered to put up a plaque detailing each donation, but then encountered the leaden hand of bureaucracy. We asked donors what they would like to appear on their plaques. Lady Bird had paid for a bathroom and had the charming idea of calling it The Bird Bath, but the local authority did not consider this amusing. After that, all rooms had to have standard plaques simply stating who had furnished them.

Naming tip

Do not make an official decision on naming a building in return for a large gift until the end of the appeal. The right to that privilege should be reserved for the greatest gift. If it is known early that the building is named after a particular individual or company, other donors may be deterred.

I recommend making one body responsible for policy on naming the parts of a building or development which may be the subject of an appeal. It may be the hierarchy of the charity or of the appeal; it can be a combination of both. Decisions include identifying the areas to be named, determining the prices to be asked for them and laying down guidelines for acceptable names. These must be reputable and not reflect badly on the charity in subsequent years. Any doubts on this point must be referred to the policy-making body for a verdict. Donors should be advised that if they wish to name a large area, such as the whole building or a wing of it, the charity reserves the right to name smaller areas, such as a room or ward, within it. This provides more naming opportunities. It may also be possible to allow donors to name an area of a building for a set period, such as 25 years. This is a sensitive point, but it means that the area will fall free for renaming in any subsequent appeal.

It is important that a single individual is made responsible for authorizing areas to be named, keeping the records of agreements and liaising between the appeal and donors. Otherwise it is very easy for an area to be named twice. All fundraisers must be told immediately a new area is named to stop them selling it again. The administrator may wish to give exclusive selling rights for different areas to different fund-raisers or leave the choice open on a first come, first served basis.

Change of use is another issue which must be handled with great care. Future managers may want to change the way a room is used to something which conflicts with the wishes or even ethics of the donor. As this is a decision which the recipients of the donation will have to live with for many years, it is a good idea to lay down a procedure for processing the larger donations through the appeal chairman or an appropriate committee. There must be no misunderstandings. The coordinator of this process should ensure that information on plaques is accurate and in accordance with the donors' wishes. The decision and authority to allow a donor to name a particular area at Great Ormond Street was taken by the Board of Governors. We had a list of what was available, but if we had not clearly marked on all the literature that no name could be guaranteed unless a pre-arranged checking procedure had been followed, there would have been chaos.

The building programme should show when each item will be needed. This gives donors a sense of urgency. Donors like to feel that they have contributed something specific. Either they can reserve an area which becomes the basis of their target for fund-raising, or they can ask what a given sum will provide. Different wards of Great Ormond Street's new building were named by the regional appeals among others.

The medical staff, who are always under severe pressures of time, were reluctant to draw up detailed lists of desirable equipment because it could be rendered out of date by technical progress. Although equipment can become obsolete during the time it takes to raise the money, suitable wording can explain that it will be subject to change. From the appeal's point of view, it is vital to have these details to stimulate donors to give more than they originally had in mind.

At Great Ormond Street there was debate initially as to whether it would be appropriate to seek a variety of gifts in kind for the main construction of the building – one donor to give the cement, someone else the paint, another the floor covering, etc. The Hospital decided it would be too dangerous to do this for reasons which were partly specific and partly universal. In the first place, Great Ormond Street is a Health Authority in its own right and might have had goods supplied which either did not meet Department of Health specifications or turned out to be faulty – that could have led to a real scandal. Secondly, materials for a large and complex building programme have to arrive on site at precisely the right time. Gifts in kind might turn up too late or even too early, and this might put unacceptable pressure on the contractors. It can also be an embarrassment and a difficulty if only part of a requirement is donated. For instance, I was told of an appeal in Yorkshire where only half the roof tiles were given. Matching them was extremely difficult. They had to be bought from the original donor's company – an embarrassment to both parties. Thirdly, when contractors are negotiating their prices, they take into account their deals with sub-contractors. If a substantial portion of the material was coming in at no cost, they might find the project less profitable and so less attractive. It is a complicated subject that requires careful thought.

Names and plaques

There must be no misunderstanding between the charity and donors about what may appear on a plaque. A donor may wish to name a hospital room in memory of a loved one. However, the room, particularly if it is a ward, will be used daily by patients and their relatives, many of whom will be stressed or depressed and will not wish to be reminded of death. It is frequently more acceptable to a hospital simply to name the room and omit the 'in memoriam' element. Explaining this requires tact.

The provision of carpets and furniture is not quite so sensitive. Some charity offices are fully furnished by particular companies, who are then credited on a plaque. Many charities do look to receive such items as gifts in kind. All this may seem extraordinarily petty in the context of a multi-million pound appeal, but failure to appreciate these sensitivities can lead to a disaster.

Point 13 is discussed in Chapter 18.

14. Conclusion

Teachers have a time-honoured adage: 'Tell 'em what you're going to tell 'em, tell 'em, and then tell 'em what you've told 'em'. This is worth bearing in mind when you are compiling the Preliminary Report. The conclusion should tell 'em what you've told 'em. It should re-emphasize the essential point that you are trying to express throughout the document.

End by lifting the reader's spirits, leaving him on a high. This is best done by spelling out, as vividly as possible, what the success of the appeal will mean to its beneficiaries, the community, the country and possibly even the world as a whole. The conclusion should use the excitement surrounding the endeavour to rally support. Above all, the reader should want to join in, contribute, be part of the great venture on which you are embarking.

Chapter 5

APPEAL RESEARCH

While you are collecting the necessary facts to prove the need and to make a case for an appeal, you should also be developing appeal research before looking at the feasibility of reaching a particular target. It is helpful if there is a clear precedent for giving to your type of cause. If not, you need to approach the question with great caution. Some foundations and trusts are keen to support projects breaking new ground, and some government departments favour and grant aid to pilot schemes before deciding whether to incorporate the new activity in their mainstream programmes.

The next step is to look at similar charities to see what lessons can be learned from them. I am glad to say that, unlike the cut and thrust of the business world, charities usually share a great deal of information and go out of their way to help each other. At this stage in the Charing Cross Medical Research Centre Appeal, I consulted my opposite number at the St. Bartholomew's Medical Research Centre Appeal, which was ahead of ours. By the time I was appointed at Charing Cross, Bart's had been appealing for funds for about six months. Through sharing information, we were able to avoid some of the pitfalls they had discovered through trial and error. However, because they were in front of us, they had prejudiced our chances when we approached those who had already contributed to Bart's – the City of London's own hospital!

A very useful work on the charitable behaviour of individuals in Britain is the Charities Aid Foundation's *Individual Giving and Volunteering*. It appeared first in 1992 as a successor to the *Charity Household Survey*, and is the source for information on how many people give to charity, what is the typical donation and whether giving is increasing or not.

MARKET RESEARCH

If the public is to be tapped, it is wise to carry out market research. A public appeal will be an uphill struggle for a new charity with no record and no profile. Even in the instance of a well-known charity producing a compelling case for support, market research can help check the public's reaction to your charity and profile the socio-economic groups you should target. The British Market Research Bureau produces a regular *Target Group Index* survey, which gives the results of broad research into people and attitudes on a wide range of topics, including charities. Many major research organizations also carry out what are called omnibus studies, into which other organizations can inject questions for a few hundred pounds. This is the sort of exercise that an appeal might be able to tap into at no cost to itself, with the support of a sympathetic company. Such support, perhaps delivered in the form of sponsorship, would be even more valuable if you contemplate undertaking detailed qualitative research into the public's opinion of your project or appeal. This type of research normally involves a series of interviews or group discussions. Because of the sheer time required it costs several thousand pounds. The Market Research Society Yearbook is an excellent guide.

CONSTITUENCY

It is crucial to decide early on the nature of the legitimate constituency for your appeal. This depends on the location of your operation, the scope of its activities and the identity of those who care about it. You must decide if it is solely a local appeal or whether, because of its area of influence, it is national. You must also decide if it is of interest to the general public or just a specific group. Race and religion may be relevant.

Nuffield Hospital targets appeals to those who show interest in private medicine through contributions to private health plans. It is a specific market, usually limited to a geographical area. In addition, past patients and their families have an increased warmth towards their hospital for four or five years after their treatment ends. Such appeals should not be targeted towards the general public. Preparatory and public schools fall into a similar category, although school support tends to come from nostalgic alumni and parents rather than recent leavers.

The Disability Centre run by the Queen Elizabeth Foundation for the Disabled in Leatherhead, Surrey, has a college and is, therefore, a national responsibility. An appeal for such a charity would be directed at those concerned with disability education as well as the general public. The extreme case, of course, is Great Ormond Street. Few are untouched by the plight of the sick child, so the Wishing Well Appeal could spread its net as wide as its pocket or gifts in kind – such as free advertising space – allowed.

A fruitful area for constituency research is a charity's list of existing donors. They should be researched exhaustively, profiling the type of donor, the level of gifts and the methods of giving and raising funds. It is also worth searching archives to find out more about historical donors. Relatives of previous substantial donors may be inclined to maintain family tradition. A great deal of desk research is necessary to produce accurate and comprehensive lists of potential donors, split into categories relevant to the type of donor and the level at which they might contribute. The Charities Aid Foundation publishes an annual review, *Charity Trends*, which lists the biggest corporate donors and grant-making trusts and indicates the extent of public sector support for voluntary organizations.

Those able to give major gifts are approached at the private stage of an appeal. They include wealthy individuals, grant-making trusts and foundations, companies and funding by government and statutory bodies. In recent years, one or two agencies have been set up to research and produce approach lists for charities. They keep their own databases of leading individuals and potential major donors. Use them when you need a list quickly – especially for leadership candidates – as it takes considerable time to set up your own records. You may be lucky enough to find suitable voluntary assistance, but proper guidance is still required.

Wealthy individuals

The list of wealthy individuals relevant to your cause is compiled using different techniques from that of companies and trusts. A reliable starting point is wealthy individuals already known to the charity. They can be approached for the names of further people who might be willing to support the appeal. This is known as 'widening circles'. Others can be found by consulting the annual lists of the wealthiest people in Britain published by *The Sunday Times*, and *Forbes* magazine in the U.S. It is worth combing *Who's Who* for people who have an identifiable interest in your cause. If they do, note their other activities, particularly in the business field, so that connections can be made. *The Hambro Company Guide* and *The Corporate Register* are both useful sources.

Organize a member of the appeal team to check the gossip and social pages of newspapers and magazines for articles mentioning prominent figures to see if they disclose any sympathy for your cause or related causes. During the Wishing Well Appeal, a team of volunteers looked through all national newspapers every day for references to wealthy individuals. They also checked the Appointments sections of *The Financial Times*. Do not neglect the process of checking and rechecking to keep your lists up-to-date and accurate. Everyone dies, divorce is on the increase and, at this level, honours are being conferred. All these changes should be logged; failure to do so could cost a major donation.

Trusts and foundations

The first task is to identify those that are likely to be interested in your project. The Charities Aid Foundation publication, *Charity Trends*, lists the top 400 grant-making trusts and indicates their broad areas of interest. Find out which part of your appeal they might wish to fund, what level of gifts they have given in the past and what sort of sum you might receive from them.

Eliminate from your list trusts with clearly defined objects inappropriate to your project, those where the trustees' policies exclude your project and trusts which make grants only to charities they already support. Some trusts will not give to capital projects. Go for trusts with policies matching your project and always look for a personal contact or local association.

Grant-making trusts have about £550 million a year to disburse in accordance with their Trust Deeds. The top 25 gave £121 million in 1990. An important research tool is the *Directory of Grant-Making Trusts*, which the Charities Aid Foundation publishes every other year. It lists about 2,500 trusts with incomes of more than £1,500 a year, arranged alphabetically, and includes their aims and names of the correspondent and trustees. The directory includes all restrictions of which CAF has been notified by the trustees. A cross-referencing system shows the types of work funded or considered. The Directory of Social Change also publishes useful reference books, *Raising Money from Trusts* by M. Norton and *Guide to the Major Trusts* by L. Fitzherbert and M. Eastwood. Another useful source of information is FunderFinder, a computer programme available only to charities and non-profit making organizations. It helps voluntary groups identify the appropriate charitable trusts for a given need. It has more than 1,000 names in its database, and the computer disks are updated every six months, incorporating any changes to the policies of the grant-making trusts included.

The Charity Commissioners maintain a public register of charities in England and Wales. They also hold public files which contain the founding document of each registered charity and a copy of the charity's annual accounts, where provided. There are tens of thousands of grant-making trusts, many of which are not listed in these directories because of their small size and local concentration. Their contribution to local and regional appeals can be very significant (see Chapter 32).

The register can be inspected at the Charity Commission's offices in London, Liverpool and Taunton. Inquirers about Scottish charities should contact the Inland Revenue Claims (Scotland). Inquiries in Northern Ireland are handled by the Charities Division of the Inland Revenue or the Charities Branch of the Department of Finance. The register is now computerized, which alleviates the problem of misplaced files and ensures the availability of information at all times. In addition, directories of foreign foundations (see Bibliography) can be found at your local central library or at the London office of the Charities Aid Foundation.

From these sources you can draw up a list of trusts whose Trust Deeds and policies allow them to give to your appeal. Although the Deeds put strict legal limits on a trust's activities, policies can change and should not initially be considered as an insurmountable barrier. A policy of geographical preference, for example, is not always rigid. Trusts which announce that all their income is committed need not be ruled out, unless they indicate a timescale beyond your appeal's. When they have fulfilled their current commitments, they must disburse future income elsewhere. Consequently, the first list of trusts should include all possibles. Dropping or upgrading a 'possible' is a judgment to make at the approach stage. Beside the name and address of each trust, the final list should show the names of the correspondent and trustees, relevant policies, size of typical donation and how and when each trust should be approached. It is important to note the name of any trustee who is on any of the charity's other lists and any who are known personally to members of the appeal panels.

Companies

It is not difficult to compile the first list of target companies. All the information is available in such reference books as *The Times 1000, The Hambro Company Guide,* Jordan's *Top 4000 Private Companies* and, from the Directory for Social Change, *The Guide to Company Giving, The Corporate Donors' Guide* and *Major Companies and Their Charitable Giving.*

It is important to realize also that the larger gifts may not come from the larger public companies. The biggest companies' budgets are often heavily committed to secondments and other long-term arrangements, so that in, say, the top 400 companies there is great competition for the relatively small amount of money that is still available. Private companies or public companies with private company characteristics, notably strong central control, are often better prospects. Such companies will often be among those most recently founded and there is also just a chance that they may not have been approached before.

There are so many potential corporate donors – the Wishing Well Appeal logged around 3,000 for our purposes alone – that a computerized database is essential. It is important to stress the need for accuracy when loading the information into the computer.

The main details for the database are the company's name, address, telephone number (with direct lines if applicable), fax number, names of the chairman and chief executive, comparative size of the company (usually ranked by turnover and total assets) and financial performance. Recent press cuttings will give an indication of how well the business is performing. The entries should be classified: we used the sector categories found in *The Financial Times*. The classification should be cross-referred to an alphabetical index. Take care to record any company name changes. A copy of *Who Owns Whom* (Dun & Bradstreet) helps to ensure that you do not write to a subsidiary of a parent company which you have already approached. While this point applies in the main, there are some exceptions. Some subsidiaries of large companies are themselves sizable organizations with their own boards and charity budgets. Familiarity with company details will show whether other directors should also be logged. Any director's name which appears on more than one list should be noted. So, too, should any directors linked with the charity. A separate directors' index is a useful way of tracking these connections. *The Corporate Register* (Hemmington Scott) and the *Directory of Directors* (Reed Information Services) log individuals' directorships. Some will also appear on your list of wealthy individuals. Some companies have their own associated grant-making trusts, whose trustees must also be noted.

One staff member or volunteer should scan the press each day for changes, promotions, deaths, resignations, mergers, takeovers, etc. It is vital to be as up-to-date and accurate as possible. *The Financial Times* carries a daily appointments column, usually on its back page, while *The Times* records deaths on its Court and Social page. This also includes lists of those attending lunches, dinners and memorial services. Further death notices are to be found on the adjoining page of classified announcements. Remember, when researching lists for approaches to individuals, companies or trusts, each approach is made through an individual. Therefore, it is wise to research his influence before a meeting. Apart from holding the purse strings of a major company's charitable giving, he may also be a trustee of a grant-making body which supports your type of cause.

Government and statutory bodies

The National Council for Voluntary Organizations (NCVO) has produced a comprehensive list of Central Government Departments which make grants to voluntary organizations. They include Education, the Environment and Health. The government has published a long and detailed report – *Efficiency Scrutiny Review of Government Support to the Voluntary Sector* (HMSO 1990) – which includes, as an appendix, a thorough guide to what each department will and does support. Because the report is all-encompassing it may reveal new areas of potential support of which you were unaware.

The Department of Health was obviously the appropriate department for the Wishing Well Appeal to approach. Indeed the Hospital had a legal duty to inform the Department of the Appeal through its Special Health Authority. Things may not always be so clear. The Home Office has a Voluntary Services Unit which can advise, and this is where research should begin.

In addition, there are non-governmental bodies which can make grants – for example, the Arts Council, the Countryside Commission, and Regional Arts Associations. The NCVO also lists more than 100 local authorities with voluntary sector liaison officers administering local grants. Local Councils for Voluntary Services can be approached as well.

Grants are available from the EC, although very few are allocated for voluntary organizations. They can, however, contribute large sums if your project qualifies.

EXISTING AND POTENTIAL LEADERSHIP

The next step is to look for suitable leadership. A charity's trustees must form an important starting point in looking for leadership – they have a duty to provide help and contacts. It is imperative that they feel committed to the leadership that emerges.

The quality of your charity's existing leadership may obviate the need to recruit outsiders, but this is unlikely. Usually, a charity needs different kinds of people to run the show on an ongoing basis from those required to make a special push for appeal funds. One of a fund-raiser's first activities is to ask the charity to put together an authoritative list of supporters, noting the type and degree of their influence and their previous involvement with the charity. This can include business people, trustees of charitable trusts and foundations, wealthy people, politicians and celebrities.

The degree of influence available to the charity can be extended by finding out whom these people know and how well they know them. This second list of contacts is a further avenue to recruiting the leadership needed for approaching each category of potential donor. Once the lists of potential main donors have been compiled, the aim is to try to recruit a respected leader for each category that research has shown should be targeted for the appeal. By the time the main leader – the appeal chairman – has been recruited (and a great deal of work goes into his selection, as can be seen in the next chapter) he should be given a list of possible leaders to approach for each donor category.

The quality of leadership available to a charity is all-important. This is one of the main factors to review when assessing whether an appeal is likely to succeed. If a charity has no existing links with the great and the good, then it is always a major problem to recruit the highly placed individual who can make the difference between success and failure. It is interesting, however, that charities often think they have no such links with the establishment, but diligent research usually uncovers one – probably via a series of stepping stones: A knows B, who plays golf with C, whose brother is deputy chairman of a major company. Another way of looking for influential links is to enlist the help of the local authority, government departments and politicians. It sounds laborious. It is. But this work is an essential piece of the jigsaw puzzle that goes to make up a successful appeal.

Pinpointing potential leaders is often undertaken by the appeal's fund-raiser, but the approach should ideally come from the chairman of the charity or another honorary officer – rather than from a paid member of staff or a fund-raising consultant. It is a good rule, yet sometimes there is no alternative but for the fund-raiser to have a go.

I was trying to set up an appeal in Chelsea to raise funds to pay for additional facilities at an old people's sheltered housing scheme. I was working for Help the Aged and they had no links or influential supporters in this district. My research identified Mr. Chelsea himself – The Earl Cadogan – as the ideal leader, but I was told he was shedding charitable work rather than looking to acquire more. Undaunted, I tried to work out how I could obtain a personal introduction to Lord Cadogan. When I found that his agent's surname was Patterson Morgan, I thought I had hit on a link as I had attended evening classes in public relations with a man of the same surname who worked for the Central Office of Information. A quick telephone call revealed that Patterson Morgan was my friend's brother. I had my introduction and the stepping stone I had been seeking. There was a happy ending, as I persuaded Lord Cadogan to become Chairman of the Appeal. You might say it was all down to luck. I would have to agree that luck played a central role, but the right setting had been created by careful research.

FEASIBILITY

Before planning a fund-raising campaign, it is logical to take soundings as to whether it is feasible to raise the money necessary to realize the proposed project. This also helps to point to what sort of target should be fixed for the appeal. Business people whom the appeal will be trying to involve will be reassured to see that the charity is going about this process in a professional way to ensure that those who give their time and effort are not embarrassed in the end by a failure.

Another consideration is the economic situation of the country. We were very lucky with the Wishing Well Appeal in that we had made all our approaches and received commitments to major gifts before Black Monday, when the London stock market fell more than 10 per cent. We went public with our appeal eight days later and were virtually unaffected. If the crash had happened before our private appeal, it could have been very damaging indeed, as many large donors would have held back. No one could have predicted the severity of the collapse, but a number of commentators had pointed out during the summer that the market was becoming dangerously overheated.

Recession, international political developments and even the threat of war must be considered when drawing up an appeal timetable. It was especially difficult to persuade any leader of industry to accept the chairmanship of a major appeal during the Gulf War. At a time of recession, it is not easy to ask business executives to spend time on charity work; their first responsibility must be the efficient and profitable management of their companies. Deciding whether to launch a major appeal during difficult times depends on the urgency of the need and the emotional pull of the cause. If these are not sufficiently strong, it may be better to wait until the climate is more propitious.

Whatever the economic background, I strongly advise against splitting an appeal into two or more separate segments. It may be very tempting if, say, a building is being erected in two phases, or to raise money for equipment separately from the building finance. However, it requires almost exactly the same work for each stage as a single appeal for double the amount of money. With any capital appeal, detailed planning and structuring is needed if you are to have the best chance of success. It is not advisable to have one appeal for stage one and then approach everybody all over again for stage two. Major donors do not want to be approached twice for the same appeal. It would also be most unwise to launch another public appeal for at least eight to ten years. The public's interest is stimulated by new charity appeals and will not readily return to one that has already been aired.

As a general rule, it is easier to raise £10 million if the target is £20 million than if the target is £10 million because donors often give in proportion to the total target. If you are going to go to all the trouble of researching, structuring and running a major appeal, then you should ensure that the charity is given the impetus to achieve its objectives over the next five or more years.

However, it is possible, without going against the principle, to use phasing as a means of establishing clear priorities in a development programme and of giving the appeal committee confidence in achieving a large target. Gifts are still sought in relation to the overall target, but phasing allows the setting of interim deadlines or targets with which the committee may feel more comfortable. If it is done carefully, it can be extremely effective.

When I was appointed at Great Ormond Street, I knew that the previous appeal for the Hospital had been in the 1930s. By chance I came across a four-page pullout describing that project in *The Times* of November 1934. Our team felt that we had created some innovative ideas for fund-raising but our predecessors had thought of many of the same ploys, including naming areas. As Viscount Astor, the owner of *The Times*, was a Vice-President of the Hospital, it is likely that the space was provided free or at a reduced rate. The appeal called for £400,000, the equivalent of nearly £13 million today. The supplement explained how readers could help and what donations of sums from £5 to £10,000 would buy. There were words of reminiscence on childhood by the author, J. B. Priestley, and a catalogue of the Hospital's annual workload, including 127 cases of rheumatism and heart disease, 24 hip dislocations, 194 cases of hare lip and cleft palate and 3,666 removals of tonsils and adenoids. The Prince of Wales was reported as declaring: *Nothing short of a complete reconstruction will enable the Hospital for Sick Children to maintain its great traditions.* There was even a crossword puzzle with appropriate clues; the solution could be obtained only by sending a donation. (The Wishing Well Appeal did not think of that one!) One reason for such a tremendous response to the Wishing Well Appeal was that the Hospital had left a 50-year gap since its last appeal.

Having ensured that the target is not ridiculously high, the task of charities is to identify exactly what they need to provide the ideal service for their beneficiaries and go for that, initially. The costings and feasibility exercises bring that target into sharper focus. Then the charity has to make the difficult decision as to exactly how much to try to raise through a one-off appeal, not forgetting that it should also help subsequent ongoing fund-raising by raising the charity's profile. All too often, charities are timid; they may be frightened of failure and attempt only the minimum because they are aware of all the dangers. Nevertheless, if those involved in an appeal are determined enough and prepared to stick at it, whatever the obstacles, it is unusual for the appeal to fail totally – assuming that the target is a reasonable one. I touch wood when I say that those with which I have been involved have always gone over target. I do not suggest that a charity should take on impossible missions; the blow to morale after a failure is too big a deterrent. Of course, luck plays a part. Napoleon said he liked all his generals to be lucky. I think all appeal directors have to be lucky and – more importantly – to believe in their luck. But there is a much more scientific way of generating luck – through intensive research.

Take into account, too, appeals for similar projects. The NSPCC Centenary Appeal took place about a year before the Wishing Well Appeal. We learned all we could about the sort of response it had received and much appreciated the help given to us. Since the Wishing Well Appeal, at least ten other children's hospitals, a score or more of other hospitals and countless other charities have consulted Great Ormond Street to help plan their own appeals. It is also important to find out about other appeals that may coincide with yours. A clash can be very damaging.

Finally, the dedication of those involved with the charity and how hard they intend to work to ensure the success of an appeal are crucial factors. Speak to as many as possible of those concerned to satisfy yourself that they believe in the cause and are all pulling together.

All this background information provides a hook on which to hang the appeal target. Sometimes it may suggest that the charity would be wise to try to achieve less through an appeal, and sometimes the reverse. All projects vary and require an open mind. There are no fixed rules about this. After careful and detailed research to justify the chosen target, optimism is the vital ingredient for success. All this research is going on while the project details – including costings – are being developed. Because there are so many imponderables, it is wise to keep the appeal target flexible for as long as practicable. This gives the project development team longer to cost the scheme in greater detail and the fund-raisers longer to look into feasibility.

It is embarrassing to change the target in the middle of an appeal. Before joining the Great Ormond Street Appeal, I had been involved in raising £5 million for medical research. I felt it would be possible to raise £20 million for Great Ormond Street. However, once we had produced detailed plans for what was required, the Hospital realized that it would need £50 million – £20 million from the government and £30 million from the Appeal, after allowing for inflation and other factors. By the time this became clear, we had sufficiently researched the feasibility of raising money for the Hospital to feel that even this would be possible. There could be no promises, however. Any fund-raiser who promises to raise a certain amount by a set time through a one-off appeal is walking on quicksand. I could only point to what had been achieved in the past and explain that our proposals were based on that previous experience.

One way round a sticky phase is to extend the period of the appeal. We planned a two-year public appeal with the Wishing Well, although I always hoped that we could complete it in one year. When we reached our goal in 14 months, everyone was delighted, whereas if we had promised to do it in one year, we would have been seen in a very different light. It is similar to preparing budgets: always plan for the worst scenario and then try to improve on it!

Remember that the various participants in this discussion will have different priorities in establishing an appeal target. The charity will normally want to raise the highest sum, but the chairman of the appeal will be more concerned to agree an achievable target. If he is the right person, he will feel his reputation depends upon reaching it.

--- *Chapter 6* ---

LEADERSHIP

The initial leadership for an appeal usually comes from the trustees of the organization needing the money. A steering or study group should be formed. This comprises two or three key representatives from the charity and several known supporters with varied disciplines, including influence and business acumen. You might involve a company chairman or director, an accountant and a solicitor. In certain programmes you might want to add an architect or surveyor.

It is wise to keep the membership of the steering group flexible and allow it to grow as new leadership is identified. Sometimes the appeal chairman may emerge from the steering group. In other situations the chairman is identified, recruited on to the steering group and gradually 'absorbed' until such time as he is so committed and involved that he is prepared to take on the full role of chairman.

Once the steering group's objectives have been achieved, the group should stand down and hand over to the newly formed appeal management structure. However, some of the steering group usually join the appeal organization.

Steering group's objectives

1. To prove the need and make the case for an appeal (see Chapter 4)
2. To decide an appeal target (see Chapter 5)
3. To look into the range of possible legal entities for the planned appeal (see Chapter 9)
4. To find the seed money to get the appeal off the ground before fund-raising commences (see Chapter 3)
5. To obtain access to professional fund-raising advice
6. To contribute to and agree the Preliminary Report

The recruitment of the appeal chairman and obtaining professional fund-raising advice are discussed further in this chapter. However, it must be understood that, even if you have access to the perfect chairman for your appeal, he will not wish to take on such a commitment unless he feels he can turn to suitable fund-raising advice. Equally, the appeal target and the legal entity should remain flexible until the appeal chairman has had his say.

A charity should think twice about its planned appeal if some of the trustees do not agree with the proposed action. In looking for leadership or links to potential leadership, a fund-raiser often interviews all the trustees, sometimes individually. It is surprising how often they disagree. If the charity itself cannot unite on the correct course of action, it has little chance of persuading others to become involved. The result may be half-hearted. So the first job is to get a consensus and then to ensure that all the trustees give it wholehearted backing. This was certainly the case at Great Ormond Street when I joined because the management knew that the future of the Hospital was in jeopardy. The idea of holding an appeal to meet the Hospital's pressing needs was conceived in 1983 by Caroline Bond, Chairman of its Governors. However, there was concern about how much money could be raised, which would affect what building could be done. This was to be explored further through research.

HOW TO FIND AN APPEAL CHAIRMAN

The need to raise a large sum puts a high premium on enlisting leadership of the right calibre. Credibility is all-important and stems from the people who personify the appeal to the outside world. The appeal chairman's most important contribution is asking power – the ability to successfully ask key decision-makers for substantial contributions to an appeal. This means he will have to be able to give or influence the giving of a lead gift himself. People give to people as much as, if not more than to causes. If your child asks you to sponsor a charity walk, your decision rarely depends on the charity. The same applies to trustees of charitable foundations and company chairmen, who may have vast sums to dispense. They will want to back a success, for failure will redound on them, implying an apparent lack of judgment. But it is very difficult to refuse to help a colleague or a friend and even more difficult to decline if the approach comes from the chairman of your firm's main customer!

The only possible exception to the chairman of a major company is 'old wealth'. The head of a well-established, wealthy family is also a suitable choice for appeal chairman. The Duke of Westminster, for example, chaired, with great success, the Centenary Appeal for the NSPCC.

It is important that the whole appeal is not built around one individual. Otherwise, the campaign is vulnerable to collapse if that key person falls under the proverbial bus. The Stoke Mandeville Hospital appeal has had a high profile link with Sir Jimmy Savile, a tireless fund-raiser, adroit manipulator of the media and one of the fittest men of his age. Were the worst to have happened, the appeal might have been in difficulties.

However, Stoke Mandeville is convinced that it was a risk worth taking. Sylvia Nicol of the hospital's Spinal Unit said: *I don't think you can have a successful appeal without a figurehead. We certainly couldn't have done it without Jimmy. If he had had some disaster after the appeal was launched, I think the momentum would have carried us on, almost because something had happened to him. Every time he mentions Stoke Mandeville on television, money pours in.*

Ideal qualities for an appeal chairman

1. A close existing link with the charity. This may be difficult to find.
2. He should be chairman or chief executive of one of Britain's biggest companies. *The Financial Times* and other national dailies list these in their share price tables, and magazines, such as *Management Today*, regularly publish rankings of companies by size, turnover, profitability and so on. Naturally, this choice will be scaled down if you are recruiting for a local or county appeal, where you should seek to attract an influential business person within the relevant catchment area.

   Many successful appeals have chosen key leaders from particular sections of the population, such as bishops, eminent physicians, admirals, brigadiers and the local mayor. My view is that most of them, while adept at allocating funds and being responsible for spending a particular budget, have little experience in making the decisions necessary to raise money. This requires a very different discipline, so it is better to look for someone who already has a successful track record in business.
3. The company should be in a profitable sector. The above publications give regular sector analyses. Companies in activities with many suppliers, such as retailing, are a good choice.
4. He should have national standing and be well respected by what is still known in Britain as the 'Establishment'. Unless he is a heavyweight, he cannot persuade heavyweights to serve under him on committees.
5. He should still be active. The newly retired may have more time on their hands, but will already have lost some of that vital asking power. Even those near to retirement are doubtful candidates, as they may not be able to return favours. They can make ideal deputy chairmen.
6. It is more important that he is well respected than well liked. The person who is liked by everyone will probably not be tough enough for this job. Many otherwise ideal candidates dislike fund-raising because they say it loses them friends. Equally, organizers should be wary of appointing a wealthy individual who sees the chairmanship as a route to respectability. If his standing is in doubt, that may inhibit contributions and could cast a shadow over the appeal. Such a person should be recruited as a major benefactor rather than as the appeal leader.
7. The leader needs to be an effective chairman of meetings and tough enough to force the pace. In some cases, such as academic appeals, he may also need to be intellectually rigorous – not just bright.
8. He should be prepared to give the job sufficient time. It is always said (in my experience correctly) that a busy person can always find the time for extra work. Recruiting a team and agreeing strategy involves hard work. After that, if he is a good delegator, he can limit his input as he sees fit.
9. He should not recently have been involved in another appeal, as he will have used up a lot of good will.
10. A good choice is a person who has just risen from chief executive to chairman. He has more time to play the ambassadorial role and may want to be seen to be making a major contribution to the charitable sector.

So there is always room for a different point of view, but I prefer to take the safety first approach and eliminate as much risk as possible by having many influential people supporting the campaign. Then it will matter less if one or the other of them drops out, for whatever reason.

THE ROLE OF THE APPEAL CHAIRMAN

I have tried to list all the key roles which the appeal chairman would fulfil in an ideal world. Clearly there will always be exceptions to each of these points.

1. To accept, on behalf of the charity, responsibility for achieving the appeal target.
2. To use his influence and standing to the maximum benefit of the appeal. If the appeal chairman is to be in the best position to raise money, he will have been responsible for obtaining a major gift from his own organization (or giving one personally).
3. To gather around him a high-level team of similar leaders in their fields to help him run the appeal and make personal approaches where necessary. The right calibre of chairman will not accept a ready-made committee.
4. To agree a strategy for fund-raising with a clear objective and plan of action.
5. To supervise the strategy.
6. To help select and work closely with the appeal director, who will set up and run the appeal office and implement the strategy.
7. To ensure close liaison between the charity and the appeal.
8. To assist the charity with its own business plan if required.

It is not always easy to find someone who has all the right qualities and can carry out these demanding tasks. Detailed research is necessary to draw up a short list of likely people. Discuss the list with a few prominent industrialists who have been involved in charity work and put the names in agreed order of priority.

Great care should be taken over how a potential chairman is contacted. At all costs, rejection should be avoided. An appeal which has been turned down by several potential chairmen can acquire a lasting stigma, however valid its cause. It is worth researching a candidate's concerns before attempting the summit meeting, which should be undertaken by someone whom he respects. This is enshrined in the principle that like should approach like. The call should come from someone whom the candidate wants to please. Make it plain that the legwork will be taken care of and that the appeal chairmanship will be a pleasant and fulfilling experience which will do his own prospects no harm.

This may sound like an extraordinarily complicated gavotte, but it really is worth the trouble. The right approach can make the difference between success and failure. The process can take many months. It is important not to be rushed and to wait for the right person. This time is never wasted; valuable information, which can eventually be put to good use, can be acquired. A potential chairman who declines the post may feel that the least he can do is generate a suitably large gift from his own company.

When setting up a meeting, the 'door opener' should say merely that he wishes to seek advice. Depending on the response, that may be all that is looked for, but often the meeting can enthuse someone who previously was determined not to become involved. The 'door opener' may take along the appeal director to answer technical questions and, if the opportunity arises, to explain in person what would be expected of an appeal chairman. It is important to keep the meetings small and low-key at this stage.

Recruitment

The procedure leading up to recruiting a potential chairman should be carefully followed, as it can easily go wrong.

- Wait until the project details make sense and satisfactory answers can be provided to questions that are likely to arise.
- Having ensured that he is approached on the appeal's behalf by the person most likely to convince him, invite him to see the site, building or whatever is relevant, and to meet those responsible for running the charity and the project.
- Assure him that, should he take on the role of chairman, he will have access to the necessary fund-raising advice.
- Assure him that few meetings will be required and that the appeal officers will do all the legwork.
- Make it clear that the appeal is a discrete activity with a specific objective and defined time commitment – i.e. it has an end.

CONSULTANT OR APPEAL DIRECTOR?

Sooner or later, a charity considering a one-off appeal will wonder whether it should be advised by a fund-raising consultant or should try to appoint an appeal director straight away. It is unusual to find both the expertise needed and the right candidate for the appeal director in one person. Moreover, if it were possible, it would be very expensive as fund-raising consultants command high fees. As the consultant is likely to take a step back once the appeal gets under way, he can be expected to provide dispassionate advice of a different nature from someone who is going to be running the appeal over a period of years.

In most instances, fund-raising consultants advise on the feasibility of reaching the target and what should be done to prepare for and plan an appeal. Then their job is over. Some consultants put in their own campaign director on a short-term contract to run the appeal, replacing the consultant. At the end of the appeal, the campaign director hands over to someone more suited to running the ongoing fund-raising operation. From the charity's point of view, I believe that it is prefer-

---

Warning

All too often, trustees heave an enormous sigh of relief once the fund-raising consultant has been appointed. 'Thank goodness, he'll now do the fund-raising,' they say, 'that's that taken care of'. A great deal of misunderstanding arises from this attitude. The consultant only advises. The officer appointed, together with the trustees and high-level volunteers recruited to run the appeal, actually carries out the fund-raising.

able for it to appoint its own staff member. This avoids the risk of split loyalties and ensures continuity after the appeal. However, ideal candidates are not easy to find.

Charities want to know exactly what they are letting themselves in for when they take on a fund-raising consultant, but it is difficult to generalize. A proper feasibility study will take a consultant at least three months to carry out. It will involve considerable research into the project, from whether the trustees are fully behind it to interviewing potential donors. It may also include initial fund-raising strategy. The cost varies enormously depending on what is being offered – and by whom.

It is important for the charity to obtain a clear view of what advice it needs at each stage, so that its management can take the lead in determining what is required – and then shop around for it. However, it may be difficult to acquire a sufficiently clear view without first listening to a consultant. The process has to begin somewhere, preferably with a definite aim in mind. With the steering or study group, a consultant will look at the fund-raising proposition to see if it will make sense to a major donor. He needs to assure himself that there is a convincing case for an appeal. He looks at the feasibility of raising the funds and helps to prepare the Preliminary Report on the appeal. Approaches are made to several potential major donors to see what their response would be to an appeal. If the answers are negative, the consultant will advise accordingly and suggest modifications, or he may advise against the appeal altogether. He will not encourage the appeal organizers to continue with a potential failure, as he will not want to be associated with it. A consultant may also pull out if the trustees cannot agree on the way ahead. But in most cases, after suitable preparation, the consultant arrives at a basis on which the appeal can proceed. The charity will then be near to deciding what the appeal target should be.

The consultant's role can cover all or part of the preparation of the appeal strategy. He can help specify the type and numbers of staff needed, assist with recruitment and then provide an ongoing advisory service to the appeal director, if necessary. Consultants can be very useful in the latter role – once the execution of an appeal strategy has begun, it is easy for all those closely involved to be sidetracked from the core strategy by new ideas, perceived changes in the environment etc. Review meetings, which include a consultant, maintain an objective view. The consultant commands respect from the trustees and appeal committee because he has been involved in determining the strategy from the beginning and this allows him to inject a sense of challenge and authority into meetings in a way staff members often cannot.

HOW TO FIND A CONSULTANT

In Britain, the pioneer of the idea of using peer-group asking power to raise charitable donations was an American called Colonel Lewis Wells. He set up the Wells Organization in Britain in 1958, probably the first fund-raising consultancy. Soon afterwards, Dr. Michael Hooker left Wells to set up a competing agency with Lord Craigmyle. Their principle was to use social and business influence. In most cases, they recruited people with asking power on to a committee that raised the money, as opposed to paying staff to approach potential donors. This was very effective because it meant that the individual brought his influence directly to bear on potential donors. They might be neighbours, the donor might be a major supplier or somebody owing a big favour.

Until a few years ago, the phrase 'professional fund-raiser' had poor connotations in Britain. There were misgivings about people being paid a salary for charity work rather than providing voluntary help. They were derided as making money for themselves on the back of a charity. At the worst, professional fund-raisers – whether salaried or paid freelance fees – were given a dubious name because of the activities of a few fraudsters. In the early 1980s, Iain Scarlet ran a series of stories in *The Sunday Times* about the misdeeds of so-called fund-raisers. In fact, they were not fund-raisers; they were opportunists selling advertising space in charity brochures and taking 65 per cent or more of the proceeds themselves. It was right that they should be exposed, but from that came the realization that something should be done to improve the image of fund-raising. A steering group set up the Institute of Charity Fund-raising Managers (ICFM). The Institute produced a Code of Conduct and started to encourage professionalism in all types of fund-raising. It is now very successful, having nearly 2,000 members who are proud to call themselves professional fund-raisers.

The ICFM provides professional support and training for fund-raisers at all levels and offers its members a forum for discussion, opportunities for contact with other professionals and a regularly updated information service. Its head office is in London and there is a network of regional groups. Training is provided at three levels; a training programme leads to the Institute's Certificate. Members of the Institute are committed to its Codes of Practice, which cover such areas as schools, lotteries and consultants' contracts.

There is nothing to beat finding a consultant through a satisfied customer. Otherwise, charities should go to the Institute, which issues a list of fund-raising consultant members. The fund-raising staff of all charities should seriously consider joining the Institute; membership will put them on the inside track and update them on the latest developments in fund-raising. The Institute's training courses are essential for would-be professionals. Another body to consider is the Association of Fundraising Consultants, which has its own code of conduct and represents some of the U.K.'s most established fund-raising consultancies.

CODE OF CONDUCT

The Institute of Charity Fundraising Managers and the National Council for Voluntary Organizations (NCVO) have jointly produced a booklet designed to assist charities in finding a suitable fund-raising consultant.

It recommends that a short list of candidates are asked these questions:

1. Their relevant qualifications and experience
2. Their willingness to work for the recruiting charity
3. How soon they would be available
4. How much time they expect to commit and over what period
5. Estimated charges and payment intervals
6. Likely expenses
7. Their view of the charity's target
8. Names of charities willing to give references

9. Whether they have a standard form of contract
10. What provision they would make for early termination of contract and discharge of outstanding obligations in that event.

The ICFM and the NCVO advise charities to examine the answers to these questions carefully, paying particular attention to candidates' specific intentions and other commitments. Take up all references and ensure that donors' cheques are made payable to the charity not the fund-raiser.

Good consultants are in great demand. Despite the recent improvement in standards, big names, often reputable consultants, still get new business and then put in a junior to follow it through and effectively be the account manager. My advice is always to meet the person who is actually going to be working with you. Make sure that you respect his record, that you get on with him as an individual and that he is sympathetic to your cause. It is essential that the chemistry is right. It is very helpful for a charity to see more than one potential fund-raising consultant. It should provide them with a good brief and ask them to come back with outline proposals of how they would proceed. The charity should be careful not to encourage candidates to come up with a plan for the sake of it, without having all the necessary background.

I take a long time to immerse myself in a project before coming up with an appeal strategy. As well as knowing the project as its leaders see it, it is essential to view it as their constituency sees it, whether the beneficiaries of the charity, its supporters or the government department with which it works. Before my appointment, Great Ormond Street Hospital was in touch with two fund-raising consultants who were working together, advising the Hospital on how to prepare for a one-off appeal. This was enormously helpful to me because the Hospital was able to avoid many common errors. The consultants stressed the importance of coordinating the Appeal's activities with the Hospital's other fund-raising activities and not approaching potential major donors before the planning phase was complete. I was then brought in to create the Appeal strategy for the approval of the Executive Committee and to set up the Appeal and run the office. The consultants played the role of primary educators, saving me considerable preliminary time and effort in agreeing ground rules.

REMUNERATION FOR CONSULTANTS

There is general opposition – from the Charity Commission, the ICFM and the Association of Fundraising Consultants – to any suggestion that consultants link their remuneration to the size of funds raised. Apart from any ethical considerations, paying commission would hardly promote good relations between a consultant and an appeal's staff and volunteers. It could be a significant deterrent to donors; no major donor would give a large sum if he knew that a proportion of it was going into one person's pocket. To prevent the appeal being damaged, such an arrangement would have to be kept secret and no charity can afford to be party to any arrangement not open to inspection. Payment of commission also leads to lack of clarity about what should be rewarded and when. In the case of covenants, for example, should commission be paid for all four years to which the covenant applies, even though the consultant might be employed for only one year? When should the commission be paid – up front in year one or annually over a four-year period? Some trusts, before making a donation, ask for confirmation that no fund-raiser connected with the organization is paid on a commission basis.

It is usual to pay a consultant a fee, which can be based on undertaking a certain study, drawing up a particular strategy, or on time. Fees vary considerably, according to the standard of the consultant and his experience. Bear in mind that a good fund-raising consultant covers a wide spectrum of activities. He should advise on the feasibility of raising a target by reviewing both potential and past sources of funds, and existing and future leadership. He will help to draw up the strategy to achieve the appeal's objectives and may become further involved in helping to recruit and train staff. These activities vary in their relevance to the sums raised, but they do have a value. As in most other forms of consultancy, a fee is the most appropriate way of expressing this value. Consultants' remuneration is addressed in the Charities Act 1992. The Act requires that all dealings between a 'professional fund-raiser' and a charity *must* be conducted in accordance with the terms of a formal agreement. In addition, a general indication has to be given of the method of calculating the remuneration of any such professional fund-raiser in all solicitations for funds made by the fund-raiser. Exactly what constitutes a 'professional fund-raiser' for the purposes of the Act, and how to comply with this legislation, is considered in Appendix 8. The application of these provisions must be considered and dealt with as one of the first priorities in any fund-raising initiative.

THE QUALITIES OF A CONSULTANT

Consultants should be alert. They must listen and understand before pronouncing, and they have to be able to take the trustees and other leading people at the charity along with them every step of the way. No matter what the charity's requirements are, if it is thinking of raising a large sum, there is no substitute for experience.

The first quality to look for in a consultant is undoubtedly political awareness. A fund-raiser is like a lion tamer; he is surrounded by others who are bigger than him and can tear him apart. He has to be able to stand up to them with strong and cogent arguments. Unless consultants can withstand unjustified challenges, they can easily be pushed around and bullied into less than ideal decisions. This often manifests itself in undue haste to find an appeal chairman. Trustees sometimes get cold feet after two or three potential candidates have declined the job and may then be tempted to make a less than ideal choice. The problem for the fund-raising consultant or the appeal director is to stand up to trustees or governors and say, 'Look, I'm sorry, but if we do what you are proposing, the success of this appeal could be in jeopardy.'

Giles Pegram, Appeals Director of the NSPCC, often talks of the role of his consultant in the NSPCC Centenary Appeal. *He never let us lower our sights, accept second best. He helped us keep our nerve during the planning stages when more money was being spent than raised. He constantly challenged our thinking. It was sometimes difficult, but it was invaluable.*

The trustees of a landscape park restoration project I was advising had nearly got to the point of selecting the wrong type of chairman. I became unpopular by resisting the mooted appointment. As a result of persuading them to wait, we eventually recruited Peter (now Lord) Palumbo, the property developer who became Chairman of the Arts Council. It was almost unnecessary to launch a major appeal after that because, when it mattered, he always seemed able to bring in a friend or contact who could fund a particular folly or planting project.

Consultants may sometimes have to insist that a charity's plans must be altered. I was asked to give advice to a university college. The Master explained to dinner guests how far they had progressed in planning their appeal. One of the first steps proposed was a get-together of all their alumni to raise funds. Telling those attending the dinner that whatever they did, they must cancel that event was very embarrassing for me. The invitations had been printed but not sent out. It was awkward, but in the end I convinced them that the smaller sums would come from the alumni and that they should always go for the big gifts first. They had got it the wrong way round. This is a common error.

Another well-meaning mistake is to accept the offer of the opportunity to run a charity concert when an appeal is still in the private phase. It can be very damaging to embark on such a public exercise because it may ruin the impact of the appeal. The main danger is the 'vaccination effect'. An individual or organization may make a donation to such an event, perhaps by buying tickets. If he is later approached privately for what the appeal organizers hope will be a much more substantial donation, he can fairly respond that he has already given – in effect, he has been 'vaccinated' against further donation.

These are examples of what consultants can be expected to contribute by way of advice but only if they have personally suffered the consequences of the many potential pitfalls and have the courage to stand their ground and steer a high-powered board or committee around those dangers.

GETTING THE BEST FROM YOUR CONSULTANT

All too often I see staff members handling their consultants in a way that may lead to an uncomfortable relationship. The staff member should look to his consultant for wise counsel and support at all times. It should be a mutually beneficial relationship. It is easy to see how the relationship can go wrong.

Remedies

Choose as wisely as you can and, having done so, believe in your choice and work at the relationship to make sure that you get the best out of it for your appeal and to achieve a happy working environment for you both.

You need 101 per cent of your consultant's ability – so make sure you have his loyalty, too. This means treating him much as you would any other member of the team, but there is a difference. He may be more senior than you so, even though you must monitor his work carefully, make sure it is done with tact, respect and sensitivity. By the same token, a good consultant will treat every staff member with respect – whatever their status.

Do not forget to thank him and show that you appreciate his input – as you would any other helper, paid or unpaid – and do not forget to invite him to your charity's social and staff events.

Prejudices

- Stories circulate about consultants charging high fees for a less than adequate service – and some will be true – but remember that there are also a number of consultants who enjoy lasting and good relationships with their clients. I know of one who has worked with one major charity for the last 12 years; a long relationship, based on trust, respect and mutual confidence.
- As with the appointment of any individual, you should interview your consultant carefully and take up references. Once you have taken him on, believe in him and give him the backing he needs to do a good job for you. If you undermine his position, you diminish his ability to carry out the role you have appointed him to do.
- Some staff feel that needing a consultant to advise reflects negatively on them.
- No individual can be a specialist in every area of expertise required to guide an appeal. Seeing your consultant as an extension of what can be achieved for your cause is the most positive way to approach the situation. If you give support and loyalty to the consultant, it will be returned.
- Another negative factor faced by some consultants is resentment, from their opposite number on the charity's staff, of their level of fees and the fact that they charge on a time basis.
- Consultants' fees are high in comparison with a staff salary, partly because they are usually very experienced people in great demand. In addition, as well as the consultant's time, the fee has to include a proportion of all his costs – secretary, office overheads, etc. It must also include time spent on his operation's administrative matters or 'pitching' for new business.

Although their main input is at the beginning of an appeal, most consultants wish to be kept in touch and to know how things are progressing after their contract ends. At the celebratory occasions, after you hit the target, do not forget to recognize the part they played in helping you get there.

THE APPEAL DIRECTOR

Being an appeal director is all to do with handling people, seeing opportunities and using vision and imagination to solve problems. The choice of a particular individual is entirely dependent on the constituency of the cause, so look for the sort of person who will fit in. A housing association and The Game Conservancy Trust would need directors with different qualities, although I have given voluntary advice to both. An appeal director needs sensitivity and the ability to recruit and motivate people. A talent for public speaking is useful. Staff have to work all hours, which is possible only by creating a good spirit in the office. To some extent, this happens naturally because the people who work for charity are usually motivated. That is why they are willing to work for less than they could earn doing the same type of job on the open market. However, once the honeymoon period is over, it is up to the appeal director to sustain morale and enthusiasm.

There are few people with the qualifications to be the ideal appeal director. Charities must advertise for exactly the type of person they need in terms of character, personality, background, education, interpersonal skills and experience of previous appeals. If the choice they face is between fund-raising experience and calibre, I would advise them to opt for the latter. As long as the candidate has the motivation, he can acquire technical advice, go on training courses, and be supported by a consultant for a period – but you cannot give people calibre. If the ideal candidate is not available, then management ability should be the deciding quality. An experienced manager can get to know the fund-raising business quickly and can exert leadership to hire and keep a team that will provide the missing elements. Nevertheless, this is second-best and depends on the size of the team. If it is a small team, it can work closely with a consultant, but a less experienced director would have difficulties in leading a team of more knowledgeable fund-raisers.

I think that one of two backgrounds is desirable for an appeal director. One is administration and the other is marketing. Administration – the ability to manage – has to be at the heart. The appeal director's desk is where the buck stops for every administrative problem, from finding a chairman to scrounging another typewriter. He is responsible for setting up the management systems, ensuring that tax and legal matters are covered and obtaining financial advice. The appeal director smooths the path for chairman-to-chairman donor approaches by working out who is the best person to make the approach, and getting the donor to visit the site of an appeal beforehand so that he really understands the project and feels emotionally involved. The fund-raiser should arrange that rather than trying to elicit money himself. His asking power will almost certainly not be strong enough, unless he happens to be a close contact of the potential donor.

Marketing is very important, too. Fund-raising is about marketing ideals. Marketing is about finding the market for a product, refining that product to make it more acceptable to its customers and selling it. The prime product in an appeal is the project for which the money is needed, but it would be wrong to ignore the emotions that a donation can generate. Tugging at those emotions is a vital task if the appeal is to fulfil its potential, for they are all part of the package the donor is buying when he gives. However, marketing is only one of many skills that an experienced fund-raiser calls on for a one-off appeal. It is not sufficient in itself, however brilliant the ideas with which a marketeer might dazzle a selection committee. Furthermore, the professional manager can usually hire or recruit voluntary marketing expertise, so administrative skill, leadership and an ability to manage have to be at the heart of an appeal director's essential qualities.

The wisdom of appointing a part-time appeal director depends on the type of project, its emotional content and the level of funding required. When I was involved with The Guinness Trust, I was finishing off its appeal two days a week while I was starting a new appeal for Charing Cross Medical Research Centre three days a week. I continued with this arrangement for a year and then ran the Charing Cross appeal for four days a week. In the main, I advise charities to go for a full-timer; buy all his attention and, with a bit of luck, the fund-raising will be completed sooner. Nevertheless, fund-raising takes its own time. Rushing increases the chance of failure.

As a rule, the appeal director should adopt a lower profile than the appeal chairman. Some appeal directors may want to use the project to enhance their career profiles. This can be dangerous because the chairman will usually be a better spokesman. The appeal director should work behind the scenes, guiding and advising the high-level people and getting them to make the contacts, open doors and so on because their names and influence make the chances of success much higher. The appeal director will step forward as spokesman if the chairman is not available to do so or if the line of questioning has to do with the appeal's administration rather than its overall direction.

I can vouch that being an appeal director is one of the most stimulating, challenging and varied jobs imaginable. The only downside is when, as quoted by the appeal director of a very large charity, 'after an exhausting day at work, I tell someone at a party what I do. "Oh, how fascinating," they say. "But what is your proper job?"'

CHAIRMAN OR DIRECTOR FIRST?

In most cases, I advise appointing the chairman first – if he is top calibre. He carries the overall responsibility for achieving the target and part of that responsibility is to acquire the right resources to do so. Prime among those resources should be the appointment of an appeal director capable of helping to draw up and carry out the strategy devised for the appeal. The chairman can make sure that he has the right working relationship and chemistry with the candidate appointed as director. The relationship between the chairman and the director is vital to the success of the appeal; the two must work closely as a team. When I applied for the Wishing Well Appeal post, I was interviewed by a panel that included Lord Prior as Appeal Chairman, the Chairman of the Board of Governors, the Chairman of the Special Trustees, the General Manager of the Hospital and a management consultant who was there to ask the tricky questions! This gave me the opportunity to meet the wider team with whom I would be working. I found it helpful that Jim Prior had been appointed before me.

The appeal director devises the basic strategy; the power and influence of the chairman pushes, or preferably eases it through. A director appointed before his chairman can be in a rather exposed position when starting up a new appeal.

I was particularly fortunate in the Wishing Well Appeal's choice of chairman. It could have been a problem if the Chairman had tried to hassle and rush his fences, which someone with a different temperament might well have tried to do. Taking that essential time to get the facts and to test the water made all the difference to our Appeal.

However, if an appeal is experiencing delay in finding a suitable chairman, it may be wise to go ahead with the appointment of a director. This means that much of the planning can proceed: project research, appeal research and the feasibility study into raising the funds.

TO WHOM SHOULD THE DIRECTOR REPORT?

It is essential that an individual reports to only one person to avoid misunderstandings and confusion. Otherwise a subordinate can play one superior off against another, has difficulties about priorities and can generate bad feeling between the two bosses, who in turn cannot tell how well the subordinate is performing. The staff member responsible for the successful management of the one-off appeal must report to the honorary chairman. And careful thought should also be given to the roles of the ongoing charity's chairman and chief executive and their counterparts in the appeal organization. The charity management will normally wish to fit the fund-raiser into their team. However, the chairman recruited to ensure the success of the appeal will quite naturally expect to have total jurisdiction over the appeal's director or chief executive.

In the one-off appeals on which I have worked, I have nearly always reported directly to the chairman of the appeal. However, it was necessary for me to have very close liaison with the chief executive of the charity. This was especially successful in the Wishing Well Appeal, where my opposite number was the General Manager of the Hospital, Sir Anthony Tippet. We were constantly in touch as it was essential that I liaised with him on all matters pertaining to the Hospital, as opposed to the Appeal. We had to agree who would be permitted to visit the Hospital and when, and how we were intending to present the Hospital and its activities in Appeal publications. Nevertheless, it was and always will be difficult to have two parallel organizations running alongside. This is usually best overcome by some of the charity's trustees or governors being on the executive committee for the appeal. In the case of the Wishing Well Appeal, I initially suffered from all the common problems of a 'them and us' attitude between the Hospital and the Appeal staffs, but this diminished considerably with the appointment of Sir Anthony; as we worked well together, he could make immediate decisions on urgent matters and he eased my way in dealing with Hospital staff.

A fund-raiser has to encourage the charity to take actions that sometimes go against the grain in order to maximize marketing opportunities for the appeal. Quite correctly, the charity will wish to guard its name, but there is always a balancing act between the sensibilities of the charity's staff and supporters and the danger of the appeal falling below potential. One way around this problem is to set up a separate legal entity, probably a charitable trust, to handle fund-raising and marketing for a specific objective. The trust can then have its own trustees and chief executive. However, this does not obviate the need for close liaison with the operational side of the charity. The problem never goes away. All organizations require different types of people to run them and they often have difficulty relating to each other. Tensions can arise in large charities between social workers and fund-raisers or marketeers. The fact is that they are usually different types of people, who need to adopt distinct methods and approaches if they are to do their best in their respective roles.

RECRUITING PANEL LEADERS

Once the appeal chairman has been recruited, his first step is to draw together his inner cabinet of close, loyal friends and associates to look at the wider circle of contacts and see whom they should recruit to head the different appeal panels.

It is rare for a chairman to have the ideal basis to make a personal approach to every potential leader involved in an appeal. Usually his inner cabinet will help. In the Wishing Well Appeal, we initially recruited top people closely connected with Lord Prior and called them the Advisory Council. They turned into an informal steering group for the Appeal. Once we had recruited the right people, the Advisory Council was disbanded and those involved moved to the Executive Committee or the panels. Once again, extreme care should be taken as to how these individuals are approached and motivated to care about the cause and the Appeal. Great Ormond Street was lucky enough to be able to invite them to the Hospital so that they could understand the importance of its work before being asked to play a part in ensuring its future excellence.

Business people are often called in to act as charity doctors, rather like company doctors in business but, faced with handling volunteers rather than employees in key positions, they often find it difficult to use methods that work in business. It is not nearly so easy to wave the big stick if people are voluntary. One of a fund-raiser's first jobs is to assure business people that, unless they use their skills in a determined and no-nonsense manner, the appeal has little chance of success. It is impossible to run an effective operation of any kind, including a charity, if people try to remain friends with everyone all the time. It has to be a professional operation, although friendships and alliances will flower. I have frequently heard top businessmen say that after undertaking the running of an appeal, they find that people cross the road to avoid them – but that depends on how people are asked to help. It would be easier if they saw this not so much as asking a personal favour, but as sharing the opportunity of doing something really worthwhile for the community.

Treasurer

Another key leadership post for an appeal is the treasurer. The ideal candidate for a large national appeal is the chairman or senior executive of one of the major banks or building societies. A smaller or local appeal would still be well advised to select someone linked to a well-known financial institution, but perhaps of a less elevated status. The appointment immediately signals that the appeal is likely to be soundly financed; this fosters confidence among potential donors. A suitably senior candidate also indicates that the financial establishment tacitly approves of the appeal's aims. Less obviously, a prominent figure as treasurer is capable of taking over the chairmanship if need be.

CONCLUSION

The public does not realize how much is contributed to the success of major appeals by the unstinting efforts of leading business people in this country. It is impossible to calculate the value of their time and know-how (although the recently published *Report on Volunteering* produced by the Volunteer Centre did try to do this), but in my experience, industrialists who accept the leadership of appeals enjoy the process and consequently enhance the quality of their lives and personal standing. Both factors have a knock-on benefit to their companies, which more than justifies the sacrifice made by their shareholders.

That is not to say that the businessmen do not have heartaches along the way. They do. Setting up an appeal is similar to the start-up stage of a business, which top entrepreneurs are continually rehearsing with new projects within their corporate empires. Less easy for them to reconcile is the uncertain and often ambiguous hierarchy they encounter in an appeal through the mix of voluntary and paid staff. At least in business responsibilities are fairly clear cut.

Nevertheless, all the appeal chairmen with whom I have worked treasure their memories and are left with a sense of fulfilment. I remember Sir Robert Clark (when he was chairman of the Hill Samuel Group) saying 'never again' at the end of the Charing Cross Medical Research Centre Appeal. As a result, I did not initially try to recruit him to chair later appeals I helped. Imagine my dismay on discovering I had made a terrible mistake for he immediately immersed himself in other charitable work – proving that he had really enjoyed the process and intended to do more to help the community. His experience in this field makes him an extremely valuable advisor to others considering taking the plunge. He is only one example of a business leader who has successfully transferred his skills to the charitable sector. Such people are to be prized and cherished, for they have the ability to recruit and inspire other talented businessmen to follow their example to the benefit of every deserving cause.

Chapter 7

APPEAL STRATEGY

Previous chapters have looked at the merit of the project plans and the reputation of the charity. They have discussed researching actual and potential supporters and reviewing the feasibility of raising the funds required. Later chapters examine further topics for research, but at this stage it is possible to make preliminary decisions. Based on the response so far, fund-raisers can gauge the level of the appeal target for which it is prudent to aim and put together the initial plans and strategy for the appeal itself.

OBJECTIVES

The first step is to review and agree the objective of the fund-raising exercise. This may be simply to raise the required funds through a one-off appeal. It may be to use an appeal as a vehicle to raise the profile of a charity during and after the campaign or to facilitate its role and recruit more volunteers or ongoing donors. Whatever the objectives, they must be clearly established and agreed at the outset. The Great Ormond Street Redevelopment Appeal was designed to raise enough money to fund the new, five-storey block – the building as well as the equipment and furnishings. We also aimed to leave the Hospital with a legacy of a vastly increased donor base.

STRATEGY

Having agreed the objectives with the charity's leaders, the fund-raiser looks for the necessary strategy to achieve them. The previous stages that I have described explain the different exercises necessary to collect the facts required before a fund-raiser can map the appeal's strategy or master plan. This includes deciding whether to have a public appeal. Your cause may be little known and not very emotive to the public, in which case a public appeal may not be worthwhile. Your research should help you decide. If your project is highly emotive or universally accepted, you can budget for generating a considerable proportion of funds during the public phase.

Fund-raising is easier to control at the private stage. You can select likely donors more precisely and explain the reasons for the appeal individually. If it is modest enough or sufficient large gifts are obtained, the appeal target may be reached through this avenue alone. As a result, some appeals do not plan to go public at all. Once the appeal is public, even if it is planned to the ultimate degree, the appeal directorship inevitably loses some control in return for the greater exposure and the increased revenue-generating potential entailed.

I produced the Great Ormond Street Redevelopment Strategy Appeal Document nine months after I had been appointed in April 1985. It can take that long. However, the essential elements of the Appeal had been incorporated in the first Preliminary Report, which was issued in October 1985.

The seven key factors of the strategy

1. We decided to use peer group fund-raising. This means recruiting highly placed voluntary individuals to make personal approaches on behalf of the Appeal.
2. We created a well-tailored structure of panels and committees, ensuring each section knew the overall objective, its part in the master plan, its own guidelines, territory, range of activities and target figure.
3. We used sophisticated marketing techniques to ensure that our message reached the widest possible audience. By recruiting honorary leading experts in the field, we planned to create a positive message and to keep our appeal constantly in the public eye.
4. We aimed to raise at least one-third of our target sum before launching the Appeal to the public.
5. We aimed to obtain a substantial government contribution for the Appeal to overcome any criticism that we were doing its job.
6. We aimed to attract major donors and to offer them specific parts of the building to commemorate.
7. We aimed to keep costs and staff to a minimum by involving the maximum number of volunteers at all levels and obtaining gifts in kind wherever possible.

STRATEGY DOCUMENT

The main objectives of the appeal and the grand strategy for achieving them should be contained in the Strategy Document. It is the master plan for the whole operation, so it gives an overview without going into too much detail. It is usually prepared by the professional fund-raiser concerned for the approval of the governing body of the appeal. The Preliminary Report includes the beginning of the strategy for the appeal and is used to recruit leadership. Once this has taken place, an expanded strategy must be agreed so that clear fund-raising principles and the proposed methods are understood and agreed.

The strategy document should cover the appeal objectives, the honorary and staff structures of the appeal, an explanation of the roles of the panels, information about potential sources of funds, target sums to be raised from each, the legal status of the appeal and who is responsible for raising, investing and spending the funds.

The Strategy Document should set out a linear programme, showing how the appeal phasing is split between the planning, private and public stages. It should include reference to the need for personal approaches, making sure the private phase is kept private and that there is no publicity in advance of the public launch. It should be so comprehensive that every person involved in the project and the appeal should know precisely what is expected of him, whether as an individual or as a member of a committee or panel. The overall strategy should be broken down and applied to each operating unit of the appeal, so that goals can be set and performance measured. This document can then be a constant reference for the leadership to assess progress. It should be supplemented with an action plan for each activity panel.

The Strategy Document is the crucial first step in planning and agreeing the way the appeal should be implemented. (Each of these areas will be covered in more detail in Parts III and IV.) The version produced for Great Ormond Street Hospital included a comprehensive project brief to committee members. Without an in-depth knowledge of the Hospital, its needs and the plan for the appeal, the voluntary fund-raisers could not be suitable advocates for our campaign.

The project brief should describe the background, the problems, the solution, a breakdown of the costs and details of government involvement. It should also include information about the charity's qualifications to undertake the project, and about the team selected to do the work. There may also be answers to difficult or political questions which may arise – so that all supporters speak with one voice. A concluding section should sum up the scale of the task, the effect and likelihood of reaching the goal and the value of the project to the community or the nation. This information will be continually up-dated, extended and refined for the succession of documents which will be needed during the Appeal.

APPEAL TIMING

Most appeals can be split into a minimum of three phases: planning, private appeal and public appeal. However, the time necessary to prepare an appeal can vary substantially. Every project is different. This decision must depend on the circumstances. The Wishing Well Appeal took well over a year before launching its private appeal, although we had achieved at least £4.5 million in pledges before initiating the business appeal.

Lord Prior, our Chairman, was keen that we should be well prepared in every way before launching the Appeal, so he gave us time to evolve the right strategy and listened carefully to advice on this important issue. We hit the deadline for the public launch when we said we would, but this was more to do with keeping the story out of the press to achieve maximum impact when we went public.

In any document I wrote during the preparation phase, I emphasized that we did not want any publicity initially. There were two reasons for this. The first reason is the 'vaccination effect', when a donor, having given an unsolicited small gift, usually prompted by reading about the appeal in the press, is effectively 'vaccinated' against a further approach. So it is wise to delay the public launch of the appeal until all such potential donors have received a personal approach at the highest level. The second reason for delaying publicity is to ensure that the appeal can be seen to be a success from the very start. Nothing succeeds like success and people do not like to back a possible loser. Having a large sum in the bank forestalls that fear.

A wise appeal director produces an appeal programme calendar which contains time for his panellists to make their personal approaches to potentially large donors. He must do his best to convince all concerned that they should stick to the deadlines if the appeal is to succeed. However, he will know that appeal work will rarely be the first priority in the lives of the influential people involved. Honorary fund-raisers can seldom approach all the people they say they will in the agreed time. It is then best to delay the launch until all potential major donors have been approached personally. A sample appeal calendar is shown in Appendix 5.

APPEAL STRUCTURE

Once the appeal has identified potential sources of funds and agreed a strategy for approaching them, it needs a clearly defined structure if it intends to recruit honorary staff with specific qualifications to do the asking. Each group, panel or committee needs to understand the overall objective and master plan and where its operation fits into the whole. Their authority, responsibilities and reporting channels must be clear and each unit needs to produce a plan of action that includes a timetable and financial target. Although each of these operating units is advised by the relevant staff member, it is important that they have considerable input to the creation of the master plan. This gives them a feeling of proprietorship towards the final version, so that they feel fully committed to it and responsible for its successful outcome. The Wishing Well Appeal's organization chart is shown in Appendix 1.

Warning

I prefer to avoid referring to 'committees' because many business people automatically shy away in the belief that they are merely time-wasting talking shops. On the other hand, they do like to feel they are being placed in a like-minded group as they do not want to be left holding the baby. They do need the assurance of backing from a good staff member to ensure that they are plugged into the rest of the appeal management system.

The first step in structuring an appeal is to decide upon the body legally responsible for its outcome. Great Ormond Street Hospital has a body called the Special Trustees, appointed by the Government to handle all charitable funds sent to the Hospital. In 1984, the Hospital's Board of Governors and Special Trustees set up The Great Ormond Street Trust for the Hospital for Sick Children to undertake the Redevelopment Appeal. It was chaired by William Clarke, then the Director of the British Invisible Exports Council (now British Invisibles), and its members included some of the Hospital's Special Trustees. The Appeal Trustees, as Mr.

Clarke's body became known, retained responsibility for handling and investing the funds received through the Appeal, while delegating to one of their members (Lord Prior) full responsibility for raising the sum required. Jim Prior had first been recruited as the Appeal Chairman, but was then appointed an Appeal Trustee to consolidate his legal status.

Royal connections and respected names

The gracious agreement of Royalty to become Patrons is a great advantage in fund-raising. Not all charities are lucky enough to receive Royal patronage although many would aspire to such high-level support. Their patronage is not usually attached to the appeal but to the project or charity itself – and then only if the charity is well respected and seen to be on a sound footing. The Wishing Well Appeal was an exception; HM The Queen is the Patron of the Hospital, so the Prince and Princess of Wales very kindly agreed to be Patrons of the Appeal itself. We knew we were asking a great deal in requesting them to consider accepting that position. Usually only female members of the Royal Family have a formal connection with hospitals, but we felt that any child in the Hospital was a parent's problem, not just a mother's, and that there were no better known parents than the Prince and Princess of Wales.

The archives contained a precedent. From 1901 to 1920, the then Prince and Princess of Wales had been Vice-Patrons of the Hospital and further research revealed that the Royal Family had been continuously involved with the Hospital since its inception, when Queen Victoria became its first Patron. We produced a detailed story of this involvement, beautifully written by Jules Kosky, the Hospital's Assistant Archivist. This story was illustrated, printed and bound at no cost to the Appeal and sent to the Palace with our request. We were really delighted that the Prince and Princess accepted and their full-hearted involvement in the Appeal was one of the crucial factors in our success.

Some appeals collect well-known people as patrons largely to associate their names with the appeal rather than to take an active role. This can be very effective in giving a suitable seal of approval to a project that may not be so well known. However, I do not suggest that a charity should recruit a long list of inactive figures for fear of creating scepticism rather than reassurance.

Appointing a president and vice-presidents is a further device for attaching well-known and well-respected names to an appeal. Such titles usually indicate that those concerned give their names rather than active service. In the case of the Wishing Well Appeal, we spent a long time researching who might be suitable to be President of the Appeal, while we got on with approaching potential Vice-Presidents. The Vice-Presidents we wanted were the leaders of the British political parties, the leaders of the country's main religions and the presidents of relevant medical institutions. We also approached the Lord Lieutenant for Greater London and the Lord Mayor of London, both of whom played an active role in the Appeal. We were lucky enough to recruit all those we wanted, with the exception of the politicians. The choice of Vice-Presidents was obvious in that we wished to demonstrate that the Appeal had been rubber-stamped by every relevant sector of the community at the highest level.

We never appointed a President for the Wishing Well Appeal. We were looking for a very popular public figure, probably a familiar television personality, who was not about to get into some sort of trouble and ruin his reputation! We did not succeed. We approached two people without success and finally decided to leave the slot vacant, but to keep an open mind in case we came across an individual who seemed ideal. So the reader may be reassured to know that the Wishing Well Appeal did have its failures. However, as we had Jim Prior as Chairman – a distinguished figure in his own right – it was less vital to fill the post of President.

Business Panels

Lord Prior recruited a strong group of top business people on to the Advisory Council (see Chapter 6) to steer the initial progress of the Appeal. They assisted in recruiting more of their peers to sit on the Executive Committee or the Business Panels and also gave the Appeal valuable early credibility. Half the Executive Committee were chairmen of the different panels and half were key people from the Hospital, including the Chairman of the Board of Governors, the General Manager, a leading medical consultant, the Chief Nursing Officer and a representative from the Special Trustees. When suitable people had been recruited to serve on this body, the Advisory Council was stood down and its members served on the other panels or the Executive Committee.

Many appeals have only one Business Panel but we decided to have two, splitting the City from Commerce and Industry. This gave us two slots for top names to take leadership in this area. The panel Chairmen were each responsible for recruiting a high-level team, including representatives from most of the key business sectors. The City Panel embraced the clearing banks, merchant banks, insurance companies, other leading financial institutions and the professions. The Commerce and Industry Panel covered such sectors as food and groceries, drapery and stores, chemicals and plastics, leisure, property, brewing, pharmaceuticals and many others. Each panel member, solely or with a small group of helpers, was made responsible for deciding who should make the approaches for help and donations in his field. Their specialist knowledge ensured that the most favourable approach was made. The Appeal Office paved the way by supplying panel members with a list of relevant companies, indicating where other panel members had contacts. (This is covered in more detail in Part III.)

The Marketing Panel

The task of the Marketing Panel is to create and implement the overall marketing plan of an appeal. This should include:

1. Obtaining a full brief on the charity, its current role, its problems, its needs and the planned project to be funded by the appeal.
2. Refining the appeal message.
3. Creating the appeal publicity package: logo, house style and literature, together with
    i. an advertising schedule
    ii. a public relations programme

iii. films, videos, TV and radio appeals

4. Creating opportunities for the merchandising programme, joint promotions (linking products or services with the charity), and sponsorship opportunities.

5. Trying to obtain free specialist services and gifts in kind to keep costs to a minimum (almost all these marketing costs were contributed to the Wishing Well Appeal).

6. Approaching further relevant companies in their sector.

Special Events Panel

The Wishing Well Appeal's Special Events Panel was set up to assemble a series of profitable key events. After the Appeal was launched, the panel screened the flood of special events opportunities put to the Appeal. It was charged with ensuring that the Hospital's reputation would be protected and that any event would generate sufficient funds to warrant expenditure. It concentrated on events which raised around £100,000 net of expenses, passing smaller events to the regional groups. This panel looked for a variety of events and intended to use them not only to raise money but to heighten awareness of the Appeal. In all cases, the objective was to try to find suitably qualified volunteers to run events on behalf of the Appeal, guided and monitored by the staff member in question, the events having been vetted by the Appeal's Special Events Panel in the first place.

Regional groups

We set up a network of regional groups, based on county boundaries, to take advantage of county pride. Greater London groups were organized by boroughs. Although initially we intended to have one central chairman helping to find chairmen in the counties, this was eventually undertaken by staff members. Their efforts were usually backed with a letter from the Lord Lieutenant of Greater London to the Lords Lieutenant of the counties or the Mayors of the Greater London Boroughs, explaining the links they had with Great Ormond Street. Another essential part of our strategy was to use clubs, societies, associations, schools, the armed forces, the police and other organizations to spread the message for us and to ask each to take us on as their charity of the year. Schools, which proved especially supportive, were approached on a county basis by our local groups through County Directors of Education. Private schools were approached through their own umbrella organizations, such as the Headmasters' Conference and the Girls' School Association.

Regional groups can play a vital role in supplementing the information on potential donor companies at appeal headquarters. London-based appeals often overlook the potential among companies in the provinces which, perhaps, have the characteristics of being private or quasi-private and have not previously been approached for a major gift. The same applies to wealthy individuals. The Prince's Youth Business Trust has done much to pioneer this strategy which has been very successful.

PROJECT ADVISORS

The people whose task is to spread the message and raise funds must be guided every step of the way by the charity or project's managers. The appeal literature must be vetted to make sure that it is accurate and puts over correctly the philosophy of the charity. The managers should also ensure that those who run the charity's services understand the objectives, progress and problems of those involved with fund-raising. Not everyone welcomes a group of people brought in to do a one-off job which, while it lasts, will take over much of the high-profile and glamorous side of their long-standing charity work. 'I'll believe it when I see it,' was the way some viewed the Wishing Well Appeal's chances of success.

At my request, Great Ormond Street Hospital set up a group of medical advisers to help the Appeal office produce accurate publicity material which took account of the staff's feelings. The group included leading medical consultants, the Chief Nursing Officer, the General Manager of the Hospital and the Dean of the Institute of Child Health. Well-written material cannot be produced by committee so, in practice, the General Manager was responsible for clearing what was written after carrying out essential consultation. Through the group, Hospital staff came to understand the needs and problems of fund-raisers. We in turn learned about the sensitivities and needs of the Hospital. In addition, the group arranged for us to give regular briefings to Hospital staff. My staff and I took every opportunity to talk at internal meetings in the Hospital, giving up-to-date information and asking for comments and suggestions. I had a similar group at Charing Cross Hospital, advising on scientific and technical matters, and that worked very well too, though occasionally some of the more recondite professional statements had to be interpreted for us.

COORDINATING EXISTING FUND-RAISING

Coordination is very important in fund-raising, but this extends to more than the fund-raising for the appeal. It is also vital that the new activities of the appeal are carefully coordinated with any existing fund-raising taking place for the charity on an ongoing basis.

Imagine a special team brought in to set up a centenary appeal for an ongoing charity, which already has volunteer fund-raisers and staff members covering different types of fund-raising. Special care must be taken to make the existing fund-raisers part of the appeal master plan and ensure they are given their own role and target. In hospital appeals, where I have had considerable recent experience, the new one-off appeal must take very careful note of existing fund-raising which is supporting research, buying equipment and meeting numerous other continuing objectives. It is important that a proper record is kept of this information, preferably on computer, so that it can be cross-referred with your appeal. (See Chapter 10.)

The pressures on many of those concerned can make it difficult for them to appreciate the need for careful coordination, but if there is a free-for-all, in which new and existing appeals simultaneously approach the same donors, these donors can be forgiven for washing their hands of the entire charity. Busy people cannot be expected to understand the difference between two projects on behalf of the same charity and will feel with justification that the charity itself should be orchestrating approaches. If it cannot sort out such a fundamental matter, how can a donor have confidence that his money will be spent wisely? This corrosive thought is dangerous enough to jeopardize a large one-off appeal.

If a small appeal approaches the same donor as a large appeal, both for the same charity, there is again the risk of 'vaccination'. A small gift to the minor appeal means that the donor is not likely to give a larger sum to the main appeal. You might even say that it gives him a good excuse to get out of giving a large gift. That is why it really is necessary to explain these harsh truths to all of those with a vested interest and to encourage them to put the greater good of the charity before the individual good of their own particular interest or appeal.

On one occasion I was trying to encourage an effective, long-standing fund-raiser to agree to coordinate fund-raising for a particular one-off hospital need. I was told severely that if I inhibited her fund-raising in any way, she would leave the hospital and raise money for another in the same field. She could not understand the point I was making and was not prepared to agree that we might damage each other's work if we did not dovetail our activities. As the person in question was not a major fund-raiser, yet did a very valuable job for the hospital, we were forced to turn a blind eye and cross our fingers that nothing dreadful would happen. Luckily, nothing did, but it so easily could have. It is a delicate but necessary balancing act between a clear but tough policy and the bad feeling which might be caused by reining in an individualistic and highly-motivated fund-raiser.

In the Charing Cross Medical Research Centre Appeal, I tried to explain that the biggest potential for the large, one-off appeal – wealthy individuals, top companies and large trusts – should initially be reserved for approach by the Research Centre Appeal team. This caused great resentment among many other Charing Cross fund-raisers because some were not going to benefit from the Research Centre. They were dedicated to their own causes and could not see that their smaller fund-raising task would affect the main appeal. It took a very stiff letter from a top insurance company, refusing to support the appeal because we had not got our act together, to prove the point I was trying to make. At the same time as the Research Centre Appeal had approached the insurance company with a brochure that included the different lines of research that we were helping to support, so one of those lines of research with its own charity had approached the same company. The two sets of documents arrived simultaneously. The letter I received was an enormous help in explaining the dangers of not tackling the thorny problem of coordinating fund-raising.

British hospitals have a lot to learn from the United States in this area. The Americans seem to have educated donors to understand that a hospital not only relies on their support for ongoing needs, but also requires an additional gift should they ever need to launch a major one-off appeal. Consequently, they avoid many of the problems we have encountered.

CHECKLIST

1. Decide on objectives of the appeal
2. Decide on key strategy
3. Produce project brief for voluntary fund-raisers
4. Produce Strategy Document, to include the above and:
       Honorary structure and staff posts
       Potential sources of funds
       Targets for each source
       Legal status of appeal and responsibilities
       Linear programme
       The need for personal approaches
5. Hold publicity until public appeal (if there is to be one)
6. Form group of appeal project advisers
7. Coordinate appeal fund-raising with other charity fund-raising

Chapter 8

MARKETING STRATEGY AND INITIAL DOCUMENTS

Project research, appeal research, leadership considerations and the appeal strategy are all closely allied to the marketing strategy.

Marketing is a frequently misunderstood concept. Many people believe it is all to do with publicity, hype and razzmatazz – and so it can be – but its scope is much wider. According to the Institute of Marketing, 'Marketing is the management process responsible for identifying, anticipating and satisfying customer requirements profitably.' How does this apply to a charitable appeal? In effect, a charity has two very different classes of 'customer': the beneficiaries and the donors. Although its main mission is to provide for the beneficiaries, the only way to achieve that is to consider donors' needs as well. The latter is the central theme of Ken Burnett's book *Relationship Fundraising,* which I refer to in the Bibliography. That, in charity, is the majority of the marketing role. It involves bridging the gap between providing a much-needed service or facility and finding the resources to do so.

Does this mean that fund-raising is part of marketing in charity management? I believe it should be, but I do not think many in the voluntary sector, other than the largest charities, have yet become that sophisticated. If fund-raising is part of marketing, then it is a very specialized form. A marketing generalist would have to learn the peculiarities of fund-raising before attempting to assemble a marketing strategy for an appeal. It is a question of adapting – not just adopting – commercial marketing techniques. All too often marketing people assume that the best fund-raising technique is to tell the world that the charity needs funds. This book has already explained the pitfalls if careful targeting of private donors does not take place first. Nevertheless, I believe that a marketing background provides an ideal grounding for a fund-raiser: both subjects are to do with communications and strategic planning. However, in recent years, the designation Marketing Manager in the voluntary world has often applied to the activities of a charity trading company, using such business methods as mail order catalogues, charity shops and joint promotions.

Marketing is a fundamental and crucial part of the one-off capital appeal, even if the appeal is strictly private. The fund-raiser should certainly help to identify, anticipate and satisfy the needs of those supported by the charity when reviewing the case for an appeal, but he is solely responsible for the injection of the required funds, without which there would be no provision in the first place. This is achieved through a combination of fund-raising and marketing techniques.

I knew at the start of the Wishing Well Appeal that the use of sophisticated marketing techniques would be essential. There are few slants or ideas in fund-raising or marketing that have not been tried before. However, with creativity and flair, a fresh image can be created to communicate urgency and set a bandwagon rolling. That was our objective for Great Ormond Street. With so many special appeals constantly asking for funds for very deserving children's charities, we knew we would have to work hard to catch the public's imagination if we were to achieve what was then the largest financial target ever attempted by a one-off appeal. Hence our reliance on marketing experience. Many admired what we created; some resented it and called it slick. The indisputable fact is that the Appeal achieved its objective and led the way for other charities to realize their full potential.

STRATEGY

Marketeers need to be very fully briefed before they can draw up a serious marketing plan for an appeal. They need to know the answers to all the questions covered by BROADSWORD in Chapter 4. Essentially these are:

• The background and reputation of the charity.
• The planned project – what to benefit whom?
• Who cares/might care – an audit of donors and supporters to date and potential donors
• What are their giving habits?

The strategic marketing decisions to be undertaken must answer the following questions:

• What audiences should be targeted?
• What message should be communicated to different audiences?
• What identity should be projected?
• What products should be offered (methods of giving)?
• What communications methods should be used?
• What timing is envisaged (the overall appeal programme)?
• Evaluation – ongoing and final review

Alternatively, one can adapt the conventional marketing approach of the four 'Ps'.

The four 'Ps'

PRODUCT: the unique selling proposition of Great Ormond Street (the children, the tangible cause, the need, the Royal Patronage, etc.)
PRICE: the target (seen to be achievable and motivating, and set at the right level for a targeted donor or group of potential donors)
PLACE: where you will pitch your stall (strategy for media and publicity)
PACKAGING: public presentation of the product (identity, logo, name, advertising messages and fund-raising mechanics)

The first audiences towards whom the marketing operation is directed are usually potential chairmen, patrons and trustees. Then marketing factors are used to decide whether the appeal should be addressed to a private or public audience – or both. This centres on who cares about the cause and on identifying potential donor categories. The message to communicate must be carefully considered, researched and rehearsed with different versions for different audiences.

Creating a suitable identity, if it does not already exist, is pivotal in the attempt to communicate that an organization is becoming more vital or professional. In turn, this helps to ensure that the organization is regarded more seriously. If the marketing objective is blanket coverage, then an easily recognized house style is one of the most effective tools with which to achieve it.

Public and private?

One of the biggest decisions of any appeal in the planning phase is whether to have a public as well as a private appeal. (The question is debated in Chapters 7 and 11.) The key to making this decision is the involvement of individuals who have relevant marketing experience. These marketeers will form the Marketing Panel, the activities of which are discussed in more detail in Chapters 12 and 17. The Marketing Panel's role is very different during each phase.

Before and during the private appeal, this panel should help to create and coordinate the case being put to potential donors to ensure consistency. In the later stages of the private appeal, the Marketing Panel will also be responsible for drawing up the promotional campaign for the public appeal, including the appointment of appropriate staff and outside agencies for the marketing activity. All these plans should be set out in the Marketing Strategy document which is prepared for the public phase.

Methods of giving

You should consider which methods of giving you wish to put before your potential donors. Appeal organizers should be aware of the main methods of giving available to donors as these will be linked to the strategy to be used and will have implications for the tax and legal structure of the appeal. You will want to promote tax-efficient methods of donating, but will you suggest that people become involved in special events, joint promotions with companies, purchasing goods or donating time? These are key planning decisions which are discussed later in the book. (Potential methods of giving and fund-raising techniques during the private and public appeal are listed in Appendices 2 and 4.)

STRUCTURE

The marketing dimension of an appeal must be carefully structured and professionally carried out. If expertise is not available, then the structure may have to be modified. No single person can be expert in all marketing disciplines, so a team of experts is required. The main skills necessary cover general business principles, marketing, advertising, public relations, sales promotion, copywriting and design. You might like to add media links, film production and others. This expertise may be available to you through honorary input, agency support or staff with suitable qualifications. In the case of smaller appeals, this might mean the local businessman, local editor or company press officer. A one-off appeal is more likely to attract voluntary contributions from outside experts. I recommend assembling a team of such talents, serviced by a staff member with good knowledge of the overall subject. Just like commercial concerns, larger charities commission input from advertising and public relations agencies. The difference in a capital appeal is that it is possible to obtain this input voluntarily, usually by invoking the pulling power of the cause itself or the asking power of one or more of its commercial supporters. However, this is just one way to get the job done. There are many others depending on available resources.

The Charing Cross Medical Research Centre Appeal solved this problem in an unusual way. Through our Chairman, Sir Robert Clark (then chairman of the Hill Samuel Group), we were lucky enough to recruit Len Heath to chair the Publicity Panel. Len had been in advertising and marketing for many years and was chairman of a number of creative service businesses, all of which he had helped to found and develop. Notable among them was Imagination, one of the world's leading companies in design and special events. He was, therefore, able to pull together a multi-disciplined team of talented volunteers, all interested in the charity, and they met our promotional needs very effectively.

Getting Great Ormond Street's message across was an enormous challenge, so we gave it a high priority. We were fortunate to recruit Bob Clarke, then Chief Executive of United Biscuits (Holdings), who has since been knighted. He headed the Marketing Panel and brought in the right people for the job: Eric Nicoli, the current Chief Executive of United Biscuits, the late Sir Ian Trethowan, one-time Director General of the BBC and chairman of Thames TV, Alan Kilkenny, co-founder of the Grayling Company (one of the U.K.'s leading public relations consultancies) and John Farrell, Chief Executive of International Marketing Promotions, a large British sales promotion company. Frank Pearce, then Public Affairs Director of Midland Bank, joined as a result of Midland's involvement. Peter Bagnall, who was Joint Managing Director of W. H. Smith, joined the panel to give advice on publishing. Ed Ram of Sky Sites, part of Mills and Allen, contributed valuable input on outdoor advertising. We were approached by Collett Dickenson Pearce and Partners, one of Britain's major creative advertising agencies, who offered honorary services and put forward John Salmon, the Chairman, Nigel Clark, Vice-Chairman, and Sue Holliday, Account Manager, to represent them.

This was the outstanding team I worked with to draw up the overall marketing strategy for the Appeal – a very stimulating experience. I believe they were a little stunned when I explained the enormous area I hoped they would cover on our behalf – not advising me how to do it, but doing it themselves. They did more than I could have hoped for and, best of all, they enjoyed it.

We have seen the full scope of the marketing role and this is how it spans the three phases of an appeal.

1. Preparation
   - receiving a clear project brief
   - receiving full information on previous donors and the way they helped

- reviewing who cares (considering market research to find out): selecting the target audiences
- deciding on the messages, propositions to be communicated and how
- creating an appeal identity (house style, logo, stationery)
- helping to produce an up-to-date Preliminary Report

2. Private appeal
   - producing the fund-raising tools: literature, audio visuals, videos, display panels, speech notes
   - advising on the staging of key presentations
   - preparing the marketing strategy and budget for the public appeal

3. Public appeal
   - marketing plan for public consumption
   - publicity plan
   - publicity tools
   - promotions
   - support publicity for special events and some regional activity

Each of these areas will be discussed in the appropriate part of the book after a more detailed look at the marketing activities to be carried out in the preparatory phase of the appeal.

MARKETING PREPARATION

Before your marketing experts can make a meaningful contribution, they must be fully briefed on the need for the facilities for which funds are required and why this should be funded by an appeal. They will ask searching questions which will sometimes help you address and overcome weaknesses in your argument. They cannot possibly advise you appropriately unless they have a clear understanding of the answers to all the relevant questions (see Chapter 4).

Market Research

When the Marketing Panel is being briefed and is researching the charity, project and appeal, they should consider commissioning market research to obtain feedback on the general image and reputation of the charity (see Chapter 5). Market intelligence is essential. People working for a charity tend to be so caught up with their cause or need that they assume the public knows as much as they do. In fact, market research will almost certainly show that the public has a vague and probably distorted picture of the work of the charity. The marketing plan must start by recognizing where people are in their understanding and not where you want them to be. The panel can then help to develop and refine the appeal message for different groups of people. They take all the facts and produce the most convincing case to put to the government as to why it should give more, to businessmen who can use the appeal as part of their corporate responsibility programme and to the public to make them feel that they should join the crusade – strongly enough to want to make a contribution of money and, possibly, time too.

The Marketing Panel's next job is to help prepare the documents referred to previously – the Business Plan if this does not already exist, the Preliminary Report (which includes a detailed project brief) and any other literature, or communications tools, required at this stage, including videos, slide presentations, display panels and other back-up material as necessary. Once again, these will vary according to the people for whom they are intended.

Creating a house style

After you have identified the people you wish to target, a house style to encompass the tone and personality of the appeal can be created. This is the corporate identity of an organization in its internal and external communications. The design, colour and typeface of all communications, from letters to brochures, should have a recognizable livery which comes to identify the organization in people's minds. It should be carefully created to be in keeping with the organization, reflecting the key characteristics of the desired public profile.

A properly designed environment can give authority and credibility to an organization's statement. An ill-conceived design can all but destroy the same statement. The Redevelopment Appeal adopted the distinctive blue colour long associated with Great Ormond Street. We wanted a house style that was consistent with the organization and its aims. Part of this was encapsulated in a new logo.

Logo

A logo is usually the most recognizable part of a house style. It is the trademark or brand which epitomizes the organization. Logos have become increasingly popular. Some tend to follow fashion: house-like designs for building firms, hands around matchstick children for caring charities.

It is worth noting that while logos are important to marketing-led appeals – especially if there is to be a public phase – they are not always relevant to the specially targeted big gift appeal.

When relevant, a logo should be used in a consistent way on all possible items, including stationery, literature, exhibitions, fasciae, publicity material and promotional goods. Our aim with the Wishing Well Appeal was to get our little face cropping up all over the place to the point of saturation. It was not easy to introduce a new and modern design to an establishment with traditions dating back to the 1850s, especially as it already had a well-loved logo (depicting a mother and child) of great relevance to the Hospital.

When we started work on the Appeal, we noted that there were about three different versions of the Hospital's existing logo. It was a complicated design and would not reduce in size with clarity. We decided that it would be best to develop a new and separate house style and logo for the Appeal. This allowed us to create exactly the right image for our Appeal without upsetting the many thousands of people who loved the traditional design. We needed a logo which clearly expressed the purpose of the Appeal in a form that could be printed on any item of any size.

The idea of a child's face drawn by a child was John Salmon's. From the very start, he had a clear idea of what he wanted to achieve and we looked to the Great

Ormond Street children themselves – those well enough to attend the Hospital's school and playgroup – to draw the sort of face he had in mind. We were warned that this might not work, as sick children often draw pictures which illustrate their state of health. That is exactly what happened. The pictures we received, although very good, did not meet John Salmon's objective, but one had a big smudge under the eye – and that triggered the idea for a teardrop. So, in the end, the children played a vital part in the logo design.

The next version of the 'teardrop' logo was designed by Neal Godfrey, Collett Dickenson Pearce's Art Director. It depicted the tear and the smile typical of the children that come to Great Ormond Street. It was a very clever concept in a form which could be easily recognized in any size. Some people loved it and some hated it, but the final version, developed after the agency had been asked to soften the face a little, won broad acclaim. A few small touches made all the difference in creating the face of a friendly little character with whom we could all associate.

It was not part of our house style policy to use the 'teardrop' logo on its own. The slogan 'Help Great Ormond Street Get Better' was an integral part and was used to overcome the fact that we had created a new, unknown logo. The more we tied it to the well-known name of the Hospital, the more we could communicate accurately the identity of the new face.

Slogan

While an appeal's logo is its identity stamp, the slogan should be a constant incitement to action. It can be the opportunity for an ongoing charity to start something new and exciting. Interest flags unless it is actively revived. The challenge is to dream up a slogan that is catchy and original, without detracting from the identity of the charity. The YMCA headed its international fund-raising effort with the line 'Why Care?' and the names of both The Save the Children Fund and Help the Aged are in themselves slogans. The St. John Ambulance Brigade has recently updated itself with the slogan 'Over to you, John', specifically linked with a publicity campaign appealing to everyone in the country called John.

The slogan 'Help Great Ormond Street Get Better', which was invented jointly by Collet Dickenson Pearce and International Marketing Promotions, was not immediately popular with the Hospital. It was felt to imply that the Hospital was sick and this was thought to be at odds with its reputation as a centre of excellence, respected the world over. We had to point out very tactfully that if we could not openly admit that something about the Hospital was far from healthy, we would have no reason for launching an Appeal. I am delighted that the Hospital continues to use the logo for its fund-raising now that the Wishing Well Appeal is over.

The appeal name

It helps everyone if a short, snappy name can be invented for an appeal. If you do not develop one yourselves, you will probably find that the press shortens it anyway. You should always ensure that the name you want to use is not already being used by another organization. It is worth checking, too, that no one is using a similar name that could be confused with it. You can check manually using the telephone directory and other directories. Official checks for this purpose can be made at Companies House and the Charity Commission. Under the Charities Act 1992 (section 4), which came into effect on 1 September, 1992, the Commissioners have the power to require a charity on registration (or within 12 months) to alter its name if it is seen by them to be the same or too like that of another charity. They have an additional power, without the 12 months time constraint, to require a charity to alter its name if it is seen by them as being likely to mislead the public as to the true nature of the charity's purposes or its activities in pursuit of those purposes.

Ideally, the appeal name should promote the name of the charity itself. So why did we not choose a name incorporating Great Ormond Street from the start? We knew that we were going to have to use a separate name to differentiate funds intended for the redevelopment from those for the Hospital itself, which has always relied on voluntary contributions to provide additional equipment, research and parental support. During the private stage of the Appeal, we developed the 'teardrop' logo and used a name which fully described the purpose of the Appeal: Great Ormond Street Children's Hospital Redevelopment Appeal. It said it all – but what a mouthful! We racked our brains to try to find the catchy, simple name we needed, but our public relations advisers gave the thumbs down to every idea. They said the Gosh Appeal was an old-fashioned word and the Peter Pan Appeal was too illogical a connection. So it went on.

Then one day John Farrell brought me an idea for a joint promotion with Harrods. The visuals showed a banner saying 'Harrods Wishing Great Ormond Street Well', and beside it was a wishing well in which customers would be encouraged to throw spare coins. To John's surprise I jumped to my feet crying, 'That's it! – that's what we've been looking for!' It took him some time to get any sense out of me and to realize that he had given me the idea to call the Appeal 'The Wishing Well Appeal'. Instinctively I knew it was right, but I had to convince everybody else. Undoubtedly, there would be votes for and against, but we were up against a deadline and had to make a decision urgently. I asked Jules Kosky, the Hospital's Assistant Archivist, to see if there had ever been any reference in the records to a wishing well. He had become used to me by then and did not look too surprised at such a strange request. I was the one who was surprised – and delighted – when he came back with a photograph of the old wishing well fountain which used to be in the garden behind the original Great Ormond Street Hospital building. It had long since disappeared, but the archives recorded that children used to throw coins into the fountain to wish for good health.

I was very relieved when eventually we had the agreement of the Marketing Panel and the Executive Committee. Some felt it was corny, it did not tie in with the logo and it did not promote the name of the Hospital. They were right, but no solution in such a subjective area is ever ideal. However, we did have the policy that wherever it was used, the title 'The Wishing Well Appeal' was always alongside the words 'for the redevelopment of Great Ormond Street Children's Hospital'. Perhaps most important of all, it was an idea which appealed to children – who made up a large proportion of our fund-raising army.

Finally, I would recommend that if sufficient funds are available, proposals for logos, slogans and the appeal name should be researched initially among potential donors. This will ensure that the right message really is communicated.

An appeal's name should have relevance to the cause. The Wishing Well Appeal's justification for what was thought to be a catchy name came later, through the work of a diligent archivist, who discovered the photograph above of the wishing well fountain. It used to stand in the gardens of the original hospital and children would throw coins into it to wish for good health.

A logo should have a simple design so that it can be easily recognized, even in a reduced size. The Wishing Well Appeal's 'teardrop' logo depicted the tear and the smile of the brave children cared for by the Hospital. (Copyright 1989 Great Ormond Street Children's Hospital Fund)

Legal protection of the logo and name

As an original artistic work, the logo developed for an appeal is automatically protected by copyright on creation. There are no formalities and no registration requirements. The copyright owner is, in the first instance, the creator of the logo, irrespective of the fact that it was commissioned by a third party. Consequently, the copyright in the logo should be formally assigned in writing to the appeal. The copyright owner has the right to prevent others copying the work without his permission.

Protection is also afforded to the goodwill associated with the appeal name and logo. In certain circumstances, it is possible to bring so-called passing off proceedings against a third party seeking to exploit a confusingly similar name or logo. This depends on the aggrieved party being able to demonstrate goodwill attaching to its name or logo.

Registering a logo as a registered trade or service mark is a lengthy process, taking upwards of two years from the date of registration. However, this does not prevent the use of the logo in the intervening period. Nevertheless, there are considerable technical difficulties involved in charities obtaining trade or service mark registrations, and multiple registrations in respect of a wide range of goods and services will usually be necessary to provide comprehensive protection. The lack of trade mark protection does not prevent 'passing off' proceedings being pursued.

Having used our teardrop logo for over a year, we had a nasty moment when a supporter told us that another charity had selected a very similar motif as a result of a design competition. No charity wants to be in dispute with another whose objectives it respects, but a confusion over house styles could have dissuaded companies from linking our logo with their products. As a result, serious damage could have been done to the value of our brand. Turner Kenneth Brown, our honorary solicitors, advised us that although the similarity was obviously unintentional, the law concerning 'passing off' would probably apply.

Naturally, we intended to do everything possible to resolve the position before resorting to legal action. We were a little disconcerted to find that the late Robert Maxwell was chairing a fund-raising panel for the other charity. It was an uncomfortable situation – especially when Mr. Maxwell sent £10,000 to our Appeal, this being money awarded to him from his latest legal dispute! However, I am glad to say that there was goodwill on both sides and once the similarity was acknowledged, the other charity decided not to promote the new design.

DOCUMENTATION

Any properly organized appeal, however small, needs to communicate effectively with its leadership, its workers and the outside world. The conception and progress of the appeal must be recorded in a series of documents so that all legitimately interested parties can see the need for the appeal, the likelihood of its success and the strength of the organization that is asking for funds. These documents are a formal written expression of what has been discussed in the earlier chapters of Part II, as well as the subsequent progress of the appeal. By committing their ideas and decisions to paper, a charity's leaders can see more easily where they are going and can debate that direction in an informed and rational manner.

Initial documents to consider

Business Plan
Preliminary Report
Appeal Strategy
Appeal brochure
Appeal Progress Report and Accounts
General appeal leaflet

There is a distinct order in which the principal appeal documents should be produced, even though they will evolve and develop as the appeal progresses. The Business Plan should come first to ensure that the charity itself is fit to set up and undertake the task of organizing an appeal. Secondly, that should be distilled into a Preliminary Report for the purpose of selling the appeal to potential leaders and those donors who are likely to be most sympathetic to its aims. Thirdly, a mature Appeal Strategy should be written. Fourthly, the appeal brochure (see Chapter 12) should be produced for potential major donors to read after a face-to-face meeting with an appropriate representative of the appeal. A condensed version, in leaflet form, follows for general use during the public phase of the appeal.

These documents can be supplemented by progress reports and brochures concentrating on particular aspects of the appeal, depending on the publicity thrust dictated by the marketing strategy. Remember that registered charity status must, by law, be clearly identified on all public and financial documents, stationery and fund-raising literature (see Chapter 9 and Appendix 8 on the Charities Act 1992). It is an offence to claim your organization is a registered charity when it is not. Equally it is essential to distinguish clearly between the charity's identity and that of any trading company, even though the same house style may be used. Further, if the appeal has its own legal entity, the trustees have a statutory requirement to produce material such as an official annual report (see Appendix 8).

CONCLUSION

The image presented by a charity's messages sets the tone for the whole appeal. Many charity publications look as if they have been produced for pennies because their supporters believe funds would be better spent on the cause. But if the literature is dull and uninteresting, it will not be read. Even the meagre sum and time spent on it will have been wasted. The trick is to produce economically (possibly through sponsorship) publications which make your target audience read them. They should give the impression that the charity is professional, imaginative and deserves support. As there are so many charities vying for attention, the quality of their presentation has to be first-rate to match the image the charity wishes to project.

Chapter 9

ORGANIZATION, LEGAL AND FISCAL ASPECTS

An essential component in the preparation for any charitable appeal – however big or small – is a thorough examination of the legal and fiscal ramifications. This includes the type of organization you will need to establish to carry out your objectives. Appeal organizers will want to adopt the structure that minimizes the charity's liability to tax, but even that is not a simple matter. Successive governments, aided by the Inland Revenue and the Customs and Excise Department, have ensured that there are a series of trade-offs limiting the number of black-and-white options. So it is best to adopt a top-down procedure, moving from the general to the particular. That is the approach I have adopted for this chapter. Questions affecting individual fund-raising initiatives, such as trading, are dealt with in the relevant chapters.

I cannot stress strongly enough the importance of obtaining up-to-date and authoritative advice on all these matters. There are many excellent books on the subject, including *Charitable Status* by Andrew Phillips (Interchange Books) and *Charities: Law and Practice* by Elizabeth Cairns (Sweet and Maxwell). However, even an extensive reading programme can be only a preliminary for detailed discussions with lawyers and accountants thoroughly steeped in this complex and constantly changing field. Do not forget to budget for these advisers' fees from your seed money. This chapter does not, therefore, pretend to be the last word on the subject. Rather, it is designed to be a guide, pointing out the strategic considerations which should be borne in mind and the pitfalls awaiting the unprepared.

Legal advice is usually sought during the start-up phase of any enterprise. It is also required in conjunction with many of the activities handled by a fund-raiser. Consequently, when you are setting up an operation in order to raise funds – as with a one-off appeal – your legal adviser is absolutely crucial to you. I can truly say that Nigel Wildish, Managing Partner of the Wishing Well Appeal's honorary solicitors, Turner Kenneth Brown (TKB), held my hand on legal issues every step of the way. The advice of his practice was sought in so many areas that its input represented a substantial contribution to our appeal.

With the arrival of the Charities Act 1992, legal advice has become even more necessary for charities. Its full implications need to be absorbed and note taken of when each part of it is enacted. To assist readers, up-to-date details are given in Appendix 8.

Five principal reasons for establishing a separate charity

1. The division of functions between a charity and appeal trust removes the stigma of begging from the parent charity. Fund-raising activity takes place at arm's length, under a separate chairman, staff and team of volunteers. This helps to stress the urgency of the appeal and enables a second body of supporters to say: 'We have given to the charity and we would like you to give.' It is harder for the charity's own chairman and trustees to put the case in that way.

2. The appeal trust acts as a financial control between the donor and the parent charity. The appeal trustees have a special responsibility to their donors, whom they have specifically asked for contributions and commitment. Of course, the parent charity's trustees would be under the same obligation, but it is presented more vividly under the aegis of an appeal trust.

3. The appeal trustees do not need to become actively involved in the day-to-day policy and management of the parent charity. They can provide continuing and objective attention to the attraction of gifts of capital, gifts in kind, legacies and other forms of giving.

4. The existence of a separate income and expenditure account and annual balance sheet enables the public to see what has happened to its money more precisely than if it were swallowed up in the more general accounts of the parent charity. If the parent charity were to fold or change character, the appeal trust's funds would remain insulated from such upheaval.

5. It can help to avoid the sensitive question of seniority. If a charity is setting up a new structure for an appeal, it is best to leave the final decisions until the wishes of the new appeal chairman have been taken into account. The structure may be crucial to his decision to be chairman. Most charities realize they have to recruit the big guns to pull off a large capital appeal. This means recruiting people who may be better known and more influential in some ways than the trustees or existing supporters of the charity. It may be tactless to ask a leader of industry to serve 'under' lesser-known people. The separate structure avoids this potential difficulty.

SHOULD YOUR APPEAL BE ESTABLISHED AS A SEPARATE CHARITY?

Fund-raising by itself is not a charitable objective under English law, and simply to raise funds for an existing charity does not qualify that activity for charitable status. While careful managerial arrangements can create discrete activities within the framework of an existing charity, there are advantages in setting up a separate charity for large capital appeals. To qualify for that separate charitable status there needs to be a discernible object other than purely to raise funds for an existing charity. A new charity can be created, therefore, if an appeal is for purposes other than the general objectives of an existing charity. Those other purposes may be new or limited to particular objectives, such as a specific project, of the existing charity.

Great care must be taken in formulating the charitable objectives of any such new charity. Where an appeal is for a specific purpose, such as for erecting or restoring a building, the Charity Commissioners recommend that it should say what will happen to the money raised if it is not enough for the purpose or if too much is subscribed (see the Charity Commissioners' leaflet CC21 *Starting a Charity*, mentioned in the Bibliography; also see Appendix 8 – Schemes).

It can be argued that, in practice, these are mere presentational matters of little real consequence. Nevertheless, such nuances can make a tremendous difference to the willingness of donors to respond to an appeal, however compelling the substantive case.

If the ongoing charity already has a large fund-raising operation, it may not be so desirable to set up a separate appeal trust. This is because the new appeal activity must be carefully coordinated with the existing fund-raising organization. In that event, funds received for the purposes of the appeal must be kept apart from general funds and, preferably, in a different bank account.

DEFINITION OF A CHARITY

Despite the existence of charities for hundreds of years, English law has not formulated a precise statutory definition of 'charity'. It has, however, developed four main categories of charitable objects and, for a charity to be recognized, it must fall within one or more of them. They are:

- Relief of poverty
- Advancement of education
- Advancement of religion
- Other purposes beneficial to the community in a way recognized as charitable (e.g. public utilities, protection of the public, protection of the environment).

These are classifications used by the Charity Commissioners, the Courts and the Inland Revenue in deciding whether a particular organization qualifies for charitable status.

REGISTRATION

All charities must be registered with the Charity Commissioners unless they have neither any permanent endowment nor the use or occupation of any land and their income from all sources does not exceed £1,000 per year. (Prior to the Charities Act 1992, the income limit from property, including investments, was as low as £15 per year.) In addition, there is a class of 'exempt charities' which do not need to register and which are listed in Schedule 2 to the Charities Act 1960. These include a number of universities, medical schools and other institutions. Furthermore, certain charities are 'excepted charities' which are excepted by regulations from the requirement to register with the Charity Commissioners – these charities include funds held for Boy Scouts or Girl Guide Associations. In fact, previously, where exempt charities were allowed voluntary registration, they will now have to de-register and will not be able to quote a reference number.

Unless therefore your charity falls within these exceptions, it will need to be registered and thus qualify for the all-important charity registration number. Quite apart from the intangible but priceless benefit obtained from displaying that registered number, as a result of the Charities Act 1992, any registered charity whose gross annual income in its last financial year exceeded £5,000 must show its registered status on virtually all official publications. These include all fund-raising literature, cheques, invoices and receipts. Anyone issuing or authorizing the issue of a document in breach of this section is committing a criminal offence, so all fund-raisers *must* ensure compliance with this provision which became effective on 1 January 1993. (See Appendix 8.)

Remember that separate, autonomous, regional committees may find that they have to register in their own right. There is a narrow dividing line in determining whether groups ('friends of...') form part of the parent charity and so should have their income consolidated into that of the charity, or whether they are truly separate entities.

ORGANIZATIONAL STRUCTURE

All charities need a 'governing instrument' which, among other matters, sets out the objects and administrative powers of the charity. The form of the governing instrument varies according to the nature and requirements of each charity. Broadly speaking, a charity will be one of the following types of organization:

Type of Organization	Governing Instrument
Trust	Trust Deed/Will
Unincorporated Association	Constitution or Rules
Company (normally limited by guarantee)	Memorandum and Articles of Association

A comparison of these principal structures is given below. They all have advantages and disadvantages, so it is a matter of deciding at the outset which form will best suit your purposes.

The people who have the general control and management of a charity are known as 'charity trustees', regardless of whether it is a trust. They are subject to more stringent obligations than the trustees of private trusts. One of the most important of these is that charity trustees cannot normally be paid for their work, although they may be reimbursed for reasonable out-of-pocket expenses.

No matter which structure is adopted, the charity trustees cannot be absolved from their absolute personal liability. Remember that the expression 'charity trustees' is defined by the Charities Act 1960 as 'the persons having the general control and management of the administration of a charity' and, therefore, covers not just the trustees of a charitable trust but also the directors of a charitable company and the management committee of an unincorporated association.

The Three Principal Structures For a Charity			
	Trust	*Company Limited by Guarantee*	*Unincorporated Association*
Flexibility i.e. ease of alteration of consitution	With careful drafting trustees able to vary administrative terms	Companies Act 1985 permits alteration within charitable objects as long as procedural hoops observed	Flexible insofar as able to tailor closely to individual cases
In all cases the Charity Commisioners' approval is required to any alteration of a charity's objects.			
Persons in in Control	Trustees • self perpetuating therefore continuity • powers well established at law • transfer of assets needed on changes of trustees unless Custodian Trustee or trustee body incorporated under Charitable Trustees Incorporation Act 1872 • delegation restricted	Directors – • involved in running charity • corporate identity • corporate structure: delegation by directors to committees, etc • members have voting powers	Membership – • difficult to identify those responsible on ultimate disposal of assets • assets cannot be held in name of association, holding trustees need therefore to be appointed • consents of all members may be required
Costs	No significant administrative costs	Administrative costs • annual fees • Companies House correspondence • Company secretary • AGM	No significant administrative costs unless tracing membership

In all cases, as a result of the new accounting, auditing and reporting regime introduced by the Charities Act 1992, charities require an independent examination at the very least and, if gross income and/or total expenditure is over £100,000 in any one year, they require a full report and audit. Similarly, all charities need to prepare and file an annual report and accounts with the Charity Commissioners.

PROCEDURE FOR SETTING UP A NEW CHARITY

Establishing a charity is not just a matter of forming a company and registering it at Companies House or executing a Trust Deed. Almost all charities must be approved by and registered with the Charity Commission and negotiations with the Commission may be necessary.

The approval and registration procedure should usually be completed within about four months, although the Commissioners may be prepared to expedite matters if it is necessary to establish a charity urgently. It is important to ensure that the charity has been fully established before fund-raising activities are undertaken in its name. It is also crucial that the objects and powers of the charity are fully defined at the outset, as fundamental alteration will probably need Charity Commission consent.

Approval and registration procedure

1. The appropriate structure for the charity is decided and the relevant governing instrument is drafted. Legal advice will be required on the structure and on the drafting, in particular that of the objects clause. This will need to fall within one or more of the main heads of charitable objects referred to above.

2. A questionnaire obtained from the Charity Commission is completed by the promoters. This covers areas such as the proposed activities of the new charity, details of proposed charity trustees, methods of fund-raising, what professionals will be involved and what sort of staff, if any, will be employed. This enables the Charity Commissioners to obtain a detailed picture of the proposed organization and to ensure that its intended activities will match its objects.

3. The completed questionnaire is returned to the Commissioners together with two copies of the draft governing instrument for their consideration.

4. The Commissioners consult the Inland Revenue as an interested party and give the Revenue an opportunity to object to any proposed registration.

5. After agreeing any necessary amendments, if both the Commissioners and the Revenue approve, the Commissioners invite registration of the organization as a charity and send the promoters a suitable application form.

6. The governing instrument should be completed in the appropriate manner and a certified copy sent to the Commissioners, together with the completed application form. (If the new charity is to be a company, the usual formalities for the creation of a company need to be complied with at this stage.)

7. The charity is entered on the Register and the promoters will be advised of:
   - the registration number;
   - the details of the charity as recorded on the Register; and
   - the requirements that the charity must now fulfil (e.g. reporting and accounting).

Scotland and Northern Ireland

The Charity Commissioners are defined by Section 1 of the Charities Act 1960 as the Charity Commissioners for England and Wales; their jurisdiction does not generally extend to Scotland or Northern Ireland (although the Charities Act 1992 has extended some of the supervisory powers of the Commissioners to certain Scottish charities). There is no formal registration procedure for charities in Scotland or Northern Ireland. Any body in Scotland wishing to represent itself as a charity must be recognized by the Inland Revenue as charitable for tax purposes. The Inland Revenue in Edinburgh maintains a public index of Scottish bodies which are recognized as charitable. Charities in Northern Ireland are the responsibility of the Department of Finance and Personnel. Charities in the Isle of Man or the Channel Islands are not required to register.

Disaster funds

Whenever funds are established for the benefit of victims of disasters, an early decision must be made as to whether such funds will be dealt with as charities and/or as discretionary trusts. In such cases, charities can be seen to be unduly restrictive, despite their tax advantages, since charity trustees are generally restricted in their ability to provide for their beneficiaries beyond providing relief from financial need. By contrast, trustees of discretionary trusts are not constrained by any such legal restrictions. It is sometimes beneficial to establish both a charitable fund and a discretionary trust fund. However, the distinctions between the two make it imperative to obtain early professional advice.

The Disaster Appeal Scheme (United Kingdom) has been established by the British Red Cross. It is designed to provide a set of procedures and mechanisms which any local authority and/or individual faced with a major disaster could use promptly to establish a disaster appeal fund. Additionally, there is a comprehensive book on the subject, entitled *The Administration of Appeal Funds*, by Roger W. Suddards (Sweet & Maxwell 1991).

The Wishing Well Appeal

The Wishing Well Appeal qualified for separate charitable status since the first object in its trust deed was 'the relief of sickness among children', which was therefore potentially much wider than merely the support of Great Ormond Street Hospital. The Deed then specified particular ways in which that general charitable object could be pursued, including promoting and advancing the charitable activities carried on at the Hospital, the rebuilding of the 19th-century section of the Hospital and the construction of a new building there (together with provision of appropriate plant, machinery and equipment). It was that wider element of discretion which meant that the Wishing Well Appeal qualified for separate charitable status.

Trustees were chosen for the new charity from those already helping the Hospital. When Lord Prior was recruited to be Appeal Chairman, he was happy to become a Trustee of that new body. This was ideal, as it allowed close coordination between the Appeal and the Hospital. It also entrenched Jim Prior's legal status and authority as a charity trustee.

TAX IMPLICATIONS

Generally speaking, the income and capital gains of a registered charity are exempt from income tax and capital gains tax, provided they are applied for charitable purposes. Take great care and obtain professional advice if your appeal is to engage in any significant trading activities, such as the sale of Christmas cards. Such activities are generally not regarded as charitable and, therefore, are not exempted from tax. So-called primary purpose trading (i.e. trading exercised in the course of the actual carrying out of a charity's primary purpose or carried out by the beneficiaries of a charity) is permissible both for charity law and tax purposes. Any other trading of a significant nature may need to be hived off to a subsidiary trading company, which can then covenant its profits back to the charity. (See Chapter 23.)

Covenanted income from individuals

If individuals enter into Deeds of Covenant to charities, the income is received by the charities net of basic rate tax deducted at source by the taxpayer. It can then be reclaimed by the charity. Higher rate tax payers can benefit by reclaiming the difference between the basic rate and higher rate of tax, at present 15 per cent. Try to avoid any covenants completed jointly by husbands and wives. Warn individuals in any literature you provide that covenants should not be given by non-tax payers. Joint covenants or covenants for non-tax payers may lead to a donor having to pay the basic rate tax to the Inland Revenue – not a way to make yourself popular with donors. (The various methods of giving by covenant and one-off payments are addressed in Chapters 13 and Appendix 2(a).) The Inland Revenue has issued a very useful Charity Tax Pack, including detailed guidance notes. It is obtainable from Claims Branch in Bootle (see Appendix 10 for the address).

Investment income

Any tax deducted at source on such income can be recovered by charities upon submission of the relevant tax vouchers. To avoid the necessity of repayment claims, investments can be made in common investment funds established under the Charities Acts which are, in effect, unit trusts specifically restricted to charitable bodies. Such funds pay income gross. Now that the services of the Official Custodian for Charities are being wound down (except in the case of land), the use of such common investment funds will, no doubt, increase dramatically. Again, proper professional advice should be obtained. (See also Investment Decisions, below.) Interest on bank and building society deposits is paid gross, provided that charities produce evidence of their charitable status.

VAT

Charities are not entitled to any general exemption from VAT. If charities carry out sufficient 'business activities' (as defined for the purposes of VAT) then they should register for VAT purposes. The registration level from March 1992 was £36,600 per year, but this level changes frequently and should be checked.

Registration for VAT has the advantage that VAT can be reclaimed on the supply of goods or services to the organization insofar as this is attributable to taxable activities by way of business. Conversely, however, VAT must be charged on all VATable goods and services provided by the organization to third parties. The impact of VAT on the charity's fortunes depends, to some extent, on the fund-raising strategy. If an appeal organization expects to be involved in considerable corporate-related fund-raising, VAT will be a less important concern as the corporations will be VAT-registered and can reclaim the VAT they are charged. If your appeal strategy is based mainly on fund-raising from individuals, however, the imposition of VAT will discourage them. You must bear this in mind when deciding on your VAT position. Indeed, this is such a highly specialist area of taxation that professional advice must always be obtained. Initial background reading is contained in H.M. Customs & Excise VAT leaflet 701/1/92 *Charities* (obtainable from your local Customs & Excise office).

Uniform business rates

Although you may be lucky enough to be given the use of premises, many appeals have to acquire their own. You should check with the local authority as soon as you acquire the premises, but under the local Government Finance Act 1988 there is mandatory relief of 80 per cent against the uniform business rate. The mandatory relief applies:

- if the property is occupied by the charity and is wholly or mainly used for charitable purposes; or
- if the property is used wholly or mainly for selling goods given to the charity and the money from the sales, after paying expenses, is passed to the charity.

In either case, a charging authority has power to waive the rates completely, at its discretion. Non-domestic property exempt from local rating includes agricultural land and buildings, places of religious worship, church administrative and ancillary buildings, church halls, and property used for the disabled. In all cases, charities must pay water and sewerage charges in full.

A trading subsidiary can never obtain rate relief. This is because it is a 'for profit' entity. It chooses of its own volition to covenant a proportion or all of its profits to the parent charity and, in doing so, obtains tax relief on Corporation Tax, but that is the limit of its relief.

Council tax

With effect from 1 April 1993, the new Council Tax, introduced by the Local Government Finance Act 1992, replaced the Community Charge. This does not affect the non-domestic rating system. Most hostels and residential care or nursing homes run by charities will continue to be subject to the Uniform Business Rate. Where properties are subject to Council Tax, there is mandatory relief of up to 50 per cent if all the residents are patients in residential care and nursing homes or care workers in such homes. The discount also applies to residential properties occupied by religious communities whose principal occupation consists of prayer, contemplation, education, the relief of suffering or any combination of these and whose residents have no income or capital of their own and are dependent on the community to provide for their material needs.

FINANCIAL MANAGEMENT, CONTROL AND REPORTING

The role of the trustee is to improve the efficiency and effectiveness of the charity, in order to ensure that the organization continues to be more 'successful'. Success for a charity is not as simple a term as it is for a profit-making institution, where it consists largely of seeing if the bottom line is in the red or in the black. A charity's activities, as well as its financial performance, need to be carefully measured, monitored and evaluated. Management is a matter of good information systems and reporting structures which send the necessary data quickly up the line to where it can be constantly checked against financial controls and other efficiency criteria. The charity trustees have the responsibility of evaluating the result, that is, of judging the overall efficiency of the charity's procedures and its success in meeting its objectives – and, if necessary, making changes to enhance both. While some of the information may be required for statutory purposes, it is fundamental to the success of any appeal that the organization has good information systems, strong financial controls and efficient reporting structures.

Management information

In evaluating the efficiency of the charity's organization, trustees and senior staff need to consider both the quality and quantity of the data being measured. It must, for example, include relevant non-financial operational information. There must not be so much data that it causes bottlenecks in the system and becomes counter-productive. Some areas which are critical to the success of the organization are:

- budgets, forecasts and cash flows showing income (and other resources available to the charity) and expenditure;
- performance indications of ongoing activities;
- information on donors and recipients, present and potential; and
- key ratios and reports on significant events.

There are many relatively inexpensive computer software packages available on the market which enable you to produce all the above information in suitable formats. (See Chapter 10.)

Budgeting

Budgets are an essential ingredient of planning an appeal. The budgeting process involves the correct allocation of income and expenditure. It is of particular importance where it is necessary to match variable income against fixed commitments, such as with a building project. All managers, not just financial staff, should be involved in budget setting. The final agreed budget for the period will be used as a benchmark against which future performance can be measured and operating parameters defined.

The budget should be prepared before funds are raised, as the charity must know how much seed money it will need in advance. It is usually updated annually, depending on the length of the appeal. An ongoing charity often prepares its budget by considering the previous budget, inflation and future plans. This process, while simple and less time consuming, may not be relevant to the one-off appeal for which the budget needs to be prepared from first principles. Budgeting expenditure during the planning and private stages of an appeal is fairly straightforward. The main cost is usually staff and possibly accommodation, unless the charity has been able to find rent-free offices for the duration of the appeal – a gift in kind which may be made available by a corporate supporter. However, trying to budget expenditure accurately for the public appeal is almost impossible until you are just about to enter this phase and have assembled all your detailed fundraising plans. A revised budget often is prepared at this stage.

Initially, the appeal will not know whether all or part of the promotional costs will be contributed as a gift in kind. It is usually wise to budget for the essential costs and then hope to reduce these by attracting contributions and gifts in kind. If no offers are received by a pre-determined date, the budget should reflect that the costs will need to be met. In the Wishing Well Appeal, we budgeted for our needs, knowing that we would seek to attract gifts in kind. We knew that if we wanted to have a large promotional impact, we would have to find a sponsor, as donors are always very sensitive about large budgets for this expenditure item. All our advertising campaign space costs were, in fact, paid for by a donor.

Predicting specific income by precise timings for a one-off appeal is much more difficult than predicting expenditure. It is always useful to consult those who have had recent experience with a specific appeal about their cost-to-income ratios. Charities with ongoing fund-raising operations have less difficulty in anticipating what a given year's income will be. They have considerable management information and can assess previous years' incomes, analyzing their sources.

The budget must include a cash flow projection, even if it cannot be very accurate at first. This exercise may produce a need to allow for bank interest payments if you find out that there are gaps in the cash flow which will have to be met with borrowing. The cash flow exercise itself is quite simple. Each item of budgeted income and expenditure should be listed in likely chronological order of arrival or departure. In that way, the organizers can calculate what the net outgoing or income will be for each month. It may be a rough estimate – certainly at first – but it will be better than not doing it and it could alert the appeal office to the chances of financial difficulties. Any gaps in cash flow, which this type of management information may reveal, can be used positively when approaching donors since it reflects the urgency of need at a particular time.

Forecasting

As an appeal develops, and time horizons come closer, it becomes more possible to plan for income because of pledges falling due, covenants and so on. It is essential to make regular forecasts to take into account actual results to date and revised estimates for the future to ensure that the appeal has the resources to meet its plans, i.e. income to meet expenditure. A forecast of the cash flow position should be completed weekly. Unexpected fund-raising opportunities often arise at the last moment. The financial system should provide for that. The appeal office may suddenly be offered a film premiere at short notice. After checking that there are people to run the charity's side of the event and that the cost-to-income ratio for that event makes financial sense, then the forecast should account for extra expenditure, outside the parameters of the budget, so that it can be readily identified.

Internal control

The objective of an internal control system is to ensure adherence to management policies, safeguard the assets and secure, as far as possible, the completeness and accuracy of records. A sound system of internal control is essential with an appeal because of high public accountability and expectations and the trustees' duties and responsibilities in meeting these.

One area which requires close scrutiny is the handling of cash (see Chapter 30). To give confidence to donors in a national appeal, it is worth recruiting a top name from one of the major clearing banks as honorary treasurer. Local bank managers are ideal for smaller appeals. The Wishing Well Appeal was extremely fortunate to recruit Sir Kit McMahon, who had just become Chairman of Midland Bank after being Deputy Governor of the Bank of England. That put the full weight of Midland Bank behind us from the early stages, leading to phenomenal pulling power in a range of ways. When setting up new appeals, I have always tried to ensure that the appeal office passes the funds to a suitable body, selected by the trustees, to hold the money. That body acts as paymaster, monitor of the appeal's budget, and carries out the investment decisions made by the trustees before the money has to be passed to the charity to be spent.

Banking decisions

Most charities hold their current account with one of the leading clearing banks, all of which offer a comprehensive range of financial services for money transmission and investment. I recommend an early visit to the manager or executive who will be handling your appeal money, even if a senior member of the bank has agreed to sit on one of your panels or committees. The personal contact is well worth the effort, for a national appeal almost always involves a large number of complicated banking questions. The points you should look out for include ready and rapid money transmission and favourable rates and methods of transfer of surplus funds to a deposit account. Keep the minimum in the current account or open a high-interest cheque account. Try to have all charges waived, if necessary by invoking the assistance of an influential trustee. Once your deposits exceed £10,000, you should be able to take advantage of high-interest money market accounts.

Midland Bank's 2,000 branches in England and Wales were geared up to accept the public's donations to the Wishing Well Appeal with special paying-in slips displayed in Wishing Well Appeal holders. Two of their key people were seconded to help with money sent to the Appeal headquarters in Great Ormond Street. Brian McCarthy, one of the Midland's computer experts, spearheaded the creation of a system to record all donations, and Jean Punter and an army of office staff and volunteers handled the vast amounts of cash and huge numbers of cheques sent to the Appeal. Sir Kit arranged for the bank to cope with the post for the first three months after the launch, when we were analyzing the public response and gearing up the Appeal office accordingly. In that period, Midland staff opened 73,000 envelopes containing more than £3.25 million and dealt with more than 3,000 credit card gifts.

Investment decisions

The law enjoins charity trustees to take special care of funds. Under the Trustee Investments Act 1961, some provisions of which may be altered following the Charities Act 1992 (see Appendix 8), trustees must in all cases diversify the charity's investments and make them suitable for the needs of the charity. That sounds daunting, but happily another clause in the same Act insists that the trustees take advice when making certain types of investment, as well as restricting the types of investment that can legally be made. You need to establish the extent to which your charity's investments will be governed by the Act – refer to your governing instrument; if it is a modern one (which it will be if you are setting up a new appeal trust), it will probably include wider powers of investment than those in the Act.

Ethical considerations may be relevant to investment decisions. The law in this area has been clarified by the recent highly publicized case of the Bishop of Oxford and Others v. The Church Commissioners. The ruling in this case made it clear that charity trustees can only allow ethical considerations to override financial considerations where investment would be directly contrary to the objectives of the charity and applying such restraints would not result in a 'substantial' financial loss. For example, therefore, it would be permissible for a cancer research charity to avoid investments in tobacco companies. The prime duty of charity trustees remains, however, to maximize the financial returns for their charity.

Investing appeal proceeds is a specialist role for which experts are required. Some experts offer a tailor-made investment service for charities. They have to use great caution. It would be badly received if, having raised £2 million for a £5 million target, the trustees were then obliged to announce that they had lost the majority of the money on the Stock Exchange and could they please have more to replace it? Midland Bank were the advisers to the Wishing Well Appeal and Sir Kit McMahon became Chairman of our Investment Committee. He placed the funds on high-interest deposit and eventually negotiated a £20 million investment over two years at a very favourable rate. In spite of the unpredictable times during which the Midland handled the majority of these funds, they still managed to raise 5.3 per cent of the Appeal's £42 million target through interest and investments. That shows what can be done with an active and willing bank, but the key principle should be not to expose your hard-raised funds to avoidable risk. A financial disaster will be remembered long after an investment success. Be sure to have interest paid gross – before deduction of tax – as it is a time-consuming administrative nuisance to reclaim it.

Expenditure on the charitable cause

It is fundamental that everyone concerned in an appeal knows how the money is to be deployed. This must be identified at an early stage. Expenditure should be approved by the trustees after due assessment of projects and applications from would-be recipients for money. This should be accompanied by regular reporting on and monitoring of how the money has been used to see if further funds are appropriate. In most appeals it is the responsibility of the charity to spend the money which has been raised. This was the case at Great Ormond Street Hospital, whose job it was to provide an investment sub-committee with a cash flow statement showing when money would be needed for the items that were to be paid for by the Appeal, as opposed to the government. Nevertheless, fund-raisers take on a specific task to raise money for a specific objective and as long as they know that this is being adhered to – in other words, that the money is being spent on the items which the donors expect – then they have fulfilled their responsibility.

If a charity cannot spend its funds on the purpose for which they were raised and no provision was included to enable funds raised to be used for another charitable purpose, it must consult the donors before changing the use of those funds, or return the money to them. The Charity Commissioners can make an arrangement to apply the proceeds of such a failed appeal, a problem which arises most often in disaster appeals. By the same token, surplus funds can present difficulties if no provision is made for the possibility of such success. Therefore, although capital appeals raise more if they are for specifics, you must leave scope in your literature as well as in your governing instrument for the widest possible use of the funds raised. If not, you may have to consult with the Charity Commissioners regarding the possibility of their making a scheme to deal with the situation (see also Appendix 8 – Schemes).

The annual report

It is a statutory requirement of the Charities Acts that the trustees of a charitable trust keep statements of account. (Charities established as companies are required to do so by the relevant Companies Act.) The government, the Charity Commission and the accounting profession have shown their concern over charity accounting practice, and the minimal details required, and guidance has thus been issued. (Details are provided in Appendix 8.)

SORP 2

The Statement of Recommended Practice on accounting by Charities (SORP 2) was issued by the professional accounting bodies' Accounting Standards Committee in May 1988. It sets out recommendations of the way in which a charity should report on the resources entrusted to it and the activities it undertakes. These recommendations are not mandatory but charities are encouraged to follow them and to state in their accounts that they have done so. There have, however, been many advances in charity accounting since the original SORP was published and, accordingly, a revised SORP is expected in the summer of 1993 as a forerunner of the statutory regulations under the Charities Act 1992.

The Charities Act 1992 introduced a new accounting, auditing and reporting regime for charities. (The implications of the new Act are discussed in Appendix 8.)

The SORP 2 – and I recommend that you obtain a copy – prescribes that the Annual report of a charity should include:

- Legal and administrative details
- The Trustees' Report or equivalent statement
- The Accounts and related notes thereto.

I have outlined in brief the requirements.

SORP 2 requirements

Legal and administrative details should include details about the charity's constitution, charity registration number and address, names of trustees, members of the management committee, principal officers and names of bankers, accountants, solicitors, etc.

The Trustees' Report should contain an explanation of the charity's objectives, organization structure, mission and strategy statement, review of developments and achievements and significant events during the year, narrative review of the financial position of the charity – details of any surplus or deficit, funding requirements, commitments and obligations.

The Accounts should comprise
- a statement of financial activities that shows all the resources made available to the charity and all the expenditure incurred by the charity during the period
- a balance sheet which shows all the assets, liabilities and funds of the charity
- a cash flow statement
- an explanation of the accounting policies used to prepare the accounts
- details of the movement on and position at the end of the year of the various resources held by the charity
- other notes which explain the information contained in the accounting statements.

Essentially, the charity's accounts should be prepared in a way that gives a true and fair view of the results for the year and the state of affairs at the balance sheet date. They should be informative and not unnecessarily detailed to enable the readers to obtain a full appreciation of all the charity's activities.

CONCLUSION

Finally, without wishing to sound as if I am receiving commission from the legal, accounting and other professions, I strongly urge anyone involved in setting up an appeal to obtain professional advice as early as is practicable on all legal and financial aspects. Charity finance is a specialized area and the rules and regulations are complex. If you ensure that your adviser has the necessary specialist experience, you will find the service is cost effective. Your trustees will not thank you if you seek to save money in this respect and you then have costly problems to sort out at a later stage. A stitch in time . . . .

Chapter 10

ADMINISTRATION AND PERSONNEL

The appropriate level of preparation required for an appeal will vary according to the size of the target and whether it is to be private, public or both. A private appeal demands a great deal of personal information about potential major donors. In a public appeal, that type of information may be less significant but the volume of data will be much larger. Further advice on administration relevant to the later stages of an appeal, is given in Chapters 15 and 30.

The need to plan the office, human resources, systems and general administrative arrangements in advance cannot be stressed enough. It is just not possible to redesign or restructure the office or its systems once an appeal, particularly a public appeal, gains momentum. Time spent patching systems in the middle of an appeal is time misspent.

There is a huge premium on getting the system right, not least because you are then less likely to encounter costly surprises in your budgeting and eventually in the final amount you are able to hand over to the beneficiaries of your appeal. Remember that most one-off appeals tend to be followed by much longer-term fund-raising operations and the equipment you install may need to take this into account.

THE APPEAL OFFICE

Unless it is a regionally based appeal, it is helpful for a charity to have its appeal office in London, the headquarters location of most of the major donors that have to be dealt with personally. Charities often take offices in the capital for the duration of a national appeal if they are not already in London. Companies may provide space free. The Wishing Well Appeal offices were arranged by the Special Trustees to the Hospital, who are appointed by the government to handle all the Hospital's charitable money. When Hill Samuel housed the Charing Cross Appeal office, we had free telephone, free postage and free access to the bank's mighty information systems. We did have to move periodically from office to office, but this was always done for us over a weekend; everything was beautifully in place when we arrived on Monday morning.

To maximize the precious man hours at an appeal office's disposal, it is always helpful if people can be persuaded to come to the office, rather than have the normally very few appeal staff spending valuable time in travelling to other offices. This is not usually too much of an imposition if the office is centrally located. Nevertheless, one must always be prepared to fit in with the extremely pressurized diaries of the high-level people who will be responsible for the biggest donations. It is especially helpful if the appeal offices are near the project location, as potential donors first see over the site before 'talking turkey' in the appeal office.

A charity appeal needs no unusual facilities. If extras are available at no cost, so much the better. It is a great help to have space for meetings. However, charities are usually lucky to have space for a desk, let alone a meeting room. It is highly desirable to have a clearly identified reception area in order to filter donors satisfactorily. In the early days of the Wishing Well Appeal's public phase, donors had difficulty making themselves known to our staff through the throng of shoppers. A reception area allows the appeal staff to give donors a cup of tea and thank them properly. Should the appeal office not have a suitable space, it may be possible to borrow a vacant shop or bank branch.

Appeal offices should not expect anything other than a bare cell, but it can work out differently. At Great Ormond Street, our volunteers worked out of a tiny converted basement. The Hospital always had to come first, so the Appeal Office was at the back of the queue for a facelift – until the Princess of Wales agreed to visit the Hospital in December 1987. The Princess very kindly said she would tour the office to encourage our hard-pressed staff and volunteers. When the visit organizers saw the basement, they were dismayed. There was no question, in their opinion, of the Princess being asked to view such cramped accommodation. Nevertheless, undaunted, she did, stooping as she descended the rickety stairs – but those stairs were at least carpeted. We had been asking for a carpet for two months; with a Royal visitor in the offing, it arrived as if by magic! The visit gave the staff an enormous fillip. We were short-staffed, they were hugely overworked and the thought that the Princess of Wales cared enough to shake them by the hand and take an interest in their work was an inspiration. The carpet was appreciated, too.

HUMAN RESOURCES

It will be apparent to anyone slightly acquainted with charity work that there are at least as many women as men active in the voluntary sector. Hence, at this stage, I would like to reiterate the point I make on the subject in the Author's Note. I have used male pronouns in general references and terms – such as chairman – merely for editorial ease.

Assessing the level of staff needed for an appeal runs on from the level of funds required, the cause, the potential donor constituency and the strategy devised to raise the required target. The one-off appeal offers maximum opportunity for using peer group fund-raising, so a structure should be devised to share responsibilities in a well-coordinated fashion. The members of the fund-raising panels are volunteers – very important maybe, but volunteers nevertheless – who can give the charity time only when their busy business lives allow. So there has to be a core at the heart of this activity and that is the paid staff.

It is essential to ensure that top-level volunteers are left with as little legwork as possible. This role is usually undertaken by staff, but the staff's function is much wider than that. Depending on the level of the staff member, his activity will usually involve planning his area of interest with the appeal director, researching the ideal panel members to try to recruit and working out the best line of approach. This is followed by the preparation of a draft plan of action and budget for the relevant panel of volunteers to approve and then advising the panel chairman every step of the way. The staff member will try to delegate most activities, if this can be done wisely, while at the same time watching over the operation and being ready to take a grip should something go wrong or a volunteer cry off at the last moment.

Dealing with people at this level demands a certain maturity on the part of the staff member, who must be courteous and positive at all times, even to the extent of being charming to the volunteer who fails to appear and so jeopardises the success of a major event. This requires real professionalism and the ability to recruit, guide and motivate supporters throughout. What a paragon of virtue, you may say: perhaps we are not quite that perfect. . . but it helps. We expect all this from our staff, including being self-motivated, working all hours when necessary, being a good team member and working for much less pay than for a similar job in business.

So charity staff are a special breed, I maintain. There are still a few who do not quite measure up to these standards. In the main, though, there is a new spirit among fund-raisers in the voluntary sector. They used to be denigrated and hence did not have a great deal of self-respect. How often have you heard people say that they would like to help a charity but did not want to become involved in fund-raising because they regarded it as rather squalid? Yet it is a fact of life that no charity can fulfil its mission without the financial wherewithal. Fund-raising has always been an art, but with information technology it is becoming increasingly scientific, producing a more professional attitude among fund-raisers.

Many support staff in business, especially secretaries, are on top of their job, but working in such a highly technical field that they have no hope of career advancement. These sorts of people are among those I try to attract to the voluntary sector because it offers them the chance to grow as far as they are able. Fund-raising is easy to understand, even though the learning process never ends. I am proud to say that some of my secretaries have developed into assistants and then gone on to become highly effective fund-raisers. One is a fund-raising consultant. Much of the work in an appeal office can be handled by secretaries and clerical workers and these, too, must be selected with care. They should be well-organized and methodical individuals who can also represent the public face of the appeal. Often they are the first point of contact with the public.

Training

Ongoing charity departments can afford to give regular training to their staff – essential if the profession is to grow and to attract top calibre people. Lack of time and money mean that the one-off appeal must usually concentrate on finding the candidate with precisely the right qualifications for the job when needed. Usually, the only training provided is to teach staff about the charity, its activities and the project for which the appeal has been launched. This is far from ideal. My own view is that all staff, at whatever level, for ongoing fund-raising or for the one-off appeal, should be allowed time for training as a norm. I believe this is not just a problem we have with staff working for appeals but a subject which is not taken seriously enough in this country.

Nevertheless, training in Britain's charity fund-raising is growing apace. Many courses are offered by the Institute of Charity Fundraising Managers and others, including the Directory of Social Change, Open University – Non-profit Organizations Course, and The National Council for Voluntary Organizations. The Chartered Institute of Marketing diploma includes an optional course on fund-raising, while the Cranfield MBA course offers the opportunity to specialize in not-for-profit income generation. Information on regional courses and community development can be obtained from your local Community Service Volunteers Office. It is also heartening to see that management colleges, such as Ashridge, are offering part-bursary places to charity staff. Initiatives such as these are changing the face of fund-raising in Britain and raising the levels of professionalism and morale at the same time.

As the qualitative substance of lesser known courses varies, however, it is wise to take references beforehand. Some fund-raising consultants also provide in-house training as part of their service. This can often be much cheaper than sending large numbers of people on a course and the training can be specific to the charity concerned.

Motivation

Staff motivation is a crucial part of an appeal director's role. If staff are prepared to work long hours at modest rates of pay, the least they deserve is the feeling that they are closely associated with their cause and that the contribution from each and every one of them is appreciated. Many staff are already well motivated when they are recruited, while others may need to see for themselves before being inspired. It is surprising that charities often keep their fund-raisers away from the rock face but they need to care deeply and be informed if they are to infect others with zeal. I learned the value of this lesson in the late 1970s when I was Director of the Local Groups Department of Help the Aged. During my research into the needs of the elderly, I visited some of the worst living conditions in London and was horrified by what I saw. I am ashamed to think that people can be left in such squalor in this day and age. It had such an effect on me that I decided I should share this appalling knowledge with my new recruits as part of their induction. I had a team of mainly retired forces personnel. They made excellent fund-raisers because of their knowledge of people and, as many already had pensions, they could manage on the low salaries we offered in those days. There was a Grenadier Guards Colonel, an Air Commodore, a Brigadier and a Deputy Lieutenant for Essex among the team. Tough types, you may think – but they, too, were horrified by what they saw, and I believe the experience helped to give us the crusading spirit we needed to encourage people to support the Greater London appeal we ran to support the building of further sheltered housing schemes for the elderly.

Recruitment

Recruiting is becoming more and more of a problem. There are simply not enough experienced people available – especially appeal directors with a successful and relevant track record. So charities are often forced to recruit people from business who have suitable skills in finance, administration and marketing, but no knowledge of fund-raising. As with any field, it is important to produce a clear job description and to draw up a candidate specification of the type of person you are seeking. There are recruitment agencies, such as Charity Recruitment, Charity Appointments, Charity People, or Execucare. Several headhunters now specialize in the charity field, handling some of the top jobs. It is sometimes possible, through a business link, to find a top headhunting firm prepared to look for a candidate as its contribution towards the appeal. This will certainly save you considerable funds, but there is a disadvantage: inevitably you will be a headhunter's second priority client.

It is wise to remain a little flexible as far as the job description is concerned. You may have the opportunity to recruit someone who does not quite cover everything you had specified, but who has a wealth of additional talent which could be put to good use. The weak area can be supported, perhaps by a voluntary expert. The priority should be to ensure that the team has the collective knowledge required.

Appeal directors should beware of recruiting an individual who has precisely the right qualifications for the post, but is a solitary or prima donna figure. It is better to take on someone with slightly less expertise who is a good team mixer. However, when the appeal pressure is building and you desperately need to fill the post, there is a great temptation to make this mistake. The only possible exception is the highly creative, individualistic type, who may be temperamental and may not fit in quite so well. If his input is really valued by the team, allowance can be made. With careful management, the operation can really benefit from such a contribution.

Staff meetings

Special care needs to be given to holding regular staff meetings. This can be particularly difficult when the appeal gathers momentum, but if you do not keep everyone up to date with progress, it is easy to duplicate effort or to cut across each others' bows without meaning to. All staff members, at any level, can be ambassadors for the appeal if they know how their own part in the operation fits into the whole. The flow of information must go – and be seen to go – in two directions. It is important for management to receive information from staff in the field about how management policy is being accepted or otherwise, to encourage new ideas and the like. Field staff should know that their feedback will not fall on deaf ears.

Personnel policy

In the early stages of an appeal, staff are the main cost. So each position must be carefully planned and filled only when the appeal has reached the appropriate stage. All the normal personnel policies and procedures need to be established before staff are recruited, although these may be amended with the input of the appeal director. It might be a matter of just slotting into the same system as the umbrella charity or it might involve setting up a new system. As has been mentioned, fund-raising staff are often paid at a slightly higher rate than the general charity staff, especially if they have been brought in on a short-term contract and do not have the benefit of job security and a pension. In these cases, it is often preferable to set up a separate body to handle personnel matters to avoid any bad feeling.

Serious thought should be given to the type of contract to be offered; for example, whether it should be for a fixed length of time or whether it should be open until notice is given. One of the reasons for this is that fund-raising staff may otherwise obtain certain legal rights which would make it difficult to end the contract once the appeal is finished. Other matters which must be considered include salary structures and the type of benefits that fund-raising staff should be entitled to, the detail of contracts, such as hours of work, location, sick pay, holidays, and disciplinary and grievance procedures, job evaluation, insurance, PAYE, National Insurance, assessment reviews and such usual personnel matters. Deliberations on policy are better undertaken before any problems arise and to ensure uniformity. Similarly, proper legal advice on the contracts should be obtained in advance to prevent problems arising.

Staffing and volunteers

Many people do voluntary work because they have recently retired, been bereaved or are just plain bored and need a purpose in life. More women are going out to work and more are being encouraged to do so in the future, which makes finding volunteers less easy, especially for one-off appeals which are often based in London. On the other hand, the recession has increased the number of redundant executives, for whom voluntary work is the best chance of avoiding demoralization and retaining self-respect. Charities can always use business and professional expertise of every description and a number of agencies exist to steer volunteers to where they are needed.

When I started at Great Ormond Street, I had only an administrator and a personal assistant, both brought with me from my previous appeal. We were at the research stage and so we recruited three excellent voluntary office researchers. They were an ex-civil servant and headmaster, a buyer, and a Citizens Advice Bureau worker. They accomplished the mammoth task of setting up all the records of major potential donors – wealthy individuals, companies and trusts – as well as helping with a wide range of other activities. All volunteers, no matter what part they play, are VIPs and should be trained as thoroughly as staff (see Chapter 30). The staff member's role is to make the work interesting and the experience rewarding and fun for them.

We could not have managed without volunteers without doubling our expenses, which would not have been acceptable. An enormous amount of time and trouble is taken by charities researching lists, names and contacts. If all this had been done by paid staff with the appeals I have run, the costs-to-income ratios would have changed radically for the worse. It is amazing what can be done through voluntary input: truly, many hands make light work. When I set up an appeal in the Royal Borough of Kensington and Chelsea and wanted to produce a comprehensive list of wealthy people in the area, we split a copy of *Who's Who* between five volunteers who went through each section pulling out the names and addresses of people living in the Royal Borough. This very valuable list was produced at no cost to the charity and we raised the money long before we had approached all the names on the list.

In the Wishing Well Appeal, staff built up to eight during the business appeal, then to 12 before the public appeal, backed by 50 carefully trained volunteers. Midland Bank staff handled all our mail for the first three months of the public appeal. Appeal staff numbers rose to 34 once we took over handling the mail because of the enormous amount of work the bank had been doing for us at no cost to the Appeal, and in response to the torrent of queries from the general public. Most of the new staff taken on were volunteers who had been doing administrative work for us. They had made themselves indispensable and fitted naturally and easily into a paid role. This is an excellent way for people to move into the charity field because they can demonstrate the right motivation if they are prepared to start on a voluntary basis. Chapter 30 includes an illustration of the staff structures we used.

Finding volunteers

Agencies, such as the Volunteer Centre UK and the National Association of Volunteer Bureaux, place volunteers with charities. REACH (the Retired Executive Action Clearing House) provides a free service which finds part-time, expenses-only posts for retired business or other professional people who want to use their skills to help voluntary bodies with charitable aims.

These are obvious ways of finding volunteers, as are advertisements in the media. One's imagination will suggest other, less obvious, ad hoc approaches.

At one stage of the Charing Cross Medical Research Centre Appeal we had free office accommodation within Hill Samuel, the merchant bank, near the Barbican in the City of London. As we wanted volunteers, it occurred to me that there were probably quite a few people recently retired or perhaps at a loose end, living in the large Barbican complex. Some of them might be prepared to contribute time to a worthwhile cause, while working as part of a team. We found what channels of communication existed between the administration at the Barbican and the flats, and arranged for information about the voluntary positions to be posted on notice boards and delivered through letter boxes. We had a very encouraging response.

Volunteers can present themselves in the most unexpected circumstances. During the Wishing Well Appeal, I went to a party given by neighbours who worked for the Foreign and Commonwealth Office. There I met Helen Kelly, whose husband was also in the Foreign Office. She showed great interest in our work at Great Ormond Street and said that she would like to help. One often hears people say this sort of thing but they do not always mean it. It was not until I met her again at another cocktail party in the same house that I realized she really meant what she said. Here was somebody who was used to entertaining for the Foreign Office and had been a bursar. To my amazement, she contributed four days a week as a volunteer helping with our international appeal and made herself so indispensable that, eventually, she became my personal assistant on our staff. She left us only when her husband was posted to Finland; we were very sorry to see her go.

Secondees

Secondees from commercial companies can be a useful source of expertise, but it is important for the charity to stipulate precisely the role it wants a secondee to fulfil. Vague calls for someone experienced in administration or sales are liable to lead to disappointment on both sides. At the same time, the charity should not expect to obtain the services of exactly the person it had in mind. Companies are most willing to second those who are near the beginning or the end of their careers. The 40-year-old senior executive is usually far too valuable to release on a secondment. The Action Resource Centre, a registered charity, provides a consultancy service for secondment of people to the voluntary sector. Based in London, it operates with business people, employers and voluntary organizations. ARC is working hard to promote early and mid-career secondments, business volunteers and development assignments. In the last case, the secondment period is measured in hours (typically 50-200), often on a day-a-week basis, and is related to a single, clearly defined project. ARC monitors and evaluates the assignments, which have proved to be excellent training for staff with potential.

SYSTEMS/COMPUTERS

When it came to setting up our office systems, the Wishing Well Appeal was advised by a computer group called Scicon, now part of General Motors of the United States. Midland Bank seconded a computer expert to help develop our system. Since the Appeal ended, systems have developed to the point where it may be a disadvantage to be advised by someone who is used only to big computer systems. Also, as a general rule, do not accept a donated system unless it is exactly what you want. The money you would save in accepting such a system will be spent in adapting it to the way you want to work or spent in working in an inappropriate way or with inadequate information.

What size of system?

The size of the system you will need depends on the volume of transactions that will pass through the system rather than on the amount of money you are trying to raise. This dictates the number of terminals, the storage capacity and processing power required. It is very difficult to suggest how much should be spent on a computer system because there are so many variables, although the overall cost of computing has fallen and continues to do so. As a very broad rule of thumb, you might expect to spend between £3,000 and £6,000 plus VAT for each user on the equipment and software at the present time. Be prepared to write this off over three to four years and to reinvest as necessary. The larger the system, the lower the cost per user should be. However, a small appeal can set up a very simple single terminal system for about £1,000 if no specialist software is used. It may sound expensive, but spending an average of £2,000 or £3,000 per year per user on a system is a small sum compared with salary and office accommodation costs.

Small appeals

Computers are not strictly necessary for small appeals, but they can help the staff to do their jobs faster and more efficiently. The decision will depend on the cost (capital and running expenses) of the system and whether the staff have used computers before. Computer systems now are easier to operate than they used to be and people may not take long to learn to operate a simple system, especially if each staff member has a clear, precise job specification. Even the smallest one-off appeal will benefit from having a word processor and keeping names and addresses on a simple database.

If your activities and/or your budget are such that a computer system is not appropriate, you must develop suitable manual records to enable you to maintain control over the appeal's operations and finances. In the following paragraphs I refer to a number of facilities which a computer system can offer, but it is perfectly acceptable to maintain the equivalent information manually. However, just as for computers, I suggest that you obtain professional advice to confirm that you are on the right lines before going ahead with a manual system.

In a larger appeal a properly used computer system will hold all the relevant information. All the staff should use it to record their diaries, plan meetings and fund-raising events and gather data about supporters. Even the most junior staff, who may not be using the data, still need to be able to input. To benefit from such a system the staff must be trained to the appropriate level of competence.

Acquiring a system

It is easy to see that one can spend considerable time and energy on looking at systems – even more if you are not careful to plan what you want.

My advice is to write down formally what needs to be put on to computer and why. Involve others in your team in this process and if possible delegate it to someone who will be the project's 'champion' and drive it forward.

Unless you or your 'champion' has broad and up-to-date knowledge of systems relevant to the appeal, I suggest that you get help from a professional. The accountancy practices who have specialist charity teams will invariably have the right people to help. Alternatively, there are independent consultants who are members of organizations, such as The Association of Professional Computer Consultants, who are well qualified to advise.

On this particular point, be sure to use a true expert, not just a computer literate or knowledgeable person to guide you. You need someone with current expert knowledge of systems for charitable fund-raising. Such a person will be able to guide you quickly and authoritatively to an appropriate system. As a guide to his ability to work on your behalf and not just to give a standard response, find out what systems he has been involved with recently. If they are all the same, it may mean that he just churns out the same answers regardless of the user's requirements. Also, contact the Institute of Charity Fundraising Managers who can guide you to some appropriate user groups.

Fund-raising strategy/computer strategy

The computer and administration systems strategy should reflect the overall fund-raising project's strategic stages. Defining the computer budget and selecting systems can come only after you have set your targets, designed the appeal and structured its phases.

When developing your computer strategy and the stages for its implementation, you should bear in mind the phenomenal rate at which technical developments are taking place. For example, if you are not going to put an element of the system into use immediately, defer its purchase. Do not be tempted by the salesman into a bulk purchase. The shelf life of a computer before it is superseded by a later model may be between 9 and 12 months. In some instances, it may be less.

Nevertheless, you must ensure that a fundamental system infrastructure is in place which can support progressive development. Personal computer networks are useful here because you can add to a system a work station at any time, as long as this progressive development has been specified in the first place. This type of development tends to be more difficult with mini-computer style systems. One has to have a central computer system that has sufficient processing power to satisfy a stated maximum number of users. Exceed this limit or underestimate the processing demands and you will need to replace or upgrade the central unit, possibly at significant cost.

The principle here is that the initial system purchase should be just the first of many and not the one and only. Future acquisitions may not be specifically pre-defined at the outset but they should fit into an overall plan for the development of the system. Plan to add to your system regularly over the course of its life.

Finally, you should develop a written strategy and specification and not be enticed into being a pioneer to experiment with new software or technology unless it is essential to your campaign methodology.

Key points about buying your system

- Do not be cornered by technology – ensure that it can be expanded and upgraded. Avoid proprietary systems where your choice of add-on equipment and software is effectively limited to one source. Try to avoid the situation where the selection of one application program dictates or restricts choice in other application areas.
- Stick to your specification.
- Only buy what you need now, not what you may need in a year's time.
- Decide promptly and decisively. Significant discounts can be gained this way, particularly on software aimed specifically at the charity market. It is common for charities to take over a year from first enquiry through to final purchase of a system. For the systems houses, this is very expensive in terms of a salesman's time. If you can be decisive without being cavalier in your deliberations, you should be able to strike a keen bargain with the supplier.
- Negotiate firmly on contract terms and ensure that you have a fair contract which protects you as well as the supplier. If in any doubt, contact a solicitor who is knowledgeable about computer contracts.

Installation and training

The installation process is a good reason to delegate the computer issue to an assistant. It is time consuming and can benefit from your management involvement and overview from time to time. Before anything is delivered ensure that there is an implementation timetable in place and all parties are clear about the division of responsibilities. Also be prepared to get involved, to show willingness and to understand the systems that are being put in place.

Some organizations are tempted to consider training as an optional item or to pay lip-service to it by taking just the basic course for selected staff. Training is not a luxury – it is essential at the outset and on a continuing basis. Modern software is a treasure trove of facilities and time-saving tools and techniques. These have to be learned and understood. While some staff may be able to pick up part of what they need to learn from the manuals, most are just too busy or too frightened to learn through experimentation. All staff benefit from training courses and refresher and advanced technique courses. All too often the investment in systems is wasted because staff are only scratching at the surface due to lack of knowledge.

Which facilities?

The basic software elements are word processing, a fund-raising database, an accounting package (if you are looking after the accounts within the appeal office) and a spreadsheet for preparing budgets and presentations. There are many packages in each category, some of which are more widely used than others, so it is worth checking whether your staff are familiar with any.

Word processing

Dedicated word processors have been made obsolete by personal computer-based word processing programs. These may be used in conjunction with laser printers which can print between four and 12 pages per minute – or even faster. At six pages per minute, a laser printer can generate over 2,500 pages in seven hours – over 12,000 single page letters in a week. The letters can be made to vary automatically, depending on the contents of the database. Strict controls and authorization procedures are, therefore, necessary to ensure the targeting and appropriateness of any mailshots that come from the fund-raising office.

Fund-raising database

There are at least half a dozen standard programs to choose from and they are constantly developing. Very simply, they enable supporters to be selected and grouped according to a huge range of criteria. The basic data you hold must be appropriately comprehensive and, above all, accurate for your own benefit and to comply with the Data Protection Act. Under that Act, if you have personal information about a living individual, you must hold that information only as long as you need it and you must ensure that it is up-to-date and accurate.

Accounting

Accounting software is now relatively inexpensive and extremely easy to use. You need to understand the basics of bookkeeping to use these programs and to produce accurate reports with confidence, so take advice on accounting systems, their implementation and the controls, checks and balances that need to be in place.

You will also need to consider how trading operations through a separate trading company will fit into the donor database and the accounting systems. You may need to deal with accounting for VAT on aspects of your fund-raising that are not exempt, such as general sponsorship of the appeal.

I will say no more on this topic now other than to stress that you should ensure that you have selected a program which will produce information relevant to your purposes. The prime purpose of an accounting system is to provide reliable management information with the minimum of fuss. This is now embodied in the Charities Act 1992 (see Appendix 8) which requires charities to keep accounting records showing and explaining all their transactions.

Spreadsheet

Modern spreadsheets are much more than clever calculators. All are able to take numeric information and turn it into charts and graphs. Many provide the tools necessary to prepare presentation materials and summaries of detailed data.

Optional facilities

A range of programs beyond the basic facilities can play a significant role in the appeal office. A selection of these is listed below with brief comments.

Database

A general purpose database can be extremely useful for cataloguing purposes. For example, research material may be quite voluminous. A simple computer-based indexing system can be an effective tool. Resist the danger of individuals in the team setting up their own databases without reference to others. You will soon find data being duplicated; this is both inefficient and almost guarantees inconsistencies.

Do not allow personal information to be kept in more than one place. Otherwise, you will almost inevitably omit to record a change of address or something similar, which may lead to the supporter's confidence being lost.

The same database system can keep details of volunteers and suppliers.

Desk top publishing

This is one of the trickiest areas upon which to give definitive advice. To use a desk top publishing package effectively, you need to have natural talent and experience. Initially, many people considered these programs to be simply sophisticated word processing programs. This can be seen in the wide variety of charity newsletters produced in this way. In fact, they require planning and skill to be used properly.

If your campaign is going to produce extensive published materials, then this software can save typesetting costs and improve turn-around times.

DTP software needs a far more powerful computer than the average word processing program. You will need to consider this when planning the acquisition of the computers and printers.

Diary systems and electronic mail

In a busy campaign office an electronic diary system can be a real asset. Combined with an electronic mail system, it can significantly improve communications. Electronic mail is a facility for sending messages, documents, spreadsheets – in fact, anything that can be stored on computer – from one user on the system to another. Think of it as an electronic internal mail system.

These 'electronic office systems' are surprisingly inexpensive add-ons to an existing network. If you need to, you can also access them remotely from regional offices or from home by normal telephone lines.

Electronic mail is very useful for disseminating information in the office. This is not fanciful – just think about the memoranda generated during the course of an appeal. Electronic mail is far easier to handle and deal with than pieces of paper because it is all on screen and you have no physical filing to do. Delivery is also instant and highly targeted.

Event management

If your strategy includes the appeal office organizing major fund-raising events, a dedicated category of software should be considered. Anyone who has done the event management juggling act will appreciate software designed to handle invitation lists, guest lists, ticketing, place or seat reservations and the receipt of auction items, donations, gifts and ticket payments.

Many fund-raising database systems have an optional event management module. In addition, there are specialist event management and conference management packages available.

Fax software

A range of inexpensive fax software and equipment is now available. This offers the opportunity to do fax mailshots from a word processor, for example. This type of mailshot will not be relevant for reaching individual donors but is a possibility for making or keeping in contact with corporate donors. This can also be an excellent way of disseminating information around committee members, branches and distant fund-raisers.

Geo-demographic coding systems

Large mailing houses and data bureaux have, for many years, been able to offer analysis of a constituency database based upon geo-demographic factors. There are a number of systems available, all of which require a postcode as the starting point. A number of these coding systems are now available in a form suitable for use on personal computers.

The result of a geo-demographic analysis can be enlightening. A cross tabulation of different fund-raising efforts by such an analysis can help in deciding how to use bought-in lists or to tailor the method or style of approach to sections of your constituency.

Information providers

Information providers range from specialist fund-raising databases of press cuttings about the great and the good, to on-line information containing business credit rating data and information extracted from Companies House.

During the research phase, access to on-line systems such as these can be invaluable, but they can also be very expensive.

Mail order systems

It is unusual for a one-off appeal to get involved in large scale mail order activities. If this is an avenue to be explored, then there are a number of specialist suppliers of mail order packages for handling telephone orders and coupons from off-the-page advertising. In addition a number of the fund-raising database systems have optional mail order modules.

The alternative is to use a company which specializes in handling the orders for you. If you are considering this course, ensure that the details of your supporters are transferred to your main fund-raising database. A supporter who spends £100 through your Christmas catalogue feels that that money is going to your appeal, just as if the £100 had been given as a straight donation.

Mailsort

The Post Office currently provides significant discounts (between 13 and 25 per cent) on bulk mailings (normally more than 4,000 letters or 1,000 packets) if you have a high level of postcoding (90 per cent plus) and you sort, bundle and bag the mailing in a strictly defined sequence. You also have to produce a report on the mailing for the Post Office in a standard format.

To take advantage of the Mailsort rebating schemes you will have to use a Mailsort package or a computer bureau to do the sorting and analysis. These packages are now widely available as separate application programs or as optional modules in fund-raising database systems.

Payroll

Even the smallest appeal office will have people on a payroll. If possible, it is probably best to get this done by a third party, such as your umbrella charity, your accountant or a friendly corporate supporter, such as a bank.

If you need to run your own payroll, there are many packages to choose from. It is imperative that you have a maintenance agreement with the payroll software house because of its critical nature and the legislative changes that occur.

Personal contact management packages

These software packages or hand-held devices are the equivalent of a Filofax. This category of software can be very useful and cost effective for a small appeal or for highly targeted fund-raising.

For the larger campaign, where the database is the hub of the fund-raising effort, these packages (aimed usually at commercial sales people) can be counter productive if the basic rule of maintaining donor information in one place is jeopardized because additions or changes to the information are not being passed back to the central database. However, as working tools for individuals they can be effective.

Personnel records

I noted above the uses that a general purpose database may be put to in the appeal office. There are cases where the level of information and reporting warrants a more specialist and tailored approach. A good example is the personnel records database.

There are a number of good personnel systems available. These should be considered if the size of the appeal office is likely to become significant and the appeal a long-running one.

Postcoding

Fundamental to using geo-demographic software and using Mailsort is to have a database with a high level of postcoding.

All available systems are based on the Post Office's PAF ROM compact disk which contains the entire database of postcodes and addresses. It is possible to say, for any particular postcode, what the address will be or to enter an address and discover the postcode.

A number of proprietary systems have been built on the Post Office's database, which allows an address to be analyzed, a postcode to be allocated automatically, and the address to be corrected to the Post Office's preferred form. Complete and accurate data is an essential starting point for eliminating duplicate addresses and preventing them from creeping on to your database.

Project management

Project management software is a class of program which has been created to design, monitor and manage complex tasks. Typically, these programs are used in the construction and defence industries to plan and cost projects in fine detail. They are generally quite tricky to use but could be invaluable for planning major media, PR and fund-raising launches and coordinating resources. The alternative is a wall planner which is possibly easier to use!

DONOR DATA

Data Protection Act and confidentiality

It is important that all fund-raisers are fully acquainted with the provisions of the Data Protection Act 1984. The Data Protection Act covers only computer records. Manual records are not included unless there is an intention to computerize them or they are indexed by a computer system.

In addition to the Data Protection Act, there are EC proposals which, if enacted, will limit the capture of personal information for fund-raising purposes to those

---

Data protection principles

1. Personal data shall be obtained and processed fairly and lawfully.
2. Personal data shall be held only for one or more specified and lawful purpose.
3. Personal data held for one purpose shall not be used or disclosed in any manner incompatible with that purpose.
4. Personal data that is held shall be adequate, relevant and not excessive in relation to the purpose for which it is held.
5. Personal data shall be accurate and kept up-to-date.
6. Personal data shall not be kept longer than is necessary for the purpose for which it is held.
7. An individual shall be entitled to be informed by any data user whether he holds personal data about that individual, to access any such data and, where appropriate, to have that data corrected or erased.
8. Finally, appropriate security measures shall be taken against unauthorized access to, alteration, disclosure or destruction of personal data.

people who expressly permit this data to be held. As one would expect, this is being strongly resisted by U.K. charities.

Under the Data Protection Act, you are required to register your sources and uses of personal data with the Data Protection Registrar, Springfield House, Water Lane, Wilmslow, Cheshire SK9 5AX; telephone: 0625 535777. The Registrar's staff are knowledgeable and helpful and will send appropriate information pamphlets and forms on request.

The Data Protection Act embodies a number of data protection principles. All are good data processing practice and are worthy of note. I have paraphrased them on the previous page for brevity. You should refer to the pamphlets available from the Registrar for the detail and full interpretation.

Donor records

Discussion of personal data leads me to the heart of an appeal's system – the donor database. Although your appeal may be a one-off, you can be sure that someone is going to inherit your database as a very valuable legacy. The system and the data you collect, therefore, are worth managing carefully. In terms of value, the data is likely to be worth more than the equipment and software in the time and effort that have been put into collating and entering the information. Therefore, I stress the need for security and back-up.

You need security to ensure that nothing untoward happens to your system, either intentionally or by accident. For example, you should be aware that computers are easily stolen, data can be erased quite easily by someone who knows what they are doing (or thinks that they know what they are doing) and people do spill coffee and have accidents with cigarettes. Security is preventative. Back-up is there to rescue you from awkward situations.

If your computer is properly backed up, for example, by copying to disk, and that back-up is very recent, the worst that can happen is that you lose a few hours or days getting back to normality when the computer is repaired. If the disk is damaged, unreadable, very out of date or non-existent, you have a problem. Like motor cars, computers break down. It is not so much a matter of 'if' but 'when'. Similarly, back-up devices like tape drives or optical disk drives can fail. You should, therefore, ensure on a regular basis that you check that you can use that back-up media. The check should be on a different machine purely to demonstrate that the back-up medium is going to be readable on another device. The original machine may be a melted mess when you want to use it in anger!

Giving and trading history

What information do you need to obtain? I start from the premise that the donor will see your appeal as a single entity. You should reflect this by recording his involvement with you just once. Donors may become upset if the left hand within the appeal does not know what the right is doing. You should be able to record, as a minimum, all of the following information about a donor, a potential donor or a 'prospect' on a single database in the appeals office:

• Name

- Salutation
- Company name (if appropriate)
- Address(es)
- Source of name
- Donations
- Pledges
- Covenants
- Gift Aid donations
- Gifts in kind
  (This can include objects such as jewellery or antiques, the donation of stocks and shares, but also the gift of time as a volunteer or the secondment of an employee.)
- Purchases
  (Even though he has not given an outright donation, your supporter has given money to you by way of a purchase, for example, of mail order goods.)
- Earmarking
  (It is important in two respects to record any or all of the above as restricted funds. The first is that you have accepted the gift as having a condition associated with it and you must account for it accordingly. The second is that you can correspond in future with the donor about the fund or project that he has supported in the past.)
- Legacy data
  (Although not as important in one off-appeals as for long-term appeals, keeping track of promises of legacies is useful, even as just a measure of an individual's commitment to your cause. It can also be useful to have systems in place to keep track of and chase monies due from solicitors when a legacy is given and probate is being obtained.)
- Contact history
  (A comprehensive history of past contact, by telephone, post, fax, or in person can be particularly relevant and important in capital campaigns. A contact history is also the appeal's memory bank.)
- Cross-referencing between donor records
  (This ability, otherwise known as networking, is very important in enabling you to structure your approach to major potential donors and sponsors. It allows you to record who knows whom, the strength and basis of the relationship. Astonishing interrelationships can be gleaned as research information is built up.)
- Diary
  (A diary system is a good example of how appeals staff can record their activity and contact with donors. The system can also act as a reminder and follow-up system.)
- Contacts
  (Important contacts who do not warrant full donor records – for example, a donor's personal assistant or the names of his children.)
- Notes
  (The system should allow for notes to be recorded about a donor. These may include details of academic, military, business and voluntary work histories, memberships of clubs and so on.)

- Analysis and constituency coding
  (To allow your income to be analyzed into meaningful categories, your donor records will need to contain sector categories to allow this to be undertaken. Examples of these categories include age, nationality, education, career or profession, interests, geo-demographic coding, wealth coding, business sector, membership of fund-raising panels, etc.)

Plan very carefully what information you will need to collect. It is easy to set goals that are going to be impossible to achieve in practice. The requirement to collect detailed personal data on all supporters can spawn a massive research and data entry task that merely results in an incomplete and unsatisfactory set of data and a research team bogged down in detail. If the research and the detail are necessary to your fund-raising approach, make sure that you have the resources – human and electronic – to make the task achievable.

Financial information needs to be held in a way that allows you to analyze income by source, amount, geographical region, method of giving, frequency of giving, geo-demographic sector and so on.

The system should also allow you to extract information about the dates of a donor's first and latest payments, the number of gifts and the donations received on a monthly, yearly and cumulative basis. In addition, statistics such as highest and lowest donation are also useful.

INTEGRATING REGIONAL FUND-RAISERS

A thorny issue, particularly where autonomous fund-raisers are operating around the country, is ensuring that systems are in place to support their efforts and avoid duplication, yet, at the same time, still operate efficiently and economically. The problem is that as appeal coordinator, you need to ensure that the local fund-raisers have the information they need while being able to have immediate and accurate information about the appeal. You also need to prevent a local fund-raiser from asking for £500 from an organization when you are lining up the company for a £50,000 gift!

ACCOUNTING RECORDS

It is crucial to have comprehensive and accurate financial records. Eventually these will include details of cash collection and control, and how the appeal organization handles cash as it rolls into the headquarters. The Wishing Well Appeal received about £50,000 a day in the post: cash, cheques, postal orders and even valuable goods, such as an antique watch worth £900. Consequently, it is important that wherever cheques or cash are being handled, there are at least two responsible people opening the post. Then they can confirm with one another what has been received. A written record of all cash and cheque donations must be rigorously maintained and reconciled to the banking and accounting records. This minimizes mistakes, and disputes can more easily be resolved. It is also essential that the staff undertaking the activity are protected from suspicion of theft. Donors frequently write letters saying that a cheque or even cash is enclosed, yet forget to enclose it. In such cases, a note must be made on the letter and countersigned by both people responsible. This problem rarely arises at the preparation and private stages of an appeal, but can be a real headache in the throes of a major public appeal.

The bankings must be recorded and analyzed so that everyone, especially your Appeal Executive, knows how much has been donated that day, week or month. The detailed analysis of this income should flow from the donor database, producing vital management information, such as the types, sources and sizes of gifts, company donations according to the various panels for the City, industry, and so on. Covenants and Gift Aid receipts will need to be recorded separately, so that they can be accurately reflected in the overall figures and the tax claims made.

Covenants for the Wishing Well Appeal were handled by the Charities Aid Foundation. The CAF provides a comprehensive service available for all charitable appeals. For a fee it can also handle a number of other forms of appeal donation, such as credit card payments, cheques and Gift Aid. Where membership subscriptions are appropriate, whether covenanted or not, these can also be administered. Many charities now administer their own covenants and Gift Aid donations and correspond directly with the Inland Revenue Claims Branch – Charity Division – about recovery of income tax. While claims may be made up to six years after the chargeable period to which the covenant relates, it is advisable, for economic reasons, to claim repayment of tax as soon as any significant sum is recoverable. Copies of the relevant claim forms can be obtained from the Claims Branch.

It is important that all covenant and Gift Aid records are kept in a safe place and that copies are made. The Inland Revenue needs to scrutinize each original deed when the first claim for recovery of tax is made.

Paymaster service

A substantial and long-running appeal has to bear in mind another parallel with a normal business: the need to maintain a staff payroll and to pay bills. I usually arrange for the payroll to be handled completely separately, so that the fundraisers are not involved. Hill Samuel voluntarily performed this service for the Charing Cross Medical Research Centre Appeal. We were very fortunate in the Wishing Well Appeal that Midland Bank took over the paymaster function, which involved paying staff remuneration and invoices that had been signed by authorized executives. The Midland physically wrote the cheques, settled the bills and kept the accounts.

I think it is best if expenditure is handled through an organization which is separate from the appeal office and that it also monitors all expenditure against budget. For smaller appeals, a separate department of the appeal office may suffice.

INSURANCE

The administrator of any charity should be particularly mindful of possible insurance requirements, including the following:

- the Employers Liability (Compulsory Insurance) Act 1969 insists that all employees must be covered in respect of injury and disease.

- separate public liability insurance against accidents is necessary in   respect of volunteers, who are not employees.
- volunteers or employees who drive a vehicle for a charity must be insured against third-party risks. This involves telling the insurer the name of each driver and the purpose of his journeys.
- a charity should check that any building it occupies is insured against the cost of rebuilding. Shop leases should be checked to see if the windows require specific insurance.
- special events, indoor and outdoor, must be covered against third-party claims. The basic premium is a matter for negotiation but, at the Wishing Well Appeal, we found it was not unduly high. The negotiations will be based on an estimate of the likely number and type of events in a given year. The insurer will probably need two weeks' notice of each event, its nature and location, and the expected number of spectators and/or participants, and will reserve the right to load the premium for any it considers particularly risky like:
  – cancellation of events.
  – theft of almost anything to do with the charity.

This is not an exhaustive list, so do take advice from a reputable insurance broker or other financial intermediary. I discuss further the issue of third-party insurance in Chapter 25.

Appeals should take out third-party insurance for fund-raisers. While it may appear to be taking caution to extremes, it is precisely the one-in-a-million chance that can ruin the enterprise, quite apart from the impact a real disaster would have on the reputation of the appeal and the charity on whose behalf it is acting. As it is so unlikely that the worst will happen, the cost of this insurance is modest. The public phase of a major appeal can involve tens of thousands of people, sometimes at a single event. In those circumstances, there is always the possibility of something going awry.

The Charity Commissioners have agreed recently that in appropriate cases a trustee can obtain insurance, paid for by the charity, for a policy to cover a trustee from personal liability for acts either properly undertaken in the administration of a charity or undertaken in breach of trust but under an honest mistake. Trustees proposing to take out such insurance should contact the Commissioners for further information.

In the Wishing Well Appeal, we arranged an overall insurance policy at a reasonable rate. We had to telephone the insurers and ask if the policy could cover a specific event. That gave the insurers the opportunity to look at the risk each time. If they were not informed about an event in advance, it was not covered.

CONCLUSION

The administration unit is the nerve centre of the appeal. Inefficiency in this quarter can seriously damage the reputation of an appeal. I have seen this problem create a general loss of confidence in the effectiveness of an appeal, especially among the busy top business people who lend their support. They are used to top grade back up in their work and have every right to expect the same service from an appeal.

CHECKLIST

1. OFFICE
   -find and prepare suitable office accommodation,
    furniture and equipment.

2. HUMAN RESOURCES
   -decide personnel policy.
   -recruit and train staff/volunteers/secondees for private appeal phase.
   -arrange regular staff meetings.

3. SYSTEMS
   -produce a strategy.
   -write a specification (listing required facilities).
   -decide on information systems and computers.
   -appoint a project manager.
   -use expert adviser and vet purchase and maintenance contracts.
   -make sure training and systems maintenance costs are budgeted for.
   -register your database with the Data Protection Registrar.
   -security – be sure to back-up your database.

4. GENERAL ADMINISTRATIVE ARRANGEMENTS
   -arrange comprehensive insurance for fund-raisers and appeal office
    facilities.
   -arrange paymaster system.
   -review other arrangements which need to be set up and
    administered such as supplies of stationery, literature and
    promotional items.

Part III

THE PRIVATE APPEAL

Chapter 11

OVERVIEW

The private appeal may be all an appeal intends to do to raise the funds needed. It is the rifle shot, as opposed to the buckshot approach. The advantage is that it can be more precise and easier to control, but preparation and research are still the keys to success. This involves holding back until the formula is right – until you have the facts to prove the need and the right asking power has been recruited. The private appeal targets the potential major donors – statutory bodies, wealthy individuals, companies and grant-making trusts. It is the only way to raise major gifts effectively.

WHY A PRIVATE APPEAL?

You might decide to restrict your appeal to the quiet approach if another similar charity is in the middle of a major public appeal; I have heard of many hospitals doing so. Alternatively, you might be raising funds for a specialization within a hospital, and going public would prejudice other appeals in the same hospital. Equally, it may be that you want to sew up the appeal as soon as possible and you may have the right contacts to help you do so. Finally, yours may be an unpopular or unemotive cause, which appeals to comparatively few. These are all reasons for going no further than the private approach. However, by doing so you miss the opportunity to raise your organization's profile and educate the public about your cause and your charity's role. This has many knock-on effects. As well as not taking advantage of the additional fund-raising potential of a public appeal, the raised profile would help in many other areas, such as recruiting staff and volunteers, government relations and local community integration.

There are two reasons for holding the private appeal before the public appeal. First, it ensures that you have raised a fair proportion of your target when you launch publicly so you are an immediate success. This is very popular with donors. Secondly, it allows you to approach all potential major donors on a personal basis. This avoids the 'vaccination effect' whereby a potential big donor sends, say £500, after reading about the appeal in the newspaper. If he had been approached correctly, the gift might have been ten times bigger. However, as he has given once, it is difficult for the appeal to approach him privately to seek a more substantial donation. He has been 'vaccinated'. This is such an important principle that it bears repeating.

REVIEW STRATEGY

Naturally, the strategy of the private appeal is an extension of the strategy for the whole exercise. The Wishing Well Appeal's overall strategy is fully outlined in Chapter 7, but in summary it was:

1. To use peer group fund-raising
2. To create a structure of panels and committees for specific tasks
3. To employ sophisticated marketing techniques
4. To raise at least one-third of the target sum before launching the appeal to the public. (It might be half or even two-thirds for a less popular cause.)
5. To obtain substantial government funding
6. To keep costs and staff to a minimum
7. To build the charity's profile and its donor base for ongoing fund-raising.

This strategy allowed us a year to complete the private appeal. During the feasibility review, one of the main activities is to analyze the likely response from potential donors. Based on this, it is possible to derive a target for the amount you can expect to receive from each category of donor. An average response might be as shown here. Examples of actual appeal results are included in Chapter 34.

Category	%
Wealthy individuals	15
Grant-making trusts	35
Companies	20
Gifts from the public	25
Interest from deposits	5

There may also be statutory funds forthcoming. The breakdown will vary for different appeals depending on the size, target donor base, timing, etc. The Wishing Well Appeal received more from wealthy donors and less from trusts.

The first three categories are approached for major gifts during the private phase, although unsolicited responses also come from them during the public appeal when companies are targeted for a more visible type of assistance. The broad figures should be broken down until a target is set for every approach. As you are not going to hit the target with each approach, you must raise the overall target to allow for under-achievement. By carefully thinking through the justification for any given target, it is easier to obtain the initial donors' support and acceptance of this procedure. They, in turn, will be approaching others for gifts. The part played by pacesetters is crucial. Early big gifts will raise sights and stimulate larger gifts.

Structures

The best structure for your appeal will be indicated by research into the donors you will probably attract. If you are using peer group fund-raising as a strategy, it is essential that you structure your appeal carefully, so that voluntary fund-raisers know their role and the part their committee or panel is playing in the master plan. This applies especially in the private phase. The aim must be to recruit influential people on to one or two panels to assist with approaches to companies, individuals, trusts and statutory bodies. All these categories are approached via a contact point, so the charity should try to recruit those most able to generate a positive response to the appeal, ideally those who have already pledged a substantial gift themselves or from their own organization. (Appendix 1 shows the Wishing Well Appeal's panel structure.)

Private appeal – Sequence of events

Devise structure to fit target groups
Pinpoint leadership in target groups (panel chairmen)
Panel chairmen recruit panel members (to give and approach others)
Produce plans of action for each panel, including setting targets
Solicit lead gifts from panel members
Circulate lists of potential major donors, broken into manageable batches
(for researching these, see Chapter 5):
   companies
   wealthy individuals
   grant-making trusts
Allocate who approaches whom
Chase panel members' approaches
Record results of approaches
Hold private 'thank you' events
Create the plan for the public appeal (if relevant)

There is a logical development from one stepping stone to another during this sequence. Many are developed simultaneously. This is one of the few parts of an appeal which you really can control; that is certainly not the case during the public phase because of the numbers of people involved.

WISHING WELL PRIVATE APPEAL RESULTS

By the time the Wishing Well Appeal launched its campaign to the public, £9.5 million had been pledged against the target of £30 million (excluding the government's £20 million pledge). If we had been able to count all the verbal promises, as well as those received in writing, this pledged figure, excluding government input, would have been nearer £15 million. Normally, when you draw up your programme for the private appeal, you set your sights on a particular date to launch publicly – say, nine months to a year after the private phase commences. When the

Wishing Well Appeal reached that date, the process was not complete and we still had some potential major donors to approach on a personal basis. In such circumstances, it is usual to delay the launch date to ensure the best result by avoiding the 'vaccination' effect. However, we were having so much difficulty keeping the plan for the Appeal out of the press that we still stuck to the original launch date. I must add that that is no reflection on the companies and individuals who were contacted later.

---------------- *Chapter 12* ----------------

MARKETING

This chapter explains the activities of the Marketing Panel in preparation for and during the private phase of an appeal. It should be looked at in conjunction with Chapter 8, which explains the marketing role to be undertaken whether a private or public appeal is envisaged. As the private phase of an appeal involves individual approaches to those in a position to make substantial gifts, the Marketing Panel helps and supports the communications process at every level. The fund-raising professional will advise on how the approaches should be allocated, but the marketing back-up will give advice on what arguments should be deployed to convince a potential donor, the setting of the request for funds and special presentations when necessary. It will produce the appeal brochure, audio-visual and display material, and add creativity to the production of speech notes, fund-raising letters and even trust submissions. There is no point in having this expertise at your disposal if you do not use it fully to improve your performance and give your appeal a definite edge over its competitors. It further helps if the copywriter is given opportunities for direct contact with the 'product'. Tony Brignull, the copywriter at the advertising agency used by the Wishing Well Appeal, toured the Hospital with his colleagues and interviewed parents and staff, which helped him to produce outstandingly good copy.

At this stage, professionalism really shows and has a very positive effect on the top-level people you intend to involve. They are used to working with efficient and effective professionals and will respect you for displaying the same attitude. They will then feel happier to link their names and reputations with your organization.

APPEAL BROCHURE

After the overall strategy and the specific marketing strategy have been agreed, an appeal brochure must be produced. The appeal executive or management committee, which formulates the strategy, then starts to recruit chairmen for the panels and committees; they, in turn, recruit the members they need. These approaches, which must be carried out personally, are still backed by the updated version of the Preliminary Report. That document is used while top names are recruited and the fund-raising and marketing strategies are drawn up and agreed. As these leading names will become the fund-raisers for the appeal, they need the right tools for their job; the appeal brochure will be their most effective aid.

The brochure's principal purpose is to provide written support for a personal approach to someone capable of giving a major gift. Brochures are expensive and should not be used if an appeal leaflet would do just as well. They will normally be handed over at the end of a meeting or sent to follow up a personal approach to wealthy individuals and companies who have been asked to contribute. I do not recommend using them in the case of grant-making trusts, which should have specially produced submissions tailored to address their particular objectives.

Appearance

The appeal brochure's appearance depends on the image of the charity, the particular project and the target. If it is a small community project, then a single colour in addition to the black type can be used creatively to give the impression of a lively publication and, therefore, a lively, but cost-conscious organization. To save money, line drawings may be used instead of photographs, but the brochure should not look amateurish. The image must be proficient and professional, for the aim should be to produce a really effective sales document. Most of the recent appeals that I have been involved with have gone for a full-colour production because this fitted the standing of such projects as the Wishing Well Appeal and the Charing Cross Medical Research Centre Appeal. However, it is important that the brochure does not look plush or luxurious, but business-like and to the point. It should follow the agreed house style for the organization, using the correct typeface and logo if applicable.

I believe that A4 is the most useful page size for a brochure, although many creative organizations will suggest an unusual size because it stands out. We used an unconventional size for the Wishing Well Appeal brochure. It succeeded, but some people were unhappy because it felt awkward to handle – precisely the point that the advertising agency argued as a plus factor. On balance, I received enough complaints to believe that it is more helpful to those having to deal with the subsequent correspondence to stick to A4.

Content

It is important to break up the story as much as possible with small headings so that a busy businessman flicking through the brochure will find answers to his questions easily. It is wise to use your most prestigious name to introduce the appeal – a Royal Patron or the appeal chairman. This gives a very good impression at the outset. In addition, there should be a synopsis of the whole story on the front page for the busy executive who might only have time to read that far and then turn to the back to pull out the covenant or other form to take appropriate action. It is also a good idea to include as many illustrations and photographs as possible to communicate the message to the reader in the most compelling way. It really is true that a good picture can be worth 1,000 words.

The case should be presented by covering the background, the problem or challenge, the solution, the cost and how the funds will be raised. You will be using much of the information collected for the Preliminary Report. The back flap should include a suitable covenant form and ways in which donors can help, as well as appeal names. It may be worth including a big gift schedule – a table showing what number of gifts you need at what level in order to to hit the target. (This is explained in Chapter 13.) It requires experience to calculate, but it is a very useful method of planning which approaches should be made when, to which potential donors and for what size of gift. The back flap should also include information that is susceptible to change, such as areas of a building available for naming or fellowships available for sponsoring. It can then be altered as items are claimed and others are introduced.

Make sure all literature clearly explains how you intend to use the funds raised if you should go over or under your target. If you do not, the situation is regulated by the Charities Act 1992 (as explained in Appendix 8 – see Schemes).

For especially busy people and for those who pass the brochure to the chairman of their appeals committee, it is worth attaching a single A4 sheet called the Statement of Appeal. This is a précis of the whole story and is what the secretary of an appeal committee often presents to that committee. It saves them time, which they appreciate.

Names

The brochure has to include the names of all relevant people. It is usually safe to print the names of all of those connected with the project and the charity in the brochure itself. However, it is often a good idea to print all names specifically associated with the appeal on good quality card; this can then be put in the flap at the back of the brochure. The reason for the different treatment is that important new people may constantly be joining the appeal and their names must be included in the brochure in recognition of their contribution and for the standing of the appeal. Hence the need to leave the production of the brochure until just before the private appeal commences.

Length

The brochure should be kept as short as possible consistent with doing justice to the subject. Remembering that it is being used to solicit the larger gifts and will be passed to very busy people, who usually have much too much to read. One of the most effective brochures with which I was associated was published in connection with the Charing Cross Medical Research Centre Appeal: it contained only 12 A4-sized pages. The Wishing Well Appeal brochure ran to 20 slightly larger pages, mainly because it was felt that the impact would be enhanced by more generous use of photographs. The keynotes in each case were clarity and brevity.

Sponsorship

Some people complain about charities spending too much on glossy publications. I recommend that the appeal brochure be sponsored so that this criticism can be avoided. In the case of the Wishing Well Appeal, we were extremely fortunate that all those connected with the production of our brochure contributed their services at no cost. The whole operation was spearheaded by the advertising agency Collett Dickenson Pearce, who did the outstanding creative work and found others to contribute photography, typesetting, plate making, printing and paper. Consequently, the production of the Wishing Well Appeal brochure cost the Appeal nothing.

Another way of defraying the cost of the brochure is to find a sponsor who will pay for it as his company's contribution to the appeal. This is an attractive option to companies because of the public relations value, as their gift will be highly visible. However, because it carries public relations benefits tax may be payable (see Chapter 28). It is important to ensure that the company name does not turn off other potential donors. Nevertheless, this option does allow the charity to keep more control over the production of the brochure and ensure that it is produced to its exact specifications.

OTHER DOCUMENTS

At the appropriate time, each of the activity panels will produce its own plan of action. These should describe the parameters of their responsibilities and how these fit into the master plan, their proposals for meeting those responsibilities and the targets for each part of their operation. In addition, there should be a programme calendar showing how their activities fit into the overall programme for the appeal. (Appendix 5 shows an example.)

Progress report and accounts

This document can be the official Annual Report which, if your appeal has its own legal entity, is the statutory responsibility of the trustees (see Chapter 9). Alternatively, it can be more a marketing tool, produced in addition to the Annual Report, to inform donors of progress so far and to encourage more support. In this case, it will include only a synopsis of the accounts, as agreed by the auditors.

It is necessary, however, to produce some kind of regular progress report for circulation during the private appeal. In the Charing Cross and Wishing Well Appeals, we produced an attractively designed Progress Report and Accounts at the end of the private appeal phase. This gave the accounts after one year's operation, repeated the Appeal message and reported progress. It was especially useful in persuading those who would not contribute to the Appeal until they had seen a set of accounts.

PREPARATION FOR THE NEXT PHASE

During the private appeal the Marketing Panel should allow sufficient time to prepare the public campaign if there is to be one. (See Chapters 17 and 18.) That is inevitably more complex and requires experienced advertising and public relations skills. Flexibility is also a crucial factor as, very often, adjustments must be made in response to new developments. Time spent on preparation now will be rewarded several times over when the public appeal takes off.

It is important to avoid publicity during the private phase of an appeal. That must be kept bottled up for use at the launch of the public appeal, to avoid diluting its impact. The private appeal relies on personal approaches. As publicity can rarely be kept completely sealed, it is wise to plan how to respond to a leak. One damage limitation technique is to steer any threatened media story to the need for action – the cause – as opposed to what you are going to do about it – the appeal. After all, the fact that you will be launching an appeal some time in the future is not normally regarded as much of a story. Nevertheless, your continuing media relations operation should include a list of difficult or sensitive issues and how they should be handled if raised. All media enquiries should be referred to an agreed official spokesman appointed by the appeal executive.

Chapter 13

MAJOR DONORS

Experience has shown that, on average, about 60 to 80 per cent of appeal funds come from 10 per cent of the donors. The private appeal is the phase when potential major donors are approached on a personal basis, starting with those in a position to make the largest gifts. Chapter 5 shows how to research donor categories. This chapter looks at the ways in which they should be approached – first generally, then specifically. Chapter 14 deals separately with the appeal to the business sector.

The inexperienced fund-raiser often imagines that major donors just pop up during an appeal, winkled out by the publicity generated. In some instances this may be so, but the main difference between the expert and the inexperienced approach to a capital appeal is planning for major donors. After all, if you can receive all the money needed by your charity's appeal in one gift, think of the time and money you will save. So that is where your thoughts should start. Compare the effort necessary to raise a net £50,000 from a special event with the time to construct a careful approach to a major potential donor. It is much easier to research who has the money and sometimes parts with it for your type of cause and simply to ask for the funds required, than to go through all the uncertainties associated with trying to raise the same sum by organizing a special event.

So, at this stage, a great deal of time goes into tracking possible major donors, researching how they should be approached, ensuring that your case is convincing and working out what you can offer them in return by way of accreditation (if that interests them).

STRATEGY

Contacts with grant-making trusts and wealthy individuals should be put in motion as soon as the charity believes it has assembled its case and suitable introductions are available. Grant-making trusts could provide at least 30 per cent of the income of the average private appeal. It is wise practice, therefore, for the fund-raiser to try to make as many personal contacts as possible with the correspondents or directors of grant-making trusts well before the business appeal gets under way in earnest. Trusts are passive recipients of proposals, whereas businessmen certainly are not. Businessmen want to be told exactly what you want them to do as soon as they are approached and this takes a great deal of thought. The distinction between the two sources, however, is becoming more difficult to define, reflecting increasing corporate support through corporate charitable trusts as well as the personal trusts of successful business people. Having researched the potential big donors and made informal personal contact where possible, you should delay an official approach until the Business Panel members have been appointed. Approaches must be made using the best key to the door and there will be many links from which to choose among your Business Panel members and potential major donors. The appeal organizers must ask panel members to name all likely contacts, so that a planned campaign of approaches can be drawn up.

Schedule of gifts

Research will have revealed which individuals, trusts or companies have given large gifts to projects similar to yours. Taking time and trouble to ensure a warm approach to these prospects is a top priority. In anticipation of such potential lead gifts, as we have seen, it is possible to split the target so that 60 to 80 per cent of your funds come from the larger gifts. If the total target is £10 million, the top gift might be £1 million, scaling down as shown.

Gift Guide for Donors		
Gifts		Revenue (£m)
1 x £1 million	-	1
2 x £500,000	-	1
4 x £250,000	-	1
6 x £150,000	-	0.9
10 x £100,000	-	1
20 x £50,000	-	1
30 x £25,000	-	0.75
40 x £10,000	-	0.4
50 x £5,000	-	0.25
		7.3
Other gifts		2.7
TOTAL		10

See Appendix 3 for a further example of a Gift Guide for Donors with Gift Opportunities alongside.

The shape of the donation profile you seek will depend on feedback received at the feasibility stage and the project's general appeal to the public. When you have worked out a scale that you feel is relevant to your project and charity, then look for the likely donors, starting at the top. If possible, the cost to the donor of naming areas or other potential objects of donor recognition, such as a research chair, should be geared to the sums you are seeking. Naming one wing of a building might be worth £1 million, while a fellowship might rate £500,000.

If, on the other hand, you are organizing a well-publicized disaster appeal, you would expect to receive a greater proportion of funds in small gifts, i.e. a flatter pyramid of giving.

A schedule of gifts is a positive way to help your appeal committee focus on the level of gifts necessary to fund the project. In most cases, the schedule will help to raise sights considerably, but I do not recommend sticking to such plans too rigidly. I have known some fund-raisers who operated more than one gift schedule for donors to the same appeal. The advantage is that, if carefully researched, potential donors can aspire to one of the lead gift levels shown. The disadvantage is that it needs careful handling to ensure that there is a clearly understandable reason for the two versions, i.e. a gifts guide for different sectors linked to their ability to give. Such a situation requires sensitive handling to avoid causing offence. At Great Ormond Street, we started with a single schedule, but soon had to change it as a result of a challenge by Vivien Duffield as described later in this chapter.

A gift schedule is also a useful tool when you are approaching someone you hope will be a mega-donor. You will need to explain that this is the schedule of gifts you must attract if your appeal is to succeed. It will then be quite clear what your potential donor should do if he wishes to take the key role!

A useful rule of thumb is that the lead donor rarely gives more than 10 per cent of the total target. The appeal can always set a higher target if the committee calculates that a potential donor might consider a greater cash sum. Most donors do not wish to hog the limelight. Cater for those who do by creating more limelight! The answer is to do your homework so that you have some idea what a donor could give if so disposed, based on what he has given before. You can never plan for the unexpected. What you can do is to lift your expectations!

HOW TO ASK

It is advisable not to make any approaches for gifts until all the facts have been assembled so that you can make a really convincing case. That sounds very obvious and very easy; it is far from that. Months of planning and research are necessary to get to this stage. I stress months. It is tempting to overcome the initial uncertainties by dashing off to land the big donation that will guarantee the appeal's success. Resist that temptation at all costs. The months spent in preparation will be handsomely repaid.

The right key to unlock the door is fundamental. At this stage of the appeal, before the general public is involved, it is a question of people – whether companies, individuals or charitable trust funds – giving to or via people. The first rule is that approaches during the private appeal should all be made on a personal basis. A letter is one of the weakest forms of approach and should be used only in support of an earlier personal visit.

Much depends on the type of cause. At Great Ormond Street, we asked the best link person to invite the potential donor to tour the Hospital with him and meet some of the key people at a modest lunch afterwards. This was ideal because it used the pulling power of the influential contact to invite the individual. He then

A helpful fund-raising tool is the ability to show potential donors tangible evidence of the problem to be remedied. The decrepit staircase above in Great Ormond Street's 100-year-old building did just that. When dropped, a heavy piece of equipment fell straight through the middle of the stairs, leaving a gaping, dangerous hole. (Photograph: Keith Waldegrave)

had his heart strings plucked – visiting the Hospital and seeing the children – before we tried to loosen his purse strings! Heart strings, then purse strings.

The visit was planned carefully and, if possible, we would find out if our visitor was interested in any particular area of medicine. If so, that department would be included in the tour and we would try to arrange for the relevant consultant or professor to attend the lunch. Even the exact route to be taken would be thought through with care to be sure we gave the right balance. Not only did we have to achieve the right balance for the donor, we also had to ensure that we did not always take people to the same wards, which would have put excessive pressure on their staff. We worked out a rota so that different wards were visited at different times. Emotive case histories, the problems of parents without suitable accommodation, the high-tech equipment used, the broken staircase and the all-embracing care given by doctors, nurses, chaplains, school teachers, social workers and volunteers all played their part. Guests would often be joined at these lunches by the Chairman of the Board of Governors, the General Manager of the Hospital, the Chief Nursing Officer and a senior consultant or professor of the Institute of Child Health – an impressive array of our top brass. In that way, important visitors had the chance to ask leading questions before deciding to what extent they wished to help the Hospital. In some cases, after lunch they would go over to the Appeal Office to look at the different ways in which they could help. Not all charities have the same favourable circumstances for projecting their cause, but they should review the ways they have to convince and influence and use them to the full.

Whatever your cause, it is wise to try to convince your potential donor of the merits of your case well before the question of a donation is raised. Not only is close contact between a donor and the cause more effective, it is also more satisfying for both parties. Once you have forged a link, maintain the contact. If a donor gave funds to name a ward at Great Ormond Street, there would be a close long-term relationship between the donor and the staff and children of that ward. This ensured that the donor really felt appreciated and, through closer involvement, was likely to give further support if needed.

Do not forget that major donors ask in-depth questions and also like to know what their gift will buy or name. This is why you should prepare a list of nameable areas, if this is feasible, and a general shopping list at an early stage. There are many ways of commemorating important gifts; time and care are needed to ensure that the charity can show that it is truly grateful for substantial donations or support.

Some fund-raisers recommend launching the private appeal with a high-level reception or similar event to which top people can be invited. This is done sometimes to recruit leadership as well as donors. The guests are addressed by a key speaker who will tell them about the charity, its needs and the appeal, asking the audience to help. This event is followed a few days later by individual visits to the guests to ask them how they might be prepared to help. This has the advantage of securing involvement and occasionally cash at an early date. The disadvantage is that, if they have not been carefully handled, it is easier for them to agree to the minimum. Another difficulty is that, this early, there are usually insufficient available people of suitable standing to undertake the vital follow-up operation. If that is not done quickly, the contact can go cold. I prefer to ensure that an appeal approaches important people at the highest possible level on an individual basis.

The big splash is, however, an option to be considered in the right circumstances. This might be to hold such a function towards the end of the private appeal. In this case, you would invite a majority of actual and a lesser number of potential donors. Potential donors will be strongly influenced to give because the majority already has – and at the right level. Also, by then, there will be more appeal 'ambassadors', who have already given, to follow up each guest's response.

KEY TARGET GROUPS

Wealthy individuals

The master list of likely individual donors, including as much background as possible on each of them, is drawn up during the preparation phase. The most important information is the link between wealthy individuals and the appeal's contacts or committee members. It is not enough to find out if they know any of these people; you must ascertain how well they know them and how much they are prepared to ask of them, so that the approach can be made through the best contact. A pincer movement by two supporters may be considered if the potential donor is very important.

Do not rush. Do not make an approach until you have established the best link. Then learn what sort of people they are; whether they are more likely to appreciate VIP treatment or a low-key approach, whether they look for donor recognition or favour an anonymous method of giving. If possible, try to involve them in getting to know those concerned with the charity, visiting the project.

In all cases, the approach must be handled sensitively. The wrong attitude can turn off wealthy individuals, who are subject to few of the pressures that apply to companies or trusts. It is entirely up to them to decide if they want to give. Therefore, the process from first approach to donation can take several months or even years; but it is worthwhile. I was involved in an approach for Great Ormond Street where the whole process took well over three years, largely because we had to search hard to find the right intermediary, but in the end the gift was several million pounds, so the time and effort were more than justified.

Trusts

Some trusts suggest applicants make an initial telephone call. This is sensible and useful. Try to discover what information the trust requires and in what form. Other trusts avoid telephone approaches and will consider applications only if they are submitted in writing. Either way, elicit the guidelines and follow them carefully. Keep your application brief and addressed personally to the correspondent. Demonstrate that your organization is well equipped to carry out the project and is not relying on others to do its work. It is important to try to make personal contact with the director or correspondent of the trust. Some trusts find this helpful, but others try to keep applicants at arm's length. However, do your best to develop a relationship with the trust. This can make a great difference to the eventual response and shows that you are completely open and have nothing to fear from probing questions.

Some directors of trusts resist their trustees becoming involved with the projects, but it is much the best arrangement from the appeal's point of view. In other cases, trustees specialize in different types of cause and may even vet the projects themselves. Look for any links between your panel members and the trustees in case they are able to lobby on the appeal's behalf to bolster your formal submission.

It is a good idea to find out whether the director or correspondent and his trustees would like to visit your project and meet some of the people running the charity. Put the trust on your mailing list for invitations, annual reports, press releases, etc.

The official line of approach to trusts must always be officer to officer. Some trust directors guide and advise applicants on how to lobby their trustees, but this is rare. Approaches must be cost-effective. Do not spend £100 applying to a trust which normally makes grants of £50. Do not be deterred by a declaration that a trust's funds are all allocated – they have to be reallocated at some time. It is worth finding out the idiosyncrasies of the larger ones, so that the appeal can plan its approach in a manner that is precisely in tune with their requirements. Trusts are grateful to applicants that take the care to be professional. A great deal of their time is wasted by people who apply fruitlessly, when their cause is totally unrelated to the trust's objectives.

Top ten U.K. grant-making trusts (1990/1991)	
Name	Grants £'000
1. Wellcome Trust	71,700
2. Tudor Trust	19,836
3. Gatsby Charitable Foundation	16,249
4. Royal Society	14,223
5. Henry Smith (Estates Charities)	11,687
6. Leverhulme Trust	10,990
7. Garfield Weston Foundation	9,944
8. Wolfson Foundation	8,636
9. Baring Foundation	7,666
10. Monument Trust	6,571

Source: *Charity Trends 1992* (Charities Aid Foundation)

The table shown here does not include the broadcasting trusts, such as the ITV Telethon and the BBC Children in Need Appeal. Further information about these appeals can be found in Chapter 18.

Large trusts are in a position to give hundreds of thousands of pounds to one project if it is really up their street, so it is essential that approaches to them are correctly handled and precisely targeted. Find out when they need to receive a submission from you; this is usually in good time to be circulated before their next trustees' meeting. Ascertain the maximum and minimum number of pages they regard as acceptable, how many copies they would like and even how it should be presented. I never send brochures to trusts unless they specifically ask for them, as they normally require something geared to their personal needs. Some ask for a report and accounts or other documents and will not consider your project without them.

Unless you are told not to, it is often a good idea to accompany the application with a background note. It should contain:

1. An introduction, describing your appeal and, briefly, its origins
2. The name of your appeal's chairman and director
3. The size of your organization
4. A statement of the problem you seek to overcome
5. Your intended solution
6. How much money you need
7. How you intend to raise that sum
8. A realistic budget, containing a detailed forecast of costs
9. Whether you are asking for a simple grant or continuing help
10. How it will be spent
11. Who will benefit
12. A copy of your charity's latest annual report and accounts.

Some of these items may be required in your formal submission, but do not rely on the trusts to jog your memory. The object of this covering letter is to encourage the trustees to read your submission, preferably with sympathy and understanding.

Livery companies

There are 99 livery companies and new ones are formed from time to time. They can be approached for funds in the same manner as grant-making trusts. An unannounced approach by letter is a last resort if it has not been possible to find a personal contact with a senior member of a livery company. The 12 biggest, headed by the Mercers' Company, are the prime targets. Some have beautiful halls which make impressive venues for events. They are available for hire, often at special rates to charities.

Local charities

Some trusts are bound by their constitution to operate only within certain localities. These are known as local charities and should be combed for additions to your list. This is discussed more fully in Part V, Smaller and Local Appeals.

Statutory and non-governmental bodies

The various governmental departments have different procedures for applications but all require the same basic information, much on the same lines as that for trusts (see above). The decision will ultimately be made by a minister, so direct lobbying will be possible only in the minority of instances where your chairman happens to know him or a mutual friend. An indirect approach can be made through a friendly MP, starting with the one representing the constituency in which your appeal is based. In any case, write to him to tell him of your application and to ask for his support. He may be able to discover when the minister is about to make his decision so that you can step up your lobbying at the critical time.

If the nature of your appeal allows long lead times, you should try to develop an understanding with officials on the relevant committees. This is particularly appropriate to EC grants, always long drawn-out procedures. Officials make recommendations to ministers and are thankful for being well briefed, and there is the possibility of aligning your plans more closely with theirs. In this way, you can even influence the budget forecast and make life generally easier for the senior officials.

Lord Prior's government contacts were invaluable to the Wishing Well Appeal. He knew precisely how to obtain the maximum government input and cooperation in the most proper manner with many positive results. As our Appeal target increased, he was able to ensure that the government's contribution rose with ours.

Local authority decisions are normally made by the appropriate committee. The relevant meeting will also certainly be open to the public. You can discover the names of the councillors on the committee and perhaps arrange to meet some of them beforehand. Seek permission to address the committee.

Nowhere is it more important to cultivate individuals than in approaching the European Commission. Any approach will be a lengthy business, so you will have plenty of time. Begin by looking at the areas of current EC funding to see if your cause can be aligned with one of them. You may have to change the name of your cause or give it a different emphasis to bring it alongside, say, the Social Fund. You will need some advice on this and also whether you should go through British government officials or contact Brussels directly. The National Council for Voluntary Organizations can help. The essence of this exercise is to find the name of an official who really can forward your case. Talk to him, take his advice on presenting your case (there may be an application form to be completed) and give him the names, if you can, of any distinguished patrons, perhaps a Commissioner or your MP.

TAX-EFFICIENT GIVING

It is important for a fund-raiser to recommend that panel members and donors seek professional advice about tax-efficient methods of giving. Various schedules identifying net and gross equivalents of income and the savings available to the donor and the charity may be obtained from the Inland Revenue. The main options available to individuals are listed here. Similar details relevant to companies are listed in the next chapter. (For more information on this specialist area of giving, see Usual Methods of Giving listed in Appendix 2, Tax-Efficient Giving Examples in Appendix 2(a) and the Bibliography.)

Deed of covenant

A deed of covenant is a legal undertaking to give a fixed sum of money to the appeal every year for at least four years. The sum may be specified as a cash amount (gross or net of tax) or as a percentage of income. The appeal can then reclaim tax at the basic rate. This effectively makes a gift about one third as much again at no extra cost to the donor. Note that higher-rate taxpayers, not the appeal, recover tax paid in excess of the basic rate. Donors who do not pay tax – and this is a possibility now that spouses are taxed separately – would still receive a bill from the Inland Revenue for money paid over in the form of reclaimed tax (which, of course, has not been paid). So neither the deed of covenant nor Gift Aid (explained below) is appropriate for non-taxpayers.

Deposited deed of covenant

It is possible to enter into a deposited covenant. The donor pays the full amount provided for in the covenant as a lump sum in advance and the appeal reclaims the tax annually over a minimum period of four years. In such circumstances, it is usual to have a letter of waiver which will be used by the charity in the event of the covenantor's death. Since the introduction of Gift Aid, this sort of covenant has become less popular.

Gift Aid

A gift of £250 or more, net of basic rate tax, can be made to the appeal under the Gift Aid scheme. The appeal then reclaims the basic-rate tax. The donor needs to be sure that he has paid enough tax to cover the amount the appeal can reclaim. Higher-rate taxpayers can reclaim the extra tax, as with a covenant.

Charities Aid Foundation Services (CAF)

CAF offers individuals and companies the opportunity to make their charitable giving in as simple and tax-efficient a way as possible through a CAF Charity Account. CAF reclaims all possible tax on the original donation and adds it to the donor's account. Distributions can then be made to the charities of the donor's choice by using a personalized CAF voucher book, which resembles a cheque book.

Giving assets

Assets, such as property and shares, may appreciate in value and attract capital gains tax, but if they are given directly to the appeal, neither the donor nor the appeal has to pay the tax. VAT, however, may be payable by the donor on donated business goods and equipment. As from August 1992 the value for VAT purposes is the current purchase price of the goods.

Legacies

A bequest is not a very appropriate way of giving to a time-limited one-off appeal. However, where the appeal is raising money for a capital project, there are ongoing maintenance costs which can be covered by a bequest via the parent charity. Charitable bequests are free from inheritance tax. They can be made in various forms. It is a good idea for people intending to make a bequest to seek

advice from the appeal and their own solicitor. (This method of giving is also discussed in Chapter 29.)

LEAD GIFTS

I have already recommended that, early in the appeal, you should draw up a
schedule listing the major or lead gifts you hope to obtain. These can sometimes
emerge as a result of the feasibility study carried out following the preliminary
interviews with potential donors to see what they would give were there to be an
appeal. They are usually linked to the supporters who are helping to set up the
appeal. They are one of the most important building blocks and need to be
cemented as early as possible to rebut sceptics who say that it is a bad time to
launch an appeal. There are always plenty of these.

Usually the lead gifts are pledged by members of the appeal committee, led by
the chairman. They can hardly approach their friends and colleagues unless they
have given or obtained a substantial gift themselves. This is always a delicate
matter for the fund-raiser to convey to the appeal chairman. After all, is he not
already undertaking the most important appeal role? You have to be very brass-
necked to talk about this touchy subject at such an early stage, but do it you must.

Lead gifts were especially important for the Wishing Well Appeal because we
were attempting to raise a far larger amount than had previously been attempted
by a one-off appeal. The chairman of a clearing bank and other leading business
figures said that the target we had in mind was absurd so we badly needed to show
such people that we had already made a start.

The most crucial lead gift for the Wishing Well Appeal came from the government. We knew that some would say that charitable money should not be raised
for NHS hospitals. The legal position was that, from their beginnings, health
authorities had been empowered to accept and retain voluntary donations and
could set up trusts to do so. The Health Services Act 1980 took it a stage further and
empowered them to seek funds. Many of the business leaders we had involved initially stated that they would not take part unless approximately half the target
were forthcoming from the Department of Health and Social Security (now the
Department of Health). So Lord Prior approached the Department. After detailed
talks, the prospects started to look encouraging. In the meantime, several other
potential lead givers had been consulted and had pledged substantial sums conditional on the government's input. Therefore it was with great relief that we
received confirmation that the DHSS would contribute about half the capital costs
of the redevelopment. In order to give us time to raise funds we had elected to pay
for the second tranche of the money needed, so we had to bear the impact of inflation on our portion. We also aimed to raise £2 million for the Institute of Child
Health. So, by the time we launched the Appeal, the government had pledged £20
million to our £30 million, which was an enormous incentive to the businessmen
involved. We had also agreed with the DHSS that, apart from such initial costs as
fees, they would fund the items that were less attractive for donors to name, such
as the boilerhouse.

While negotiations with the Government were in full swing, we were wooing
the Variety Club of Great Britain. It is known to care for children and to be an excellent fund-raiser. Michael Samuelson, then the International President, had been

closely involved with Great Ormond Street for over ten years. Through him, the Hospital made early contact with Trevor Chinn (now Sir Trevor), Chairman and Chief Executive of Lex Service, who – like Michael Samuelson – was an influential member of the Variety Club. Both had helped since the idea of the Appeal was first raised, so we had the best possible introduction to the Variety Club. Nevertheless, the senior members rightly expected and received a full-scale presentation to convince them that they should play a major part in the Appeal. This took place in the recently refurbished Hospital Theatre.

It was certainly worth all the trouble we took to produce a special version of the Preliminary Report, display boards, a panel of top-level speakers at the presentation and a full tour of the Hospital. As a result, the Variety Club pledged that it would raise £3 million towards our target. It was the Appeal's first big break. The Variety Club not only met its pledge, but also helped us in many other ways throughout the Appeal.

The first major donation received by the Appeal was £500,000 from Mrs. Jean Sainsbury. This showed great confidence in our ability to raise the funds and stimulated others not only to pledge sums of money, but also to hand some of it over! In our search for initial donors or pledgers, we received outstanding advice and assistance from Sir Trevor Chinn, who was a Vice-Chairman of the Appeal. He brought to our Appeal extensive experience in fund-raising and knew many of the people we wished to approach for lead gifts. At a very early stage he also pledged a hefty gift from Lex Service. This gift dramatically raised our sights in terms of what we could expect from company gifts. Through Sir Trevor we met Vivien Duffield, the late Sir Charles Clore's daughter and Chairman of the Clore Foundation. She played what might have been the most significant part in ensuring we received enough lead gifts for such a mammoth appeal. She has had a great deal to do with charity fund-raising and said she would pledge £1 million to the Appeal if we could find nine others to do likewise. She could not have helped us more. When approaching potential major donors, we had the perfect reason for stating the amount of money we hoped they might give. We did not quite achieve nine other donors at £1 million each, but I am delighted to say that the Clore Foundation paid £1 million anyway.

Our biggest single gift was received in a most unexpected manner. Sitting at my desk one day, going through correspondence, I read a very warm letter to the Appeal Chairman from Garry Weston, Chairman of Associated British Foods. The letter explained how Mr. Weston's family, his trust and company employees felt deeply about the work we were doing at Great Ormond Street and hoped we could accept the attached cheque. I could not believe my eyes when I saw it was for £3 million. I was even more incredulous, half way through the appeal, when he followed this with a further £1 million donation.

Chapter 14

THE BUSINESS APPEAL

Enlisting businessmen to help with charitable appeals is a time-honoured tradition. As long ago as 1858, George Augustus Sala wrote of Great Ormond Street, *At the sight of the children, no hard-hearted business man could not shed a wee tear.* Businessmen may not themselves be wealthy, although many are, but, above a certain level, they all have access to wealth, either through the authority to order some of their company's funds to be diverted to charitable causes or through their network of contacts to influence wealthy individuals. Above all, their credibility as directors of substantial enterprises is a valuable quality from which a charity can benefit by association. That credibility can be directly tapped by asking them to serve on appeal panels so that they can contribute their management expertise to your deliberations.

These considerations make the business aspect of a private appeal particularly important. It can lay the foundations of an appeal's organization, meet the immediate requirement for funds from private sources and provide the platform for its fund-raising in any subsequent public appeal. I assume that the reader has become thoroughly acquainted with the points I have made on preparation in Part II before embarking on this vital phase.

Strategy

1. To raise the maximum funds from major businesses through carefully arranged personal approaches and by setting targets broken down by sector and donor.
2. To use high-level businessmen as fund-raisers, advised and serviced by the appeal office with access to professional fund-raising expertise.
3. To use the influence of panel members to assist and facilitate approaches to wealthy individuals, statutory bodies and grant-making trusts, as well as to other companies.
4. To handle panel members, donors and potential donors in such a way that they enjoy the experience and are kept in touch with the charity's needs and progress. They will then be more likely to back their support in the private phase with further help in the public appeal.

STRUCTURE

Panel chairmen and members

What sort of chairmen and members should be recruited for the panels and how does one go about it? To begin with, the appeal office researches a list of key individuals in the relevant activities. The chairman must be well respected by his peers and the establishment generally and more than capable of pulling together a top-level team to help approach potential donors. Having recruited him, the appeal office should then produce a list of the key business sectors and, say, the top three leaders in each. For the City, one would group clearing banks, merchant banks, insurance companies, institutions and livery companies, etc.; for Commerce and Industry – retailers, brewers, car manufacturers and so on. It is difficult to decide which category applies to some conglomerates so the best bet is to stick to their classification in the share price tables at the back of the *Financial Times* – a yardstick that is generally understood and accepted.

One or more Business Panels?

Many private appeals decide to have one Business Panel to make company approaches. The members usually prefer this arrangement because it gives them contact with a wider range of businessmen and so offers great scope to enhance their own networks. It is difficult to lay down a general rule, simply because every appeal is different. If you believe that you will reach your target without exploiting every available contact, this factor may not be crucial. If prospects are more limited, give careful thought as to how to structure your business appeal. A charity which aims to benefit the homeless would put particular emphasis on companies involved in the building industry and create a special group to plan the best strategic approach to them. Medical research charities would adopt a similar attitude to the pharmaceutical industry. The appeal for the Prince's Youth Business Trust had 28 industry sector committees. The 1991 Royal Marsden Hospital Cancer Appeal had just one panel dealing with approaches to the City and Industry. However, the Royal Hospital for Sick Children in Edinburgh had a Commerce and Industry Panel and another panel for Banking and Finance.

In the Wishing Well Appeal we split the City from commerce and industry, which allowed us to involve two top people instead of one as leaders. The late Sir Patrick Meaney, then Chairman of The Rank Organization, led the Commerce and Industry Panel, and Lord Rockley, then Vice-Chairman of Kleinwort Benson Group, headed the City Panel. The members of those two panels were selected with an eye to their links with wealthy individuals and grant-making trusts, as well as their business contacts. In my experience, really wealthy people are not very clubbable. They expect – and get – very individual treatment. To some extent, the same is true of the largest grant-making trusts, which require specifically tailored approaches.

So the structure which saw us through the private appeal was:

The Advisory Council, which acted as a steering group until its members moved into

- The Executive Committee, or one of
- The panels for Marketing, the City, and Commerce and Industry.

LEADERSHIP

The qualities of leadership required for the business appeal are similar to those required for the chairmanship of the appeal (see Chapter 6). The role of the panel chairman is to bring to bear the full influence of his company and to recruit a team of his peers from the appropriate sectors of industry or the City. His panel must agree a plan of action and he must motivate, support and nudge them to carry it out.

The members will need to be convinced that the cause is worthwhile and that the fund-raising job is being tackled in a businesslike and effective manner. They will also need to know exactly what they are being asked to commit themselves to. They should be assured that there will be very few meetings, but should be aware of the points listed below, which are common to nearly all appeals of this nature.

1. They should each bring a major gift from their companies, personal resources or elsewhere.
2. They should be prepared to approach at least six similar people face-to-face.
3. They will be expected to advise the appeal office how best to approach other companies in their sector based on their in-depth knowledge of their own market.
4. They must use their influence to promote and support the appeal at every suitable opportunity.

In suggesting which names should be invited to join a panel, the appeal office should have researched their directorships and links with grant-making trusts and wealthy individuals. Indeed, the dividing line between wealthy individuals and business donors is often blurred, as both may serve on the same panel. In most cases, however, it is preferable to group like with like or some members of a panel may be placed at a disadvantage. This is a good reason for the rule that every member must be able to produce a pledge from his own organization before approaching others to give. Difficulty could arise if this pressure were lessened by one or two committee members becoming exceptions to the rule. I also believe that, once they have obtained a major gift from their own organizations, committee members should make a personal contribution to the appeal. They are all in a position to do so and it demonstrates an essential personal commitment to the cause.

Researching whether a businessman is already actively involved in charitable fund-raising is also crucial. It is usually best to avoid such potential panel members so that you are not poaching from another charity and because it is likely they will already have used up a considerable amount of goodwill.

Charities should always offer donors a suitable form of recognition even though it may be the last thing some want. Many commercial donors need to be able to see a tangible benefit to their businesses in terms of public profile or employee morale.

I believe it is a fund-raiser's task to find out potential company donors' marketing strategies, to understand how their involvement in the appeal would fit and to suggest ways of ensuring they receive due credit for their contributions. This might mean holding a press conference or reception to mark the opening of a unit, widespread publicity when a company has sponsored an event, a special presentation for the members of their staff who have raised the largest amount and, if appropriate, a visit to the site or project.

Other ways of conferring benefit

- When senior businessmen work together on aspects of the appeal, they come into contact with people they might not otherwise meet. This high-level networking can lead to business spin-offs. A chartered accountant might meet company chairmen who could turn into clients or suppliers may meet possible customers.
- A newly appointed company chairman, if he has risen through his firm, may need to widen his circle of contacts. Serving on an appeal panel or committee is an effective way of doing so.
- Not only is the prestige of a company enhanced locally by being seen to be lead sponsor of a local project, but the 'halo effect' enhances the standing of the staff in the community.
- By working together on an appeal, company employees get to know others in their firm whom they might not otherwise meet. The experience can be stimulating, competitive, exciting and rewarding to each individual. It may also offer chances to catch the chairman's eye.
- Most of all, voluntary work gives people a sense of being part of their community, extending their range of activities and thereby becoming more complete and rounded individuals.

If a charity treats its supporters properly, encouraging, reinforcing and – especially – showing appreciation of what they do, it will often be able to maintain involvement beyond the duration of the one-off appeal.

PLAN OF ACTION

Each panel must have its own plan of action, which incorporates the relevant section of the master plan. It is usually drawn up by a staff member and then refined before being agreed by the panel members. It will include a review of the master plan for the entire appeal, a full project brief for panel members, defining their role, territory and specific objectives, and a strategy showing how these will be achieved. The panel should set targets for each sector and individual approach, looking at the prospects for the panel, sector by sector and even company by company. This is best distilled into a programme calendar, which can be referred to at every meeting to check progress and pinpoint delays. The appeal office will produce detailed desk research on different businesses' past performance and likely response (see Chapter 5). This should be supplemented by the more intimate knowledge possessed by panel members.

Setting company targets

Part of the strategy for the panel will be to obtain a predetermined level of gift from the selected lead donors before approaching others. Later donors will tend to fall in behind the leaders and give a proportion of the starting sum. Target-setting was approached by the Wishing Well Appeal from two different directions. Desk research gave us figures showing what companies had given to charity in the previous year. Assuming that business prospects had not radically varied, it was reasonable to aim for a gift of 10 per cent of that charity budget. Another method is based on a percentage of the company's profits. There is an organization called The Per Cent Club, which has more than 300 corporate members committed to giving at least half of one per cent of their pre-tax profits to community and charity projects.

The Wishing Well panel representatives from each sector, knowing the general business scene, suggested what should be forthcoming from their trade or industry. After negotiation, these became the targets. Setting individual targets within those sectors was greatly assisted by the desk research provided by the Appeal Office. The objective was to make sure that there was a well-reasoned answer to any executive approached when he asked how much his company should give. Even if he did not enquire, we asked the panellists to suggest tactfully the exact level of gift to ensure targets were reached.

Corporate giving

Companies give to charity for many reasons. It creates goodwill, helps relations with employees, promotes a caring image through a practical demonstration that the company accepts its responsibility to the community in which it trades, and it associates the company with a cause for which it has sympathy.

Many larger companies have their own charitable trusts or maintain units responsible for community relations, corporate affairs or social policy, whose job is to disburse funds in accordance with company policy. Otherwise, companies can transfer some or all of their charity budget to a Charities Aid Foundation account and distribute it to charities of their choice, using CAF's personalized voucher book system. Very large sums may be involved – BT, BP and National Westminster Bank each gave more than £10 million during 1991, for example. Total corporate giving in the U.K. has been estimated at more than £200 million a year.

TAX-EFFICIENT GIVING

There are several ways in which companies can give tax-efficiently. Here I list those appropriate for a private appeal. Those more suitable for the public appeal are discussed in Chapter 28. (For further reading, see Tax-Efficient Giving Examples in Appendix 2(b) and the Bibliography.)

Gift Aid

This scheme has made it possible for companies to donate large single cash gifts each year and to deduct the donation from profits before tax. There is no maximum limit to the amount they can donate and, while close companies must donate £250 or more, there is no minimum limit for most publicly quoted companies.

Covenants

Companies may enter into covenants. The conditions are similar to individual covenants, but the tax efficiency is greater for the company. It is allowed to deduct the gross amount paid under the covenant from its profits before calculating its corporation tax liability. It then deducts tax at the basic rate from the gross amount donated and accounts for this to the Inland Revenue.

Gifts in kind

These can be very useful to charities. Office space, furniture and equipment are very welcome, as the Wishing Well Appeal found. Sometimes the loan of a van can help overcome a crisis. VAT is payable by the donor on donated goods and equipment based on the purchase price value of the goods.

Secondments

One of the few ways of giving which increases during a recession is the secondment of middle and senior managers to work in the voluntary sector. The usual arrangement is for the employer to pay the secondee's salary for a fixed period; the charity normally pays other expenses. (This method of giving is discussed in Chapter 28.)

Interest-free loans

Companies may provide interest-free loans or loans at preferential rates. These do not have any taxation implications as far as companies are concerned because the company has merely lost the potential for earning income from the money it has lent. However, a company must have some assurance that the loan will be repaid. In many cases the company may waive the loan at a later stage. The company should also ensure that its Memorandum of Association confers the power to make such loans.

ALLOCATING APPROACHES

The allocation of approaches is a painstaking, detailed, but crucial activity. It is not easy to ask leaders of industry to wade through long lists of companies and to mark their contacts, but that is what you must do. Use a lot of encouragement, cajoling and tactful chasing. The top 1,000 companies you have selected should be split into batches of 200. Each batch should be circulated to reveal contacts and to note the closeness of those contacts. I suggest the following shorthand.

A = I know him very well and will approach
B = I know him less well but will still approach
C = I know him slightly
D = he is a supplier to my organization

A combination of A and D is the best contact if the businessman concerned is prepared to approach a supplier for a charitable contribution. Many do, but some feel it would weaken their trading relationship with their suppliers. It depends on the relationship in each case and the preference of the individual, but the major customer-to-supplier route is bound to be more effective than supplier-to-customer or competitor-to-competitor. At this stage of the appeal, there is a lot of paper flying around. Whatever you do, write the name of the committee member on the list before it is sent out. It would be a catastrophe if it were sent back and separated from the compliments slip which recorded the sender's name. I learned that from bitter experience.

Sector leaders

I usually advise the chairman of a Business Panel to select the most important business sectors and to recruit a leading individual to cover each. This is not because these people should necessarily approach their own sector, but to act as the appeal's adviser on the best method of approach for each company in that sector. There are fund-raising consultants who recommend that sector representatives should be entitled sector chairmen, and be responsible for approaching all company chairmen in their area of commercial activity. It is a very tidy way of organizing the appeal but, to my mind, it is against business principles. Competitor would be approaching competitor, which is not sensible. There are exceptions to this rule, such as the brewery trade and property developers, where a different ethos applies.

The sector leader comes into his own when allocating approaches. He will know a great deal about his competitors' activities and relationships and is usually the best one to advise. As the approaches have to be shared, this exercise takes considerable time and skill. The panel chairman usually assembles a small group of his members to decide on the allocation of approaches. In some instances, it is best to work a pincer movement, whereby more than one person influences the potential donor's decision.

Panel members then receive their allocation sheets from the appeal office, and a note of the target gift size for each potential donor. Each approach must be made on a personal basis, sometimes involving the staff. The best arrangement is for the person being approached to meet some of the people concerned. In the case of a building, it is helpful if he can visit the site and meet the charity officers. If no building is involved, potential donors should meet the charity officers before embarking on any talk about gifts. Corporate donors usually give in proportion to the total appeal target. In some cases they give in relation to each other's gifts.

The level of gifts we received from pace-setters for the Wishing Well Appeal was all-important. We knew we had to receive at least £100,000 from each of the top corporate donors, such as BT and British Petroleum, in order to hit the target. I am glad to say they did not let us down. This process was assisted by the lead donors we had at this stage and by the pledge from Lex Service for £150,000. At that early stage, the top company gift of over £184,000 came via Sir Peter Reynolds, then Chairman of Rank Hovis McDougall. The pace-setter principle is so important that fund-raisers have been known to return gifts that fall well below the desired level. This is not a policy I advocate, although there was one gift from a major company to the Wishing Well Appeal which we kept very quiet about for some time until there was no longer the danger that it might affect others' decisions.

STAFF ROLE

As we have seen, the staff's role is to do everything necessary to service the Business Panels. This includes desk research, investigation into potential leadership and panel members, drafting the plan of action, producing approach lists and updating them, recording results of approaches and all the legwork required to alleviate the panel members' very busy schedules. The senior staff member must be a very competent administrator, who can encourage leading businessmen to wade through long lists of potential donors and, without causing offence, chase them to ensure that the panel keeps to its programme.

Training or briefing voluntary fund-raisers is a necessary step. Some leaders of industry are excellent fund-raisers, while others are apologetic and afraid it will lose them friends. It is important to make sure that they have all the relevant facts at their fingertips and that they know support is available from the appeal office. Their attitude should be that they are giving their contacts the chance to contribute, rather than saying, 'I really am sorry to pester you about another charity, but any small amount will do.' Too many fund-raisers like that, and your appeal has no hope. On the other hand, a fund-raiser cannot expect to change someone's fundamental character, so sometimes the answer is to embolden coy volunteers with a more persuasive partner when the approach is being made.

Once a panellist has approached a potential donor on a personal basis, he needs to follow up that initial contact by sending a brochure (discussed in Chapter 12). The appeal office must also provide a single sheet entitled Statement of Appeal, which contains a précis of the appeal message. As previously explained, this makes it much easier for the company's hard-pressed charity committee secretary to understand the case so he will recommend it to the committee all the more enthusiastically. The appeal office should also provide the panellist with a suggested covering letter. This should be typed on the panellist's own company letterhead, not the appeal's, to underline the business status of the panellist who is making the pitch on your appeal's behalf. Panellists should also have instant access to advice on the different advantages to companies which can be obtained through the various methods of contributing.

HANDLING MEETINGS

If you recruit a chairman of a multi-million pound company, you expect him to be able to chair a meeting with ease. However, this is not always the case. If a panel chairman waffles, the appeal director should find ways of accelerating the agenda and making sure the meeting covers the necessary ground in reasonable time. Most businessmen will not agree to join an appeal if it entails lots of interminable committee meetings. They tend to hate the word 'committee'; it has an unfortunate connotation of pointless timewasting, especially in the context of charity. I prefer to use 'group' or 'panel'. Part of the deal with panel members is that there will be very few meetings, as the fund-raiser will deal directly with them to chase progress and provide back-up. Beware of members who want more committee meetings.

They probably do not have enough influence and have joined partly to make better contacts.

A skilful chairman should run a meeting efficiently while allowing others to have their say if they have something germane to contribute. He should have a clear idea of the meeting's purpose and the talent to make everyone feel involved, consulted and motivated. A little competition between members on these occasions is no bad thing. So some appeal panel chairmen tend to go round the table asking members to report on their progress. It is surprising how many approaches take place just before such meetings!

Motivating and thanking

The chairman will develop his own way of motivating and encouraging his team – holding private dinner parties at different stages, perhaps. He should keep in close touch with his panellists and ensure that they are well briefed and up to date on the charity, the project and the appeal. It is often worthwhile holding a special reception at the end of the private phase of an appeal to thank those who have worked so hard to bring in what is usually the majority of the funds needed. The fund-raiser should never forget the panellists' wives, husbands or other partners, ensuring that they too are invited to such occasions and to tour the site of the subject of the appeal. The panellists' secretaries are another important source of goodwill. They should be kept in touch with the charity, invited to visit and thanked for the immense amount of behind-the-scenes work so many of them do.

I believe that one gets the best out of highly talented volunteers if they are given a task which they are well suited to handle and allowed to do it their way. This assumes, of course, that they are prepared to let their activity be coordinated with other appeal activities and that you are in a position at the appeal office to keep a careful eye on their progress. In such cases, these volunteers should be given due credit and shown the real gratitude of the organization for their achievement.

Towards the end of the private phase of the Wishing Well Appeal, our Royal Patrons allowed us to hold a special reception at Kensington Palace. In the presence of the Prince and Princess of Wales, its purpose was to thank all the major donors and to encourage some possible substantial donors who had not yet committed themselves. We also invited some key individuals we hoped would play an important role during the public phase of the appeal. It was a private occasion to prevent media curiosity. We tried to keep in close touch with supporters during the Wishing Well Appeal. Not only did we wish to see credit given where it was due but, if possible, we wanted such people to feel valued and recognized. We felt they would then be more likely to become long-term friends of the Hospital.

It is a matter of fine judgment and taking time to give the personal touch wherever possible – such as enclosing signed letters from top people with invitations to dinners or receptions, all private occasions at this stage of an appeal. Some appeals bring together a special group to decide how to thank different categories of supporter. If there are only a small number of invitations available to, perhaps, a Royal Garden Party, it is a good idea to ask a group of people to make a joint selection to avoid any feeling of unfairness, which would ruin the whole purpose.

DON'T GIVE UP

The final point to make about the private business appeal is that you should never give up. Even if you receive a refusal letter, write and thank them for it. I have worked for some tremendous appeal chairmen – two of the best declined the appointment when first asked and subsequently changed their minds.

A potential donor to the Wishing Well Appeal had been in discussions with us for four months regarding a possible gift of over £1 million. He then wrote to say he regretted he did not wish to proceed. Imagine my disappointment if I had left it there, but I did not. I went to the wife of the person who had made the approach on our behalf, for she also knew the would-be donor. We had lunch and she said she would try to revive the matter. Three months later we had the gift confirmed. So I guess the motto is 'If at first you don't succeed. . . stick with it!'

Chapter 15

ADMINISTRATION AND PERSONNEL

As the appeal progresses, so the appeal office's administrative systems develop and require more attention. While they must be set up at the preparation stage, problems always arise from unexpected developments and the systems must constantly be kept in good order. Much of the work may be laborious, but it is essential if the best results are to be achieved from approaches and if your panel members are to receive the standard of service they deserve. Following the preparatory topics discussed in Chapter 10 and the operational requirements arising from aspects of the private appeal, this chapter describes the systems and arrangements necessary for effective administration of a private appeal.

LISTING

> **Priority Approach Lists**
> 1. Times 1000
>   Top 250
>   2nd 250
>   3rd 250
>   4th 250
> 2. Private companies
>   Top 200
>   2nd 200
> 3. Wealthy individuals
>   Top 50 (other than with trusts)
>   Others
> 4. Grant-making trusts
>   Top 50
>   2nd 50
>   3rd 50
>   4th 50
> 5. City Livery Companies
>   Top 12
>   Others

Busy businessmen have to wade through copious lists of companies, wealthy individuals and grant-making trusts. It is a good idea to split these into manageable units, to keep your panellists sane and to stagger the follow-through work which will have to be handled by the appeal office. A standard approach is to create Priority Approach Lists (PAL) and divide them as shown on the previous page.

APPROACHES

It is important to look separately at the administrative work necessary to support the approach process. Each member of a committee must mark a list of target companies, indicating the nature of his contact in the company and whether he would be prepared to make an approach.

The appeal office must compile a master approach list. This is a mammoth catalogue of all the companies to be approached by the appeal. The companies should be listed down the left-hand side of the page, and the names of panel members along the top. The replies from the panellists, indicating whom they know and how well, can be tabulated as the basis for the eventual allocations schedule. From this information sector leaders of banking, insurance, shipping, engineering, etc., decide which panellist should approach which target. The decision is based on the importance of the potential donor, his relationship with the panellist and the necessity of sharing approaches among panellists to spread the work load.

The appeal chairman should form a small group to decide who should be approached by whom. Then a personalized list should be distributed to each committee member. This provides all necessary background information on each prospect. Produced by the appeal office, it includes any previous links with the charity. Copies should be kept at the appeal office, preferably on computer. The layout of the sheets or cards sent to the panellists should include columns on which they can record the date of each approach and its success or otherwise; amount received, absolute refusal, conditional refusal, decision deferred and when to re-approach. Panellists must keep the appeal office informed of the outcome of their forays, together with copies of correspondence.

Sometimes the appeal office may find that the cheques for the appeal, although requested by a panellist, are sent to the appeal office. You should then ensure that a copy of the accompanying letter is sent immediately to the relevant committee member so that he can send his own letter of thanks. If the cheque is sent to the committee member, he must send a copy of the letter with the cheque to the appeal office.

Areas to name/shopping list records

It is most important that one person is made responsible for recording which areas of an appeal building have been named and which items of equipment have been purchased by a specific donor. The same person will also take care of the necessary correspondence to ensure that the wording on any plaque is correct.

Keeping up to date

The staff member servicing the business appeal should be sure to collect as many relevant business news cuttings as possible and to keep completely up to date with developments, especially concerning the companies and other organizations connected with panellists and potential donors. Intelligent sifting of such material can prevent embarrassment, particularly when two companies are in conflict over a business matter. The cuttings and related material should be put on file. It is also important, once the company approach lists have been produced, to make sure that company names and addresses and the title and position of each contact are updated. There is little more irritating to a senior executive of a company which has gone through the internal agonizing over a name change to see that change blithely ignored by an organization seeking a donation. Equally, every change of someone's title, however small it may appear to the outside world, is a step in that person's career to which due recognition must be accorded. If it is a promotion, it is only courteous to show that the appeal is aware of it. If it is a demotion, then the individual will not wish to be reminded of his previous higher status.

In my early fund-raising days, when I was working with the Earl Cadogan on an appeal in Kensington, having delighted me by saying that he would agree to be the Appeal Chairman, he made me promise that all letters he was asked to sign would be carefully checked to ensure they were absolutely correct in terms of titles, designations and addresses. Of course, I reassured him that this would be so. Imagine my horror when I was let down by my Swedish secretary, whose English was slightly imperfect. She produced a pile of letters for Lord Cadogan to sign, addressed to, for example, 'Mr. George Smith Esq.'. I do not think I ever quite lived that down with Lord Cadogan, as I should have personally checked those letters before passing them on. I had not done so and paid the penalty in terms of my credibility. I am glad to say that he continued to chair that appeal, and very successfully too, but I did risk his goodwill, and understandably so.

FILES

A separate file is required for each panel member. It should contain personal details, personal gift information, and an approach list. Separate files are needed on his company and any trust or wealthy individual he will be approaching. All contact should be logged, preferably on computer, from the moment a name comes up as a serious prospect for the appeal.

Some appeal offices use a card system instead of making lists of approaches. Each company has a detailed card carrying all relevant facts about the company and the appeal's contact there, including the names of directors. Space must be left to add information as the appeal and the approach progress. One copy of the card goes to the contact panellist and another remains in the appeal office. It should be tagged against the panellist's name, so that progress can be checked – and chased! Once there is a result from the approach, the card is moved to another box entitled 'Gift' or 'Refusal – See Later' or 'Refusal – Absolute'. Even if you are running a comparatively small appeal, however, a modest personal computer system will do the job better.

Another method of dealing with really important targets is to compile a list of all names that crop up in connection with the appeal: trustees, wealthy individuals, directors and relevant executives of major companies and so on. If all those are collated in one coordinated alphabetical list, it is possible to see where one person is not only chairman of two major companies but is also perhaps trustee of a very important trust. You will automatically see networks emerge, highlighting the degree of influence each person in the network commands. This operation is handled effectively by several software packages.

STAFF

To run a successful big-gift campaign or private phase of a wider appeal, the organization needs a well-disciplined person who can pay close attention to detail and who should always try to set up an approach at the highest level. He should also have tact and the ability to get more out of high-level people than they initially intended to give, in terms of time, support and even money. However, as has been explained, it is helpful if the staff member accompanies the peer-group fund-raiser when he approaches a potential donor to be available to explain the background to the appeal's fund-raising strategy. Ideally, the staff member should not attempt this alone. A suitable background for this type of role ideally involves a good knowledge of the business scene and experience of dealing with business people at all levels.

The following diagram shows the staff structure used by the Wishing Well Appeal at the time of its private appeal.

Wishing Well Appeal staff structure at the time of the private appeal

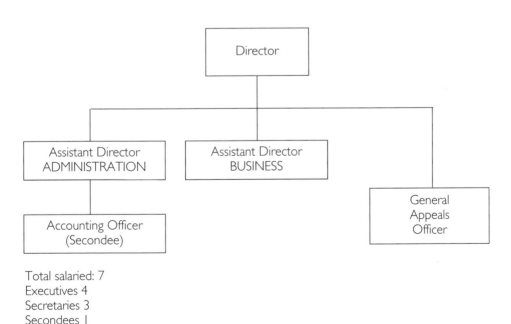

Total salaried: 7
Executives 4
Secretaries 3
Secondees 1
Backed by 4 volunteers

OFFICE FACILITIES

Well before the private appeal reaches its conclusion, the increased organization which will be needed to run a public appeal should be assessed – if that is your next step. This involves ordering more telephone lines, finding space for more desks, telephones, computers, filing cabinets, stationery supplies, promotional material and other office paraphernalia – as well as additional volunteer helpers!

Public events can have unexpected consequences. If too many advertisements appear at the same time, it may not be possible to handle the resulting flow of responses. The transition from a private to public appeal is a difficult one to manage. People's roles and relationships will inevitably change, creating possible stresses, strains and disappointments, unless careful forethought is given. That is why you should devote as much time as possible to planning this development in your appeal.

Part IV

THE PUBLIC APPEAL

Chapter 16

OVERVIEW

The public phase of an appeal is when you beat the drum and make the maximum noise. Everything you have done has been in preparation for this phase. Usually, the general public will believe that the public launch is the start of your appeal, whereas it is, in fact, the final coat of gloss to put a good finish on all the layers of undercoat.

Some appeals remain private – perhaps because their causes do not attract the sympathy of the public at large or because a similar charity has just gone public with an appeal or because they have had bad publicity which can be explained only in face-to-face meetings with potential supporters. There can be many other reasons for deciding against a public appeal. However, apart from being a major source of funds for any charity, a public appeal has many merits. It raises the profile of the cause and the charity, which will lead to increased support for the appeal. If the appeal has a fun image, people can enjoy being involved, store happy memories and become long-term supporters. Rather than expecting the government to provide, the public can take a direct part through the charity. In effect, they become stakeholders and the charity is immeasurably strengthened through this wider ownership. Can you imagine the outcry if the government had tried to close Great Ormond Street Hospital immediately after the Wishing Well Appeal? So a public appeal helps the charity become part of the life of a nation, be more fully understood and remembered by all those who were involved.

An enormous amount of planning and research takes place before the public phase. Without planning, the organizers risk considerable embarrassment as any mistake or disaster will take place in the glare of publicity. The research for the public appeal is carried out during the private phase. It is a matter of developing all the potential sources not approached for lead gifts in the private phase. It is about developing what has been referred to as the constituency for the appeal; this entirely depends on the particular project and whether the appeal is national or local. Our aim with the Wishing Well Appeal was to reach as wide an audience as possible. This meant splitting the public into sections to ease communications before deciding how to involve them in the Appeal.

It is worth remembering that the broader the public appeal, the greater the cost of raising funds. Clearly, local group fund-raising is not so efficient as big gift fund-raising in terms of the cost-to-income ratio. This does not make it less important when you consider the PR and awareness benefits and the large sums raised. Trustees must be briefed that the broader spread of the the public appeal will necessitate greater initial investment and running costs.

Each of the fund-raising activities covered in this part of the book requires detailed research, so it is easiest to explain this in conjunction with the activity in question, be it carried out by national organizations, regional groups, special events or schools.

STRATEGY

Having worked out which fund-raising techniques are available for your type of appeal (see Appendix 4(b)), you need to plan your strategy and establish panels of volunteers supported by appropriate staff to develop the different activities. These matters are addressed in this part of the book and discussed in conjunction with the experiences of the Wishing Well Appeal and others. If there are people determined to carry out a particular type of fund-raising on your behalf at no cost to the appeal itself, there is no reason why you should not encourage them to do so (as long as they have been suitably vetted). In the main, however, this phase involves the promotion of types of fund-raising which earn the highest returns for the appeal in the most favourable manner. These aspects are discussed in some detail in the following chapters. The appeal must strive to put over a sense of fun and excitement – fun-raising – so that a bandwagon effect is created and everybody wants to join in.

The public appeal involves several phases. Firstly, there is a high profile launch if you can achieve it. Hitting the headlines requires creativity. Maintaining press coverage requires a constant drip-feed of stories, with planned high spots along the way, to keep people interested in your appeal and to remind them that it is still going on. The intensive follow-up to the launch may go on for as long as a year. It is followed by the top-up phase.

There is no single way to carry out this latter phase. It all depends on the circumstances – the amount of money still to be raised, the type of project and cause. Sometimes it even means bringing in new blood to look at the situation and to provide new impetus. I was able to do that in Kensington, where a geriatric day hospital had raised a lot of money but was experiencing difficulty in reaching the target. I had set up a committee, chaired by the Earl Cadogan, to raise money to provide sheltered housing schemes in the Royal Borough of Kensington and Chelsea. A change in the law meant that it was no longer needed as the funding was fully provided by the government. I had a splendid committee with no job to do. I would not normally advise picking up a committee formed for one purpose and moving it over to complete a different project, but it worked very effectively in this instance. The committee was able to complete the appeal for the St. Mary Abbots Geriatric Day Hospital.

A last push is often required to refocus the appeal and bring new impetus if it is flagging towards the end. Conclude your campaign with a finale – finish with flair and recognition of those who made major contributions. All these phases are discussed in more detail in the following chapters.

Thermometers

A common mistake made by public appeals is using a thermometer. You see them exhibited outside churches, hospitals and schools. I agree with large boards explaining the need for an appeal, but a thermometer will catch you out in the end. First, it is no longer an imaginative idea. Second, and more importantly, it usually sticks a little way below the top and you are then publicly embarrassed and have to admit that you are having difficulties raising the last tranche. By this time everyone is somewhat sick and tired of your appeal and feels that somebody else should put his hand in his pocket. I know others argue differently and there will always be exceptions, but without a thermometer you are free to put out as many messages as you like as long as they are factual. You may declare what you have deposited in the bank. You may add the pledges made and even the interest you have received on the money from the bank. The more flexibility you have, the easier it is to react in the best interests of your charity.

It is essential that your supporters and staff are kept in touch with progress, thanked for their achievements and encouraged and motivated to attempt yet greater feats. This requires regular briefing sessions, 'thank you' receptions and newsletters. Your supporters should be advised of developments – good and bad – before public announcements. They will be known to be involved with your charity and can act as well-informed ambassadors if they are kept fully in the picture. One word of warning: it is important to achieve impact with some announcements. If one newspaper, radio or TV station gets a story before the rest, it can kill the possibility of wider coverage. Therefore, it is wise to tell your supporters of developments only just before you make public announcements. No matter how confidential your briefing sessions, it is amazing how quickly the story gets out. If your charity has a high profile, like Great Ormond Street's, the next thing you know, one journalist has a scoop.

Succeeding with an appeal does not just involve raising the necessary money, but raising a team that does the work and thoroughly enjoys the experience, feels appreciated for what it has done – and has a slight feeling of regret when it is all over. If you can achieve this, those people will tend to feel long-term loyalty to the charity and continue to help, if not at the same frenetic pace. This certainly happened with the Wishing Well Appeal (see Chapter 31).

Many of the regional groups had planned events for dates after the announcement that the target had been reached, so naturally they were disappointed as were the Appeal Office volunteers, because a way of life which they had enjoyed was coming to an end. Something similar happened at the end of an appeal I ran to save a home for elderly ladies in Buckinghamshire from closure. Under the chairmanship of John Paterson, then High Sheriff of the County, we formed a fund-raising panel made up of one leading individual from each of the main towns in South Buckinghamshire. Many of them had not known each other before, so the appeal widened their horizons. They really knew how to run a good party and, quite apart from raising the funds, they thoroughly enjoyed themselves. I have not forgotten the chairman thanking his committee for all it had done and saying that, in a way, it was sad they would not be meeting regularly in the future. The charity saw its opportunity and the committee was transformed into a Friends of the House group to visit and support the residents and have at least one annual get-together.

Chapter 17

MARKETING

Marketing is a key element in any large one-off appeal, particularly in the public phase. The central point that such an appeal has to offer potential donors, rich or poor, is the persuasiveness of its cause. To the extent that marketing is a refinement of selling, it is essential to sell the reasons for donors to put their hands in their pockets and pull out coins, notes and cheque books.

A public appeal must have a coherent and thoroughly debated marketing strategy, preferably created with the help of leading experts in the fields of graphics, advertising, public relations, sales promotion, publishing, licensing, special events, and field and regional fund-raising. It requires the sustained co-operation of anything from half a dozen to several hundred people. They must all know what is expected of them and how their contribution fits into the whole. Above all, timing is crucial. An event, activity or initiative that takes place outside the agreed sequence might be highly damaging to the success of the appeal. It is vital to ensure that those involved in this aspect of the appeal are in agreement. Significant splits will be readily visible to the outside world and could damage the appeal's effectiveness.

The point is illustrated by a very tempting offer to the Great Ormond Street Hospital from a major newspaper. The Hospital, rather than the Appeal, was offered the chance of a £1 million campaign in this newspaper over Christmas 1986 – the year before the Appeal was to go public. However tempted the Hospital might have been, the Appeal's executive committee knew that it would damage the impact we hoped to make over the Christmas period immediately after the public launch. People would say 'we gave to this last year'. It could have dented the overall reaction the Appeal achieved and, although £1 million is serious money, it had to be seen in the context of the original £30 million target and the £54 million we eventually raised. So, with regret, we turned down the proposal. It was a difficult decision and one the newspaper found extremely hard to understand after they had made what, on the face of it, was a very generous offer. In retrospect, all those concerned with the Appeal and the Hospital who saw the response we had from the public in 1987 – after we had not previously asked for money in a major way since the 1930s – felt that they had made the right decision.

In Chapter 8 I explain how to produce a marketing strategy, structure and house style. Chapter 13 examines the marketing input in support of a private appeal, which, in the main, is the production of the appeal brochure. This chapter covers the marketing activities required for the preparation and execution of the public appeal. Whereas marketing has a support role in a private appeal, it is pivotal when the appeal is aimed at the public.

Contents of the marketing strategy document

1. A synopsis of the preliminary report (Chapter 4)
   - Project brief
   - Appeal objectives, strategy, structure and responsibilities
2. Marketing objectives
3. Marketing structure (honorary and staff)
4. Public appeal activities
   - Local, national and international publicity (advertising and public relations)
   - Joint promotions with companies
   - Special events
   - Regional groups
   - Direct mail
   - Trading
   - Mail order (catalogues)
   - Character licensing
   - Shops
   - Other
5. House style guidelines
6. Promotional material available (posters, videos, display panels, leaflets, etc.)
7. Who's who of those involved in the appeal
8. Programme calendar

MARKETING STRATEGY DOCUMENT

You cannot work out the detail of the marketing strategy for the public appeal until just before reaching that stage. This is because you will be recruiting the necessary expertise during the preparatory and private stages, as well as reviewing publicity opportunities and deciding on budgets. However, once agreed, the marketing strategy should be brought together in a booklet. This document should state its purpose at the outset: to outline the marketing thinking behind the appeal and the strategy being implemented, so that all supporters can receive clear guidelines on where and how contributions might most usefully be made.

It should set out the structure of the appeal organization: the operating panels formed to deal with such activities as special events, approaches to industry, schools, churches and special interest groups, and any overseas work which might be deemed desirable.

The marketing strategy document should also set out the guiding principles and considerations to be borne in mind throughout the appeal. In the case of the

Wishing Well Appeal, we pointed out that, as the Hospital was sensitive about its role as a healthcare organization, all collaborative ventures should go through the Hospital's Medical Advisory Committee. We stated that companies would want a quantitative commercial return, as well as the qualitative benefit of helping a worthy cause, if they took part in joint promotions. This demonstrated that we gave due consideration to their needs as well as to the Appeal's.

Marketing objectives

The marketing objectives during the public appeal cover a wide range of activities:

- to raise public awareness of the cause
- to convince the public that your cause is valid and your case strong
- to support the overall fund-raising plans, by raising a minimum figure through marketing activities
- to support other fund-raising activities by developing suitable publicity campaigns
- to protect the appeal's image, ensure continuity of execution and standards across all public communication material and to prevent dilution of impact through over-exposure

Some charities might add:

- to raise substantially the number of volunteers supporting the charity's regional network

Organizational structure

There has to be a chain of command which is easily understood. The list of operating panels should be readily available to the appeal's staff and volunteers, so that they can see how the different activities relate to one another. The Marketing Panel should, ideally, contain representatives from the main disciplines described above, so that their views can be heard at the highest appropriate level. By the same token, a member of each of the operating panels should be appointed to the main executive committee. (See Appendix 1 for the Wishing Well Appeal structure.)

Leadership

As Appeal Director, I was intrinsically involved in the initial work of setting up and recruiting the Wishing Well Marketing Panel with its Chairman, Bob Clarke, who was then Deputy Chairman of United Biscuits (Holdings) and has since been knighted. Through his personal pulling power and wealth of contacts, he was able to assemble a unique team of creative people dedicated to the Hospital and determined to put the Wishing Well Appeal truly on the map – and so they did. The appointment of the Chairman of the Marketing Panel usually dictates which advertising and PR agencies become involved. I often advise charities to delay making these appointments until the appeal chairman and/or marketing chairman has been appointed. In our case, the advertising agency and the main PR agency came to us of their own accord, when they heard that we were planning an Appeal.

Staff

Having taken the Wishing Well Appeal's Marketing Panel through its planning stages and private appeal, I knew we would need to take on a senior staff member to handle this activity in preparation for and during the public appeal. We appointed Josephine Lundberg, who had considerable experience in public relations. Her role was to service and develop all marketing aspects through the Marketing Panel. Before long we had also appointed a press officer to handle media relations on the Appeal's behalf (as opposed to the Hospital's). It was imperative to have professionally qualified staff handling all marketing aspects by the time our Appeal was publicly launched. Our policy was to encourage panel members to do much of the work – rather than just advising – but the staff still had to coordinate all these activities, develop specific promotional deals with companies and make sure that everything took place on schedule and to plan.

Specific activities

The marketing strategy document should describe all the main fund-raising activities planned for the public appeal and how they are structured. It should explain that each activity will have its own plan of action, which will fit in with the main appeal strategy. Contact names and telephone numbers should be included for those who wish to support a particular area of activity.

The appeal's marketing plan should be laid out, so that all concerned know what they are supposed to do. Nevertheless, I recommend that there should be a firm and unambiguous procedure for clearing proposed ideas and messages in order to maintain control at the centre. In this area, above all others, the appeal organizers will be dealing with people whose creativity and enthusiasm can easily run away with them unless they are clearly instructed to seek approval for their latest brainwave. The need for internal communication on these topics makes the Marketing Strategy document all the more important.

The NSPCC Centenary Appeal had an 'Ideas Group' which considered hundreds of possible ideas. Dozens were implemented. A few achieved press coverage; one was hugely successful and was the publicity high spot for the appeal. This was when HRH The Princess Margaret, President of the NSPCC, took part in The Archers – as herself, attending a fund-raising event in the fictional town of Ambridge. It was the first time a member of the Royal Family had taken part in a soap opera and it achieved headline news.

Marketing plan of action

The public document is unlikely to include the specific plan of action for the Marketing Panel. Having been given the areas to cover by the appeal chairman, the marketing chairman should break down the different marketing activities into groups for different working parties. Each should prepare its own plan, including advertising, public relations, joint promotions, publications, merchandising, and contributions from the marketing sector. They should also prepare a schedule of budgeted expenditure and targeted income to be included in the overall marketing plan of action. This is not as simple as it sounds; who is to say what income is generated solely by advertising or public relations? However they are part of the cost which stimulates the public response. Other areas, such as joint promotions, publishing and licensing, can be analyzed and predicted more accurately.

House style guidelines

The marketing document should be the definitive place to lay down the agreed name for the appeal and any variants or abbreviations deemed permissible in certain situations. There may be a formal name for use in legal documents and official communications with Royalty, government ministers, company chairmen and other heads of organizations but, especially if there is to be a public appeal, a catchier name may be used to capture the imagination of the public and the media. It is important to stress to everyone involved in sending out appeal messages that the official name must be used correctly. If your own people cannot get it right, how can you expect anyone else to do so?

As I have stressed previously in Chapter 4, the marketing document must also state the aims and target of the appeal. It should clearly address what fall-back position will be adopted if the target is either under- or over-achieved.

House style and logo

A major one-off appeal should have settled the question of house style before it reaches the stage of preparing for the public phase (see Chapter 8). Setting a clear and uniform style for all communications is vital from the point of view of both internal morale and public image. This – the house style – covers letterheads, forms, brochures, posters, stickers, collecting boxes, flags, banners and anything else that might bear the name of the appeal. By making the style consistent, it acts as a reminder to outsiders that this is the appeal of the moment, the one they may already have heard about and not some other similar cause. That helps to avoid confusion and channel contributions towards your appeal. It is worth taking professional advice on the question of style if you are going to take the matter seriously, as it is not easy to strike the right balance of authority and breeziness when choosing type faces and colours for both print and paper. Once the choices have been made, they should be circulated as widely as possible to minimize error.

The flagship of the house style should be the appeal's logo, or trademark. This should be the symbol of the appeal, easily printable and recognizable on all publicity items. The style and logo should be set out in the marketing document, possibly as an appendix, but it may also be a good idea to present them separately in a leaflet which can be pinned up prominently in the relevant offices. This should go into technical detail regarding type faces and sizes. An address and telephone number should be added for those who wish to obtain the artwork. Finally and very importantly, all fund-raising literature and any material that might, in any way, constitute an appeal must state that your organization is a registered charity (see Chapter 8). Not to do so is an offence under Part I of the Charities Act 1992 (see Appendix 8).

Clearance procedures

If the Marketing Panel and the appeal office are to retain control over messages and initiatives, the marketing document should contain procedures for obtaining approvals. I suggest the following rules:

1. The logo should be used only in the artwork form, as supplied by the appeal office.
2. All public phase marketing activities have to be cleared by the appeal office.
3. A minimum of two weeks should be allowed for approval of joint marketing initiatives.
4. Copy for advertisements and promotional material must be cleared by the appeal office to ensure that they are legal, decent, honest, accurate and truthful, and to ensure that they are consistent with house style.

The marketing strategy and guidelines document should include information on the type and quantity of promotional material and from whom it is available. A well-organized appeal will have a wide range of such material, including stationery, posters, display boards, leaflets, audio visuals, videos, speech notes and progress reports. (These publicity tools are discussed in more detail in Chapter 18.)

Appendices should include an organization chart for the appeal as a whole and a list of the members of the Marketing Panel with the names of their companies, their addresses and telephone numbers.

COMPREHENSIVE STATUS REPORT

The sequential timing of the appeal's activities is vital for achieving maximum impact and keeping the appeal's public profile high. It is important to avoid conflicting events and to avoid choosing dates which will mean your own event will not get suitable coverage. Research this through friendly newspaper librarians, keep an ear to the ground in the charity field to avoid clashes with other big charity events and check the Charities Events Calendars available from the Charities Aid Foundation and National Council for Voluntary Organizations. Ask all event organizers, staff and volunteers to let the appeal office know the dates of events so that one schedule can be kept and used as a status report. In the Wishing Well Appeal, we included all activities – media events, special events, joint promotions, relevant regional events, advertising campaigns, celebrity visits to the Hospital, etc. This list must be regularly updated and sent to all staff and appropriate volunteers to keep them fully informed.

PUBLIC RELATIONS AND ADVERTISING

The next chapters cover public relations and advertising, which are both essential elements in the marketing mix. However, it is worth explaining now how these techniques fit in with an appeal's marketing strategy.

The main difference between marketing in business and in a one-off appeal is that an appeal cannot afford all it would like to command in terms of spread or coverage. Yet it would be difficult to sustain a public appeal without a certain minimum level of publicity. The best approach is to plan exactly what type and degree of exposure would achieve the desired results and budget for it. Then, instead of commissioning the work, try to achieve the same goal through voluntary input. You can sometimes achieve widespread publicity in this way without paying the large sums of money required by an orthodox commercial project. On the other hand, you cannot insist on first-priority service when it comes to voluntary input. However, you should also agree what would be the minimum coverage required and be prepared to pay for it as a fall-back position. So it is something of a juggling act. Ongoing appeals for major charities cannot normally achieve the same marketing input from volunteers as a one-off appeal may be able to generate, so they usually have to pay the going rate for the job, but they, too, have to be sensitive to their cost-to-income ratio.

CONCLUSION

It is difficult to point to the one element which will make an appeal take off. It is usually the combined effect of many different parts of the strategy, working together and maintaining a high profile. Let's not forget luck – needed in abundance to ensure that another story does not steal the headlines on the day you launch or the day after one of your biggest events. So many things can go wrong with any widely publicized event that you need luck to get through it without unfortunate publicity that might alienate the public from your cause. That is where planning comes in: planning for good luck, if you like, and planning how to minimize damage if luck turns against you. These aspects will be developed further in Chapter 18.

When it does all come together successfully, it is an enormously exciting experience. The Wishing Well Appeal certainly had its problems but, if you talk to anyone who was involved, their main recollection will be of the uplifting experience of seeing what seemed like the whole country respond to the Hospital's needs. Many of the Appeal team look back and think that they will never experience that degree of excitement again.

Chapter 18

PLANNING THE PUBLICITY CAMPAIGN

A public appeal's publicity campaign is fundamental to its success. It is essential that all public relations activities are planned and organized well before the campaign's launch, with a clear view of how to time events, activities and press coverage to ensure sustained ongoing interest in the appeal.

The publicity campaign provides plenty of opportunities for injecting fun into plotting your public profile. It needs as much imagination and talent as possible, so select a group of people to act as a think tank to help you create the lively, fresh approach you need. Flair, ingenuity, a certain originality of style – even a little glitter – play their part in attracting supporters. Yet, with delicate handling, all this can remain compatible with even the most heartbreaking cause. It is crucial that it should. Band Aid, Comic Relief and the various Telethons are all evidence that cheerfulness does not rule out sensitivity and genuine compassion for beneficiaries – who often shame one by being cheerful themselves. (The Wishing Well Appeal 'face' had a smile as well as a tear.)

The publicity campaign should be planned carefully to make a sustained impact by using diverse public relations techniques: staging events, stimulating favourable editorial and news coverage, producing copy and general publicity material to communicate effectively with your different audiences in order to encourage them to support your appeal.

Make sure your publicity campaign is designed to keep you as the fund-raiser in as much control as possible. In particular, beware of any material promoting, either explicitly or implicitly, illegal activities. For example the ITV Telethon explicitly states that any collections in public places are prohibited without proper permission. The Telethon has produced a very helpful manual, *The Community Fundraising Guide,* which clearly illustrates how money is best raised by the public. Even more importantly, it explains why some methods should not be used!

STRATEGY

Every facet of a large appeal needs to have its own plan of action. One of the most crucial of these is the publicity campaign. It must address the following:

What is the plan?
What tools will be needed?
Who will implement it and how?
What will it cost?

What is the plan?

Deciding the objectives of your campaign and what your messages will be is an essential starting point to planning any strategy. As with any other part of your appeal, you must decide at the outset what you wish to achieve from a publicity campaign. The Wishing Well Appeal wanted to encourage the public to give or raise funds to help pay for a new building on the Hospital site to ensure the future standing of the institution. To achieve this, we had to send a variety of messages:

1. Explaining the problems and the dangers they caused
2. Detailing the proposed solution
3. Stating what it would cost, what the government would contribute and why it could not fund the whole scheme
4. Specifying what the public was being asked to do.

Press coverage versus advertising

Editorial
- Has to include one or more news items of real interest to the audience unless it is a feature article
- Potentially much more convincing than advertising, because if the target media accept your point of view, it will be published with that extra endorsement, giving it added credibility
- Carries the potential risk that your chosen medium might not see your message the same way you do and may, therefore, present it in an inaccurate or less favourable light
- Low cost

Advertising
- Gives the advertiser control of the message
- Impact can be increased by an arresting visual treatment
- Advertiser controls timing
- The message can be tested to ensure that it produces the desired impact
- Much higher cost (although this may be underwritten by a supporter or sponsor)
- Reader scepticism because it is only your view

It is useful at this stage to compare the merits of buying space with those of press coverage. Press coverage is free, after allowing for staff time and costs of materials, but you have less control over the end product because your message has to go via a third party – the newspaper, radio, or television station. Advertising – paying for space – is more straightforward. It consists of deciding how to allocate a fixed budget to achieve certain results: to heighten awareness, inform or persuade. Once the decisions have been made, it is then a matter of bringing creativity to the task of making the messages as effective as possible (see Chapter 19). The main points of comparison between the two techniques are shown here. However, they are not mutually exclusive and most campaigns contain elements of both.

What tools will be needed?

Any strategy needs to review the wide range of PR tools available. Some of these will be detailed later in this chapter; for now, it is useful to note that at the planning stage of an appeal strategy you should review the potential for using techniques as diverse as press conferences, editorials, logos, video presentations and radio and television interviews. The scope for using these methods will differ according to the nature of each appeal.

If you are going in for a public appeal, you will probably want to create as much of a splash as possible. This means trying to attract the national media to give it editorial coverage. If your appeal is specialized or will benefit only a small section of the population, you should concentrate on channels of communication that target your message more accurately. Otherwise you will waste time, effort and money. For the purposes of this book, it is probably best to explain how to aim for the maximum, as long as the reader realizes that a smaller or more specific appeal should adapt its plans accordingly.

To give maximum backing to an appeal, the communications strategy should include a high-profile launch aimed at reaching every member of the population. This is not easy, as not everyone reads newspapers, listens to radio or watches television. So every possible medium should be used to bring home your message. Chapter 21 explains why dealing with national organizations helps an appeal to reach a wide number of people in a personal way. As a general rule, it is best to use a well-known and respected figure to act as your spokesperson. Do not be afraid to ask your VIPs or celebrities to play an active role. Remember, they must be fully briefed so that they really know what they are talking about. Celebrities are often asked to attend functions purely to raise the profile of the function, without knowing what to do once they are there. (See Chapter 25.)

While aiming to interest and involve the press in our plans for the Wishing Well Appeal, we had to take great care to protect the privacy and the interests of the children treated at the Hospital. The hard-pressed staff also needed shielding from the glare of publicity. The staff contributed enormously by explaining the Hospital and its work to supporters and dealing with cameramen. However, we had to be careful that they were not overburdened by this.

Having decided on the messages to project, you must decide to whom they are to be addressed and how they are to be delivered. That is, which are the target media, what is the most effective strategy for approaching each and what are the methods they will use to communicate with the public.

Who will implement it and how?

When developing a new appeal, planners should consider whether professional advisers may be attracted to the campaign. In many ways, participating in such projects is wonderful free PR for these agencies; do not be afraid to approach them and ask about the possibility of pro bono advice.

There are several ways of collecting the know-how and pairs of hands necessary to put together the marketing role (see Chapter 17). Such skills can be drawn from in-house staff, agency support or a combination of both. The Wishing Well Appeal's solution, under the chairmanship of Alan Kilkenny, co-founder and then Chairman of the Grayling Company, was to assemble a panel which included representatives from eight major PR consultancies. This was an incredible achievement in its own right! Only the special pull of a cause such as Great Ormond Street could have brought such deadly rivals round the same table to work in harmony. This panel was serviced by suitably qualified staff – the Head of Marketing and the Press Officer. As each activity was identified as requiring public relations support, so the work was shared among the panel members job by job. It was a phenomenal response from the public relations sector. The resulting flood of press coverage was a just tribute to their dedication and the very real concern of the media in the well-being of the Hospital and its patients.

What will it cost?

A detailed budget to incorporate the costs of the essential publicity work should be prepared. You should then see if some of this can be met by corporate supporters. If support is forthcoming, additional initiatives may be within your reach. It is interesting that the Sick Kids Appeal for the Royal Edinburgh Children's Hospital spent £443,330 on advertising and promotion, representing 45 per cent of the total cost of running the appeal. Their policy was to pay the rate for the job in this area, to ensure they received a first-class service. The cost of the Wishing Well Appeal's advertising campaign was a very similar figure (although it was paid for by a donor and the media owners).

Towards the end of the Wishing Well Appeal, I received a call from a reporter who said that he had totalled the cost of all our publicity. The figure came to £6 million and he felt it was a disgrace that we had frittered away so much of the public's funds in this way. He wanted to know what I had to say about it. Of course, all I could do was to thank him for the useful research statistic and assure him that it had, almost without exception, been achieved through gifts in kind. Somehow I do not think this was what he wanted to hear.

TARGET MEDIA

Media are the conduit for delivering your message. One of the first stages in a PR exercise is to select which media are most relevant to your organization. Several companies publish directories, updated regularly, which give a complete list of national, local and special interest media, including information on their editorial content, circulation and the names of relevant correspondents. Two useful reference guides are *PR Planner* and *The Hollis Press and Public Relations Annual*. Other suppliers, including Pims UK Ltd. and Two-Ten Communications Ltd., offer a wider range of services, which can cover media selection, press release production and distribution, and a press cuttings service. The latter is an essential management tool to check all references in the press to subjects of interest to your charity or campaign.

As a campaign continues, it is important that the master media list and all reference sources are updated regularly. Journalists change jobs and there is no better way to ensure that a press release ends up on a spike than to release it to a journalist who switched desks three months earlier.

A large-scale appeal will want to attract television, radio, national and local press coverage, as well as feature articles – assuming that you have a story of sufficient merit or that you have staged an event which will attract widespread attention. You should approach specific magazines and other media to which your event has some relevance – not forgetting the local press applicable to the birthplace or home of someone featured in your story. This media list will be the all-important target of press releases and feature articles about your charitable cause. It will vary with each news release, depending on the content of the story.

The main media targets for the Wishing Well Appeal

National and local television and radio
National and local press
Specialist press:
 Medical
 Architectural
 Building trade
 Women's
 Children's
 Parents'
 Charity
 Marketing

What newspaper, television and radio journalists want are stories of real interest to their audiences. That is not necessarily the same as stories of interest to you as charity appeal organizers or even the same as the sort of story you would like to see published. Although they do publish 'good news' stories, journalists are usually looking for an element of drama – and that often means some form of conflict. In the case of Great Ormond Street, we wanted to stimulate favourable press coverage of the Hospital, its work, the redevelopment and the Appeal. This involved responding to press queries on specific patients (where families agreed, of course), announcements of developments in childcare, discoveries in areas of medical research, a foundation stone laying ceremony by a Royal Patron and a press visit to see the redevelopment work in action, accompanied by a presentation on progress and examination of the latest plans and model. Initially, we were looking for a combination of media and fund-raising events to keep our profile high. Sometimes, advance publicity was helpful, as it encouraged more people to take an interest or participate in an event, so adding to the amount raised. For example, we organized a photocall on the steps of St. Paul's Cathedral to promote the idea of running in the London Marathon in support of the Appeal.

Television

Editorial mentions on television are a very effective and cheap form of PR. Television news editors need a number of national and local stories for daily news programmes. If you think you have an item which might be suitable, get in touch with the news editor to whom your story might appeal. It will help if you can offer a good spokesperson who might be interviewed or give a brief, clear statement. 'Good' in this context means adroit enough to slip in an implicit appeal or even a telephone number. However, it must be recognized that news editors usually avoid direct appeals in news bulletins and, unless the interview is live, such comments may well be edited out.

If you are lucky, you might interest television in producing a feature on your cause. This could be a valuable fund-raising tool during the appeal. The Wishing Well Appeal benefited enormously from the BBC TV documentary *A Fighting Chance*, which was broadcast on 30 December 1987. It dramatically captured the progress of four children at Great Ormond Street. It did not flinch from the truth in that not all the stories had a happy ending, but there could have been no more effective medium for portraying the essence of the Hospital to a large audience of potential donors. The telephones rang constantly from the moment it ended until the early hours of the New Year, with people offering to help. The video tape of the programme was also a highly effective way of reinforcing our message at every available opportunity.

Appeals

A charity which wants an appeal on television should apply to the BBC Appeals Advisory Committee (AAC) which advises the BBC in this area. The AAC accepts only one application in any three-year period. It decides which applications are to be successful and whether time is to be given on TV or radio. If your application is successful, it is important to let your supporters know as soon as you know the date of the broadcast. The broadcast should be followed up immediately by advertisements in the press, including the *Radio Times* and *TV Times*. There are now both a Charter and Recommendations for the conduct of broadcast appeals which should be followed. Copies can be obtained from the Manager, Donation Taking Services, Broadcasting Support Services. BSS is an independent educational charity which provides various services including publishing, running helplines, as well as donation-taking services required by any broadcast appeal. It works with the BBC, Channel 4, ITV and satellite companies.

Telethons

BBC Children in Need

Children in Need is a charity which aims to help children and young people under 18, using the funds raised by the BBC Children in Need appeal. The appeal broadcast takes place in November each year on television and radio. The huge sums raised enable the trustees to make thousands of grants, ranging from relatively small amounts (£100 in one case) to hundreds of thousands of pounds. Each year, assessors consider large numbers of applications for grants and recommendations are made to the trustees through regional committees.

The Children in Need appeal transmitted just after the launch of the Wishing Well Appeal might have been a marvellous vehicle to promote our cause but, after detailed research, we realized it would be better not to be included. We felt that supporters would give substantially in response to publicity naming Great Ormond Street, not realizing that the Wishing Well Appeal would receive only a share of the donations. The separate launch and the popularity of the Hospital would produce larger sums and avoid confusion. In general, smaller appeals do relatively better from multiple appeals such as Children in Need.

ITV Telethon
The Wishing Well Appeal did benefit from the ITV's 1988 Telethon (see Chapter 26). Since 1988, Telethons have taken place every two years and have raised over £60 million. Telethon is committed to supporting small local charities via its regional trusts, in addition to national ones, and does the latter through the Independent Broadcasting Telethon Trust (IBTT) which agrees the national priorities for each Telethon and coordinates the work of the separate Telethon Trusts. These bodies, one for each ITV region, consider all applications from charities in their own area and allocate funds to them. A key principle of Telethon is that all the money raised in a television region stays in that region. Requests for grants have to be made on application forms provided by the trusts, each of which can derive its own regional priorities from the specific needs of the region.

Comic Relief
So far, Comic Relief has raised over £75 million through three Red Nose Days. The fund-raising costs are covered by sponsorship in cash or in kind so that all the money donated can be used on charity projects. Applications for grants are assessed by Charity Projects, the parent charity, which also distributes the funds.

Some of the funds are used in the U.K. on projects to help older people or young people who are disabled, homeless or drug addicted. The remainder goes to finance projects in Africa judged to be of long term help with health, education and agriculture. Where possible, in Africa or the U.K., projects are designed to help people help themselves.

Radio

Television is a very powerful medium and tends to overshadow radio. In fact, radio has a great deal to offer the fund-raiser. News editors are always on the look-out for newsworthy items. Tape recordings, preferably with a celebrity's voice, can be made and distributed to producers by the charity or via the United News Services for use as stop-gaps. If you involve celebrities, it is best if they have had personal experience of the charity. Radio stations round the country used Bel Mooney's touching interview about the support she received from Great Ormond Street when her child was there. If you are really fortunate, like the NSPCC during their Centenary Appeal, you might even arrange to get a mention on a radio 'soap'.

Appeals
The best-known radio appeal is *The Week's Good Cause* which is on Radio 4 at 8.50 am on Sundays. There is no guarantee you will be allotted the time, but you should

certainly apply to the BBC Appeals Advisory Committee. In the lifetime of a one-off appeal – say, two years – not more than one acceptance is possible, so care should be taken to make the programme a success. The producer who will be responsible for your programme will discuss it with you and provide technical services. A celebrity presenter, someone with established audience appeal and credibility, is vital. In addition, Capital Radio runs an appeal called *Help a London Child* and many local radio stations run appeals to benefit local charities or to promote a special event.

PR TOOLS

Press conferences

You can always call a press conference if you feel that there has been a major development of sufficient interest to justify it. Invite the press to come in person to hear your story. In return, the press will expect to be able to quiz the spokesperson about the appeal and obtain responsible answers. It creates more news if the message comes from a celebrity skilled in public speaking, who can answer questions which relate directly to your cause. Careful briefing is necessary. Someone senior in the appeal, who can, perhaps, also chair the conference, is needed for more general questions.

The location of the conference is very important. It should be accessible and, if possible, interesting. There should be access to telephones. Prepare a briefing pack to send or deliver to journalists who do not attend the conference. Try to schedule the press conference for the morning to allow all journalists attending to make their copy deadlines.

If you want wide coverage, do not give an exclusive interview or let one journalist have details before the others. However, in response to one-off enquiries from journalists who want to write about your appeal, try to find an angle which is exclusive to them.

Photocalls

A press conference, especially with a well-known personality, can provide photo opportunities. Other photocalls can be arranged by setting up a stunt of some sort – anything that will provide an unusual or exciting picture. Special events can be used for this purpose. Pictures of supporters handing over large cheques to a celebrity are hardly unusual and do not warrant national press coverage unless the celebrity happens to be in the news for some other reason – not always one favourable to your cause! Local newspapers often include one or two photographs of cheque presentations, but it is best to try to do something unusual to make a special occasion of it if you want coverage. An update on the funds raised for a cathedral spire would be unlikely to be reported in the national press, unless it were extraordinarily successful – or a mammoth flop. On the other hand, a stunning picture of or from the spire might get there on photographic merit alone.

Press releases

Ideally, you should recruit public relations expertise to issue press releases on

The visit of a charity's Royal Patron during the private appeal phase can produce very valuable footage for a film or video for use in the public appeal stage. The Prince and Princess of Wales' visit to Great Ormond Street was included in the BBC TV's documentary 'A Fighting Chance'.

Almost all fund-raising events need sustained and special advance publicity if they are to achieve their full potential. Creating an imaginative photo opportunity is one way to do this. The Wishing Well Appeal aimed to attract more runners through a publicity stunt on the steps of St Paul's Cathedral before the 1988 Mars London Marathon. About 1000 runners eventually raised £1,500,000 for the Appeal. (Photograph: Keith Waldegrave)

behalf of your charity. If not, it is important to learn some of your recipients' requirements before you waste time sending them stories they may not want to use. First, be sure that your story is sufficiently newsworthy to warrant inclusion in a publication. This will vary with different publications; what interests *The Independent* may be of no relevance to a specialist publication like *Charity*, and vice versa.

Second, you must present the facts in the way a newspaper can easily use; they rarely have time to plough through your deathless prose to unearth the one nugget of information that will make a story for them. Many like to be able to put your release straight into the paper, virtually unchanged, especially if they are up against a deadline, so do your best to tell your tale in something like a newspaper's style. You can buy textbooks on newspaper writing.

Hints on writing press releases

- Put the most important facts first
- Keep it as brief as possible
- Include a contact name and telephone number at the end
- Answer the questions who? what? when? where? how? and why?
- Photograph captions should have no more than one or two sentences
- Double-space your text and leave wide margins
- Don't use flowery language
- Short words and sentences are best

Third, do not assume knowledge. Your charity may be the most important organization in the world to you, but the journalist who picks up your press release may never have heard of it. Add a sheet of background information, giving a potted history of the charity, its aims and achievements. It will help him develop his own version of the story with a basis of solid fact. As the press is so crucial to an appeal, it is also wise to collect some journalistic friends of your charity to meet those handling the appeal and to receive some regular updates. They can also be taken to visit the site, if appropriate, so that they can understand the cause more fully. Their influence and support can be enormously helpful and they can advise how to handle situations, including potentially adverse news.

Advertorials

These are a cross between advertisements and newspaper editorials. Essentially, they are features or feature spreads that look like editorial matter to the casual eye, but which are paid for or sponsored. They are, therefore, under the same degree of control as an advertisement. They can be a useful way of putting a full, accurate and beneficial view of your story before the public in a manner that is easy to read and absorb. The space will be headed 'Advertising feature' but it looks like editorial matter and may include advertisements of support from your charity's main commercial donors to help pay for the space.

Photographic and film library

A crucial part of any public relations operation is commissioning and storing photographs and film. If you commission a photograph, you must agree in advance with the photographer who owns the copyright and the detail of what you plan to produce. Copyright will belong to the photographer unless he assigns it to the charity in writing in the commissioning contract. If the charity is not the owner of the copyright, the extent to which it can use the photograph should be clearly set out, together with any ongoing payment obligations.

A picture story is a good way to keep your appeal in the public eye and, once again, specialist knowledge can save a great deal of time. Public relations practitioners or a picture editor can give invaluable advice. Newspapers and magazines are always looking for good photographs. Try to anticipate the timing of your own events and how that schedule fits in with other current events which might detract from your story.

Make sure your system for storing and filing photographs is well prepared before the appeal is launched. It is useless to own a wealth of photographs suitable for a range of publications if you cannot lay hands on them when you need them or if the captions are mislaid. Once the appeal gathers momentum, you will be flooded with all sorts of items and no one will have the time to sort them properly. Above all, observe this golden rule: every picture must have a caption gummed – not pinned – on the back. It should identify the people or buildings in the shot and state the month and year, if not the actual day, it was taken or received. You may think that you will always be able to date a picture by looking at it, but memory can play surprising tricks. Once your photo library starts running into the hundreds, you have no chance if you do not date the photographs as they are received. The caption should also include a contact name at the charity.

Essential picture library details

* name, address and telephone number of the photographer or owner (if it was taken by an appeal supporter or a newspaper)
* information on copyright ownership
* caption

Videos, audio visuals and speech notes

If these are attractively produced, they will encourage as many people as possible to give speeches extolling the appeal and propounding its message. In these days of electronic communication, do not overlook the power of the individual to persuade his fellows in open session. The personal touch can powerfully stimulate response, but it is far more effective if it is backed by well-researched, professionally produced verbal and illustrative material – flip charts, slide programmes, overhead projectors and speech notes. The easier you can make it for potential speakers, the more will come forward and do a better job for you. At the Wishing Well Appeal, we produced a video linked to the objective of the Appeal, its progress and the ways in which viewers could help. This was a very convincing fund-raising tool and we used it in many different settings. It was presented by Martyn Lewis, the television news presenter, a great supporter of the Hospital and a member of the Appeal's Marketing Panel. The video was produced at no cost to the Appeal. We also produced a series of slides and speech notes which were especially useful to our local groups.

Display panels, models and leaflets

These can be very helpful in enabling potential supporters to see exactly what the appeal is trying to do; they give you an excellent means of getting your message across. Professionally produced panels can be mounted on display units and transported to various sites for inspection, either on their own or as part of a promotional event. Be creative about where you display these panels. For example, the Upper Waiting Hall in the Houses of Parliament hosts regular exhibitions of art or photography related to particular causes or appeals. While this entails a ballot of MPs and requires a long lead time to organize, such a location generates additional publicity.

You will need to obtain some suitable, transportable units. You may even draw up standard posters for each panel, so that you can economically run off a number of copies to be kept in regional locations.

The public relations unit will also be asked to produce a leaflet to replace the brochure during the public appeal. It is a cheaper version which tells the essential story of the need for the appeal and how people can help. Other leaflets on different methods of giving, such as the Give As You Earn scheme (see Chapter 28), may be needed. Regular progress reports and possibly a newspaper or newsletter should be used to keep staff, volunteers and donors involved and fully informed.

STAGING THE APPEAL

Launching the appeal

The launch of the appeal plays a key role in the creation of momentum and development of publicity. One of the most effective ways is to hold a press conference. It saves the organizers having to answer the same questions several times over and creates a sense of being an important event by confirming to each of the reporters present that here is a story in which their rivals are interested – assuming they turn up! The conference can be part of a social occasion set in a prestigious location. The timing and location must be convenient for the principal media to give them the best opportunity of providing full coverage. This argues for holding the conference in London in mid-week, with a late-morning start running into an informal lunch. A reception for VIPs can be held that evening.

These principles governed the launch of the Wishing Well Appeal. We held a press conference at the Institute for Child Health, the Hospital's research and teaching arm, fronted by a panel of speakers representing clinicians, architects, Hospital management and the Appeal. As they left, journalists were given a press pack which contained a press release, speech notes, background notes, and photographs with captions. There were leaflets and display panels to support the story. What made the event special was that the Appeal was launched by the

Prince of Wales via a satellite link to his home in Gloucestershire. It was the first time His Royal Highness had done this, which helped to ensure that the launch received maximum coverage. Jonathan Dimbleby hosted the conference to explain that the Appeal was being launched to the media because we realized that they were vital to its success. Jonathan's presence was doubly relevant because one of his children had been a patient at Great Ormond Street.

This detailed and professional operation, with different versions of the press release sent to different types of media throughout Britain, was handled by in-house staff with the guidance and back-up of the Grayling Company, who undertook responsibility for the whole exercise as their contribution towards the Appeal. Professional advice on the planning of such high-profile events is often essential. PR consultants will be able to direct you to other specialist experts who may be co-opted into contributing their services free as well. Equally, they will ensure that the details of an event are handled in the proper way, and should guarantee the highest standards.

Much thought was also given to a photocall to see if we could produce relevant and striking picture opportunities to depict the essence of the Appeal. In the end, we involved many children's characters, together with a Walt Disney version of Mr. Wishing Well. The resulting photograph was not widely used by the press, as they were much more interested in the involvement of the Prince of Wales. Nevertheless setting up a suitable picture story should be thought through very carefully. As with so much else, professional advice is most important, as it is so easy to detract from the message which the appeal organizers wish to convey.

Follow-through

The momentum generated by the launch should be maintained with a drip-feed of suitable newspaper stories to sustain the public's interest. These might cover the progress of the appeal, developments in the project for which you are raising funds and events being held to support the appeal. The events may be designed specifically to catch media attention, such as the visit of the Princess of Wales and Jimmy Tarbuck, dressed as Father Christmas, in December 1987, two months after the Wishing Well Appeal launch. This reminded people about the Appeal in the vital run-up to Christmas. It merited a front-page photograph in most of the following morning's national newspapers. News items may also be created around the appeal's fund-raising activities.

If an appeal has had widespread coverage, you may have to consider the dangers of overkill. While this may seem like a dream at the outset, it can become a real problem. If you are in danger of alienating your supporters with too many news stories, it may be worth thinking about restricting media coverage to events which are expected to raise substantial sums of money and which rely on publicity to achieve their targets. It is a fine balancing act, requiring sensitivity and the ability to see others' points of view. Those responsible for the appeal's publicity should constantly review events to see which have the potential to hit the headlines and, therefore, require PR back-up. In addition, you must try to manage these events so that they do not clash or cut across one another's impact. For that matter, they must not clash with events organized in support of other appeals. The Charities Aid

Foundation produces an events calender which carries the latest information supplied by charities on their fund-raising and publicity events.

Planning the programme of events should include every highly visible activity: events, joint promotions, advertisements and issuing news stories. This will give a picture of the back-up publicity to accompany any activity – a good selling point to help persuade potential sponsors or joint-promotion partners.

INTERNAL PR

With so many demands on your time in responding to press inquiries, supporting events and organizing media coverage, it is easy to overlook the importance of internal PR. Good communications with staff and volunteer fund-raisers is vital, as they make the appeal happen. This, too, needs its own strategic plan. Managers must hold enough meetings to keep staff motivated and informed and to ensure that there is a two-way flow of information and opinion. That is the best way of catching problems early, as well as learning of bright ideas that might otherwise be lost. Special presentations and regular meetings with regional volunteers are necessary to keep them informed about what is going on at national level and to recognize their different input and needs. Relations between the appeal and those charged with serving your beneficiaries must be carefully nurtured to obtain maximum co-operation.

A newsletter or newspaper is a good means of reaching these audiences and giving them a sense of common identity. It can inform, ventilate response, give credit to those who have made a noteworthy contribution, circulate press releases on achievements and new developments in the project and even answers to negative publicity – before informing the press and general public.

HANDLING PRESS ENQUIRIES

Your appeal must decide at an early stage how press calls should be handled and issue a policy paper so that the entire team is aware of the procedures. You may decide that all queries should be routed through one experienced or suitably trained member of staff. His role is to collect the details of the call and the journalist's requirements and deadline. It may then be a matter of discussing these with the appeal director, who will decide how to follow up the enquiry and who will be the charity's spokesperson. This system allows the charity time to think about the enquiry and to research the relevant facts before responding. However, if you are running a large-scale appeal, there will rarely be time to make decisions on individual calls so you will need a different policy.

Press queries about the Wishing Well Appeal were fielded by the Head of Marketing or our PR Manager. The General Manager of Great Ormond Street Hospital handled enquiries to do with the running of the Hospital, while Lord Prior or I handled issues relating to the Appeal. Other specific questions on special events or regional appeals were answered by the relevant senior staff member.

One temporary secretary, who had not seen our policy directive, gave me a fright when she proudly announced that she had answered a press call because she knew the answer – or thought she did. She was offended when I explained the correct procedures. Factual questions must be answered truthfully but journalistic enquiries are seldom as simple as that. Unless you are in a position to know the impact of your words, there can be dangers. What my temporary secretary did not realize was that some press enquiries are not as innocent as they may seem. When we had some negative publicity about Great Ormond Street supporters collecting funds near another children's hospital – not at our instigation – a national news-paper asked if we would arrange for our supporters to have their photograph taken with collecting tins immediately outside the hospital in question. In that case, I do not think the charity officer taking the call would have had to be too senior to realize that the outcome would hardly have been helpful to the Appeal or sensitive to the other hospital's feelings.

Adverse publicity

It is not easy to cover this complex subject briefly, but a charity and an appeal must not be caught off balance and attempt to rely on crisis management. There should be a carefully devised method of adapting plans to meet any challenge to the charity's good name. This must include a detailed plan of how to react to a crisis. Most notably, perhaps, it is essential that a handful of trusted spokespersons are clearly identified with all the relevant phone and fax numbers (with 24-hour access if necessary) included. It seems obvious to point out that you should check facts before responding to any press enquiry. If your organization really is at fault, it is best to come clean – make the admission and explain how the situation arose and how it will be rectified. Journalists will rapidly detect a cover-up.

Another tip, just as difficult to put into practice, is that it is best not to insist on a correction if you are falsely accused in the press, unless you have an open-and-shut defence on a matter of prime importance. The correction merely repeats the false claims and is likely to appear days or weeks after the original error, often in an obscure corner of the publication. It is a sad but unavoidable facet of human nature that no one likes admitting mistakes and journalists are well-versed in min-imizing any damage to themselves (rather than limiting damage to you).

CONCLUSION

Some charities do not begin to understand the power of the press, or if they do, they see it as a threat and ignore the muscle it can wield in the promotion of a cause or course of action. At the Wishing Well Appeal, we were well aware of the media's potential. Our plan was to work with them as partners, secure in the knowledge that they, too, would care about sick children – as would their readers, listeners and viewers. This is why we launched the Appeal to them, as our mouth-piece, and finished it that way as well. They did not let us down. In fact, I should pay tribute to the media for their warm and sometimes generous support in their own right, not only in their professional work but also as donors and activists. I really believe that the care and attention we devoted to our PR, which generated great loyalty and support, did a vast amount to ensure the Appeal's success. It is true that the media started to give us a hard time towards the end – as a result of the Appeal's very success. They love an underdog, but start looking more critically at a venture which seems to be standing on its own feet without apparently needing much outside help.

─────────── *Chapter 19* ───────────

ADVERTISING

It has been said that 'An advertisement isn't an advertisement unless it affects people and causes them to do something. It's money down the drain.'

In Chapter 4, I discussed the importance of project research – the need to collect all the relevant facts in order to make the case for an appeal. Similarly, it is essential to undertake the necessary research before deciding whether to use advertising as a marketing tool for your fund-raising campaign.

To begin with you need to understand the public's awareness of your cause or charity before deciding what you want to say to them and what action you want them to take.

DECIDE WHAT YOU WANT YOUR ADVERTISING TO ACCOMPLISH

Advertising is just one of the marketing tools available to fund-raisers. First you must define the role you want it to play in your overall campaign. It can tell people about your appeal and leave it at that. This is currently termed 'image advertising' because the manner in which the advertisement is expressed and designed will inevitably create an image in the reader's mind.

Advertising can motivate people to support an appeal by organizing or joining fund-raising activities, it can encourage people to write to their MPs, or it can recruit people to the cause. You must decide what you would like your advertising to accomplish and then make sure that it is produced with this purpose clearly in mind. If you try to achieve more than one of these things you will limit the effectiveness of your advertising. So decide what is most important and communicate it clearly to your advertising agency.

At the Wishing Well Appeal we took the same view as our advertising agency, Collett Dickenson Pearce (CDP), that it would be best to encourage individuals to raise funds rather than simply send a donation. For every one direct donor, there could be a hundred buying a sales promotion or attending an event in aid of the Appeal. Awareness and impact were the key objectives. This could not have been

so if there had not been a range of other catalysts (sales promotions, regional committees, national events) to convert intention into action.

DECIDE WHOM YOU WISH TO ADDRESS

Some appeals (Poppy Day, for example) are addressed to virtually everybody and
the only limitation on the media that can be usefully employed is the money available. Usually your audience is effectively limited. For example, it makes no sense
to advertise a local appeal in a national medium. Decide who is your primary audience and tell your agency's media planners. They will work out a media plan
which will reach your audience effectively at the lowest cost. They will also tell
you how big (or long, in the case of broadcast media) and frequent your advertisements can be.

HOW ADVERTISING WORKS

Advertising must touch basic human motivations. Everyone wants to protect
themselves and their families. Everyone wants to be attractive. Everyone wants the
approval of their peer group. At first glance, it may seem difficult to relate any of
these to charity advertising.

Obviously, charity is giving to those in need. The act of giving in itself may
relieve the guilt some people feel because life has been good to them. On the other
hand, people who, apparently, can least afford it make contributions perhaps
because they have been close to the problem the appeal seeks to relieve and understand why money is needed. 'Lightning may not strike the same place twice, but
you never know. It's better to be on the safe side,' may be the guiding sentiment.

So, as a general rule, advertising should relate the appeal to an emotion that is
likely to motivate the audience or, better still, since many people respond to a mixture of triggers, to several emotions. Just as people might buy a product because it
is tasty as well as good for them, so they are more likely to become supporters if
the ways they can help are fun as well as worthy.

People who responded to the Wishing Well Appeal felt they were helping to ensure the continuity of an invaluable facility for very sick children. Parents of children
who have been patients understood the difficulties doctors and staff faced working
in outdated conditions and they may have been motivated by feelings of gratitude
to them, but ultimately they value the Hospital for its service to their children and
to other people's. Preserving life and well-being is a primary motivation but it must
be related to the individual if it is to be effective, and the action called for must be
seen as a credible contribution to solving the problem raised by the advertisement.

The headline and picture in a charity advertisement must pull as many people
as possible into reading the body copy. The aim throughout is to stimulate a sympathetic reaction. Your agency will say that the reader should feel uncomfortable
if he does not do what you want him to do. On the other hand, he should feel guilt-
free as well as worthy if he does comply.

Perhaps the main achievement of the Wishing Well Appeal advertising strategy
(including the logo) was to make people want to 'belong' to the cause. The appeal
feels big and important as well as human and emotive. Feeling important is
another primary motivation! Advertising must get attention.

One thing is certain. If advertising does not get the attention of the people to whom it is addressed, it is a complete waste of money. Moreover it must gain attention in a way that is relevant to your message. Near-naked girls sitting on cars will usually get attention but they are unlikely to cause the reader to study copy about the performance of the vehicle. Getting relevant attention is difficult. You need advertising experts, so involve an agency from the start.

Advertising for contributions

Many charity advertisements solicit contributions, but only a minority pay for themselves. This type of advertising is far less effective today than it was 30 years ago. Every £1 invested in those days could pull in as much as £30 in donations. Today the returns are likely to be much lower. However, sometimes it is worth running an advertisement that only breaks even if it supplies you with a live mailing list of people responsive to the cause.

Be experimental. First decide whom you want to talk to and then find out which medium reaches them at least cost. Ask your agency to produce an advertisement and run it in one medium. See if it pays off. If it brings in more than the costs of production and the space, run it in as many suitable publications as you can afford. Make no further use of publications which do not return a profit.

At the same time, ask your agency to try to produce another advertisement that will out-perform the first one. When it comes up with something promising, test it in the publication which produced the best results from the first advertisement. If it does better than the first one, run it in all publications. You can continue this process, seeking better results. Of course, some advertisements will wear out and have to be replaced, but some continue to be effective for years.

As with all forms of advertising you must clearly indicate what you want the audience to do and how to do it. If you want them to telephone a pledge, make sure they have time to note the telephone number and the name of the appeal.

Although televised appeals, such as the ITV Telethon and Children in Need, have raised in excess of £20 million in 24 hours, they do not achieve this purely through spontaneous personal donations. It is the result of at least a year's work by the organizers who ensure in advance that substantial sums will be donated.

WHAT DOES ADVERTISING COST?

The advertising should cost nothing. Each advertisement should bring in more money than it costs. However, this is not always possible. Sometimes it is necessary to use advertising to raise awareness of an appeal so that other activities can bring in the money.

The costs of all media are high and fund-raisers are open to criticism if they use contributions on advertising that does not directly attract contributions. It is advisable to ask somebody with experience of advertising whether your objective is attainable with the funds available before committing any money. Remember, however, that advertising is critical in communicating the 'personality' or image of the appeal. This is the key to ensuring people have confidence that their money will be well used.

If you have a major sponsor who can put up a significant advertising budget, you can sometimes persuade newspapers to contribute space free.

Advertising in cinemas can be cost-effective, particularly if you can persuade the management to allow collections to be made there. CDP produced a script and top director Peter Webb produced a beautiful commercial at no cost to the Appeal. We then approached the Rank Organization and they kindly agreed to show the commercial in selected cinemas.

COMMERCIAL TELEVISION ADVERTISING

In the past, television advertising for charities was not an effective medium for recruiting new donors or raising funds successfully. However, in 1991, the NSPCC was successful in producing commercials which directly raised funds in excess of the media and production costs and recruited many new donors. The NSPCC experience shows that television can be a powerful fund-raising tool and could be used for both regional and national campaigns. In addition to raising money, it also creates powerful images to reinforce awareness of your cause and can help emphasize and support other marketing and fund-raising activities.

It should also be borne in mind that television advertising is subject to rigorous regulation and censorship by the Independent Television Commission through its Code of Advertising Standards and Practice. Under the Code, charities must prove their good faith and comply with requirements for content, tone and style that are mostly intended to avoid giving offence to viewers and other charities. The RSPCA, for example, was thought to be overstepping the limits of 'care and discretion' when it wanted to show a puppy walking into a steel trap. Registered charities are not allowed to politicize anyway and should not be affected by the Code in that respect. So make sure you have approval of the script of the commercial you intend to produce before you shoot, and ensure that the film makers stick to it.

CHOOSING AN ADVERTISING AGENCY

Many agencies are keen to do charity advertising because it affords them an opportunity to produce some outstanding work for a worthwhile purpose. They get a showcase campaign which they can use to impress potential clients. It is cus-tomary for advertisers to talk to a number of agencies before deciding on a short list of, perhaps, three whom they ask to make recommendations. It is a curious aspect of the advertising business that often agencies are prepared to invest time and money in these presentations to potential clients without expecting remuneration. Nevertheless, you can probably get more out of an agency if you do not subject it to this process. Talk to them, listen to their ideas about your appeal and see if they understand you and how you see the appeal developing. Look at their work for other charities and their existing clients. Ask yourself if you can work with them. Talk to them as people with whom you would like to have a long-term connection.

Apart from the ability to get along with one another, the most important things to look for are talent, commitment and enthusiasm. They may offer to work for nothing if the idea of the appeal excites them and they believe you will implement their proposals without unnecessary changes. If they employ very good people, they may not be able to afford to do that but they may be able to persuade their suppliers to reduce production and art costs. They may even be able to get you some free space or time, or a free commercial production. Do not, however, put too much emphasis on free service – it makes it more difficult for you to demand more from them. You may get better work by paying their fee and then encouraging them to do more.

How should you select the agency to approach? Finding a good advertising agency is not as straightforward as it may seem. My list of suggestions follows.

- Take soundings from the senior businessmen recruited to help your appeal.
- Look for a supporter who is an important client of the agency. If you select that agency, he will be able to help you get the best agency team.
- Look for an agency with a good record in appealing to people with similar market profiles to your supporters.
- Ask to meet the team who would be doing the work. It is important that you respect their work and feel able to get on with them.
- Speak to some of their clients – and, possibly, some of their ex-clients.
- Do not be overawed by their expertise. Specify exactly what you are hoping for.

Naturally the chance of the agency providing honorary support for your appeal is enhanced if they are invited to support a client who is chairing or leading the appeal in some way.

Once you have made your choice, work as closely as possible with the creative people in the agency. Make sure they understand exactly how you are running the appeal and the part advertising is to play. Give them a clear and workable brief. Discuss it with them, if possible, to see if they think it is stated in terms which give them an opportunity to produce outstanding advertising.

Do-it-yourself copy checklist

If you find yourself having to write copy for advertisements, brochures, pamphlets and so on, you may find these points helpful.

- Write as if you were writing a letter to somebody you know. Imagine the individual you are addressing and write to him about the importance of the appeal and the difference his involvement will make.
- Short words, short sentences, short paragraphs and plenty of personal references make copy easy to read.
- Speak the truth. Check facts. Do not overestimate or overstate. If you do, the copy will not ring true and the public relations damage can be considerable.
- Initial impact is very important – if you do not get the reader's attention, the advertisement cannot work. It is essential to have a strong attention-getting headline and the right choice of art direction and illustration.
- Avoid impacted language – dense sentences with too much meaning and too few words. Do not use jargon or trendy language.
- An appeal does not get a second bite of the cherry. You must be absolutely clear and explicit in telling the reader how to respond. Do not give him more than one choice. If he is even slightly confused, the moment will pass and he will avoid action.
- Fund-raising advertisements are not about money, they are about needs. If you stress money, you will not get it. Write about the need and relate it to the basic emotional drive of the reader.
- Depending upon the treatment, talk about the solution – where the money will go!

THE WISHING WELL APPEAL

> **Aims**
>
> The Wishing Well Appeal's advertising campaign had three main aims:
> - To raise awareness of the Appeal by telling the whole country that it was happening
> - To enlist help
> - To raise funds

The Wishing Well Appeal chose Collett Dickenson Pearce as its advertising agency because it demonstrated such great enthusiasm for the project from the first encounter. The agency has a unique creative reputation and was not working for a major charity at the time. In the event it gave us its services for nothing and cajoled many suppliers into contributing as well. It would be hard to quantify the value of its contribution because you can not easily price the kind of dedication it brought to the task. The agency team was headed by Vice Chairmen Nigel Clark and John Salmon and Account Manager Sue Holliday. Tony Brignull, copywriter, and Neil Godfrey, Art Director, created the campaign which received so much attention at the start of the public phase of the campaign.

Logo

Before embarking on the campaign, we identified the need for an emotive logo to focus every communication and activity. The development of the teardrop logo began in the Hospital school and playgroup, where the agency asked the children to draw pictures portraying their thoughts on life at Great Ormond Street. One little girl had painted a smiling clown with a large purple hat. The paint from the hat dripped on to his face creating, by accident, a sad purple tear. The smile and the tear captured the emotional essence of the Hospital: the happiness and love which shine through the pain and the tragedy. Neil Godfrey developed this very simple thought. Sue Holliday recalls walking into his room during the process: *Neil is regarded as one of the most gifted, talented and sophisticated art directors in London. Yet here he was on his hands and knees surrounded by children's drawings of a face. Each one had the mouth in a slightly different place and Neil was not going to stop drawing until it was just right! The simplicity of the result belies the sophisticated judgment and hours of creativity behind it.* John Salmon – in conjunction with John Farrell of International Marketing Promotions – added the line 'Help Great Ormond Street Get Better.' It appeared on all our promotions and every kind of publicity material. In the last analysis, the posters were probably one of the most important elements in the campaign. They made the appeal a household name overnight.

Strategy and timing

Collett Dickenson Pearce argued that for three reasons the launch advertising should create a major and immediate impact. There was the scale of the advertising task, the finite nature of the fund-raising period (planned to be over two years but in fact only 15 months) and the need to weave the Appeal into the national consciousness. So the strategy was to go big and go early: big spaces, double-page spreads, posters and cinema. The timetable of the Appeal framed the campaign:

- press – autumn 1987
- posters – early 1988
- cinema – winter 1988.

Copy

The launch advertising copy conveyed the following messages:

- A unique Hospital
- An urgent need
- A massive Appeal
- Many ways to help

The advertisements suggested three ways to give: credit card phoneline, coupon response and bank giro through Midland branches.

Funding

Sponsorship of charity advertisements is excellent corporate PR and should be 'sold' to companies as a matter of mutual advantage. The Wishing Well Appeal received a generous donation of £470,000 from the Midland Bank to fund our campaign. Collett Dickenson Pearce contacted all national newspapers and persuaded them to run one free advertisement for every one paid for by Midland. That gave the Appeal the equivalent of a media spend of nearly £1 million, and Collett Dickenson Pearce concentrated this into two months following the public launch in October 1987. With donated space you need to be opportunistic. Collett Dickenson Pearce asked media owners to give when and where they could. Mills & Allen offered free poster sites in January, February and March, when there is low demand for outdoor advertising.

Campaign effectiveness

The campaign was phased deliberately to allow responses to be handled methodically. It was widely acknowledged that the Wishing Well advertising played an important role in the success of the Appeal, in terms of funds generated in the first few months and of awareness among people of all ages in all parts of the U.K.

CONCLUSION

Advertising promises much, but can deliver disappointingly little if it is not properly planned with the help of experts. It is too important to a national appeal to leave it to chance. That does not mean that the experts should necessarily be allowed to take over completely. The impact of national advertising is such that a member of the charity should be deputed to check copy to ensure that it does not unwittingly breach sensitivities. With that safety net in place, you can have tremendous fun with your campaign – and you may be pleasantly surprised by the contribution it can make.

An appeal should aim to use top creative talent to devise its advertising campaign. The photo above shows the award-winning series of highly emotive advertisements used, in double-page spreads, to communicate the Wishing Well Appeal's message throughout the media. Collett Dickenson Pearce produced these advertisements at no cost to the Appeal.

CHECKLIST

1. Decide what you need. Do you want money, help, to acquire new donors, to build a voluntary task force or to generate legacies? This decision will determine how you should communicate. An advertisement can do only one prime job at a time, so distinguish between the advertisement that raises money immediately and one that changes attitudes or informs.

2. Select your media to target potential sympathetic donors. With U.K. newspapers, it is relatively easy to select and target an audience in respect of its lifestyle, income level and political attitudes.

3. It is unrealistic for a charity spending less than £20,000-30,000 on advertising in the media to expect to be given discounts, but there is no harm in suggesting to the media owner that he could contribute by granting some free time and space.

4. Position in a newspaper or magazine is more important than the size of the advertisement in determining response. A smaller advertisement next to the crossword, where people are at leisure, have already paused and have a pen in hand to fill in the coupon, can be highly effective.

5. A full-page advertisement does not produce twice the response of a half-page. It often produces the reaction that 'if they can afford a big advertisement they don't need the money'. The Wishing Well Appeal carried double-page advertisements, but purely to make an impact for public relations reasons. They were not designed only to generate donations or other types of direct response.

6. Convert need into action. The advertisements must show clearly how the donor can act. Many only create awareness and do not make it easy for the would-be donor or helper to respond.

7. Be sure to code the coupons used in different publications so that you can judge which medium works best.

8. Do not be too clever. Ogilvy-Mather Direct produced a very simple-looking advertisement: 'Help The Aged – Make A Blind Man See £10'. It has generated substantial sums over the years. Speaking of copywriting for charity advertisements, charity advertising doyen Harold Sumption says that achievement produces congratulations, not money. Need produces money and urgency. Advertisements should say 'Do it now and here's why.'

9. Make an offer and make it in the headline: the bulk of the impact is in headline and picture. Another situation where a good picture is worth 1,000 words.

10. Be aware of the Advertising Standards Authority Code, its rules and regulations. Advertisements have been withdrawn at the last minute after all costs have been incurred.

Chapter 20

REGIONAL GROUPS

Setting up and working with regional groups was one of the most exciting and rewarding activities of the Wishing Well Appeal. We were dealing with all types of people, very often motivated by Great Ormond Street parents and ex-nurses, whose feeling for and dedication to the Hospital seemed boundless. We were building an army from scratch to fight a crusade – motivating where necessary, recruiting, training, and then working in unison as each unit became part of the big push towards our goal.

There was no regional structure in place before the Appeal began. This was an advantage, as we could pick ideally suited people who were fresh to the task. The disadvantage was that, because of the immense amount to be achieved in a short period, we had no ready-made structure which we could simply slot into our plans. As what we had to do was to some extent a textbook case, and some readers will find themselves covering the same ground, I shall describe in detail how we went about the regional aspect of the Appeal.

The regional appeal for the Wishing Well involved two separate but related areas of activity. One was supporting the national organizations who were helping us and the other was finding local representation in a particular area. Because they involve very different considerations, I have split them into two chapters. This one deals with regional appeals in general. I discuss national organizations in the next chapter.

STRATEGY

Timing

The lack of a regional network in advance of the Wishing Well Appeal was, to some extent, a self-inflicted difficulty. It was part of our strategy to maintain a black-out on the Appeal until the public launch, so that we could achieve maximum impact at that time. You cannot have it both ways: putting a comprehensive regional organization in place before the launch means that news will leak and the launch will be diluted. It is a calculation, but one in which we found it well worthwhile to sacrifice the ready-made nationwide organization. The people we needed to make that work certainly came forward soon enough after we had gone public! As a result, little work was done in advance to contact would-be local leaders until immediately before the launch, but an immense amount of preparation was undertaken, so that we could move swiftly and decisively once the gun went off.

We had little time and there were few ready-made supporters in the field. Our U.K. Field Manager, Paddy Vincent, was recruited to run the regional campaign only four months before the Appeal went public. He bought a map and pinned on it the Hospital's patient figures for each county. That clearly indicated where we could expect most support. We then had to find the people, persuade them that the cause was worthwhile, and give them a written briefing. We decided to organize our groups county by county unless there was a good reason to do otherwise. There were three main exceptions to this rule. We divided London by borough, and the Lord-Lieutenant of Berkshire asked to have his county split east and west, while his counterpart in Lincoln wanted a north-south division. A most valuable reference book for such an exercise is the *Municipal Handbook*, which gives details of each county's Parliamentary constituencies, councillors, local authority executives, and the police and fire chiefs. In addition, the chief executives and information officers in County and Town Halls were very helpful with names of local celebrities and larger local businesses. We started making approaches in those counties that held the highest numbers of ex-patients, beginning with London and the Home Counties – Bedfordshire, Berkshire, Buckinghamshire, Hampshire, Hertfordshire, Kent, Surrey and Sussex. We also went to the National Society for the Prevention of Cruelty to Children, who, three years earlier, had had a centenary appeal with a similar orientation towards children. They were kind enough to give us their contact list on which they indicated the people they had come across who had a particular flair for this kind of work.

What the NSPCC did with an already existing developed structure for a large ongoing charity was to bring in a small core group at the centre and dedicate it to their one-off centenary appeal. It was their role to support the chairman of the appeal and the Royal President, to coordinate central initiatives and to respond to enquiries. The fund-raising, particularly the regional fund-raising, was organized by the permanent staff of the charity who were given additional resources, temporary help, etc., to enable them to carry out their centenary appeal responsibilities. This avoided setting up a new structure which might have competed with their existing groups.

LEADERSHIP

First you need to have strong leadership at the centre of the appeal. This can come from a high-profile, effective volunteer in the capacity of chairman of a local group or some such title, backed by a suitable staff member. That allows the best of both worlds – the influence of the volunteer to help pinpoint and approach suitable local leadership, backed by the professionalism of a full-time staff member, ideally used to dealing with people at all levels, to implement the strategy. In the Wishing Well Appeal, the central chairman role was filled by Lord Prior, who did a great deal to help us set up our new regional structure.

Additionally, Field Marshal Lord Bramall, Lord Lieutenant of Greater London, played a vital role.

The correct appeal leadership at a local level is just as important. The local chairman is responsible for stirring regional pride and, possibly, competitiveness to raise more funds than the next village, town or county. This is a wellspring of energy that any major appeal has to tap. We did not try to make county compete with county, as their differing sizes and characters would have made this unfair, but regional loyalty sprang up naturally. In the main, it can be a positive factor for an appeal.

The regional chairmen must themselves be enthusiastic or they can hardly be expected to spread enthusiasm around their communities. They are the appeal's ambassadors and so should be able to embody the ethos of the appeal. It helps if they are well known in their communities, for then their enthusiasm will be welcomed, trusted and taken seriously. They should at least know other community leaders, be familiar with the levers of power and influence and be able to deal confidently with the media. We turned to former Great Ormond Street nurses and parents, but also to local MPs, JPs, company chairmen and heads of the local branches of national organizations.

At the Wishing Well Appeal, the Lords-Lieutenant, the Queen's permanent representatives in each county, were one of the keys to setting up the regional network. At the time the Appeal went public, in October 1987, we had only a handful of regional chairmen in place, largely because of the need for secrecy ahead of the launch. It was also much easier to recruit regional chairmen once they could see the impact of the publicity we were generating, and how much easier that would make their job. Three months later we had 27 – numbers continued to grow.

One of our Vice-Presidents was Field Marshal Lord Bramall. He kindly wrote a letter of introduction to his equivalents around the country and to the mayors of the London boroughs. The letter explained what the Appeal was about, that it was in the process of setting up a regional organization covering all the counties of the U.K., how many children in their particular area had been treated at Great Ormond Street and that Lord Bramall would be grateful if the recipient would agree to be our representative. They were all astonishingly helpful. Inevitably, some were unable to come up instantly with a county chairman for the Appeal, but they all offered valuable advice and gave most useful insights into the workings of their county. All these leads had to be followed up immediately by our U.K. Field Manager. While I strongly recommend this as the best starting point for a regional network, it does mean having staff in the field who are the sort of personalities who can generate enthusiasm in others in all walks of life. The appeal's representative must be able to answer most questions off the cuff or know where to get answers within a day or two.

Four people who became regional chairmen initially just telephoned us, inspired by the Appeal publicity. One called soon after the BBC screened the documentary *A Fighting Chance* in December 1987. At the end of that programme, a notice went on the screen saying that Great Ormond Street had launched the Wishing Well Appeal and adding the telephone number. That little plug produced 60,000 calls in the following month. One was from a Canadian who had lived in Britain for 25 years, had a lot of business contacts and was a director of the Football Association. He was clearly the sort of person who could be useful. He lived in

Croydon, South London, so we recruited him to run the Appeal in the London Borough of Croydon. He arranged for a huge cheque for the Appeal to be presented by his local MP, who happened to be the Rt. Hon. Bernard Weatherill, the Speaker of the House of Commons, whose father had been a Great Ormond Street patient. They had a grand ceremony in the very imposing Speaker's Chambers in the Commons, with Bernard Weatherill (now Lord Weatherill) wearing his full regalia, buckled shoes and all.

Structure

At the Wishing Well Appeal we were setting up regional groups for a one-off appeal with no existing groups. It is interesting to compare this with the way the subject was approached by the NSPCC, which already had a regional structure and wanted to set up additional groups to raise funds for its centenary appeal.

The NSPCC called meetings of the existing local volunteers to discuss who should be approached to chair and to sit on the regional centenary committees. Representatives of the existing committees sat on the centenary committees to provide a liaison role. This resulted in some excellent suggestions from local people who knew who was who. It also gave them real 'ownership' of the centenary structure and avoided clashes between existing volunteers with their ongoing appeal target and 'special volunteers' with their one-off centenary target. In the end, the centenary committees achieved their target. Moreover, the ongoing committees raised more than expected from their ongoing activities because they benefited from the publicity attached to the centenary. Liaison between these groups was critical.

At the Wishing Well Appeal, we left it very much to the regional chairmen to decide how they wanted to structure themselves and perform in their own counties. We gave them basic guidelines; some wanted huge committees, others wanted no committees at all. We encouraged them to manage in their own way and to tell us what they needed in support. A good many split their counties into areas and asked us to deal directly with area chairmen. So, in addition to 81 county and borough chairmen, there were another 42 area chairmen with whom we were in touch. There was a constant two-way flow of information. We had to keep a particular eye on progress and, if need be, deal directly with local organizations and voluntary groups in those areas. In the majority of cases we were overwhelmed by the enthusiasm and ingenuity of the regional organization.

It made sense to group counties together in the less populated parts of Scotland and Wales. By the time the Appeal closed, we had failed to get chairmen in place only in three areas. There were other places where we purposely avoided forming local organizations, particularly where there were children's hospitals, to minimize the risk of infringing upon their own fund-raising activities. We also kept clear of Great Ormond Street's sister hospital, Queen Elizabeth, Hackney, in East London. At the outset, each of these institutions received a letter from the Chairman of Great Ormond Street's Board of Governors, advising them that our Appeal was imminent and assuring them that we would avoid setting up Appeal groups near them. Where local organizations spontaneously formed in the vicinity of children's hospitals, we asked them not to mount high-profile events in that area, merely to coordinate and help individual local supporters such as former patients who were volunteering to help us.

It would have been wrong and most unpopular to have tried to inflict financial targets on our groups. Many of the chairmen had not attempted such a task before, and counties vary widely in their population and affluence. However, as I have underlined, all fund-raising should have targets to aim for; how else can fund-raisers know if they have done a good job and how can they share the burden of raising the funds between the various elements of an appeal?

We conducted our own research, area by area, of the local resources and previous appeals to have an idea of what would be possible. We then discussed the situation with the chairmen. In this way, many of the local chairmen officially agreed with Paddy Vincent a target they could attempt. With others, Paddy merely commented that he would be disappointed if they did not raise a particular sum. We believe we handled what might have been a very touchy subject in a sensitive way.

Our regional groups' fund-raising was stimulated when they realized that the funds they raised could be put to specific needs in the redevelopment of Great Ormond Street, such as naming rooms or buying particular pieces of equipment. The London Borough of Bromley raised £200,000 for the Appeal and later gave another £100,000 to equip the area they named. We were happy to reserve an area or an item when we received such a request from a regional group and were amazed at the enormous sums that they then raised. These were the largest gifts with the areas they chose to name:

County	Gift (£'000)	Area named
Essex	857	14 cubicles and 22 beds in general wards
Kent	644	No. 3 Operating Theatre & instrument set
Wiltshire (Thamesdown)	602	No. 4 Operating Theatre
Hertfordshire	592	A Recovery Ward
Hampshire	530	10 beds in Infectious Diseases Ward
Jersey	332	Dermatology Ward & 5 bedrooms

GUIDANCE FROM THE CENTRE

We handled each of the Appeal's regional organizations on a very personal basis, as they were keen not to feel they were under the control of a head office. They wanted personal contact, which meant going round the country to talk to them and reinforce their enthusiasm. They became friends, just like the staff and volunteers in the Appeal Office at Great Ormond Street. We made a point of treating the area chairmen in each county on a par with the county chairmen; they all needed similar guidance and all deserved a similar degree of attention. We wrote to every Member of Parliament, telling them how many ex-patients from Great Ormond Street they represented and who their local Appeal chairman was and asking them to lend support, and sent copies of these letters to the chairmen.

We gave advice and encouragement to local events for the Appeal, a large proportion of which straddled the country. Particularly popular was the idea of raising money by some form of travel from Land's End to John O'Groats. More ambitious projects took regional helpers to the Appalachian Trail in the United States and another plucky pair from London to China by bicycle.

In time, the regional section of the London Appeal Office expanded to embrace a Deputy Field Manager, an administrative assistant and a secretary, so that four people were running the country-wide network of regional organizations, as well as maintaining contact with national organizations. Together with the Field Manager, they travelled constantly and received valuable assistance from volunteers who took care of routine administrative tasks.

Guidance notes for regional chairmen

1 The history of the Hospital.
2 The objectives of the Appeal.
3 The Special Health Authority, the Governors, the Special Trustees and the Appeal Trustees responsible for the Redevelopment Appeal.
4 Central arrangements for handling donations and requests for information.
5 A model local fund-raising organization structure: president, vice-president(s), chairman, treasurer, secretary and press officer.
6 Local bank accounts and arrangements for handling funds received locally.
7 Local contact lists, numbers of local patients, press cuttings, newsletters, sources of volunteers.
8 Nameable areas in the new Hospital building, and equipment required.
9 Model notes for supporters offering to mount Appeal events, with further special events advice available from the central organization.
10 Press publicity guidelines and speech notes. We received considerable voluntary help from the PR agency Daniel J. Edelman, whose regional network assisted in some localities.
11 Guidance on how to deal with support offered by local companies.
12 Covenants.
13 Give As You Earn schemes.
14 Other methods of giving.
15 Advice on fund-raising techniques to avoid.

We gave the regional chairmen basic information to start with, including guidance notes. We produced a stock catalogue for the area chairmen, so that they could obtain basic fund-raising aids: collecting boxes, banners, posters, sashes, rosettes, T-shirts, sweatshirts, ball-point pens and many other items. Regional Committees were given order forms and identifier codes and were supplied direct by Social Service Supplies at Whitton in Essex. Videos and display panels were available on loan from head office.

We sent the regions a fund-raising pack, which included a description of the way the Appeal was organized, a practical guide for grassroots fund-raising activities and how to avoid the obvious pitfalls. It gave guidance on all sorts of matters, including the house style and the logo, the law relating to public collections and lotteries, public liabilities, insurance and VAT, and at the back there was a dossier on how to organize a range of popular fund-raising events.

FINANCIAL CONTROL

It is essential to set up a system to keep an eye on all the money being raised by the regional network of a major appeal. It is advisable to put this machinery in place as part of the preparation for the public phase of an appeal if you are confident that the scale of the campaign will warrant it.

We went to the London Society of Chartered Accountants. It was most helpful and advertised on our behalf for a volunteer who would have the time to look after our regional accounts. Within two days we received a reply from a retired accountant called Reg Samuels, who did a splendid job overseeing regional groups' accounts. Cash flow can be a major problem because local organizations are inclined to sit on funds until they have enough to make a decent-sized cheque. They tend not to realize that the appeal needs the money as it arises, however small the dribs and drabs, either to spend on much-needed items or to put on deposit to earn interest. The point is that considerably more interest can be generated by pooling the funds and investing or depositing them centrally. It is a difficult topic because local groups, understandably, like to maintain control of their own actions and the resulting funds. It has to be explained that pooling the money will be a much more effective way of benefiting the cause. Each regional group needs to appoint an honorary treasurer to keep control of the money. In the case of the Wishing Well Appeal, many of these were branch managers of Midland Bank.

In addition, there should be a comprehensive computer database to record who has donated how much, when and from where. This is a basic means of ensuring that money does not go astray, but it is also a source of morale-boosting information for the regions to tell them how much each of them has raised at any given time. It needs to be set up at an early stage because if an appeal takes off in the way that the Wishing Well did, there is very little opportunity to catch up.

Every donor should receive a letter of receipt, signed by an appropriate appeal representative. The Wishing Well Appeal also had two forms of certificate to be given to people who had accomplished something extraordinary – especially schoolchildren. Irrespective of the size of the donation, this was an effective way of marking exceptional effort on the Appeal's behalf.

As a standard practice, we offered to pay the out-of-pocket expenses of the chairman and secretary of each local Appeal group, but most declined, saying that the costs were part of their contribution to the Appeal.

COMMUNICATIONS

Money received from the regions was only part of the two-way flow. Details of people offering help to the Appeal office, by letter or telephone, were passed on to the relevant local chairman. He then knew what was going on in his area, who was heading in their direction to do things, which local parents were getting in touch and so on. Gradually we were able to direct more and more of these enquiries to the local contact point, rather than trying to do everything from our head office.

Considerable support was available to the regional organization of the Wishing Well Appeal from the London office. We asked the regions to contact us as soon as they wanted a cheque collected by a celebrity of suitable importance to reflect the enormous effort they had put into raising the money. In many cases, Lord Prior, our Appeal Chairman, visited local groups in that capacity. It involved a lot of organizing by the Appeal Office before the local appeals were running sufficiently well to find their own celebrities. Even more time was spent arranging for people from the Hospital to collect cheques. Members of the Appeal Committee, Appeal staff, members of the Hospital staff, doctors and nurses were constantly going out and collecting cheques in all sorts of places. There was a list of volunteers from the Hospital who were prepared to undertake this task. In addition, we were privileged to be able to involve the Prince and Princess of Wales in a few of the major regional events.

We also held three regional conferences during the Appeal, each consisting of a social event and a talk-in. These occasions enabled the Appeal Office to brief the regional chairmen on the latest developments, how much had been raised and how much remained to be done. The conferences gave me more of a chance to get to know the chairmen and ensure that they understood the main policy decisions. It was also an opportunity for the chairmen to ask questions and offer ideas, contributing to the decisions. Above all, it gave the chairmen a sense of belonging to a united movement, being part of a large family in which they were kept fully informed and given a clear view of how their own work fitted into the master plan. The meetings also provided the Appeal Office with the opportunity to show them how highly their efforts were valued.

We asked each regional group to keep the Appeal head office up to date with names and details of their members, and to write quarterly progress reports. Some were better at this than others. The centre sent each regional group the names of the chairmen and secretaries of the other regional groups so that they could liaise if they wished. We also asked for material that could be included in the Appeal Office's monthly news sheet, particularly news of successful fund-raising events which might prompt other counties to emulate them. The news sheet kept them informed of overall progress, policy matters, financial results and forthcoming events. It contained an update on fund-raising methods and developments, backed by a monthly diary of forthcoming events. We also produced a six-monthly newspaper reporting on activities on a broad front.

COORDINATION WITH CENTRAL FUND-RAISING

There has to be coordination between the centre and the regions in any appeal. There is always a problem about who should approach major potential donors and how. The best tactic is to approach as many such donors as possible before the public appeal is launched and, therefore, before the regional cells come into play. Several regional groups will have important companies or individuals in their constituencies. It is essential to brief the relevant chairman or secretary about any contacts already made. The regional group can take account of that if, for example, they make a subsequent approach to the donor to take an advertisement in an event brochure. It is also important to ask the counties whether they have particular links with potential donors who may have been overlooked during the private phase of the appeal. They may be able to help the central organization, or call on it to produce a suitable person to make a high-level approach if they do not have access to such a person themselves. The centre must be told of planned major events to avoid clashes. At all costs, the various parts of the appeal must avoid treading on one anothers' toes. Guidelines should be issued at the outset. Failure to do so carries an unacceptable risk of upsetting supporters.

IMAGINATIVE IDEAS

Our groups came up with many lucrative, funny, imaginative ideas. A few are outlined here:

- Dorset came up with a particularly good idea, which other appeals could adapt. They ordered a large number of candles with the teardrop logo. The plan was that everyone would light a candle and put them in their windows on a given day. The Princess of Wales kindly agreed to light the first candle in Poole General Hospital. This imaginative scheme raised £70,000 in Dorset alone.
- An enormous children's party at the Bell, Aston Clinton, was attended by Frank Bruno, Paul Daniels, the late Roald Dahl and a number of other celebrities. It was organized by our Buckinghamshire regional team and raised £9,000.
- A prestigious piano concert was given by Melvyn Tan in the superb setting of Blenheim Palace.
- An elegant fashion show, held at Woburn Abbey, included wool-clad models leading live sheep along the catwalk. Some of the sheep proved less than model animals!
- A book of Lakeland tales by Cumbrian authors was organized by the Cumbria committee.
- Members of the Jersey Lions Club undertook a cross-Channel boat trip from Jersey to Devon – in a bath.
- A race day was held at Towcester race course on behalf of the Appeal.

CONCLUSION

We could not inform our regions too far in advance of hitting our target. If we had done so, we would not have reached our goal, as Appeal activities would have been wound down and responses would have faded. We announced that we had hit the target after including pledges and gifts. Regional chairmen were invited to a meeting at the Hospital to be advised of the situation and informed that a press conference was to be held the next day. Some were upset that they had taken enormous time and trouble which could have been wasted, setting up events for the following year when the Appeal would be over.

It is not easy to see how that difficulty could have been overcome to everyone's satisfaction. However, many of the future events, where literature had still to be produced, were run to benefit other causes or the ongoing work of Great Ormond Street Hospital.

John Laing, the building group, raised £500,000 for the Wishing Well Appeal and a further £325,000 for other children's hospitals. Of United Biscuits's 30 sites,

---

Lessons

1. The computer system must be suitable for banking, mailing list and management information. If not, the information fed back to the regions is likely to be incomplete and therefore less useful. There have been great advances in computer software since the Wishing Well Appeal ended; we found our system unable to keep regional groups constantly updated on the funds received from their areas. It is important to learn from failures as well as successes.

2. If the Wishing Well Appeal had been able to arrange for all its regional groups to transmit every relevant name and address to the centre, there would have been the most powerful mailing list for the future benefit of the Hospital. Understandably, local groups like to maintain their own contacts during the appeal. Even so, regional lists should be submitted to the centre at the end of the appeal, so that they are not lost to the organization benefiting from the appeal.

3. The regional group structure of the Wishing Well Appeal could not avoid intruding on the territory of other children's hospitals or wards. We did our best to avoid such situations, but ex-nurses, ex-patients and their parents responded spontaneously to the Wishing Well Appeal and could not be told that their contributions were unwelcome simply because they lived near another children's hospital. We tried to develop an arrangement for setting aside a proportion of locally raised money for local hospitals or units. Sadly, this could not be arranged because of legal technicalities. Instead, as the Wishing Well Appeal hit its target early, many events earmarked for it were diverted to local causes and several million pounds were raised in this way.

---

many gave half the money they raised to local children's hospitals or other charities. UB's second Swimathon in 1989 diverted two thirds of its money to Action Research for the Crippled Child and Save the Children. In that year, too, the successor to our tennis event was passed to the British Deaf Association. The Variety Club of Great Britain's rag doll was used for other children's hospitals. And Jim Prior, the Appeal's chairman, used his influence to ensure that GEC – which he also chairs – sent £25,000 each to the Manchester and Birmingham children's hospitals.

In all cases, those recruited to set up and run regional organizations were asked to do so for a one-off appeal but, because Great Ormond Street has a serious need for an ongoing inflow of funds, they were asked to continue supporting the Hospital. Many did so, to the Hospital's continuing benefit.

In my experience, the people involved in the Wishing Well's regional Appeal were among the most dedicated. In many cases, their lives and those of their families were dominated by the demands of the Appeal. Also, our regional appeal centre in London did magnificently in pulling together this flood of money and information throughout the Appeal.

Chapter 21

NATIONAL ORGANIZATIONS

One of the biggest logistical problems in a nationwide appeal is disseminating information to recruit helpers. The marketing strategy can be perfect and awareness raised to the skies, but much will be wasted without suitable conduits to channel individual response. Hence, the networks of national organizations are invaluable channels for an appeal office to use to coordinate activities and keep everyone up to date with the campaign's progress. The most potent resource available to act as this distribution network is the great raft of national organizations, from the armed forces to the Townswomen's Guilds, from the Inner Wheel to the Working Men's Clubs. If they are persuaded that a cause is worth backing, they can mobilize a staggering amount of manpower – at little or no cost to the appeal. Above all, you should target groups who may have some connection with your cause. It was natural for the Wishing Well Appeal to target children's organizations, such as the Scouts, Guides and schools, and they were among the biggest generators of funds.

The Wishing Well Appeal received tremendous support from young people in all guises – youth organizations, cadet forces, Scouts and Guides, the Youth Clubs Associations, the Boy's Brigade and, most particularly, schools. Schools alone raised nearly £1.5 million, and that was only the sum that could be directly identified. The Girls' Brigade raised £35,000, which they presented to a sister from Great Ormond Street at their annual rally at the Royal Albert Hall. We received £180,000 from children who were members of the pre-school network called Tumbletots (all under-5s) and whose activities were sponsored. A number of children came with their parents when the cheque was presented.

HOW TO INVOLVE THEM

We simply approached national organizations at headquarters level. In the main they recommended us and sent the word to their branches and people in the field. Most activities in national organizations are at a regional level. In the Wishing Well Appeal, many set up a series of local appeals rather than have one national appeal throughout their organization. In that sense, the contribution of the national organizations blends seamlessly into the appeal's efforts at regional level (see Chapter 20).

On July 13, 1987, four months before the Wishing Well Appeal was launched publicly, The Prince and Princess of Wales hosted a reception at Kensington Palace for the presidents and heads of all the major service organizations, the Churches, the Rotary organization, Women's Institutes, the Round Table, several youth organizations, the Chief Inspector of Fire Services, and Chief of the Air Staff, the Second Sea Lord and the Adjutant General. A total of 27 organizations were represented. His Royal Highness talked about the Appeal and hoped they would do something for us. We pursued that quickly on an individual basis and maintained a personal link from then on.

We had lists of the heads of such organizations, to whom we wrote whenever we had to send formal communications. We also had a contact list of the working executives whom we knew we could approach more informally. It is vital to have a comprehensive and efficient filing system for names, addresses and telephone numbers that can be constantly updated. For one or two organizations, such as the Trades Union Congress, it was more appropriate to make direct contact with individual units – in that case the different unions. We received considerable help from the unions and their membership. It was often a question of identifying the most suitable person in an organization with whom we could form a working relationship. Among the Forces there was the Editor of *Soldier* magazine, the head of the British Forces Broadcasting Service, the Second Sea Lord's Charity Officer, the Personal Staff Officer to the Chief of the Air Staff, and the Aide-de-Camp to the Adjutant General, and their equivalents in other organizations. We had an extremely good working relationship with all of them, and became firm friends – which has stood the Hospital in good stead ever since.

Many organizations accepted articles from us for publication in their journals and magazines. They could commend the Appeal to their people at the grass roots and let them know the Appeal had a regional set-up with which they could become involved. Many helped the Appeal's local chairmen and local groups. It was the role of the Appeal Office to maintain active links with these organizations through named contacts. We sent them follow-up articles and letters, as well as periodic newsletters from our Chairman, Lord Prior, saying how well they were doing, and acknowledging what they had sent in. At the end we sent them all a 'thank you' letter from Lord Prior.

EXAMPLES

Scouts and Guides

Some of the national organizations made the Wishing Well Appeal their charity of the year and raised colossal sums. The Scouts and Guides wanted to buy a leukaemia ward for us in the new Hospital, for which the price was £500,000. We were delighted when they decided that they would like – unusually – to do this for us as a joint endeavour. They raised £830,000 and put the extra £330,000 into a trust to provide extras required by the ward on an ongoing basis.

To communicate with a wide audience is an expensive operation. One way to minimize this cost is to link up with national organizations, with extensive memberships, and to use their networks to widen the circles of those you approach. Many such bodies rallied round the Wishing Well Appeal, including (above) the WRNS seen presenting a cheque to 'Mr Wishing Well' (photograph: © Crown Copyright 1993/MOD), and (below) the Metropolitan Police, who raised over £300,000 through a variety of activities including fingerprinting the public. (Photograph: Fotocall)

The Police and the Fire Service

The Metropolitan Police decided to make the Wishing Well Appeal their charity of the year, and raised something in the order of £300,000. They thought of many imaginative ideas, such as selling finger printing (not something people usually pay for) and fining people for being late – a ploy that caught me when I was a few minutes behind time for a meeting at Scotland Yard. At that level of fund-raising it is possible to give further encouragement by sending supporters the shopping list of nameable areas. The Metropolitan Police said they would name the ophthalmological department. The London Fire Service, having raised £200,000, will also be naming a unit in the new building.

Forces

We had substantial help from the armed forces, who have been long-standing supporters of Great Ormond Street Hospital – as the Ark Royal Ward testifies. We made initial contact with them through their personnel officers. They were helpful in promoting the Appeal through their own forces. We had an active liaison at the regional level. We directed inquirers to their local docks, barracks or airfield; the British forces in Germany were also extremely helpful. Royal Air Force Gatow, in Berlin, acted as the focus for all the British forces in Berlin and raised £55,000 for us.

When they start moving like that, the different units can stimulate one another. Part of the proceeds of the 1988 Berlin Tattoo went to the Appeal. A Royal Artillery field regiment over there raised £21,000 through a monster raffle. German spectators at that year's Berlin Marathon were amazed to see the Gordon Highlanders taking part in the race wearing kilts, spurred on by a pipe band! At no cost to the Appeal, Katy Lewis, a patient, her ward sister and the comedian Norman Wisdom flew to RAF Gutersloh to cheer on enthusiastic supporters; the Commanding Officer of No. 4 Squadron, Wing Commander Gault, is the brother of the plastic surgeon who was treating Katy.

Paddy Vincent, our U.K. Field Manager, was born in the Falkland Islands and broadcast to the garrison on the BBC radio programme *Calling the Falklands*. He followed that with a letter to the garrison commander which produced an excellent response from the garrison. It also generated substantial support from the islanders themselves.

Back in the U.K., the WRNS made the Appeal their charity of the year. The starting point was a couple of Jingle Bears they had been presented with, which they used as the basis of Operation Jingle Bear (see Chapter 24). Another idea of the WRNS was a sponsored fish shift at Billingsgate market in the City of London at 5.30 one morning. The WRNS were rewarded for their efforts with a slap-up fish breakfast in the market's boardroom.

Clubs and associations

We received help from national benevolent organizations, including the Freemasons, Free Foresters, Buffaloes and Friendly Societies. We asked the regional chairmen to get in touch with them to draw on local loyalties. It would

Involving celebrities in fund-raising events increases the sense of occasion generated. Above, Lulu receives a £40,000 cheque from Debbie Taussig and her pony,
Dougal. Debbie was one of the 220 riders from south London and the south east
who took part in the Wimbledon Village Stables Charity Ride.

have been tempting simply to circulate the headquarters organizations, but we felt that was too impersonal and stood less chance of making an impact.

One exception to this was the Nurses League of Great Ormond Street Hospital. The Chief Nursing Officer wrote to every member of the League and we fed names and addresses to our regional organizers. Their jubilee convention was held near the start of the Appeal, so I took the opportunity to address them then. We handed out slips on which they could write their names and addresses if they wanted to take an active part in the Appeal and received a most encouraging number of responses.

SCHOOLS

The Institute of Charity Fundraising Managers has issued an extremely useful Code of Practice in relation to fund-raising in schools.

ICFM code of practice for fund-raising in schools

1 To use an appeal to offer children a positive opportunity to become involved in helping others.
2 To foster trust and honesty by putting children on their honour to pay sponsorship pledges and to hand over all money collected on behalf of an appeal.
3 To ensure that all talks given to children in connection with an appeal are pitched at the appropriate level and are both educational and non-political.
4 To contact children in or near school premises only with the prior approval of the headteacher or the head's designated representative.

The Institute advises that children should be told not to approach strangers for money: in any case, it is illegal to ask children under 16 to collect from door to door or in any public place. The charity should make every effort to ensure that parents are made aware that children should approach only friends and relatives for sponsorship pledges. The appeal should suggest examples of safe sponsors, and parents should be fully informed of the appeal's plans in relation to their children. The parents of children under 16 must be allowed to decide whether their child should participate in a fund-raising event. Incentives should be kept at a token level, such as badges, but they must go to all participating children. Rewards should not be linked to the sum raised.

Field staff should discuss with the headteacher the appeal's plans for the children, the educational context of any messages to be given to the children and the pattern of the proposed event. All details, including financial arrangements, should be confirmed in writing. There should be close and co-operative, two-way communication between the local appeal organization and each school, culminating in an appropriate message of thanks.

In addition, I recommend that an appeal consider carefully whether a potential fund-raising school and the age range of its pupils are appropriate to the appeal. An appeal on behalf of an AIDS charity, for example, is not suitable for a nursery school's involvement. Beware also of emotional blackmail, especially of under-13s. This is particularly sensitive in appeals on behalf of animals.

The appeal should then decide whether to send all target schools a fund-raising pack or general information accompanying a call for help. The package approach is expensive, but saves schools having to devise their own response. That may make it more attractive to hard-pressed headteachers. Schools are more likely to become involved if the charity provides not just a fund-raising pack, but an educational pack too, so that the children can learn through their involvement. Such a product may be a suitable vehicle for corporate sponsors.

Remember the children's own expenses. Avoid putting too much strain on their pocket money, as this may incur the ill-will of parents placed under pressure to contribute. By the same token, charities should not employ devices which encourage unhealthy habits or which may offend against religious sensibilities.

Our policy was to approach state-run and private schools through their own networks.

State schools

There are just over 100 local education authorities in Britain. Their Directors or Chief Education Officers will provide lists of state schools in their area. If yours is a national appeal, it is worth preparing a standard letter for your regional chairmen to send to their local education authority, together with publicity material. Most of the Wishing Well Appeal Regional Chairmen used the letter; one or two wrote a slightly different version if they knew the Chief Education Officer personally. The important point was that they had a model to work from. They could give it a local flavour, asking the Chief Education Officer to support the efforts in his own region rather than his receiving a more impersonal central request. The Chief Education Officers were extremely helpful.

We tried to form links with individual schools. At Elmgrove, a First School in Harrow, Middlesex, the children raised £1,156 in one term after a seven-year-old girl asked the headmistress if she could speak to the children at assembly. She told them that if they saved their Hula Hoop packets, 1p per packet would be donated to the Wishing Well Appeal. As a result of her initiative, the children crunched their way through enough Hula Hoops to contribute £55.80 to the total. A small group of children came with the headmistress to visit Great Ormond Street Hospital, which assigned them one of the areas to name – a scrub room. There were also the most humbling contributions from poor schools in deprived areas.

Private schools

The Independent Schools Information Service and the Grant-Maintained Schools Trust are good starting points for approaches to the private sector and to schools which have opted out from local authority control. Other key bodies are the Headmasters Conference and the Girls Schools Association, both of which circulated literature about the Wishing Well Appeal to all private schools. We also wrote to the Independent Schools' Association, the Society of Headmasters of Independent Schools and the Independent Association for Preparatory Schools. That gave us strong penetration of private sector schools and stimulated excellent responses. Rugby produced £18,500, Eton raised £17,000, Little Abberley Hall preparatory school in Worcestershire collected £16,000, and Cottesmore School, a prep school in Surrey, produced a further £16,000.

It was quite amazing what these schools achieved, despite their relatively small numbers of children. Some gave in kind. Downside made us their musical charity of the year, Christ's Hospital made their wonderful Dining Hall available to the West Sussex Committee for the West Sussex Wishing Well Ball.

UNIVERSITIES

We left it to the regions to approach their local universities. If the university was going to help the Wishing Well, it was usually in a Rag Week or something similar. Then it was helpful for our local people to be in touch to offer advice or assistance. The idea for the *Chariots of Fire* event (see Chapter 25) was conceived and organized by a mature student at Cambridge University.

CHURCHES

We had invited Britain's principal religious leaders to be Vice Presidents of the Appeal. These included the Archbishop of Canterbury, the Moderator of the General Assembly of the Church of Scotland, the President of the Methodist Conference, the Cardinal Archbishop of Westminster, the Chief Rabbi of the United Hebrew Congregations of the British Commonwealth of Nations and the Director General of the Islamic Cultural Centre and London Central Mosque.

We contacted the General Synod of the Church of England at Church House, Westminster, for assistance regarding the Appeal, but most of the church activity simply took off at the local level, as people naturally turned to their churches. However, the Cardinal Archbishop of Westminster held a Christmas Celebration at Westminster Cathedral. This splendid event, with proceeds to the Appeal, was brought about largely through the involvement of the Rev. Denis Murphy, the Roman Catholic chaplain at Great Ormond Street.

CONCLUSION

National organizations are a marvellous source of energy for a charitable appeal and, on that count alone, should form an important part of any public phase of an appeal. They generate enormous enthusiasm because they draw on a common sense of purpose already existing within an established organization. Once the leadership of a body has decided that a cause is worth supporting, all that goodwill is mobilized. In strictly logistical terms, one of the greatest assets a national organization can offer is its mailing list. This enables a charity to reach large numbers of people personally – including many who may not see your messages in the media. For that reason also, these wonderful bodies facilitate ongoing communication, for it can be possible to contact thousands of potential supporters through one contact point. Such is their kind-heartedness, this is often achieved at no cost to the charity.

Individuals respond to calls for help that come through organizations to which they belong: the request is more personal than if it has been received through a broadcast, a newspaper article or a poster. This is only human, for people find it more satisfying – and, frankly, more fun – to be involved in a group of their fellows. They can be reassured that the cause has been vetted by their organization before they have been asked to help and the whole exercise breathes new life into the association that takes up the appeal.

Since the Wishing Well Appeal ended, the Great Ormond Street Hospital's ongoing fund-raising office has made a point of maintaining contact with as many as possible of the national organizations so that further approaches for additional funds can be made when appropriate. This has been particularly important for those organizations who have paid to name areas in the new building and who, therefore, have a continuing interest in the future of the Hospital.

Chapter 22

INTERNATIONAL APPEALS

There are many international appeals with part of their operations – projects or fund-raising – in Britain. These tend to be formed in Britain and the United States to take advantage of charity legislation. There is no reason why a large-scale appeal for a British-based project should be confined to the United Kingdom. This country accounts for little more than one per cent of the world's total population. Of course, the calculation is not as simple as that; many of the remaining 99 per cent are too poor to consider giving, even to a local charity, let alone one that may be thousands of miles away. Of those who are in a position to consider responding to a British appeal, only a fraction will have sufficient connection or even sympathy with the appeal's aims or beneficiaries to think in terms of positive action. However, of those who are left, there are still many thousands, possibly millions, who have a family link with Britain, or who may know someone who has benefited from the facilities offered by the organization your appeal is assisting. This may include any part of the English-speaking world and we are growing ever closer to people in our fellow member states of the European Community. So it would be remiss not at least to consider whether it is worth mounting an international appeal.

As always, the first step is research: consider the aim of your appeal and what attraction it is likely to have to potential donors abroad and review whether there is sufficient justification to seek funds from overseas. If so, identify potential sources. If these inquiries give grounds for optimism, then an international organization must be formed – at home, as another specialist appeal panel, and in each target country, in accordance with local laws and practice. Generally, there is a reluctance on the part of donors towards charities based in foreign countries. Accordingly, it is usually of benefit to establish a local base through which donations can be channelled.

FEASIBILITY RESEARCH

It is always worth asking yourself at the outset, 'When was the last time I made a donation to an Amsterdam animal shelter/New York hospital/Stockholm cancer research programme/Madrid youth training scheme?' If you cannot remember or have never made such a gift, then be even more rigorous in testing whether your cause is likely to have international appeal.

The principles behind researching an international campaign are the same as for a national or local appeal. You must establish the case for an appeal – if you have not already done so – and express it in a concise, economical statement. Then set yourself clear limits on the time and expense you are willing to devote to this aspect of your appeal. Do not assume that because another hugely successful campaign had an international department, yours should automatically copy.

Research your beneficiary organization's foreign links. Has it had or does it have foreign beneficiaries, such as patients or residents? Have there been foreign employees? Has the organization sent people, equipment or technical advances to overseas countries? Can a case be made for targeting any particular foreign country? A top-down approach is often useful; start by identifying which continents and/or cultures have a link with your cause, then which countries and finally which groups within those countries.

You will soon need help in your selected countries. See whether you have access to an established network, such as alumni associations or former staff, patients or customers. Time spent in reconnaissance at this stage will help you avoid wasting time and money later. It is important to obtain knowledge of the sociological background of each country in which you are interested. Look at the arts, cinema and media. Find out what different age groups are following and doing. Research spending patterns, including the distribution of disposable income and traditions of giving to charity. Is there a pool of suitable volunteers and what sort of recognition or reward, if any, do they expect? Which are the leading non-profit agencies in each country, and what do their reports reveal about style, standards and priorities? Do not be afraid to ask other domestically based charities for this sort of information; they will probably be glad to share it with you. Before you finally decide to go international, invest in a trip to the relevant countries to get a feel for their attitudes towards your appeal. Once there, travel around and consult a wide selection of relevant contacts. If nothing else, you should aim to pick up the names of potential wealthy individuals or corporate donors. If funds do not permit such a trip, recruit someone who knows the country well and draw on his knowledge.

DONOR RESEARCH

You should make a preliminary judgment of which are the precise sections of foreign society on which you expect to be concentrating. This will be modified as your studies progress. Will you be looking only to expatriates? Do your target countries contain potentially sympathetic special interest groups, such as members of an international federation relevant to your cause? Or do you really believe that your cause is so vital to the whole community that you will attract widespread support just by passing the word around?

Sometimes it is helpful to make early contact with the Foreign and Commonwealth Office to engage its assistance and receive advice on diplomatic sensitivities. London's Chatham House (Royal Institute for International Affairs) and the Centre for International Briefing at Farnham in Hampshire are also useful starting points.

Governments

These may be thought of as including United Nations and European Community institutions and overseas government departments which have an interest in your project. All recognized nations have embassies in London and international bodies have offices there. They are worth approaching to see if your appeal might qualify for a grant. Government grants are normally specific to the charity's programme of activities and all applications have to be carefully prepared to ensure there is a correlation between the charity's and the government's objectives. Language barriers and sheer physical distance mean that this process often takes far longer than for the equivalent domestic inquiries. In the case of the European Community, it may be up to four years. It depends how strongly represented and respected your beneficiary organization is, for it is your experts' reputation that earns you a hearing, rather than peer-group influence.

Individuals

As you are approaching wealthy individuals on a global scale, you may encounter breathtaking cases of individual wealth. You must tailor your approach accordingly. A personal gift of £1 million or more is difficult to achieve in the U.K., but is considerably more likely abroad. The donor who knows enough about the U.K. to be interested will tend to be a much bigger donor. Such individuals may want to make more of a splash. The asking process has to be culturally specific. How much you ask for has to be very carefully calculated. You can risk offence more easily by asking for too little than by asking for too much, when at least you will be paying your target the compliment of assuming he is capable of giving a large sum. Approaches must be carefully worked out in advance to avoid giving offence and it is important not to place a ceiling on the potential gift. Otherwise you may provoke the reaction: 'If that is all you require, why are you asking me?'

The lead time is very important because many of these people can become regular donors. However, in some cases it can take two or three years simply to arrange a meeting. It takes planning and understanding by the charity; it is more important to build relationships than to ask for money. The whole process of asking is different.

You have, therefore, to spend significantly more time researching potential overseas donors. That leads to problems of security. Such donors will almost certainly have political or business sensitivities. To be global players, they have to be politically aware.

Another category is those people who, for tax or cultural purposes are treated as being international, but who either are based in the U.K. or spend a lot of their business or recreational time there. Many of these people are to be found on the polo, horse racing, shooting, gambling, arts and cultural circuits. Inquiries should be made of any contact the appeal may have in those circles or, failing that, their central organizations.

A further, obvious category to consider is wealthy expatriates.

Companies

There are two broad groups of companies which you should identify at the outset: foreign companies with U.K. operations or aspirations and the overseas subsidiaries of U.K. companies. There are also foreign companies which may have an interest in your cause. Research is even more important here. It is essential that you avoid embarrassing your charity through an inadvertent connection with a company whose activities are not appropriate to the charity. At the very least, you must understand the nature of the risks to which you may be exposing the appeal.

Blocked funds

Another source of funds concerns what are termed 'blocked funds'. These are funds, usually profits, that companies have declared in countries where the exchange regulations do not allow their currencies to be exported. A number of third world charities have used such funds by obtaining the agreement of the company and the government concerned so that the funds may be spent within the country to do things of interest and of help to the host government.

Trusts

Overseas trusts or foundations can be a useful source – the bigger ones, such as the Carnegie Foundation, the Ford Foundation and the Rockefeller Foundation in the United States, make very generous donations, though in restricted fields. They should be approached in the same way as trusts in the U.K. The Charities Aid Foundation has a very useful international library in its London office, which it allows researchers to use, provided they telephone first.

HOW TO APPROACH

If you are serious about an international appeal, you will need to appoint a full-time paid member of staff to take responsibility for it. He should have a record of constructive relationships within a multinational framework and should be able to speak the language of at least one of your intended target countries. Beware of perpetual international students and those who have worked for ten agencies in as many years.

You should try to obtain the assistance of a native of each country where you wish to make contact – preferably someone who is bilingual. You need resident expertise and relevant legal advice because the situation can change rapidly. You will, in any case, soon need local help to make sense of published material, such as economic reports. You need the best advisers and they should be hired in advance of your planned local launch date to give time to assess how well the person assimilates your messages and instructions. If you have chosen wrongly, you still have time to correct your mistake. There are good firms in the U.K. that can advise, but they tend to go no further than the U.S., Germany and Japan. The Directory for Social Change has books about the tax position in certain countries. Local expertise varies from country to country, but does not come cheap. Such advisers know their value and will charge accordingly, but the right person will almost always be worth it. Make sure that any local staff are paid by and report to you.

Never assume that because some people in a foreign land appear to espouse your cause, they share your agenda despite their different language and culture. The cultural barriers will be different every time. It is imperative to remember that in many countries the legal and historical background of charities is quite different. This applies to those countries in the EC which have centralized systems of civic law, unlike the common law system in the U.K. In these countries, voluntary initiatives are, as it were, tolerated despite infringing the state's prerogative to provide. In the U.K. they are still accepted as a proper sector of a democratic society and operate under the aegis of the state. It is because the state has a role akin to a benevolent patron that it is prepared to forgo certain taxes. Consequently, in the EC, there are differences about the application of VAT to charities (better to call them non-profit making organizations). So it is difficult for charities to unite across Europe, although they can form groups for an identical cause.

Subject to the advice in Chapter 9, keep your foreign organizations as simple as possible, consistent with local legal requirements and the need to secure donations. Try to obtain *de facto* control of the organization, even if you are not permitted to have overt legal control. Minimize committees, which will be harder to keep within bounds when they are at a distance and planted in an alien culture.

Find small groups of busy people who have expertise and professionalism and are unlikely to use your campaign to promote themselves. Give them clear guidelines about what you want achieved within a set time. Keep everything as specific as possible. Your lines of communication must be clear, simple and unambiguous, including your organizational and reporting structure. Even more than in your head office, cut down the scope for misunderstandings, willful or otherwise, by ensuring that everyone knows to whom they are to report and that regular reporting does take place. It must be a two-way flow of information; if you keep your foreign outposts in the dark, you can hardly complain if they lose enthusiasm. Your structures will be partly determined by the most acceptable or popular methods of giving locally. That will decide whether your man on the spot must recruit an army of tin-rattlers or whether a relatively few well-aimed approaches will do the trick for you.

STRATEGY AND STRUCTURE OF THE WISHING WELL APPEAL'S INTERNATIONAL APPEAL

The success of the Wishing Well Appeal in the U.K. was used to argue both for and against setting up an international appeal. To some, success at home seemed to justify going overseas, while others argued that that same success made a wider appeal unnecessary. We had no way of knowing at the outset whether we could sustain the high profile generated by our public launch in the U.K. The balance was tipped in favour of an international appeal by the many links Great Ormond Street already had with hospitals and other institutions abroad and the number of patients who came to the Hospital from abroad, especially the Gulf region.

Research

Our first task was to review the international links of the Hospital and the Institute of Child Health to ensure that they were strong enough to warrant an international appeal. Our International Appeal Chairman, Sir Michael Palliser, says: *I believe feasibility research is crucial. We found at various times during meetings etc. that there was too ready an assumption that quite a lot of people abroad should regard it as a privilege to donate to the Wishing Well Appeal. In practice, I think it is extraordinarily difficult to raise money for a cause of this kind, however worthy, from residents abroad. Hence I explained the need for rigorous testing.*

We decided that we should proceed on the basis of the following facts:

- 7 per cent of children treated at the Hospital are from outside the U.K. Between 1983 and 1988, 5,000 children from over 110 countries were treated there.
- In 1988, 140 doctors and consultants from 40 countries and 219 nurses from 20 countries worked at the Hospital.
- There is a long tradition of teaching doctors and nurses at all levels at the Hospital and the Institute. These include:
    - Postgraduates working for higher degrees or training in one of the numerous paediatric sub-specialities.
    - Trainees attending the courses of the Tropical Child Health Unit, which does vital work in primary healthcare, preventative medicine and education relating to infant nutrition.
    - Research fellows preparing doctoral theses and many senior physicians, surgeons and scientists, who further their knowledge of the specialist medicine and research undertaken at the Hospital and the Institute.
- Many overseas nurses receiving training in children's nursing and the specialist fields of intensive care, oncology and cardiothoracic nursing.

The combined strength of these two important institutions offers the overseas doctor, nurse or student the opportunity to confront illnesses on the wards that they have previously experienced only in theory.

This information was analyzed by country so that none was approached without full justification based on specific facts about the type and numbers of links to Great Ormond Street. Lists were researched which covered international companies with U.K. subsidiaries, American and European charitable foundations, wealthy international individuals with U.K. links, expatriates and British forces overseas. We did not then have the advantage of *The International Giving and Volunteering Survey,* a new (1993) publication from the Charities Aid Foundation, which by providing international comparisons and other information, helps in the formulation of policy and publicity.

Strategy Document

We then produced a strategy document based on the intention to launch the International Appeal several months after the main public launch in the U.K. This would prove that the home country was already doing a great deal to help itself. Also, by staggering the two events, fewer staff would be needed. However, both these assumptions are debatable, as discussed in the conclusion.

Leadership

We were fortunate to recruit as chairman Sir Michael Palliser, a director of Midland Bank and former head of the Foreign and Commonwealth Office. He was brought into the Appeal by Lord Prior, who knew him from their time in government. His deputy on the International Panel was Geoffrey Nichols, who has special knowledge of the Asia Pacific region and was an adviser to Samuel Montagu, Midland Bank's merchant banking subsidiary. There was a planning committee, chaired by Sir Michael. Half the members were Hospital representatives and half were from the Institute. Their role was to provide ammunition or justification for an international appeal – the facts and figures that spelled out the full extent of operational international links, such as numbers of international patients, graduates, advisers sent abroad and so on. They also introduced international contacts who might be helpful in fund-raising.

Many of the medical members of the committee were constantly travelling abroad, where they could act as Appeal 'ambassadors' if they were asked to help with a specific approach. In this way, we hoped to avoid burdening the Appeal with the high cost of foreign travel. I can say, with some pride and perhaps a little regret, that the cost of overseas travel was never a charge I or my staff expended on behalf of the Appeal.

The Management Committee of the International Appeal consisted of representatives from the Hospital, Institute and Appeal Office and an international regional coordinator for each of the following: the Americas, Asia, Australia and the Pacific, Europe, and the Middle East. Poorer areas were not approached. The Melbourne Children's Hospital in Australia, which has many contacts with Great Ormond Street, was in the midst of its own appeal, so we left its patch clear.

Each of the regional coordinators was particularly knowledgeable about his area, having lived there or visited it frequently.

The role of the regional coordinators

1 To review potential fund-raising resources within their area.
2 To liaise with British ambassadors in their region and seek advice as to the best means of finding a chairman for each country.
3 To identify wealthy individuals, foundations, trusts and people willing to help the Appeal.
4 To identify those who might be willing to organize large fund-raising events.

The United States

North America was treated as a special case, as raising money there requires specialized knowledge and expert legal advice is essential. To start with, the terminology is different. A U.S. charity is called an 'exempt organization', colloquially 'a foundation', and it can be in the form of a trust or a corporation. An American solicitor is someone who solicits funds, not a legal adviser, and a fund-raising counsel in the United States gives advice on fund-raising.

In addition, many states have their own practices. Charities are required to register in 31 states. In 13 states, the regulatory agency is the Department of State; in 11, the Attorney General or Department of Justice; in six, the Department of Consumer Affairs; in five, other departments. Twenty states limit the proportion of donated funds that may be appropriated to cover fund-raising costs. In nine states, fund-raisers must disclose how much of what is raised goes to the charity. In 29 states, fund-raisers must be licensed. We appointed a lawyer to help us to set up a foundation. That is the only way charitable donations can be channelled back to the U.K.

Having obtained state registration, the foundation is then required to make a federal application. For a U.S. resident to take an income tax deduction for a charitable contribution, the donor must make the contribution to an entity that has been approved by the Internal Revenue Service as qualifying under Internal Revenue Code Section 501(c)(3).

At the Wishing Well Appeal, once an exempt organization was formed, we planned to commission fund-raising advice on how to approach the Americans: their well-known generosity is so often presumed upon in a variety of tactless ways that we did not want to fall unwittingly into any traps.

The Institute for Charity Fundraising Managers has a sister body in the United States, the National Society of Fund Raising Executives (NSFRE). There is also the American Association of Fund-Raising Counsel Inc. (AAFRC), the membership of which is restricted to firms which provide fund-raising advice to organizations. The NSFRE contact address is included in Appendix 10.

Sir Michael Palliser wrote to 38 U.K. ambassadors asking for help in recruiting outstanding individuals who would lead the Appeal in their countries. The London Appeal Office provided a helpful information pack.

Support provided

1. Guidance notes explaining the strategy for the overall Appeal and International Appeal and giving up-to-date information on each country under these headings, as applicable:
   - Chairman (specification)
   - Background notes
   - Medical connections
   - Historical connection
   - Major potential donors
   - Progress made
   - Events planned
2. Fund-raising materials available – catalogues of stationery, posters, collecting boxes, T-shirts, videos, etc.
3. Progress reports on the Appeal, at home and abroad.
4. Speech notes and audio visuals.

Results

We delayed launching the International Appeal until six months after the U.K. launch to demonstrate that the domestic Appeal was effective. This strategy suffered from the drawback that the very success of the domestic Appeal called into question the need to spend the money required to set up an international organization. Nevertheless, Appeal committees were formed in Cyprus, Malta, Dubai, Gibraltar, Sweden, Spain, Abu Dhabi, Kuwait and Greece, and many unofficial groups raised money throughout the world. The strength of our U.K. public relations drive spilled abroad. The BBC World Service broadcast several programmes on the Appeal and various networks, such as the Diplomatic Service Wives Association (now re-named British Diplomatic Spouses Association), were very active on our behalf via British embassies and the armed forces.

Altogether, the Wishing Well International Appeal raised £1.5 million, including outstanding feats in comparatively small expatriate communities such as Dubai (£100,000) and Abu Dhabi (£77,000).

A reception was held in October 1988 at Kensington Palace, hosted by the Prince and Princess of Wales. When the date was agreed, the intention had been to focus on special plans to boost international fund-raising during 1989. However, by then the Appeal was rapidly approaching its target, so the occasion was used to thank those who had already made a major contribution and to encourage others to donate and help in a less structured way than we had first envisaged.

CONCLUSION

You will see that some of the general advice given at the beginning of this chapter differs from the way we organized the Wishing Well's International Appeal. This is because I have explained the best practice if you wish to set up an appeal with a major international dimension – for which a considerable time span is necessary. In the Wishing Well Appeal, on the other hand, we always knew that the International Appeal would be a minor part of our overall activity. Nevertheless, with hindsight, I would have put greater store on researching potential major international donors to be approached during the private appeal. I would also recommend launching the international public appeal at the same time or soon after the U.K. event. This is because, if your home-based publicity engine is really purring when you go public, it will break international barriers automatically – as ours did.

Chapter 23

TRADING

The very words 'charity trading' are almost a contradiction as current legislation expressly forbids most charities to trade except in furtherance of their primary purpose or when the trade is carried out by the beneficiaries. Trading by a charity may be *ultra-vires* (unlawful) to a charity's purpose and can create legal and financial problems, including liability to direct tax and VAT. Therefore, most of the larger charities that undertake regular trading activity create a separate limited company, wholly owned by themselves, which passes any profits back to the parent charity.

To comply with the law, the trading company should be operated quite independently from the charity and should obtain no beneficial loans from the parent. In other words, it should have no unfair commercial advantage over any other company. Indeed, there is a school of thought which believes that charity trading companies should have to pay a licence fee to the parent charities for the beneficial use of their names and logos. At the very least, there should be some form of agency agreement.

It is important to define 'trading'. The sale of donated goods is not considered a trade. It is, in fact, the conversion of a donation into another form – money. The law allows the occasional sale of goods by charities at events such as county fairs and gymkhanas providing they do not compete with commercial traders and the public is made aware that the profits are to be used for charitable purposes. The key word here is 'occasional' and charities which have regular events, such as dances, have been held to be conducting a trade for taxation purposes.

A charity may sell goods made by its beneficiaries or in furtherance of its primary purpose. Examples include goods made in workshops for the disabled or books sold in a cathedral bookshop. However, the issue becomes confused. A cathedral selling religious books is fulfilling its primary purpose but if it also sells souvenirs and postcards, this may be considered a trade. In this instance, it will probably need to form a separate trading company to conduct this activity legally and tax effectively.

No one should be in any doubt that trading is risky, often requiring substantial investment in stock, premises and distribution. It is a skilled business which should not be lightly undertaken by the amateur. Many charities, excited by the prospect of large profits, have found themselves close to bankruptcy with ware-houses full of unsaleable stock and huge debts incurred through mail order fulfil-ment and brochure printing. An appeal may be able to sell large quantities of T-shirts and logo items but sales can suddenly dry up and any profits will be wiped out by writing off unsold stock. Trading can also be very sporadic either because activity is geared to particular fund-raising events or because of normal seasonal fluctuations. For example, many charities achieve the bulk of their annual turnover during the three months prior to Christmas. Competition is very keen and cash flow and stock problems are inevitable unless you have an all-year-round outlet and a ready market for your goods.

High start-up costs and the long delay before worthwhile returns accrue make many forms of trading inappropriate to a time-limited appeal. If the appeal is linked to an ongoing charity, as the Wishing Well Appeal was to Great Ormond Street, there may be a case for longer-term trading, but great care must be taken not to overestimate the potential or underestimate the costs. The Wishing Well Appeal also had a very effective logo and slogan, a great bonus in getting any trading quickly established.

SETTING UP A TRADING COMPANY

Before setting up a trading company or undertaking any trading activity, a charity must ensure that it has the power either to set up such a company by virtue of a specific power in its constitution or to receive and retain shares in such a company. If the latter is favoured a benefactor can then set up the trading company and give it to the charity so that the charity does not have to invest in the subsidiary itself. In addition to the initial investment, any loans to the subsidiary will have to be made on an arm's length basis. A charity trading company must be legally inde-pendent of the appeal and they must be seen to operate as two separate, distinct entities. Even so, it is essential that the charity should retain effective control. It is also important to remember that while the trading company's liabilities are limited to the value of its assets, it does not necessarily insulate the charity against the risk of something going wrong. A great deal of adverse publicity and damage to the charity's reputation can be caused by an unsuccessful venture. Trading companies act as conduits to channel income raised from appropriate and approved com-mercial activities back into the charity in a tax-efficient manner, but they are vul-nerable to market forces and often do not have the dedicated or professional management of their commercial competitors. It is important to take specialist pro-fessional advice on how to set up, finance, manage and pass profits to the charity from the trading subsidiary.

Taxation

Any trading company is potentially liable for Corporation Tax and VAT if it has sufficient turnover. The Wishing Well Appeal followed the widespread practice whereby the company covenants all its profits to the charity. Each year's profit should be transferred in a tax-effective way, such as by covenant or Gift Aid. It is important that the payment is made before the accounting year-end of the trading subsidiary. Consequently, the payment made is based on an estimate of taxable profits. The company must deduct from each gross annual payment a sum equivalent to income tax at the basic rate and account for this to the Inland Revenue. That sum may then be reclaimed by the charity. For the company, the after-tax cost of covenanted donations is substantially lower than the gross sum received by the charity since the gross sum is allowed as a charge on income for the purposes of computing corporation tax. Hence if the company has properly passed up all its taxable profits, no corporation tax will be payable.

The Charities Commission and the Inland Revenue have expressed increasing concern about charities subsidizing loans to their trading companies, often with insufficient security. This results in a tendency for trading companies to seek external funding or at least retain a part of their profits, say 20 per cent, to fund future activities. No special tax reliefs are available in relation to profits retained by the trading company for the purpose of financing its ongoing business.

Liability for VAT depends on whether the trading company is VAT registered. Registration is mandatory where the company's taxable turnover exceeds a specific limit. If the company operates through a national network of branches which are each genuinely financially independent, then each can be treated separately for VAT registration purposes.

When discussing trading, it is important to realize that the sale of donated goods is zero-rated for VAT, therefore there is no need to charge it. However, the charity can recover all VAT inputs (i.e. charged to it in connection with the sale of donated goods – such as transport costs). Furthermore, since the sale of donated goods is not considered to be trading, these activities can be carried out without forming a subsidiary company.

Any charitable contribution, for whatever purpose, which has a commercial benefit to the donor, potentially attracts VAT. This is why charities use their trading subsidiaries to handle all financial transactions involved with joint promotions, sponsorship, royalties, licensing arrangements and any other commercial partnership deals. This includes special events income which, if it is not from a VAT-exempt event (see Appendix 7), is best passed through the trading subsidiary. The VAT implications should be carefully considered whenever a charity receives income in exchange for providing something – such as free admittance, advertising or publicity. Any such quid pro quo exchange is within the realms of trading with associated tax and charity law implications. Fund-raising methods which are of a commercial nature are discussed in the following chapters.

The subject of taxation as it affects a charity's trading subsidiary is a complicated area. It is essential to seek professional advice before engaging in any type of fund-raising activity of a commercial nature.

TRADING METHODS

Shops

Never contemplate a shop unless the financial projections indicate that it is certain to make a profit. Shops set up as profile raisers or as a service to the community invariably fail, with a subsequent loss of credibility for the charity itself. The necessity for detailed planning and professional management cannot be overstated. An operation should not be initiated unless you have evaluated the subject objectively, including a detailed assessment of the potential profit and loss. It is easy to underestimate likely running costs for services, maintenance, stock, rent of premises and insurance against fire, injury and theft of stock or takings. A 'sensitivity analysis', whereby you add 20 per cent to your estimated costs and take the same percentage from your projected sales, will show whether the project is still viable if you have miscalculated by this amount.

A shop selling only donated goods and making use of low cost or free accommodation and volunteer labour can make notable profits within a year. A shop paying rent, selling new merchandise and paying staff is a very risky proposition and requires professional management and control. It may achieve no more than a 15 per cent pre-tax return on turnover. A donated goods shop can generate 30-70 per cent returns, depending on its cost base.

Merchandise
Be very cautious about ordering large quantities of logo-bearing stock. These products sell only under certain circumstances and once an appeal is over may become a liability. Watch out particularly for dated lines, such as calendars and food, and clothing, of which you might be left with all the unpopular sizes. Even large, successful charities often off-load more than a third of their calendar stock after Christmas, thereby losing much of the initial profit.

Merchandise which is linked to a cause will sell if it is well designed, fashionable and value for money. However, individually designed products require either big production runs or incur high unit costs on low runs. It is easy to hit serious stock problems unless you have a large number of all-year-round outlets.

Competition
A major problem is competition. Competition is more prevalent during the recession as the closure of hundreds of commercial stores has paved the way for charities to open new shops and take advantage of the free or reduced rents offered by local authorities and private landlords. City trading patterns are changing; people are not in a charity shopping mood when they go into town centres – the most successful charity shops are in low rental sites, high traffic local communities. According to a 1992 survey by the Corporate Intelligence Group, there are some 5,500 charity shops in the U.K. and the number is expected to grow by 1,000 in the next three years. Oxfam, which pioneered the trend, has about 850 outlets in the U.K. and another three on the Continent. Many of the original sites are unprofitable, however, and it is important that the charity carefully consider the risk of opening shops. Some charities with loss-making shops are finding that it can be more expensive to close the shop than to continue running it.

Choice of Site
One of the most crucial factors when considering setting up a charity shop is the choice of site.
1. Sites are usually classified Prime, Good secondary, Secondary or Off pitch and rents are set accordingly. However, you may be offered a site at no rent or a reduced rent for a short period.
2. The type of merchandise sold will determine the location. A charity shop or café for instance, can rarely achieve the same turnover per foot as a fashion multiple and cannot usually justify a prime city centre rental.

3. Careful research (socio-economic, demographic, etc.) will identify potential towns, after which a more detailed examination of the target area should be undertaken to identify traffic and pedestrian flow, parking, public transport and other physical factors.

4. 'Footfall' is important and although time consuming, if you want to be thorough, simultaneous counts of the number of people passing different locations should be carried out on key shopping days at a variety of times.

5. A site next to a bus stop, post office, library, or other attraction such as Marks and Spencer can sometimes benefit from the passing trade, but beware. A few yards can cut a footfall from 50 to 5, and pedestrians in a hurry will rarely stop to shop.

6. Close proximity to other charity shops should not worry you unduly. A street full of antique shops is often the best place to locate another, since customers come to these areas looking for antiques. Of course saturation does occur and this is particularly apparent in the charity shop field as a finite supply of donations and volunteers are chased by an increasing number of shops. In these circumstances it becomes even more important to ensure that a shop is professionally presented and fills a niche in the market.

Manpower

It is best to recruit management staff with a commercial or retail background, ideally a local shopkeeper or store manager. It is easy to fall into the trap of attracting a high-powered supermarket executive, but he will probably be unfamiliar with the grassroots problems that arise in a smaller operation. Basic hands-on understanding of cash collection, stock control and presentation of goods are key requirements. A supportive attitude to the charity and a sensitivity to the needs of volunteers and customers are also important, as the shop is very often the only visible sign of the charity and can in itself provide valuable PR.

Charities vary in their policies on recruiting volunteers as sales assistants in their shops. Some charities employ only paid staff; most employ a professional manager who is then responsible for recruiting volunteers; a few rely solely on voluntary help. Increased competition is making the recruitment of volunteers and collection of donations more difficult.

Wishing Well Appeal

At the Wishing Well Appeal it was our original intention to produce a great many promotional, logo-bearing items – more for publicity than for profit, in view of the time limitation. However, the demand grew to such an extent that Great Ormond Street formed The Wishing Well for Great Ormond Street Ltd. as a trading company. All the legal paperwork was handled by Turner Kenneth Brown, honorary solicitors to the Appeal, while advice on financial control and accounts was provided by Arthur Young (now Ernst & Young).

We started what became a very successful shop, eventually taking up to £2,000 a day at the height of the Appeal with customers queuing in Great Ormond Street. We had a good site opposite the Hospital and we were able to provide competent management through a combination of volunteers and staff. We began by selling mostly donated items to help hold down initial costs.

Points to remember

- Christmas cards are always fine sellers
- People generally buy where they perceive quality and exclusivity. Indifferent merchandise will not sell just because it has the appeal logo stamped on it.
- Stock is appreciated more if it is linked in some way to the cause. Museum shops are good at exploiting this. Conversely, it is possible to alienate potential customers by offering them merchandise at odds with the charity's values or aims.

Remember, it is almost inconceivable that a one-off appeal can sensibly sustain a shop unless it is linked to an ongoing charity or the appeal is planned to continue for a minimum of two years.

Mail order

As with charity shops, a mail order operation can take up to two or three years before it generates any revenue. Returns are typically small – 10 per cent of turnover on average – unless you can rely on a large volume of donations. The biggest risks faced are those of stock control and fulfilling orders – particularly with a one-off appeal where there is always the risk of being left with dated and perishable surplus stock once the campaign is finished.

Agencies

Mail order trading can be adapted to a time-limited appeal by sub-contracting to one of the handful of firms which offer this service. The Webb Ivory Group is the best known. The appeal gets a running start and a better chance of making money. In effect, it is buying in the services which it believes will give it the most trouble to operate on its own. These might include making up its own catalogue, or such mechanical elements as warehousing and order processing. Very few charities are big enough to go it alone.

The Charities Act 1992 provides that all dealings with 'commercial participators' must now be conducted in accordance with the terms of a formal agreement. In addition, a general indication has to be given of the proportion of the consideration to be received by commercial participators in all representations they make. Exactly what constitutes a 'commercial participator' for the purposes of the Act and how to comply with this legislation is discussed in Appendix 8 on the Act.

Another option to reduce the start-up costs is to become involved with a syndicated catalogue with one or more other charities. This method results in some loss of control and you need to work with a cause that is compatible with yours. Alternatively, a full syndication is where the agency provides a shared catalogue with other agencies and simply tailors it for the individual charity by inserting a loose leaf cover and order form. This method requires no stock investment from the charity and is suitable for small organizations and short-term or one-off appeals.

In-house operations

If the trading company decides to handle all its operations in-house, it is necessary to make a list of potential buyers from its supporters – perhaps 25,000 names for a start. The products should be constantly modified to achieve the best match with the list. The products are chosen based on different criteria from items sold in the shop since mail order buyers tend to buy things they think they cannot find in shops. In a mailing, the most important factors in descending order are the list, the offer, the copy and the creative approach.

Compiling a catalogue is a task for an experienced professional, who will take from September to July to produce a catalogue for the following Christmas. Spring and summer catalogues typically produce a quarter to a third of the response rates of Christmas catalogues and are invariably unprofitable unless the risk is shared by a number of charities or the mailing (around 50 per cent of the cost) is subsidized in some way.

Buyers

It does not matter how good the creative theme and the product is if you approach the wrong audience. Mail order customers are usually women in the C2, D, E social groupings (with the exception of the Victoria and Albert Museum and the National Trust). Their main predisposition to purchase is a mail order purchasing history. The support of the charity is a secondary reason. The choice of product is, therefore, crucial.

Products

Purchasers will pay a small premium for products, but too big a mark-up for indifferent merchandise will deter support. Paper products, notably Christmas cards, give the best margins. The NSPCC earns about 30 per cent of its trading profits from Christmas cards. Recently the trend has moved away from offering traditional mail order products such as tea towels, mugs, etc., towards more upmarket, quality items, including leather goods, silver pens and glassware, which may have a discreet label saying 'sold in aid of . . .'. Campaigning merchandise can sell, but it depends on the charity's charisma and on product quality. The logo in itself can do very little to enhance sales. An ordinary T-shirt with the logo stamped on it does not become an object of beauty – unless the logo is a pleasing decorative motif. The World Wide Fund for Nature panda is a good example.

When sending out catalogues, it is important to code the order forms distributed to different segments of the buyer file; this provides valuable test marketing information. It is also worthwhile preparing several versions of the covering letter to make it more relevant and personal – the NSPCC, for example, has 20 versions.

CONCLUSION

Much of this chapter may appear negative and, indeed, the advice must be 'If in doubt, don't.' Many trading managers and staff work tirelessly, investing hundreds of thousands of pounds to end up with a 10-15 per cent return on capital at best. A 10 per cent downturn in the market can throw the whole operation into a loss-making concern.

Many ailing trading companies are propped up by the parent charity, and this practice is coming under increasing scrutiny from the Charity Commissioners (and the Inland Revenue since it is seen to be expenditure not in fulfilment of the charitable objectives). The big operators are as professional as any high street retailer and have long-term property portfolios as well as large and valuable mailing lists and substantial trading profits, but these have been developed over many years and the investment has been enormous.

I strongly recommend that you obtain professional advice. Make sure you talk to a trading professional since the techniques are very different from those used by general fund-raisers. If in doubt, share the risk. It is far better to take a small but secure commission than to be caught with a warehouse of useless stock.

Chapter 24

COMMERCIAL PARTNERSHIPS

Commercial partnerships are business transactions in which a charity and a company become partners (but not in the strict legal sense of the word) and both make a contribution to the deal.

This chapter covers a range of possible commercial partnerships: joint promotions, character or logo licensing, sponsorship, affinity cards and charity links with financial products or services – affinity marketing. These arrangements have held up better than company donations during the recession because companies benefit financially from the partnerships.

MORAL AND ETHICAL GUIDELINES

Before attempting to develop any commercial partnerships it is essential that your charity trustees produce a policy paper which clarifies the sort of associations they are and are not prepared to condone. This is a highly sensitive subject which, if not properly conceived, can lead to embarrassing and damaging consequences. The Board of Governors at Great Ormond Street Hospital issued such a paper, but every agreement still had to be cleared by the Hospital's General Manager before it was signed. He, in turn, consulted his colleagues if there was any doubt. This ensured that the Hospital was happy to be associated with the product or service and found acceptable any other conditions that had been requested.

BRAND DEVELOPMENT

Different rules apply to running commercial partnerships in one-off appeals from ongoing charitable activities. The one-off appeal has certain advantages: it can be big news. On the other hand, an ongoing charity often has a ready-made regional network and a long-established database of supporters, which can be very useful to a business partner. Either way, charities should be more marketing conscious. They should think about their cause as a brand as well as a cause. A brand needs building, projecting, protecting, supporting and sustaining. All that requires planning.

Legal advice will be required on trade mark protection and copyright owner-ship and protection (see Chapter 8). In addition, a clear set of instructions should be produced for the company on exactly how the name and logo can be used, and which trade mark or copyright claims should accompany the logo. The Wishing Well Appeal was lucky enough to secure the free services of Turner Kenneth Brown, a City of London law firm with expertise in the field of intellectual property.

ADVANCING THE DEAL

All such business arrangements must be handled through a trading company because they are often seen as trading and thereby potentially attract VAT and cor-poration/income tax. Before approaching a potential partner you need to establish clearly your minimum terms of business. In other words, what are you setting out to accomplish and what are you prepared to do and accept in order to achieve these objectives? The establishment of revenue targets should be balanced against other strategic aims and offers of benefits in kind. For example, it may be more beneficial to obtain a database of potential donors as part of your remuneration package. Once you have identified your business parameters, you will be able to negotiate from a position of knowledge and strength, taking all considerations into account.

Your terms of business should differentiate between a licensing agreement and an agreement for the promotional use of the logo on branded products or other-wise for a short period of time to meet specific objectives. This is often in return for a fee or against an amount based on consumer participation, as opposed to the true licence which gives the charity an amount on every product using the logo sold.

It is also important to draw up a standard contract. The Charities Act 1992 has relevance to all parts of the contract because of the requirement that all agreements between commercial participators and charities must satisfy the prescribed requirements. Consult your solicitors. At the very least, a standard contract should cover the factors summarized here under five sub-headings.

Definitions
Granting of the licence – what name and logo?
Duration of the contract
Territory covered – U.K., overseas?
Relationship mechanics – e.g. on what products will the logo be placed? At what price will the product be sold?
Method of distribution or promotion
Include wording to ensure the agreement does not create a partnership, in the strict legal sense

Financial terms
Minimum guaranteed return
Royalty amount and payment on account by way of advance
Basis of royalty calculation
Request for sales statement (if contract is royalty based)

Obligations
Company – accounts open to inspection; non-assignment of contract; developing and implementing the marketing plan; producing promotional literature; organizing press conferences, etc.
Charity – use of name and logo; possibly some PR; informing the membership of the commercial relationship, etc.

Control
Product and publicity approval – all aspects of quality control should be governed by the charity

Termination
Under what circumstances can the contract be terminated
Variation clause – stipulation that the contract can be changed should there be a change in the law

The advantage of a standard legal agreement, with sufficient flexibility to be used for all commercial activities, is that one or two members of staff can be trained to use it, so that going to solicitors is necessary only for exceptional purposes. Legal fees can mount up.

The operational procedures will be derived from the legal contract. I recommend that you draw up a detailed schedule which sets out clearly who does what and when – a critical path analysis – in order that both parties adhere to what they have agreed contractually. In all too many cases, confusion arises from a lack of clarity. It is, therefore, essential to include this checklist, constantly updated, at the front of your operations file.

Finally the most frequent mistake is to leave too little time to plan the strategy and get drawn into the operational phase too soon. It may be, of course, that appeal funds are urgently needed, but there is a technical dimension to joint promotions which can best be provided by advisers.

JOINT PROMOTIONS

A joint promotion is a business arrangement in which a charity associates its good name with a company's service or product in return for a financial payment – and publicity. The company, using its promotions budget (not its charitable budget), pays for this association to benefit the cause. At the same time, the link fosters a positive, caring image for the company. Joint promotions can be of immense value to both sides, assuming cause and company fit well. The charity can receive a large agreed sum and the joint promotion provides yet another way of reminding the

---

Key criteria for companies

- whether the promotions provide a positive association with the brand
- whether they have a positive impact on trade customers, such as major retailers
- whether they build positive associations with the consumer to improve loyalty to the brand
- whether they help to sell more product

Illustrations which accentuate a charitable project's history and prestige enhance the case for an appeal. The Hospital for Sick Children was founded in London's Great Ormond Street by Dr. Charles West in 1852. The above photograph shows the 1875 version of the hospital, which had 120 beds and a Chapel. Its foundation stone was laid by the Princess of Wales.

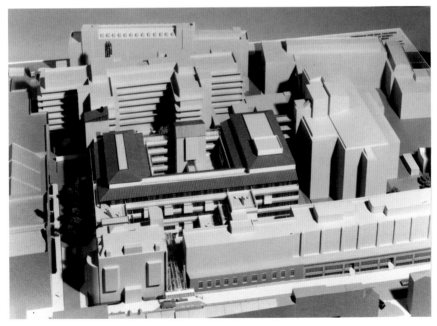

When raising funds for a building, an artist's impression or, better still, a model is needed to show to potential donors. Above is a model of the new, state-of-the-art building (with dark grey roof) funded by the Wishing Well Appeal. The building will provide a technologically-advanced environment, geared to modern paediatric medicine and care. (Thorp Modelmakers)

National organizations (with large memberships) can raise enormous sums for charity. Using their networks can also spread the message at minimum cost. The Forest Hill Green Watch (above) pulled a vintage fire engine from Sydenham Children's Hospital to Great Ormond Street, sharing the £3,000 proceeds between the two hospitals. Below, the Scouts and Cubs took part in the 'Leg Stretch' (to walk, trot, hop, run or go three-legged round a circular course) in Coram's Fields with Mr. Wimpy and staff from Great Ormond Street Hospital's Oncology Department. (Photograph: Mike Gooderson)

Occasionally, very special visits - perhaps by a charity's Royal Patron or the Prime Minister - can be used to benefit two separate fund-raising events, if carefully orchestrated. The above shows the tennis world's superstars playing an exhibition tennis match, for the Wishing Well Appeal, at the David Lloyd Slazenger Racquet Centre in the presence of the Princess of Wales. Below, at the same event, the Princess presented the City Challenge Trophy to the winning team from the Mars London Marathon two months before. (Photograph: Keith Waldegrave)

HELP SAVE GT. ORMOND ST. CHILDREN'S HOSPITAL

AN INVITATION FROM
VOLVO

Commercial partnerships with companies raise serious money and profile for charities. This advertisement invited customers to visit Volvo car showrooms. The promotion raised £168,000 for the Wishing Well Appeal. (Photograph: Volvo)

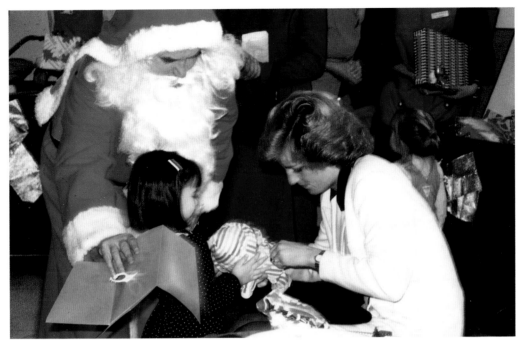

A charity may decide to hold events solely to raise its profile during an appeal. Here are two examples which were televised and achieved front page news in almost every national newspaper. Above, the Princess of Wales, with Father Christmas (alias Jimmy Tarbuck) visited Great Ormond Street children just before the Christmas which followed the Wishing Well Appeal launch. Below, three-year-old Joanne Doerffer bubbled with excitement when Michael Jackson visited the Peter Pan ward in 1988. (Photograph: Reuters News Archives)

There is very little that is new in fund-raising techniques, but imaginative and unusual ideas can give an appeal a special aura which makes it seem different and special. Above, this chestnut two-year-old was named Mr. Wishing Well by a Humberside businessman who was a member of the South Humberside Wishing Well Committee. Below, two windsurfing fanatics attempt to race the ferry crossing the English Channel. They lost the race, due to unhelpful winds, but still raised nearly £5,000 for the Appeal. (Photograph: Colin Booth)

Appeal Office staff and volunteers often work all hours for the cause. Make sure each knows his effort is appreciated. Above, this glamorous, impromptu chorus line was produced by Wishing Well Appeal staff at the Appeal office dinner dance at the end of the Appeal in a venue provided by the Institute of Chartered Accountants. (Photograph: Keith Waldegrave)

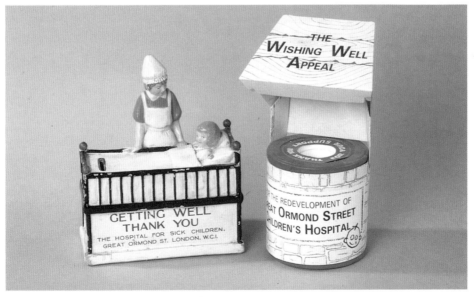

Fund-raising tools can be unusual and eye-catching. Above (left) shows the hard-to-beat collection box produced for the hospital's appeal in the 1930s. On its right is the Wishing Well Appeal's version which appealed to children and any romantic who likes to drop coins into a wishing well.

Remember fund-raising is never an end in itself - and make sure your supporters know that too. Above shows Great Ormond Street's 'place of peace' where parents and staff of all faiths go to find solace at times of trauma. This small, listed chapel was built in 1875. It has been moved as part of the redevelopment to ensure it continues to be an important part of life in the new complex. (Photograph: Ian Bradshaw)

public of its urgent need for funds. Although a joint promotion agreement may not say that the charity vouches for the product, the mere association of its name confers approval. Partners should be chosen with great care.

The partnership marketing activity must work from the commercial partner's point of view. It is more likely to work if the appeal is successful than if it is not, although this is not vital.

Many people think of joint promotions as on-pack offers, where consumers save wrappers or coupons and the manufacturer gives so much to the charity for each one received. That is, in fact, a tiny segment of the total joint promotion opportunity. One of the most exciting things about the Wishing Well Appeal promotional campaign was the number of companies and varied schemes devised to achieve different objectives for the manufacturers, but yet to raise money for Great Ormond Street.

Targeting prospects

Joint promotions can be prompted by a company, agency or charity. If the charity is taking the initiative, it has to look at the possibilities through the eyes of the target company. It is important to pick a company whose customers will be well disposed to the supporters and beneficiaries of the charity. For example, youth clubs affiliated to the charity Youth Clubs U.K. have 700,000 members. To make a good fit, this charity should look for a company that is catering for the teenage market with goods and services like jeans, pop records, or even the first bank account. The charity should ensure that the company has an impeccable reputation and positive prospects. As the charity's good name is its most valuable asset, this must not be put in jeopardy by a damaging association.

Having selected companies where you can see there would be mutual benefit, make sure you research them carefully before making an approach. Are their businesses thriving? Can you find out about the basics of their marketing strategy? Are there links between their hierarchies and yours? Have they been involved with previous charity joint promotions? Even more important, have they had any previous links with your charity?

This information will help you decide how to approach them. If you have developed an especially attractive idea with obvious benefits to a company, you can go straight to the relevant marketing director or brand manager. If you have found a higher level contact to 'help you in', then it is best to ask his advice. To be

---

What can you offer?

- Do you have details of the number and breakdown of your supporters, their socio-economic groupings and geographical spread?
- Have you produced any recent market research findings which give a third-party view of your organization's reputation?
- Are you prepared to let your commercial partners have access to your research, government links and database?
- Would you consider involving your Royal Patron or other notable contacts, celebrity supporters, etc.?

introduced by the Chairman or Managing Director will usually ensure you are heard. On the other hand, such an approach may cause resentment because of the hint of undue pressure. For this reason, each case must be assessed on its own merits.

Having chosen the target company and found out as much as possible about its marketing strategy, you should devise a scheme which would raise money for the charity and promote the company's products or services. There are many ways of doing this. Large charities, such as the World Wide Fund for Nature and the Save the Children Fund, tend to employ staff who are competent to devise and run sales promotions. Smaller charities will need to enlist the help of a sales promotions agency whose fees are usually borne by the company.

You may have to give the company a certain exclusivity in some product areas or at particular times. Feel free to negotiate – after all, both sides have something to sell. Careful consideration should be given to the impact this will have on the rest of your programme of joint promotions and fund-raising events.

Some charities will have one or two specific proposals for joint promotions to present to the companies they approach. Others may prefer to have a general discussion to learn more about the company's needs before going away to put together a proposal or two based on a detailed brief. If you are given the choice, the latter is the safer – unless you have already developed a very attractive and relevant idea.

Wishing Well Appeal strategy

It is unusual for a one-off appeal to concentrate much effort on joint promotions, but in the Wishing Well Appeal we knew we had a blue-chip brand to offer and were confident that we could set up a series of joint promotions during the public phase of the Appeal. This approach provided us with an ideal opportunity to promote the new logo for the Appeal and expand the publicity. We had a great deal of top marketing expertise to assist us with our plans, as the Chairman of the Joint Promotions Sub-group of the Marketing Panel was Eric Nicoli, now Chief Executive of United Biscuits (Holdings). He called on the early input of John Farrell, Chief Executive of International Marketing Promotions, the largest sales promotions agency in the U.K., which had been doing a great deal of work with UB.

They helped us to draw up a schedule of companies with whom we would be happy to do business, where there was a good fit in terms of image and target market, and proceeded to put together suitable and imaginative promotions for companies. The companies were then approached at the highest level. Sometimes we undertook a pincer movement: the charity officer concerned with joint promotions or the joint promotions agency spoke to the company's marketing director and a leader of industry made a formal approach to the chairman or chief executive. Depending on the particular situation, an introduction to the chairman was referred to the marketing director.

Once the Appeal achieved its own high profile, it was more a matter of vetting and selecting from the proposals put to us. We knew we would diminish our value to companies if we developed too many joint promotions, so we looked to net in the region of £100,000 for each arrangement, although this figure slipped a little towards the end of the Appeal. Some felt that £100,000 was too high, but looking to this level of funding for a joint promotion automatically sorted the wheat from the chaff and, as the Marketing Panel raised around £5 million – much of it through joint promotions – it seems that our strategy was correct.

Examples

We agonized most over the first joint promotion. It was bound to be special because of the importance of the first slot to the company and the prominence it would achieve for the Appeal. We nearly negotiated a deal worth £500,000 to the charity, but this fell through because the launch date of the product eventually did not coincide with the launch of the Appeal. Nevertheless we found an ideal replacement with Mars Bars.

Mars

Mars was, on the surface, the classic on-pack offer, generating a donation of 5p to the Appeal for every wrapper returned to the company, up to a maximum of £100,000. It was an excellent opportunity to get off the ground because Mars is such a well-publicized brand that it would send all the right messages to the promotional marketplace. Other big companies would want to get involved with the Appeal. Secondly, over 40 million wrappers would come to the public's attention, which would give the Wishing Well Appeal a mass advertising medium. So the value of the Mars link was not just the money stimulated by the return of wrappers, but also the advertising medium that it created for us, so soon after the public launch of the Appeal. It also opened the door for us to engage in conversations with Mars about other forms of joint fund-raising activity. The biggest was the Mars Marathon. Through this original contact we moved on to talking about fundraising through the Marathon, which raised significantly more than £100,000 (see Chapter 26). So there were other strategic issues at work beneath the surface.

Jingle Bear

The Variety Club of Great Britain launched its £3 million fund-raising initiative two days after the start of the Wishing Well public appeal. It started with Debenhams and Allders, the department stores, giving £1 for every bear sold over the Christmas period. The Allders Jingle Bear became a particular success, raising £100,000 by Christmas 1987. The next Christmas he was joined by a glove puppet version; the two raised a total of £250,000. Allders sold the bear for only £9.99 if customers spent £25 at Allders or Arding and Hobbs, their sister store. The WRNS used the puppet promotion as a basis for what they called Operation Jingle Bear. The stores sold out of the puppets within six weeks – and the WRNS raised £25,000. It worked wonders for staff morale because the stores carried colourful Jingle Bear window displays and everyone was happy to be helping a charity. The WRNS brought Liz Robertson, the actress, with them to present the cheque – with the help of a Royal Marine dressed as a Jingle Bear, who abseiled down the side of the Hospital!

Volvo

This was a one-off evening event in Volvo car showrooms around Britain. There were fund-raising events and the company donated 50p for every person who

An effective joint promotion with a company should offer real benefit to the charity, the public and the company concerned. Two Jingle Bears are pictured above with a WRNS representative. This Wish Well Appeal promotion – which involved Debenhams, Allders, the Variety Club and the WRNS – was spread over two years and raised about £300,000 altogether. (Photograph: © Crown Copyright 1993/MOD)

attended, with a view to increasing the numbers of people who visited Volvo dealerships. The company had a press-led activity, with attendant awareness benefits for the Appeal, which picked out the values of the Volvo brand. At that time, it was using a robot figure to emphasize the safety and robustness of the cars. So it had advertisements with the Volvo robot standing with his hand on a little girl's shoulder while she held his hand. It pleasingly united the Volvo strategy of caring and looking after its passengers, manifested in a promotional message about raising money for the Wishing Well Appeal. It showed how a really good joint promotion has more than the immediate short-term benefit: it should also endorse the longer-term brand values of the partner. Volvo hoped to contribute £50,000 to the Appeal when it initiated its programme of events – a magnificent £168,000 was finally raised.

Kodak

This campaign was about putting a smile back on the faces of the children through taking photographs. It was a photographic competition about happy children, designed to put a smile on the face of Great Ormond Street. This linked beautifully with the teardrop logo. Kodak's film processing division donated 50p for every competition entry received. It was an example of recognizing the brand-value association for the end-user as well as a short-term promotional involvement. With the money raised, which totalled £50,000, Kodak named the Theatre X-ray room on the first floor of the Hospital's new building.

The Sun newspaper

Kodak or Volvo's approach would have been wholly inappropriate here. Nevertheless, if the right deal can be negotiated, it is a good idea to have a promotion with a media owner because there is a double benefit from the publicity and the direct fund-raising. So *The Sun* operated a 'Dash for Cash', which harmonized with the newspaper's own distinctive flavour but was completely different from the other joint promotions. Our role was to recognize the newspaper's requirements, which demonstrated the importance of a flexible approach to joint promotions while adhering to the charity's principles. You must not compromise your charity's integrity or cut across its ethical values, but you should try to blend aims with those of the corporate partners.

The Sun ran a competition with Ford cars as prizes. Readers telephoned a special number every day to answer questions and the revenue from those calls was given to the charity. That raised over £330,000.

Crown Paints

This company recognized that just giving customers a warm feeling about supporting a charity might not be enough to move pots of paint off the DIY shop shelves. The company donated 5p for every 10 litres of gloss and undercoat sold during the promotional period, during which £50,000 was raised. Instead of just saying 'we'll donate on the basis of so many labels or lids', they also said 'and for every five or ten labels, we'll give the customer a free Crown Paints holdall.' So the promotion recognized that, if there is something in it for the customer as well as a warm feeling, there is an even more compelling reason to take part.

Wimpy Scouts Legstretch

This was a promotion between the Scout movement and Wimpy International, the fast-food chain, then owned by United Biscuits. All London scouts were invited to Coram's Fields, the playground near Great Ormond Street, to walk, trot, hop, run or go three-legged round a circular course. The entrants signed up sponsors, and at the end they were given a Wimpy bag containing a badge, a voucher for a free Wimpy hamburger, sandwiches and a Coke. The event raised £29,000 towards the Appeal.

Comfort Fabric Conditioner
Another warm association between the brand and the Appeal was an on-bottle promotion, a classic collector scheme. Some 7 million bottles featured a token offer, in which £1 was donated to the Appeal for every 6 tokens returned. £100,000 was raised for the Appeal.

Swimathon
When Swimathon '88 needed a sponsor, International Marketing Promotions identified the Penguin chocolate biscuit brand, as it has connections with swimming and water sports. The target market for Penguin is young children, and it was an opportunity for swimming bath managers to increase the numbers of people using the pools during a quiet time of year. It offered Penguin, which is made by McVitie's (a division of United Biscuits), an opportunity to become involved in a promotional activity which cost £140,000 and raised £689,000. Penguin was the vehicle which carried the publicity through swimming baths and schools, so the children and the rest of the public could take part in the promotion. The event received huge press coverage to the benefit of both the Appeal and United Biscuits, and there was a very positive connection between Penguin, the children and the baths. When you run joint promotions with a public face, often they spin off into activities within the organization. In this case, senior management at United Biscuits ran their own Swimathon, and the staff adopted the Wishing Well Appeal as their charity of the year (see Chapter 28).

Lessons learned

The scale and complexity of the Wishing Well Appeal meant that we were entering new territory in many areas, not least the delicate business of joint promotions linked to a short-term appeal. These are some of the lessons I drew from the experience, with the perspective of hindsight.

1. We wasted time trying to set up too many joint promotions before the launch of the Wishing Well Appeal. The experience taught me that it is best to get policy, strategy and only the first few joint promotions in place before the launch. After the launch, the response will be 100 per cent better – but it does mean taking a nail-biting risk that the appeal may not achieve a sufficiently high profile to have companies knocking on your door. On the other hand, if you sign up a huge clutch of deals and the appeal does not take off, you will be faced with some extremely disgruntled company sales directors.

2. International Marketing Promotions played a special role in guiding and advising the Wishing Well Appeal and developing many lucrative joint promotions. However, we did realize that it would not be possible for them to handle all the joint promotions put to the Appeal because some were developed by compet-

itive sales promotions agencies. In those circumstances. they dealt directly with the Appeal's marketing staff.

3. Take time to vet offers carefully. We nearly had a disaster by linking our name to a lesser-known company's new consumable product. Although we took care to vet both the company and the product, eventually we pulled out because of the unavoidable risks in that market. We decided to treat any future association with new food and drink products very carefully. The sheer volume of law on the subject demonstrates that such products are extremely sensitive to the slightest variations. We had little doubt that the company was capable of monitoring such variations, but felt that it was unwise for a charitable appeal to be sharing in such risks. To protect our good name, we should have had to monitor production on a regular basis. That was enough to make alarm bells ring.

4. The Wishing Well Appeal created a brand marketing culture. We established that we had a brand – the Wishing Well Appeal – and a logo that required a promotional programme, in the same way as Heinz Baked Beans or McVitie's Digestives. We recognized that many companies were looking for a commercial return as well as warm feelings. We encouraged the Hospital to be an active rather than a passive promotional partner. Some charities can be criticized for vanishing as soon as they have the cheque in the bank. They overlook the possibility and desirability of a long-term mutually beneficial relationship. They do not give as much support as they should. We arranged for the Princess of Wales to launch the Swimathon. Most charities have access to some kind of VIP or celebrity, but they do not bring them to promotional activities as often as they might. That is essential for maximum success in reinforcing the strength of the appeal brand.

We also recognized that, if the Appeal was going to be successful, the activities had to be structured with a degree of exclusivity to each commercial sector. We would not run a Rowntree promotion at the same time as a Mars promotion; the companies would not have tolerated a clash. It was all part of being businesslike and, therefore, attracting businesses. As a result, we had over 60 promotional activities in under 18 months.

Licensing is a revenue source, but an appeal has to have something to license. It is unrealistic to assume that it is enough to offer the opportunity for companies to use an obscure hospital or charitable letterhead. A property has to be developed. That is why we adopted the teardrop logo: it had licensing potential, as a small or large graphic, from button badges to 48-sheet posters. It is also important not to overdo licensing. The appeal logo can end up on a whole range of unsuitable or undesirable products which can tarnish the appeal's image. Licensing is not just about royalties; it is also about spreading the message in a wide sense, through constant reminders in connection with good quality products.

LOGO OR CHARACTER LICENSING

Logo licensing entails using the device both as a design and as an endorsement on a range of products. Character licensing, on the other hand, describes the situation whereby a charity has the copyright on a character such as the Mr. Wishing Well character developed for the Wishing Well Appeal. In our case we did not use our associated character to any great extent in order to avoid any confusion with our teardrop logo.

If your appeal has a powerful, attention-catching logo or slogan, it is possible to make an attractive arrangement with a manufacturer, who will put your logo or slogan on some or all of his products. The appeal will negotiate a payment for the use of its logo and will gain greater public awareness from the distribution of products whose saleability has already been established. The appeal must ensure that the labelled products are appropriate to its ethos.

The returns are attractive as long as you vet the companies and products carefully. Also, remember to structure your activities with a degree of exclusivity to each commercial sector. Too many arrangements can diminish the value to both the company and the charity.

In the case of the Wishing Well Appeal, mail order firms GUS and Kayes sold Wishing Well T-shirts by catalogue. Character licensing deals also put the teardrop symbol on mugs, pendants and badges, not to mention on the side of a Matchbox ambulance.

In order to find the right partners you should take all the same steps as detailed in the section on joint promotions. These include handling this activity through a trading company, and drawing up a legally binding agreement which is understood and adhered to by both parties and which can be carefully monitored.

The law on intellectual property licensing is a specialist area and I recommend that you seek professional advice.

SPONSORSHIP

Sponsorship is when the company, or sponsor, puts its name on your product (e.g. an event or brochure). Joint promotions are the other way around – you allow your brand (logo, appeal or charity name) to be associated with their product or service.

Many of the principles relevant to joint promotions apply to company sponsorship deals. The arrangement has to offer real benefits to the company and the charity. The policy document produced by your trustees will apply here, too – identifying companies with which the charity is or is not happy to be associated. In Chapter 25 , I give examples of companies that sponsored some of the Wishing Well Appeal's major events and examine sponsorship in more detail. In the context of dealings with commercial companies, it is worth pointing out that they can

---

Benefits of sponsorship to companies

- wide favourable publicity associated with a generous action for a good cause
- the right event can produce television coverage and a mound of positive press cuttings
- there can be prestigious tickets to offer to valued clients
- the occasion can provide the ideal setting for company entertainment, impressing clients through the role the company has played in the event
- employee morale should be boosted by knowing that their company is seen to play a valuable role in supporting the community.

Character licensing can benefit an appeal even if the charity does not own the particular character. James Driscoll (top), creator of the cartoon series 'The Shoe People', designed three special badges for the Wishing Well Appeal. He launched the Shoe People Badgathon in 1988 on TV-AM and raised over £52,000. (Photograph: © James Driscoll 1993). Another example (below) were some exclusive knitting patterns sporting the Appeal logo, designed and marketed by Wendy Wools. The scheme raised over £50,000.

benefit greatly from sponsorship with charities and, after a good experience, are usually willing to do more in the future. There is a lot at stake for them.

On the negative side, sponsorship is the first area of a charity's activities to suffer in recessionary times. Companies cannot be seen to splash out on entertainment at a time when staff are being asked to take a drop in salary or, worse still, being made redundant.

Sponsorship offers the charity real benefits, too. Major sponsorship is often the deciding factor as to whether a charity will proceed with an event where considerable seed money is required. It usually means that the charity can be sure of making a respectable profit for the activity – always a sensitive point. The sponsorship of a top company may encourage smaller company sponsors to come on board: success breeds success. From the charity's point of view, the greatest prize is to pick or create an event which is either special enough or sufficiently different to attract television coverage. This will almost ensure you get sponsorship at a sufficiently high level. However, it is not easy to receive definite assurances from television companies that they will cover an event. Furthermore, promises may be broken at the last minute if something else grabs their attention. It is advisable to contract with the television company to ensure they guarantee certain coverage; although difficult, it is possible. As usual, the appeal staff must try to please both the sponsoring company and the television station (see Chapter 25).

A company may agree to underwrite all the administrative costs associated with the sponsorship of a charitable event. Provided that the company can demonstrate that the expenditure has been incurred in the ordinary course of business, in the sense of being construed as wholly and exclusively for the purposes of furthering the trade of the organization – if only publicity value – then that expenditure can be offset against tax. The company will also be able to recover VAT from HM Customs and Excise if it is fully taxable for VAT purposes. If, on the other hand, the expenditure was incurred without the possibility of commercial benefit to the organization, then the expenditure would have to be considered as a charitable donation. In this case, the company should make the payment in a tax-effective way, such as by covenant or Gift Aid. The nature of the support may also render the activity non-commercial for the purposes of VAT and so deny the company the opportunity to recover input tax (see Appendix 7).

AFFINITY MARKETING

Affinity group marketing has existed for many years. The process involves the marketing of a product or service by a commercial organization to an identified membership who share a common interest or bond. In other words, they have some affinity so that the product can be tailor-made for their needs. Several charities with large numbers of members have developed such an affinity arrangement, typically with a financial services institution, as a fund-raising method.

Affinity marketing is a mutually beneficial, three-way commercial arrangement between the supplier of the product or service, the buyer or member and the member's umbrella organization/charity. The supplier benefits from the economies of marketing to a well-defined market segment. The member benefits in that the products and services offered are tailor-made, reflecting his hobbies, lifestyle, values, etc. The member organization or charity gains financially in that each time a product is sold; the charity receives an agreed percentage of the price.

Perhaps the best-known practitioner of the concept is the Frizzel Group, the largest privately owned U.K. Insurance Broker. Its products range from personal insurances and banking products to life and financial planning services. It has established affinity arrangements with several charities, including the sale of personal insurance to Royal National Lifeboat Institute supporters. For each insurance product sold, the RNLI receives a contribution equivalent to 2.5 per cent of the amount paid. Similar arrangements exist with the National Trust and RSNC Wildlife Trusts.

When selecting a partner, a charity must ensure that the supplier has a strong track record and that the offer to your donors or members is financially attractive as well as ethically acceptable. Research is crucial to ensure acceptable response levels. It is also essential that you can control the process; this includes drawing up a comprehensive and formal operating agreement. Time and effort are required to develop a successful partnership.

Affinity arrangements can work for smaller charities. As long as you are prepared to undertake detailed research and vetting to confirm the quality and reliability of the supplier you choose, it would be feasible for a small charity to select a local insurance broker or such other appropriate supplier as a partner for this service.

AFFINITY CARDS

Charity affinity cards, which are used like any other credit card, arise from a joint venture between a financial institution, such as a bank or a building society, and a charity. Affinity cards have no particular relevance for a one-off appeal, but may be useful in promoting the wider awareness of the underlying charity to which your cause is related.

Operation

The first charity credit card in the U.K. was issued by the Bank of Scotland in 1987. The beneficiary was the NSPCC. There are now many such arrangements; Great Ormond Street has an affinity card with the Bank of Scotland, set up since the Wishing Well Appeal. The financial deal is much the same in all cases. A small sum, perhaps £5, is paid by the bank to the charity when the card is first taken out by a supporter, and the charity receives 25p or more for every £100 spent through the card.

It is very difficult to persuade people to change credit cards or fill in a complex application form in return for £5 for charity. American experience shows that affinity cards work best where there is a real 'affinity group' – AA members, birdwatchers, perhaps – where related products can be offered to the cardholders.

A development of the affinity card is the lifestyle card, related not to a particular organization but a particular type of user, interested, for example, in health or the environment. Several beneficiaries are involved and the user can choose which of them should benefit from his transactions. In June 1992, the Leeds Permanent Building Society announced that it had paid out £3 million to three charities in the three and a half years since it introduced its lifestyle card.

Although charity credit cards can provide a painless way of soliciting funds, once the user has signed up, the charity is dependent on the users' spending patterns – not easy to predict or rely upon during a recession. You also need to ensure that the activities and policies of your institutional partner do not conflict with your own. Finally, this fund-raising method, which involves the provision of a service, is governed by the Consumer Credit Act and has tax implications, so it is essential that you take professional advice.

CONCLUSION

Some charities resent companies that seek specific benefits through helping the voluntary sector. This negative response seems unrealistic and unlikely to encourage companies to do more. They deserve credit for what they do and, if the

---

CHECKLIST

- Review moral and ethical implications: produce guidelines on the types of companies, products or services with which your charity would or would not be prepared to be associated.
- Allow sufficient time to prepare your campaign and brand carefully before it is marketed. Register the trade mark, if appropriate, and control its use diligently.
- Make sure you have access to sales promotion expertise and good legal and financial advice.
- Always consider the charity/trust law and the direct and indirect tax implications of all agreements with third parties. They are often not immediately apparent, but the consequences of errors can be disastrous.
- Handle all deals through a wholly owned, separate trading company.
- Produce standard terms and conditions of business, a standard legal contract and detailed operating procedures. Train staff to minimize legal costs.
- Select target companies to approach and research their marketing strategies to ensure they fit your charity's aims, its beneficiaries and its supporters.
- Make sure your prospective partners know you realize a joint promotion is a two-way deal, and that there will be considerable support publicity once the appeal is launched.
- Ensure that your partners do not undervalue their association with your cause, and that the contract is carefully scrutinized and negotiated.
- Set up several key promotions, suitably spaced to avoid clashes from a fund-raising or product point of view, for the first phase of your public appeal.
- Try to involve employees of your partners' businesses in adopting your cause as their charity of the year.
- Foster close and mutually beneficial relationships with your business partners to ensure they achieve positive results from their association with your charity and wish to continue the relationship.
- Produce and execute a detailed plan of action.

shareholders can be convinced that charitable involvement makes commercial sense, the company will be free to become further involved in the future.

Equally, given the chance, companies have been known to try to take advantage of the amateurism of charities which do not understand business principles. These companies get away with paying a pittance for the use of the charity's good name. Some companies try to demand the same credit for a joint promotion arrangement as for a no-strings donation. The two transactions are completely different.

Other companies constantly castigate and patronize charities for their lack of professionalism. Yet, when their marketing departments receive proposals for joint promotions, many still pass them on to the charity donations committee, which is not at all appropriate. The charity, in that instance, would have been aiming at the promotions budget, not the charity budget. Such cases indicate continuing confusion and misunderstanding in dealings between companies and charities regarding joint promotions. However, that will fade as companies deal more often with the larger, more businesslike charities and appreciate the growing professionalism of the voluntary movement.

What you can offer

The advantage of a one-off appeal is the massive support publicity it can offer its partners. To be part of that high profile is very attractive to potential commercial partners. One way or the other, you must have a clear idea of what your charity can offer the company before you can make any approach.

Chapter 25

MANAGING SPECIAL EVENTS

Special events have a crucial part to play in the public phase of a successful appeal. They help to beat the drum, bring people running to support the cause, keep the appeal's name in the public eye and allow it to bask in reflected glory. In the public's mind, they give life to the appeal, make it more than just a fund-raising exercise and create opportunities for well-known people to endorse the cause. Special events are the icing on the cake. They can also be a valuable way of rewarding staff and volunteers with an occasion they will remember and enjoy.

However, special events are not always the most effective way to raise money. The cost-to-income ratio is often high and there is a risk of loss. The failure of a special event may leave the organizers with very public egg on their faces. In addition, these projects require a high input of staff time. If this were to be fully costed, many events would barely break even, but with care and attention, it is possible to raise serious money.

Creating and running a special event is a process that thousands of appeal organizers undertake every week, but few know how to structure it to raise substantial sums. That requires professionalism. Before a charity embarks on special events, it is important to have access to expert advice. This may mean recruiting

---

Checklist for special events agencies

- Remember that the buck stops with the charity, not the agency.
- A legally binding contract should be signed, detailing who does what, when, where and how. It should also define 'break points' for the event in order to minimize the risk.
- Beware of people who tell you they have a great event which will cost you nothing.
- Outside agencies fall within the definition of 'Professional Fund-raisers' under the terms of the Charities Act 1992, Part I, and will, thus, be regulated as such. (See Appendix 8.)
- Be sure to take up references with other charities they have worked for.

somebody with suitable experience, as we did in the Wishing Well Appeal when we appointed Jane Waldegrave as our Special Events Manager. It may mean engaging the services of a specialist agency. The agency will still have to be overseen on behalf of the charity by a suitably qualified staff member.

The Wishing Well Appeal had many major events which usually managed to build on the activities of others. They were extremely varied and gave the Appeal glamour. We spaced them to achieve a drip-feed of unusual and imaginative occasions to hit the headlines and remind people that Great Ormond Street was still appealing for funds.

Special events require an immense amount of detailed planning, but they create an aura around an appeal which money alone cannot buy. In view of the complexities, I have included in Appendix 6 a budget sheet example which I hope will be of practical use to future events organizers. The Institute of Charity Fundraising Managers also produces a useful and detailed checklist for events organizers entitled *How to Sleep at Night: Checklist for Events.*

PRINCIPLES

The first principle of a special event is to offer something that people would love to go to. It has little to do with the charity's identity; people do not generally attend a special event because of the cause. The main motivation is the same as for a noncharity occasion. It has to be something they expect will entertain them. That takes flair, imagination and experience. In entertainment there may be nothing new under the sun, but it has to seem unique to prospective ticket buyers.

Experience shows that people like going to events for two main reasons. The first, trivial as it may sound, is the style of the invitation they receive. First impressions count. It must look exciting and suggest that it is part of an occasion that they will look forward to attending – and sharing with friends. That is the second factor: are they going to be with friends? Is it going to be a strain or a social event which they can all look back on with a warm glow – a glow that should also embrace the appeal? So the invitations must be targeted specifically for the event and at the appropriate guests. You may therefore have a very high-class scripted card or merely an eye-catching advertisement in a newspaper.

Flexibility in handling events is a valuable quality because they often take on their own life and may develop in an unexpected direction. When planning a programme of special events, it is a good idea to select a range of activities that will appeal to different age groups and sectors of the population. Think in terms of arranging pop concerts, sports events, fashion shows, social events, racing, ballet, opera, theatre, music, film premieres, private views and art exhibitions. Then the appeal is more likely to involve the whole country – and generate much more publicity.

Special events can also be used very effectively as a new donor recruitment mechanism. If successful, an event enables a charity to obtain names and addresses of and personal introductions to both new and potential supporters. A fund-raiser at a well-known charity followed this approach during a series of special events. At the time, the charity had no potential high-level donors on its donor base. Two years later, when a major Royal event was arranged, tickets were sold out on the basis of the list alone.

For the one-off appeal, special events carry no second chance. An ongoing charity can build on an event year by year. An appeal does not have that luxury; it may have to prepare and organize an event in six months or less. That might sound a long time. Believe me, it is not. However, when we started the Wishing Well's public appeal, we allowed ourselves two years to raise the necessary sum. As a result, we did plan to repeat some of the more successful events in the second year. However, this contingency was obviated by our hitting the target early. Having no second chance puts a high premium on the ability to filter ideas and people to ensure that the right events are chosen and that they are run by the right people. The blessing and curse of a successful appeal is that everyone wants to be part of it. Wonderful as that may sound, it does mean rigorous selection of individuals and cool assessment of the likelihood of making a profit, the prestige the event can confer and its suitability for the charity.

Before settling on a particular location for your event it is necessary to research the strengths of the particular area and venue. If you plan to use a provincial stately home, you need to find out which charities have used that venue in the past, what happened, how successful the event was, etc. Also, what is a suitable event for the locality?

There are many ways of filtering the ideas that come before you. The method some adopt is to keep pouring cold water on every idea until the best comes through. It may not always be what people want to hear, but the best idea comes through at the end – an idea that will stand up to every question. Only when you have a positive response to every question, do you know that you have a special event.

Initial questions about special events

Is the timing right?
Is it the right event?
Are you going to attract the right audience?
Can you sell enough tickets?
Will it raise enough money to warrant the planning time?

Events must be suitable and not conflict with the appeal's image. The next chapter examines the considerations behind events that are good or bad from a fund-raising point of view. Even if the style is right, there is another vital principle: a special event must be capable of raising a minimum net sum with minimum risk. In the Wishing Well Appeal, we set a floor of £100,000 per event. That was a demanding figure, but it helped us to eliminate many possibles and enabled us to concentrate on the real winners. You can spend as much time on an event that raises £10,000 as on one that raises £100,000. All charity fund-raising resources are very limited, so they must be used to their utmost. A £100,000 event is like an elephant – hard to define, but easy to recognize after you have seen one or two. Events with good potential but less scope for generating the required level of income were passed to local groups to develop, for which they received advice from the Appeal office if required.

As a general rule, it is best to insist that events are held 'in aid of' the appeal or charity. Avoid the situation where the charity or appeal is the promoter because if it falls down or there is a scandal, the cause suffers. If the phrase 'in aid of' is used, the cause at least appears to be one step removed. However, if the charity legally undertakes the contracts which set up the event – with venue owners, caterers, artistes, etc. – then it is liable for any losses arising if the event is unsuccessful. In those circumstances, the only way to minimize negative publicity (which cannot be avoided altogether) is to have formed in advance a separate, wholly-owned subsidiary company to run the event.

Avoid funding seed money

Wherever possible, a one-off appeal should avoid putting up seed money to finance special events. Committing funds under these circumstances is extremely risky. In most cases the correct sequence is to conceive the idea, recruit people who are prepared to become involved and draw up a budget of costs and potential income. It is then possible to seek a sponsor to cover the costs. There are exceptions, such as the sudden opportunity which may be so obviously attractive that it is worth taking, even if it means providing seed money. It is important to be doubly guarded; so often these last-minute opportunities can cause incalculable difficulties, largely because the time factor makes it harder to think through the proposed project in a rational manner. The guiding rule is that each event must be very carefully vetted and financially assessed. Count to ten, draw a deep breath and count to ten again!

STRUCTURE

Special Events Panel

A one-off appeal has the advantage and disadvantage of starting with a blank page in forming individual panels. There are rarely people in place already, so the organizers can decide exactly what they want. It is important to have influence, technical skill, experience and know-how for a Special Events Panel. It is possible to set up a separate panel for each major occasion because there will be only a few very large, lucrative events.

The management structure created for a special event has to be tailored to the event's requirements. As a rule, I believe more is achieved by a tightly-knit group or committee. Each member should have a specific task and a view which influences the main decisions. This group may then set up sub-groups to implement particular actions – such as selling advertising space or selling tickets to friends, colleagues and neighbours. Ticket sales may require a very large group which, perhaps, meets only twice: once for members to take their quota of tickets and once for the chairman to thank them for their hard work. Remember, the bigger a committee, the more difficult it can be to reach decisions; all members naturally want their views taken into account with respect and courtesy. A balance has to be struck, the positioning of which largely depends on the nature of the event. If the event requires the sale of more than 10,000 tickets, it is probably worth appointing a professional agency.

Regional initiatives are, of course, a different matter. There, a closely-knit community can easily be covered by an active and energetic committee to make the event a truly communal occasion, drawing on local pride and loyalties. Such emotions may also be brought into play in persuading performers and suppliers to do their very best for the sake of the appeal.

The Wishing Well Appeal had a key group of people who formed the Special Events Panel. It was co-chaired by Michael Samuelson, chairman of Samuelson Lighting, and James Gatward, then Chief Executive of TVS, the independent television franchise holder for the south of England at that time. James gave expert advice on the entertainment industry and how certain events could achieve television exposure. Our Royal Gala in Southampton would not have been nationally networked, but for him. Both co-chairmen had enormous experience in arranging and organizing special events for charity, and a wide range of show business contacts.

The Special Events Panel of the Wishing Well Appeal also included our Special Events Manager and me. Financial advice was provided by Philip Rusted, who was a partner of the accountants Stoy Hayward and organizer of the finances for the Band Aid and Live Aid concerts in the mid-1980s. Indeed, I recruited him after hearing him give a talk on those projects – a point to bear in mind for those who might be wondering how to assemble the necessary expertise for an appeal. James Gatward was supported by Graham Benson, controller of drama, Alan Boyd, director of programmes and Bill Guthrie, director of production, all at TVS Entertainment. So the panel had good all-round skills.

The members of the panel took responsibility for drawing up a Special Events Calendar for the Appeal, underlining the Appeal's credibility, checking the credentials of would-be organizers of the events and reviewing a budget for each event to ensure it raised sufficient funds at an acceptable cost-to-income ratio. They were happy to be involved in every event in some way, giving the Appeal an invaluable management continuity. It was their job to ensure that over £1 million was raised through major special events. To achieve this, they generated ideas and reviewed proposals from external sources to select events which their extensive experience suggested would raise sufficient sums. Their role was to monitor and oversee on behalf of the general appeal, and guarantee that separate groups of people were responsible for running each event.

Celebrity events may be said to need a committee of only three: the celebrity's manager and/or promoter, the owner/manager of the venue and a senior representative of the appeal. For the Foster's Classic tennis evening, the committee comprised the managers of Boris Becker, Ivan Lendl, Henri Leconte and Stefan Edberg, with David Lloyd and Charles Haswell representing the venue and two of us from the Appeal office. It would have been easy to get a large committee together for that event, as it would have given keen tennis fans the opportunity to rub shoulders with their heroes – or, at least, their heroes' managers! We might, indeed, have raised another few thousand pounds by doing that, but the additional cost of running such a committee might have been far greater in management time and other missed opportunities. However, the danger with a small committee is that, sometimes, the members have conflicting interests. This is where a strong chairman is needed. Somebody has to take a lead on decisions. It can be a big-name outsider or a staff member with sufficient clout. The overriding point is that the structure has to be cost effective, which may require very hard decisions. As it was, the Princess of Wales attended the Foster's Classic evening, we raised £161,000 and had two hours' television coverage.

A charity fund-raising event should be managed on a commercial footing at the outset and the organizers should assume that they will pay everybody the going rate. If, on that basis, the event is likely to generate a reasonable profit, costs can then be reduced to make even more money, and other people – performers and/or customers – can be brought in to increase potential revenue. Discounting supplier costs and performance fees should be tackled after making the initial financial assessment. It is no good approaching the event on the basis that if it were run on commercial lines, it would make a loss but because you have a few stars contributing for no fee it should just about make a profit. The chances are that something will cause unexpected costs and the event will make a loss. The presence of star performers may tip the balance for television coverage. They may also entitle you to increase the ticket price. They could bring in a number of other services at a discount or for nothing. These considerations are all valuable, but they should not be used as the sole justification for holding the event.

FINANCIAL VETTING

All costs must be examined before entering into commitments, whether the project has been internally generated or is proposed by an outside agency. Try to have costs underwritten by a sponsor or other supporter. Do not rely on others' calculations, which may be deliberately over-optimistic. At the preliminary stage, it is better to make the most pessimistic assumptions.

Watch out for hidden costs. If a public building is to be used for an event, the local authority or the Department of the Environment may impose charges to cover the costs of cleaners, electricians or security guards. What concessionary arrangements does the venue have and what percentage of the concessionaire monies are the organizers going to give to the appeal? These can cover anything from cash bars to selling T-shirts. There is always scope for negotiations on how much of any revenue the venue keeps and how much you receive. There may be a benevolent fund attached to the building's owner or operating company: film premieres require a contribution to the Cinema and Television Benevolent Fund and many outdoor events are attended by St. John Ambulance who expect (quite rightly) to receive a donation in return to help cover their costs. The request is unlikely to be either objectionable or onerous, but it is a factor to be aware of in advance.

There may also be unexpected staff costs: if the event finishes late, will the appeal have to pay for taxis home? That can diminish the anticipated profit from an event. Advertising is another expense that inexperienced organizers often fail to take into account in their budgeting exercises. Appendix 6 shows the main elements to consider in your budget for each special event.

The speed of developments as an event is mounted can frequently take organizers off guard. Make it a firm rule to document anything agreed verbally and follow any decision with a confirmatory letter to all concerned. This is a protection against people pulling out or changing their minds. Enthusiasm is welcome, but it is not enough to ensure an event's success. Financial control during and immediately after the event is important, too. You have to make sure that you are paying only for the goods and services you have received. It is common to have a sponsorship arrangement in which half the money is paid before and half after the event. In such situations, some event organizers arrive in person to collect the second tranche, to avoid long delays.

It is important to keep track of money due from events, particularly the many local events which may be going on up and down the country. The organizers of the Band Aid appeal had a computer database of all 375 events notified as being held 'in aid of' the charity. The events were followed up to make sure that the money which was supposed to be sent did come through. A minority of people run events supposedly in aid of charities, but do not actually send in the money. If you have been advised of events, big or small, you have to have some sort of administrative control, to know how they are advertising, how they are using the charity's name – and how they propose to give the money to you: by a presentation, simply sending a cheque through the post or other means. Establish this point and, at the same time, commit the event organizers to a deadline for delivery. Make sure that your records are comprehensive and that you ensure such hard working supporters are suitably thanked.

CELEBRITIES

The involvement of celebrities, TV personalities, actors, top sports people and so on is essential to the appeal which aims to hit the headlines. This is all part of the razzmatazz necessary to underline the national importance of an appeal, give a seal of approval and create an impression of fun and excitement. Many celebrities give an enormous amount of their time, with very little thanks, to supporting good causes and rallying supporters, usually at no cost to the charity. It is never easy for a charity to make the initial contact because most celebrities receive so many requests that they develop elaborate filter systems. Charities must find out if any celebrities have been involved with them in the past or if there are any existing links. It is easier to contact celebrities' agents, as they often have the job of fielding such enquiries. Try to make friends with agents who have special celebrities on their books and even to involve them in the appropriate appeal committee. They are then working on your behalf rather than merely prospects to be approached.

It is surprising how few people seem to understand how celebrities should be handled. You might think it obvious that they should be given VIP treatment, but many people are embarrassed to talk to them at events. If stars and their agents know that the charity understands what is required, they are more likely to attend another event organized by that body. At all times, an ambassador from the charity should be at the side of the celebrities, smoothing their way, introducing excited fans and making them feel that their contribution is appreciated. Exactly what they require and how they would like to be treated should be clarified before the event and their programme planned as if they were Royal guests. All facilities, such as transport, refreshments and changing facilities, should be taken care of. If everyone is to be satisfied at the end of the day, care should be given to choosing the right guest for the right event. It would not be wise to invite Placido Domingo to honour the winners of your Swimathon. Young swimmers may not yet have

Some celebrities become closely involved with a charity and help in a wide range of activities besides gracing certain functions. One such champion of the Wishing Well Appeal was television presenter Martyn Lewis (above), seen here receiving a cheque from a young Wellwisher. (Photographer: Keith Waldegrave)

acquired a taste for opera and might insult your celebrity by wondering who he is!

The Wishing Well Appeal Office was asked to support regional groups by helping to attract celebrities to attend events and by asking them to collect cheques on behalf of the Appeal. This proved a serious problem, as cheque collectors were needed all over the country. It was very time-consuming to find a special person to respond to each local effort. Hospital staff voluntarily took this on to begin with but, in the end, we created a series of Cheque Clinics – which were immediately a great success. Instead of finding people to go out to collect the cheques, we invited the fund-raisers to bring their cheques to Great Ormond Street once a fortnight to present them to a celebrity. People like the actors Dennis Waterman and George Cole, and the singer Dame Vera Lynn collected cheques at Great Ormond Street during two-hour sessions. The fund-raisers were delighted, as they went home with a special 'thank you' from a well-known personality. A photograph of the occasion was sent as a memento to the group which had raised the funds. It worked extremely well, except perhaps for one occasion, when we received 60 cheques in one session – which nearly destroyed the system!

EVENT SPONSORSHIP

Sponsorship can be a valuable source of revenue, especially if it underwrites the cost of an event. However, as with commercial partnerships, appeal organizations must realize that they are entering into a business relationship with the sponsor. Both sides are entitled to expect a specific return. The charity will need to establish a wholly-owned trading company through which all sponsorship activities will be handled, reflecting the commercial nature of the relationship. Before drawing up a schedule of events, appeal organizers should contact a selection of company sponsorship managers for advice. This may be at a regional or local level; it is not necessary to go to head offices unless the appeal is intended to go national. Most will not mind giving a little time to discuss common concerns, even if they do not eventually become sponsors. It is an opportunity, particularly for those who are not experienced in this area, to find out what companies like and dislike, what is and is not acceptable and where their priorities lie. They may also be able to provide useful guidance on the policies of other companies in the same industry or locality. Indeed, sponsorship-minded companies may prefer to be associated with certain types of event. If so, it can save a lot of time to adapt their off-the-shelf formula – providing, of course, that it does not cut across any of the appeal's aims and principles.

Initial approaches for sponsorship should be made on the principle that like talks to like. Your appeal panellist should contact the chairman of the potential sponsoring company. Many discussions further down the line will be required to arrive at a mutually satisfactory deal. Many companies have sponsorship agents who seek out opportunities to exploit their products or services. It may be worth speaking to the agent and warming him to your proposal before approaching the company, as the company will often ask the agent's opinion.

If you have not thoroughly researched a potential sponsor, the company's priorities, its fiscal year and promotional budgets, it is unwise to try to bluff. If there is no opportunity to prepare, it is better to go with a blank sheet of paper and be prepared to listen to what is on offer. It is important to discover the company's requirements and priorities.

However, it is a two-way business arrangement. You must be clear in your own mind about what you can deliver, such as television and press coverage, corporate hospitality facilities, celebrity attendance and so on. Once sponsors are confident about this, they will be more likely to be willing to do business with you. They may also be invited to have, say, 50 clients to a special reception with VIP attendance. The next step might be having several corporate sponsors for the event, with a hospitality area, a brochure advertisement and presentation of a representative to a VIP. Never commit yourself to deliver something you cannot guarantee. You should distinguish between soft and hard sponsorship. Soft is the provision of goods and services which effectively reduce the costs of the event. Hard sponsorship is cash in return for exposure through TV or advertising. You cannot promise Royal attendance in return for sponsorship. A decision on Royal attendance is made once the event is seen to stand up in its own right.

Television

Sponsorship is much more easily attracted if an event is to be televised. There is a very good reason for that; television is highly prized but considerably harder to deliver than anything else. It is almost impossible to be sure that an event will be televised until it happens. If a television company has paid to film an event, it is more likely that it will be screened, eventually if not at once. Of course, this applies only to feature treatments; news items are scrapped all the time.

Television is a specialized area that can make a huge difference to a particular event or even the whole appeal. A major effort should be made to recruit a top television executive on to the special events panel. The Wishing Well Appeal received tremendous assistance from James Gatward of TVS, from Martyn Lewis, the BBC TV news presenter, and from Jonathan Dimbleby, the BBC presenter. One of the first considerations is whether to seek television coverage of the whole event, highlights to be shown afterwards or advance promotion. The last is most desirable because of its potential impact on revenue from the event, but it does require the right ingredients in terms of news value or celebrity content.

Television is a very demanding medium which can result in untold publicity. To get your event televised you must be prepared to listen to and most probably accommodate the needs of the producer. The danger is that changing the event to a large extent may ruin it for the live audience who bought expensive tickets. An example, which I attended, was a performance held on an open air stage with television cameras on hydraulic ramps swinging in and out of the audience's vision in a very distracting way. Think carefully about whether television coverage really is appropriate for your event. Perhaps an idea may be to print a disclaimer on the promotional material and ticket, mentioning the fact that the event will televised. However, it seems most people love the idea of being 'on television' and so will usually forgive any inconvenience caused by the cameras. It is up to your PR representative to liaise very closely with the television producer to avoid relinquishing all control.

How to obtain television coverage

The first point of contact for independent television is the relevant network contractor, who may be an independent producer. The award of the new ITV franchises in late 1991 resulted in the emergence of many independent producers. Aim to contact the producer at an early stage in your planning process (at least six months in advance of your event) and try to get him to agree to broadcast it at a particular time. This may be difficult since scheduling underlies the whole process and the producer is contracted to show certain categories of programme within pre-arranged slots several months ahead. Try to target two or more areas for coverage which may be relevant to your event. At the BBC, the best course of action is to approach the editor of the relevant television section – the Sports Editor if you are holding a sporting event, or the Head of Light Entertainment if it is more appropriate for him.

DEALING WITH THE PALACE

Over the years, the Royal Family has developed a series of policies in regard to their many official and regular duties. As part of this, the Palace has a standard procedure which all charities are asked to adopt if they are honoured with the presence of Royalty. This is particularly relevant to the question of their attendance at functions or special events organized by or on behalf of the charity. The purpose is to ensure that all submissions to them are treated fairly and dealt with on an official basis. The Palace staff prefer to deal with one person from an appeal, usually the appeal chairman or director. However, the staff member running or overseeing the event on behalf of the appeal should also have direct contact concerning the necessary detailed arrangements. Care should be taken in selecting the right individual.

While members of the Royal Family accept invitations from charities with which they are unconnected, much of their time is spent with those organizations with which they are linked.

Royal patronage is usually granted to a charity only after it has become well established and is rarely conferred on a one-off appeal. In receiving the support of the Prince and Princess of Wales as Patrons, the Wishing Well Appeal was a fortunate exception. Approaches for patronage should begin at the highest desirable level of the Royal Family. Obviously it is best to approach a member of the Royal Family known to have sympathy with your charity's cause. On the other hand, if you are unsure about this, you can always ask the advice of the Palace Press Office. If the approach is declined, it is acceptable to write to the next member in order of precedence. A Royal Patron will indicate how many events he is prepared to attend to support your appeal in a given time span. The Prince and Princess of Wales agreed to attend two or three Wishing Well Appeal events every six months, which was more than generous. A strict selection system is necessary for any moderately successful national appeal. There is no doubt that Their Royal Highnesses could have been invited to a function almost every day of the 15 months the Wishing Well Appeal lasted. In this situation, the Palace asks charities to ensure that all applications for Royal attendance are routed via your head office, which is asked to prioritize them on behalf of the charity as a whole. At all costs, local groups or branches must be dissuaded from writing directly.

It is important to remember that no event can be submitted to the Palace if holding it is conditional on Royal attendance. It must be capable of being successful and making a profit on its own merits. However, it is recognized that Royal attendance can substantially boost the income and visibility which an event will generate.

The first question is whether an explicit fund-raising event – rather than, say, a visit to those receiving the charity's care – is suitable for a Royal presence. Assuming that the event has sufficient fund-raising potential, it is still difficult to define what is and is not likely to be appropriate. The Royal Family will not attend political events or any occasions which might subject them to embarrassment. The Palace is very receptive to innovative ways for the Royal Family to be presented, as long as they are considered appropriate and suitable.

You should write to the Private Secretary of your chosen member of the Royal Family with a range of types of events and dates where the presence of Royalty would be highly desirable from the charity's point of view. Details should include the duration of the visit, anticipated income and VIP attendance. A selection will be made at the next diary meeting of the relevant member of the Royal Family. Secondly, the event must be of a scale that can take full advantage of a Royal Patron's presence. It would be a waste of time for Royalty to attend a pub darts match – in purely fund-raising terms – because it would be unlikely to have the capacity to take the additional money which would otherwise be forthcoming.

Do not be afraid to cancel an event which a member of the Royal Family has agreed to attend. The Palace would much prefer that to attending a function which is seen to be struggling, for whatever reason. It is always possible that they will agree to a re-arranged date, if it is sufficiently far in advance. Be brave.

If you have not organized a Royal event before, you will receive every assistance and guidance from the Palace. You will be asked to produce a detailed account of the planned occasion, describing the event, its objective, budget and the exact movements concerned, carefully timed and including details of those who will be in attendance and those whom you hope to present. Remember the Palace likes new members of the team to be presented rather than the same old faces. The relevant Equerry or Private Secretary will guide you on these arrangements and, finally, before the event, he will wish to reconnoitre with a small number of people from your charity to make decisions on the spot. During this visit to the venue, he will be accompanied by a protection officer who will be responsible, with the local police, for looking into all matters of security. The Equerry will review the procedure planned for the day, the press facilities, the timing and the number of people to be presented. After this exercise, it is your task to produce a revised schedule.

Rota press

The Royal rota is designed to give all aspects of the media a fair chance to cover a Royal engagement. There is no normal size to the press party and it depends upon the size of venue. The rota is designed to control the numbers of people covering an event. For example, if the Royal visitor is going to look at a new X-ray unit there is little to be gained by giving access to a large media party in an area that will accommodate a total of ten people. While every endeavour is made to maximize coverage, it has been found that big is not necessarily beautiful. Composition is of paramount importance. In an ideal situation the print and electronic media, which includes radio, will be accommodated side by side.

While rota passes are issued by the Buckingham Palace Press Office, it is the responsibility of the respective media organizations to undertake the distribution, by 'rotation' to the media they represent. Allowance in the rota party is made for a host or house photographer or video cameraman. While press positions are fixed and agreed in advance, the host is allowed slightly more freedom of movement.

I have received a great deal of help and many imaginative suggestions from discussing events with Palace staff when plans were still at the formative stage. It was the idea of the Prince and Princess of Wales's office to have a satellite link between Great Ormond Street and Highgrove, their Gloucestershire residence, at the press conference marking the start of the Wishing Well Appeal. Consequently, the Prince of Wales was able to launch our Appeal. This was the first time such a link had been used by a member of the Royal Family and it helped to give the Appeal immediate media impact.

LEGAL FACTORS

You need to be aware of various legal issues when organizing certain types of event. I have summarized below some of these in relation to the more popular activities, but I recommend you refer to the specialist books listed in the Bibliography or seek professional advice as part of your planning process.

Bars

You may not sell alcohol without a licence, but the Licensing (Occasional Permissions) Act 1983 allows the licensing justices to grant permission for eligible organizations to do so for not longer than 24 hours, not more than four times in any 12-month period. The application has to be in the name of an officer of the appeal. A form can be obtained from the clerk to the licensing justices. 'Eligible organizations' refers to any organization not carried on for purposes of private gain, although they can be trading companies whose profits are passed to a charity by covenant or Gift Aid. Allow plenty of time. Licensing sessions are heard at varying times, depending on the locality. Your proposed premises must be suitable and not likely to disturb nearby residents. However, if you leave it too late, there is another possibility. You can ask a local licence holder to obtain an occasional licence at as little as 24 hours' notice. He may or may not donate the profits to your appeal, but even if he does not, you will still have a more inviting proposition to attract people to your function.

Entertainment

As with the sale of alcohol, it is illegal to invite the public to an entertainment without first obtaining a licence. Also, if you are going to arrange a performance of an artistic work, you may have to consider the question of copyright.

Plays

The Theatres Act 1968 requires the promoter of a public performance of a play to obtain a licence from the Common Council of the City of London, the relevant London borough council, or a district council outside London. Such licences permit the sale of intoxicating liquor without a justices' licence, providing the clerk of the licensing justices is informed. However, some local authorities will grant the theatre licence only on condition that alcohol is not sold. It is an offence to present a play which is considered to be obscene, likely to foment racial hatred or provoke a breach of the peace.

Music and dancing

A licence is required for music or dancing, whether the public takes part or merely watches. However, if the music or dancing is part of a play, the theatre licence will suffice. The law in London differs from the rest of the U.K., so you should refer as early as possible to your local authority. If you are hiring a hall, the owners should be able to advise.

Film shows

An occasional film or video show does not need to be licensed, providing the premises are for showing films on only six days a year or fewer. You must still give at least seven days' notice of the event to the local authority, fire authority and chief officer of police. If the premises are to be used regularly, whether for public or private showings, then a licence must be obtained under the Cinemas Act 1985.

Sporting contests

As with music and dancing, London's law differs from elsewhere. In both cases, however, the local authority, police and fire department must be told at least a month in advance.

Car-boot sales

These are another popular way of fund-raising for charity, but you should inform the local authority. Some require notice of any temporary market if it is not in a building or on the highway and involves five or more stalls or vehicles. Notice is not required if the proceeds are to be given principally for charitable, social, sporting or political purposes. That is fine if the car owners or stallholders are happy to hand over all they raise. If the charity is merely going to charge a fee or rent, letting the participants make as much money as they can, a licence will probably be required, at least a month in advance. You should also be aware that car boot sales will be regulated under Public Collections legislation incorporated within the Charities Act 1992.

VAT

Since 31 March, 1989 the sale of goods and the provision of services by a charity in connection with a one-off charity event has been exempt from VAT. However, there are instances where it would be better to ensure that charges raised by the charity at an event are liable for VAT. As things stand, the organizers of a one-off event do not charge VAT on entry fees, tickets or sponsorship. That is worthwhile if you are predominantly selling to the public, as they cannot recover the VAT and may be deterred by having to pay the additional tax. In that situation, it is probably worth seeking exemption and bearing the irrecoverable VAT on the event's costs; if the event is big enough, the charity should come out on top.

However, it may be better ensuring that charges raised by the charity are liable for VAT if most of the event's income is derived from other VAT-registered entities, rather than from the public, because it is likely that they can then recover the VAT you have charged. In that situation you can recover VAT on your costs. It is important to clarify that the VAT treatment of the event is not a matter of choice for the charity. If the event meets the criteria to qualify as a 'one off' event then it is automatically VAT exempt. Therefore, if it is thought that it would be beneficial to treat the event as VATable, then early planning to facilitate this is a must.

The ways to make the charges liable for VAT are to run the event through a commercial company set up for the occasion and not owned directly by the charity. Alternatively, you could arrange for the event to be part of a series or programme of events. Anyone in doubt should obtain advice and seek rulings from HM Customs and Excise, although it may well be preferable first to obtain professional advice to ensure that the position is put forward to Customs in the most favourable way.

The treatment of one-off events is important for charity appeals and is explained further in Appendix 7.

INSURANCE

It is sensible to ask the owners or organizers of the venue for an event about insurance provisions and requirements. If it is already covered by an insurance policy, the appeal or the promoters may be able to take advantage of that, either by informing the insurer or by paying an additional premium.

The Wishing Well Appeal insured with Commercial Union Assurance to cover accidents and other liabilities which might arise as a result of special events. There are several other insurers in this field, so I recommend seeking the advice of a reputable broker. The arrangement we had was that participants in an event would be covered if the event was notified to Commercial Union in advance and they accepted it as a reasonable risk. We had to declare:

1. The nature of the event – run, swim, barbecue, etc.
2. Location
3. Confirmation that the appropriate authority (police, local town hall) had given consent
4. The approximate number of people expected to attend/participate.

That left the many independent events organized in aid of the Wishing Well

Appeal, often without our knowledge. All we could do was to explain the position to our regional chairmen and ask them to make sure as many people as possible knew of the arrangement.

MAILING LISTS

Mailing lists are useful adjuncts to a special event, particularly at the outset, as they enable the organizers to target likely attenders accurately and personally. So sensitive and precious are these lists that the appeal should avoid approaching people on the same mailing list more than two or three times in a year. I also recommend that they should not be made available for use by another department of the appeal, such as catalogues or Christmas card sales. It can create dangerously negative feelings if people realize that they are being bombarded with whatever the appeal has to throw at them. Some event organizers insert breaks in computerized lists, such as false names with their own addresses, to see if the list is being misused. Lists must constantly be updated. It is dispiriting to have material readdressed from old homes or businesses for months after the change has taken place. Only personalized letters should be sent with application forms for an event, handwritten at top and tail. This may mean signing 5,000 letters, but it will produce a far better response than the duplicated alternative. After this initial stage, the commercial momentum of the event takes over from the mailing list as the driving force.

THANK YOU'S

From the day an event is given the go-ahead and preparation begins, there should be a 'thank you' page in the file. Otherwise, it is easy to forget whom to thank, so great is the rush of developments in assembling an event. Jane Waldegrave, the special events organizer for the Wishing Well Appeal, had a rule that she would always write 'thank you' letters the day before the event. The danger is that the appeal staff may be too tired the following morning, after a late night, and it can so easily be pushed down the order of priorities thereafter. It is most important that the 'thank you' process starts as soon as the event has ended – the same or at least the next day. It is crucial to sustain supporters' enthusiasm for the next event.

CHECKLIST

Guiding principles
Select events that:
- Offer real attraction to a particular audience
- Create conviviality to generate pleasant memories (and therefore charity loyalty)
- Ensure the maximum return to the appeal for the time involved and a respectable cost-to-income ratio (20 to 30 per cent)
- Do not risk the charity's good name
- Are run by trustworthy and experienced organizers
- Have the potential to achieve television coverage
- Are sufficiently prestigious or unique to attract sponsorship

Delegate wisely (duties and credit!)
- Form a small group to oversee the whole activity of special events, with a special committee for each event
- Ensure you have access to all relevant expertise: legal, financial, special events, publicity, television, merchandising, etc.
- Appoint a sound and experienced in-house special eventer

Marketing and publicity
- Involve highly creative ideas people
- Use professional public relations techniques
- Find sponsors by matching marketing objectives and getting like to approach like – chairman to chairman and marketing director to charity representative
- Keep an events calendar and ensure there is a constant flow of high-profile events, which must not clash

Finance and administration
- Check legal requirements and the need to establish a separate trading subsidiary to handle the event
- Construct a standard system for financial vetting, reviewing income and expenditure before, during and after the events
- Avoid paying seed money wherever possible
- Have clearly defined 'break points' for the event to minimize the risk
- Draw up detailed written contracts with outside agencies, which include 'break points'
- Plan for every eventuality, including dates when the event would be aborted if key targets have not been reached
- Produce detailed checklists and status reports to keep everyone informed
- Insure
- Build and protect mailing lists
- Give careful thought as to how to thank different supporters promptly.

Chapter 26

RISKS AND REWARDS OF SPECIAL EVENTS

However meticulously you plan and manage your appeal's special events, unexpected pitfalls are bound to occur. It is in the nature of such occasions. To be successful, they have to have an element of spontaneity and artistic creativity, qualities which are often most effectively delivered by people with spectacular egos to match! While I cannot prepare you for every eventuality, I can point out some of the commoner types of difficulty, so that they can be identified and dealt with as expeditiously as possible. I have included examples of Wishing Well Appeal events to make some of the points more vivid and to convey the feeling of the constant drip-feed for which we strove in order to keep the Appeal in the public eye.

In a sense, there are neither good nor bad special events. An event is either special for your appeal or it is not. Either it raises the desired sum of money and fits in with the appeal's image, or it does not. Nevertheless, there are pitfalls to avoid and qualities to pursue. Some types of event consistently prove more lucrative than others.

The best type of occasion is a large participatory event which attracts crowds of people, each raising money to reach his own personal target, heavily sponsored so that it costs the appeal little or nothing. However, this type of project is risky because everything depends on the day. Even though people may have collected sponsorship pledges beforehand, if they do not turn up to run, jump, walk, sing or do whatever may be required on the day, they will not be able to ask their sponsors for the money. The way to limit the risk is by introducing an entry fee. In the first Sport Aid, the organizers charged £5 for a T-shirt and a sponsorship form, which covered a substantial proportion of the costs. However, if they go well, these participation events can bring the most wonderful surprises and the most rewarding return. Having hordes of people doing the same thing on the same day generates enthusiasm, competition, friendship and the feeling of being part of a big event.

Outstanding examples of national projects involving very large numbers of people are the ITV Telethon, Children in Need and Comic Relief Red Nose Day. All of these projects achieve nationwide media coverage and have proved to be highly successful. Millions take part in these events each year, creating a great community feeling towards their respective causes. Telethon donated £75,000 to the Wishing Well Appeal in 1988. Your charity/appeal may plug into these extravaganzas by applying to the organizers to become a benefiting charity, or alternatively, you may offer unique assistance, manpower, or major sponsorship through a friendly contact.

Appendix 8 discusses the impact of the Charities Act 1992 on the collection of sponsorship pledges. It is important that you do not incite people to raise funds illegally, so ask the following questions:

- Am I engaging in a collecting activity?
- Am I in a public place?
- Am I, in that process, making an appeal for something?

If the answer to all three questions is yes, your activity will be regulated by the provisions of Part III of the Act.

Above all, a special event should be impressive, but different events are impressive to different audiences. Swimathons appeal only to swimmers, children and, possibly, their parents. They depend on the organizers arranging for the swimmers' heroes to appear in the water with them. So the target audience is an important consideration.

The Wishing Well Appeal naturally set out to attract the interest and concern of parents and children, as the Appeal would ultimately benefit them, but we had to go beyond that category if we were to hit our targets. Many people are impressed by an opportunity to take part in any event which a member of the Royal Family graciously agrees to attend, but the enormous pressures on their time mean they can accept only a limited number of carefully chosen invitations. Celebrity participation is important, although not essential. Many people, deciding whether to attend a ball, are influenced by the names of those on the ball committee. Above all, the event has to look impressive and run smoothly. A glossy brochure can be appropriate, but only if it generates substantial advertising revenue.

GALA BROCHURES

A show business gala, variety performance, opera or film premiere is the prime occasion on which to publish a souvenir brochure. Indeed, I believe that the main criterion in deciding whether to be associated with such an event is the degree of confidence the appeal organizers have in their ability to raise advertising for the brochure. For that is the main source of revenue, rather than the box-office takings. A gold page in a brochure in 1992/3 was worth between £750 and £1,000 – nearly all pure profit – and a brochure can carry as many as two dozen such pages.

Maximizing that revenue is hard work. It is a matter of approaching advertising agencies and public relations companies and finding out which of them carries a promotional budget relevant to such events, which has a centenary or other major anniversary in the near future, which is promoting in your area at the appropriate time and which organizations might wish to take the opportunity to burnish their image. You can also approach companies already supporting your appeal. The important point is that the big gift must be secured before asking for a further contribution, such as advertising in a brochure. Of course, in those circumstances, the

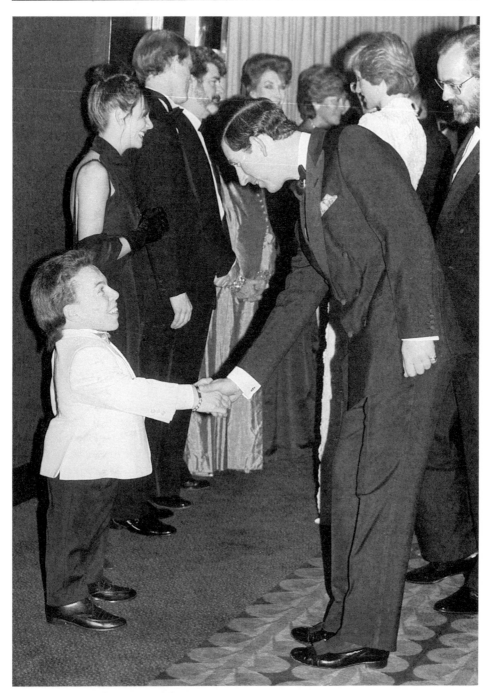

Every film has a premiere – which provides a fund-raising opportunity for charity, for the right type of film. Make it a Royal premiere and the event can be raised onto a different, more exclusive plane. Above, the stars of the film 'Willow' are presented to the Prince and Princess of Wales at the Empire Theatre, Leicester Square in 1988. The event, held as part of the Variety Club's £3 million commitment to the Wishing Well Appeal, raised £130,000. (Photograph: *The Sun*)

appeal organizers must make due reference to the valuable assistance already rendered; but they must have that help already in the bag to avoid the risk of pre-empting a bigger donation later.

An event at the Royal Opera House, Covent Garden, might merit producing a brochure in the form of a hardback book, which gives advertisers the prospect of its being retained as a souvenir for several years. People might then pay £1,500 or more to have their names printed discreetly in gold at the foot of a page. It is very much a matter of creating the right environment and I recommend seeking advice from people with professional expertise in these matters. Indeed, an appeal organizer should try to co-opt such a person on to the committee.

Whenever you wish to sell advertising space in a fund-raising brochure, it is better to undertake the activity in-house, if possible. However, it must be recognized that special skills are required for the creation and writing of scripts and delivery of the appeal over the telephone when selling space. If you appoint an outside agency, you should be aware that working on a percentage basis is normal practice in the advertising business. Some of these percentages can be very high. Never enter a relationship without first signing a written agreement which specifies what proportion of the proceeds raised will be retained by the agency and what is the minimal proportion that will come to the appeal. As mentioned in Appendix 8, all forms of direct selling activities with an outside agency, where it is paid a portion of the income from that activity, will be regulated under the Charities Act 1992.

However, a word of caution is in order on show business events, particularly film premieres. If they are not thoroughly checked, the appeal organizers might be embarrassed on the night to find that the film or performance contains inappropriate material which runs counter to the objectives of the appeal. The Wishing Well Appeal, jointly with the Variety Club of Great Britain, held a Royal Premiere of *Willow* at the Odeon, Leicester Square, in the presence of the Prince and Princess of Wales. It was sponsored and raised £129,000. *Willow* is a fantasy adventure featuring people of restricted growth – a condition called achondroplasia. As achondroplasia attacks children, the film was highly appropriate for the Appeal, but such a sensitive subject had to be vetted very carefully. We consulted the Institute of Child Health, attached to Great Ormond Street Hospital. The Institute identified a suitable sponsor, Eli Lilly, the American pharmaceutical firm. We then invited every relevant organization representing people of restricted growth to a private screening to find out their reactions to the film. It is essential to preview every film to be shown as part of an appeal to satisfy yourself that no one will be embarrassed. Instead of hiding the problem of achondroplasia, we featured sponsored case histories in the souvenir brochure for which we charged double advertising rates. It worked very successfully. A different sort of film or a less prestigious sponsor might have been damaging and that would inevitably have had an effect on future events.

EVENTS TO AVOID

Extreme caution is necessary when assessing events. Many events that seem attractive prove to be only superficially so on closer inspection. The two principal types of danger are physical and financial. Together with the Spastics Society, the

Institute of Charity Fundraising Managers is currently drafting a Code of Practice relating to dangerous fund-raising events for charities.

It is best to avoid parachute jumps. They look spectacular, but the potentially unfortunate results can easily outweigh any goodwill. We were delighted that a doughty grandmother chose to celebrate her 80th birthday with a freefall parachute jump from 12,500 feet, and that she donated sponsorship money to the Appeal. However, we were glad that we heard about her daring exploit only after she had jumped, or we would have been extremely fearful for her safety!

It is impossible to stop individuals from doing anything and giving the proceeds to an appeal – so long as it is legal. That is a long way from actually organizing the event and suffering the bad publicity resulting from injury or death. In any case, be sure you have met all insurance requirements (see Chapter 10) and taken all reasonable precautions, such as roping off spectator areas, providing litter bins to minimize fire risk, etc. Display disclaimer notices prominently in such places as car parks and be sure to liaise with the police and first-aiders. You should ensure that you arrange adequate cover for the requirements of the event.

Surprisingly, an event with more financial risk than many is the charity ball. Many charities regard these as a pillar of their fund-raising activity, but it is difficult to make much money out of a charity ball unless it is cleverly set up. Dinners, cocktail parties and dinner dances are even worse. The moment you give people something to eat or drink, profits begin to be eroded unless the event is supported by a generous sponsor. If even a few guests complain that they did not have enough to eat, they can spread dissension. So many things can go wrong with catering that the organizers have to order ten per cent extra to cover for mishaps. If food arrives late, guests have to be offered an extra drink or two to make up for the lapse; they have paid for their tickets and will resent any penny-pinching. Moreover, contingency food and drink supplies may be pilfered unless carefully supervised.

Some events meet all the requirements, yet fail to trigger a sufficient response. It is important for the appeal organizer to set targets in advance of the event itself – targets calculated in a calm and objective atmosphere before people become emotionally involved in the event. You should decide on the appeal's maximum outlay and minimum response by set dates. These usually correspond to suppliers' deadlines – dates beyond which they will expect half or full payment. The appeal is then increasingly committed. Do not be afraid to pull out in spite of the effect on goodwill. All too often, people attempt to rescue events with an expensive burst of advertising and other promotional activity but, sadly, that merely adds to the losses.

As we have seen, it is a good rule not to entertain any proposal for running an event that is not made formally in writing, with full details of costs and anticipated income and evidence that the event would operate profitably without any involvement from the charity. The only reason the charity is being brought in is that the promoter wishes to support the charity and the charity's patronage adds to an already successful event. The event must not be contingent on the charity's involvement. The sort of thing to avoid is a concert given by a little-known orchestra whose management does not think will fill the hall and who turn to a charity as a way out of its difficulty.

Any event which would happen in its own right is worth pursuing. Every film of a given quality has to have a first showing. What makes it special is to call it a premiere held in the presence of Royalty or a VIP and declare revenues in aid of a cause. Similar considerations apply to an opera, a day at the races, a Pavarotti or Domingo concert, the Summer Exhibition at the Royal Academy, or late night shopping in a major store. The common denominator is that all the principal costs have already been borne by the venue in question. The appeal does not have to pay set-up costs, organize staff or artistes, arrange lighting or a public address system. It can simply piggy-back, taking that night's profit – which should be maximized by charging extra for the tickets to reflect the significance of the occasion.

The most prestigious events require considerable advance planning because they are subject to very long waiting lists. For instance, Goodwood and the Royal Opera House require two years' notice or more. Some are effectively out of reach to the one-off appeal. Royal Ascot, for example, has a long waiting list of several years on which places are awarded by Her Majesty The Queen. There are no exceptions to this rule.

A good piggy-back example was the Penguin Swimathon, brought to us by London Youth Games. In the previous year, LYG had organized a similar event in which 2,000 entrants had raised £120,000 for St. Thomas's Hospital in London. We were delighted to be chosen as the benefiting charity. They were pleased to hear that we wished to be active partners with them to build on the success of the first Swimathon. We explored different ways to increase the event's fund-raising potential. We found a sponsor – United Biscuits – who had been involved in a similar event in the past. Its public relations company developed a public awareness campaign for the event. We helped the organizers to dramatize the event that launched the appeal at London's Queen Mother Sports Centre. TVS gave valuable advice on televisual considerations and we invited the Princess of Wales to open the proceedings.

The Swimathon involved timed swims by individuals or teams over 5,000 metres. Forty-three pools in Greater London offered 150 sessions on different days to 6,000 entrants. The event won us a place in the *Guinness Book of Records* for organizing the largest Swimathon. It was held in 26 London boroughs, raising a record £689,000. The organizers ran the event again in February 1989, but as it was due to happen after we had hit our target, we shared the proceeds with Save the Children Fund and Action Research for the Crippled Child. Since then the event has gone from strength to strength. It now involves 30 thousand swimmers throughout Britain and raises nearly £1.5 million for several charities every year. The organizers say that it was the close association with the Wishing Well Appeal which raised the event on to a different plane. It is now a mega sports event and regular money spinner for charity. However the Wishing Well Appeal swimathon in 1988 still holds the record for the average money raised per swimmer as it was £115 as against today's £50.

A similar effect can be achieved by building a relationship with a prominent individual who has strong pulling power. Instead of drawing on a particular event, the appeal is then drawing on the individual's attraction. When the Wishing Well Appeal was organizing the Foster's Tennis Classic, we knew Cliff Richard was keen on tennis and thought he might like to compère or play. We approached Bill Latham, his charitable affairs manager. He arranged for Cliff to attend the tennis event and Cliff made a valuable contribution. Later that year, Cliff celebrated 30 years in show business. Because we had established a good relationship and, presumably, made a worthwhile impression, Cliff offered to give the Appeal the receipts from the final concert he held to mark his anniversary. The evening was going to happen anyway, so we were not committed to any costs. Cliff's suppliers and sponsors were persuaded to pay several thousand pounds each to appear in the souvenir brochure for the event. The Appeal received over £127,000. We were able to repay Cliff by inviting him to read a lesson at our Thanksgiving Service at Westminster Abbey at the end of the Appeal. We thought this would attract him as he is a committed Christian, and it did, adding considerably to the occasion. So, by building a relationship, the Appeal benefited to a significant extent from the support and involvement of such a major celebrity.

PROTECTING A CHARITY'S GOOD NAME

A great deal of coordination and care is necessary to make sure that people use the appeal's good name correctly. It is tremendously valuable and must not be risked in any way. Reputation is doubly important in a one-off appeal because there are no second chances and the appeal features more prominently in the public eye than an ongoing charity. Such considerations are usually a factor in evaluating proposals from outside people or agencies.

Individuals who approach the appeal organizers must be vetted strictly and thoroughly, but also tactfully and considerately. Have they done this sort of thing before? Have they worked for charities before? If they claim to have done so, do contact those charities for a reference. The most fundamental exercise is to ask for a simple projection of income and expenditure for the event; this will eliminate more outlandish schemes, however tempting they may seem, and will give you an early indication of the proposer's reliability. However, even if the plan is taken further, the appeal must insist on constant access to the event's financial records, a right that must be established from the outset.

While financial competence is a substantial component in an organization's reputation, it can also be affected by the far more subjective matter of taste. Is an event suitable for reaching the sorts of people the appeal wishes to target? There is often strong pressure to proceed with an event because a person who is important to the appeal has said: 'Wouldn't it be a good idea if ... ?' The appeal organizers can easily feel duty bound to see that event through somehow, to keep faith with that major supporter. Ultimately, the project has to be right for your appeal and, above all, it must not seem vulgar to potential donors.

WISHING WELL APPEAL EVENTS

I have pointed out the importance, when setting up the programme of events, of the appeal organizers trying to involve all sectors of society relevant to the appeal. This is a selection of the Wishing Well Appeal's events, tabulated to show that we did try to maintain a balance.

Wishing Well Appeal events

	£ Net
Sport	
Penguin Swimathon 1988*	689,000
Foster's Classic Tennis*	161,000
London Marathon*	1.5 million
Rock	
Michael Jackson concert*	100,000
Cliff Richard's 30 years in show business*	127,000
Film	
Willow, Odeon Leicester Square, sponsored by Eli Lilly*	112,000
Variety	
Royal Gala Variety Performance, televised by ITV on New Year's Day, 1989*	170,000
Society	
Wishing Well Ball, Grosvenor House Hotel	80,000
Leadenhall Ball, sponsored by Lloyd's of London	85,000
Intellectual	
Quiz organized by Collett Dickenson Pearce	75,000
Vintage Cars	
Classic Car Auction, Brocket Hall*	561,000

* = televised

It may help to generate ideas and act as a reference point to discuss some of these events in more detail.

Fund-raising events

Vintage car auction

I was sitting at my desk one day when I received a telephone call from Geneva. The caller told me that Great Ormond Street Hospital had saved the life of his daughter a few years previously and that he wanted to do something to help the Appeal. He said he was going to give us two rare Lamborghinis and help set up a vintage car auction. After I had recovered from the shock, I realized he was serious. He was a man of about 40 who wanted to avoid personal publicity. He just wanted to help us. He managed to procure 11 cars from friends, who were equally keen on vintage cars, plus 60 additional lots. The event was held at Brocket Hall in Hertfordshire and run by Christie's, the auctioneers, who also donated the Collectors' Catalogue and a full support service. The Appeal Office then built on this man's brilliant idea. The auction was televised and produced a phenomenal £561,759 for the Appeal. I noticed the gentleman in question trying to buy back one of the lots that he had put in. His generosity was extraordinary.

In the special events arena, the fund-raiser's role is often to encourage, support and monitor the volunteer who not only has the imaginative idea, but also offers to run the show. One of the most amazing offers received by the Wishing Well Appeal was from a grateful parent who arranged for Christies to run a vintage car auction and who donated two Lamborghini cars himself. The photo above shows the 1923 yellow Rolls-Royce and below is one of the rare Lamborghinis donated for the auction, which was held at Brocket Hall and raised £561,759. (Photographs: Christies Images)

Royal Gala

We had a Royal Gala, an evening of music and comedy with a galaxy of top stars and celebrities. It was held in Southampton and attended by the Prince of Wales. The show was laid on by TVS, so the Appeal Office simply coordinated and supported in any way we could. It attracted about £75,000 of sponsorship and was televised in January 1989, raising a total of £170,000.

Quiz

This was an idea dreamed up by Gay Haines, who was then the New Business Director at the Collett Dickenson Pearce advertising agency. The aim was to find a Company of the Year through eight rounds of 20 questions per round, with topics that included art, current affairs, the City, food and wine, literature and music. The event was held at the Natural History Museum in Kensington, with Jonathan Dimbleby as master of ceremonies. An amazing 50 companies and organizations, with ten members per team, paid £1,500 each to compete. They ranged from the Houses of Lords and Commons to the Bank of England, Cadbury Schweppes, Guinness, De Beers, Eagle Star, British Airways and Beecham. It was a roaring success and the winner was *The Independent* newspaper group. We also held a raffle, for which Toyota donated a £17,000 sports car. That raised £14,000, the winner gave the car back to be auctioned for the Appeal for what turned out to be another substantial sum. In total, the quiz raised £75,000.

London Marathon

The 1988 London Marathon was a major source of funds for the Appeal. About 1,000 runners, mostly wearing Wishing Well T-shirts, raised money individually, while nearly 100 companies entered teams of three. The companies were generous enough to match pound for pound the sums raised by their team members' individual efforts. Altogether, nearly £1.5 million came to the Appeal. Any interested charity should contact the current sponsors of the London Marathon for details of the current rules and arrangements.

Remember, the collection of sponsorship pledges before the run is permissible (unless it is carried out in a public place) – collecting *en route* is illegal unless you have a permit.

Media events

A special event can be a media event, a fund-raising event or, ideally, both if your appeal needs publicity and money. Media events are calculated to generate maximum media interest, relying on creative ideas, the unusual, spectacular, imaginative, quirky, touching and often involving good visual interpretation.

The Princess and Father Christmas

On 3 December 1987, the Princess of Wales visited the Hospital to distribute presents with the help of Father Christmas, played by the comedian Jimmy Tarbuck. We wanted to generate a strong picture story at this early stage of the Appeal and worked hard to make the most of this publicity opportunity to ensure that it obtained maximum media coverage. TVS did the trick for us. They recruited Jimmy Tarbuck, provided a sleigh drawn by two Shetland ponies and wired Great

With some events, the charity has little more to do than to support and then collect the cheque! Above, Sebastian Coe and Steve Cram recreating the race around the Great Court of Trinity College, Cambridge in 1927, featured in the film 'Chariots of Fire'. The event, devised and arranged by a mature student, achieved massive publicity as well as £40,000 for the Wishing Well Appeal and £11,000 towards other children's causes. (Photograph: *The Sun*)

Ormond Street so that the Wishing Well song filled the street. We had everything but snow. Every newspaper we could lay hands on ran the story – with pictures.

Chariots of Fire

On 30 October 1988, Olympic athletes Steve Cram and Sebastian Coe dressed up in 1920's running gear to re-run the scene from the film *Chariots of Fire* that depicted the race round the Great Court of Trinity College, Cambridge, while the college clock struck 12. They raised £50,000. This was the brainchild of a mature student at Trinity College, after he had seen the BBC TV documentary on Great Ormond Street the previous December. James Capel, the stockbroking firm, put up £10,000 to sponsor the event and 1,500 tickets were offered for sale. Ben Cross, an actor in the film, was Master of Ceremonies, and HRH Prince Edward started the race.

Virginia Leng

Virginia Leng, the British Olympic three-day event rider, undertook a ride from Wiltshire which was both a media event and a fund-raising vehicle. It proved more eventful than expected. She was approached by Mrs. Jane Irwin, the Appeal's Regional and Area Chairman for Wiltshire, who realized that a well-known personality was needed and knew Virginia Leng. She was joined by every pony club on the route for part of the way and let it be known that she would do nearly anything to raise money for the Appeal. When Virginia reached the Hospital she was surrounded by patients. However, one little girl was heartbroken because she was a tremendous fan but was too ill to come down to street level. So Virginia went to her bedside – and quietly left her riding gloves on the end of the bed as she said goodbye.

Lord Mayor's Show

One annual event worth joining is the Lord Mayor's Show through the City of London every November. Although there has to be some sort of limit on the number of floats in the procession, it is a sufficiently flexible format to allow everyone who has something to shout about to take part. If your appeal has City contacts, they should be able to make preliminary enquiries. Otherwise, a call to the Corporation of London's offices will set the ball rolling.

Not only did the Wishing Well Appeal have a float in the 1987 show, but the Lord Mayor, Alderman Sir Greville Spratt, included the Appeal in his special charitable appeal – along with Action Research for the Crippled Child and the Lord Treloar Trust. It proved to be one of the most successful Lord Mayor's Appeals and raised over £1 million in all.

Towards the latter stages of the Wishing Well Appeal, we actively avoided media events because we had reached saturation point, when the public might have become tired of hearing yet more about our Appeal. Then we staged only events that would raise substantial funds, rather than going in for media events as well.

Others

Harder to keep tabs on, but heartening because of their sheer spontaneity, were the thousands of events and stunts organized by supporters who just wanted to provide people with an excuse for giving. A Dick Turpin look-alike raised £25,000 on

Fund-raising events that raise profile and money have a double benefit to an appeal. Above, Virginia Leng raised £60,000 for the Wishing Well Appeal through a five-day sponsored ride to London from Wiltshire in 1988. She ended her journey flanked by a Household Cavalry escort. Below, 'Mr Wishing Well' and nurses from Great Ormond Street are seen with their float at the Lord Mayor's Show in November 1987. As one of the three charities in the Lord Mayor's Charity Appeal, the Wishing Well Appeal received £113,000. (Photograph: Times Newspapers)

a ride from London to York, 'robbing' pubs on the way. Two businessmen raced yachts from Needles Lightship to Cherbourg. The road from Land's End to John O'Groats was pounded by a succession of bizarre journeys, from walks to a lawn mower ride.

The most practical option for the Appeal was to stimulate the offers that came to us and to build on them as much as we could. Because we were so conscious of the cost-to-income ratio, we had no intention of putting in seed money. If we could get out of doing anything ourselves, we did – as long as we could delegate wisely and tactfully oversee what was done to benefit the Appeal.

That gives an inkling of the huge range of special events undertaken for the Wishing Well Appeal. The fund-raising target for this series of activities was covered four-fold, but only by an enormous effort by many, many people. They were motivated and supported by a dedicated and talented team of only three executives and two secretaries.

CONCLUSION

Contrary to popular belief, there is nothing glamorous about organizing special events. They involve a tremendous amount of hard work and organization which might – only might – produce an event that will raise a substantial sum of money, generate valuable publicity and boost the morale of everyone concerned in your appeal. Contingency plans are necessary at all stages to deal with disappointment or a breakdown in arrangements.

There is no dress rehearsal for a special event. Individuals may rehearse their own parts, but it finally comes together only on the big night itself. However thoroughly you prepare, there will almost always be snags. You may have tasted the food and wine, and still find it different on the night. The band or orchestra may sound terrific in another hall but terrible at your venue. That PA system you used last week may not be powerful enough this time. A pile-up on the motorway may prevent your star from arriving punctually. It is vital to check, recheck and enlist the help of as many experienced professionals as you can. Despite everything, it really is worth it in the end! All you need is a cool head, resourcefulness – and an outsized sense of humour.

---------- *Chapter 27* ----------

PUBLISHING

Most people think they can write a book, given the time and the opportunity. If they become involved in a national charity appeal, they are liable to jump to the conclusion that a book will be a relatively easy way to raise money. If they were organizing a rock concert, the whole project would stand or fall on whether a suitable band could be cajoled into appearing. The appeal chairman, unless he were a rock star, would not dream of offering to step into the breach by leaping on stage at the last minute. However, if a suitable author cannot be found for an appeal book, it is all too tempting for a member of the appeal committee (or even the Director!) to volunteer to be the writer.

This indicates the extent to which normal commercial calculations so easily fly out of the window when someone suggests producing a book for an appeal. Judgment is further clouded by the fact that a well-distributed book can at least help to spread the word about the appeal, even if it does not actually make money on its own account. The appeal organizers are then entering the highly dangerous territory of balancing an actual financial loss against an intangible gain in terms of publicity. However, even if a financial loss is acceptable, no book will spread the word about anything unless people pick it up, open it and feel sufficiently rewarded by reading each page to encourage them to turn to the next.

Most appeal committees, unless they are lucky enough to include a professional publisher, have only the vaguest idea of the intense competition within the book trade these days. If you think about what is required simply to break even on a straightforward commercial book, it quickly becomes apparent that this is no easy route for a charity to follow. Depending on the type of book, at least 5,000 copies have to be sold. This may not sound a lot, but the hard fact is that most books sell far fewer. Publishers are sometimes able to sustain such losses because they reckon to make up the leeway with a minority of best sellers. Obviously, this strategy works only if an organization is publishing a large number of different titles. A one-off appeal, which becomes involved with only half-a-dozen or so at the most, will be taking a much greater risk of not hitting the jackpot. That is the scale of the problems to be overcome when considering books as appeal money-raisers.

HOW TO MAKE MONEY OUT OF PUBLISHING

There are four broad categories of book which are published by or in aid of charities as part of their fund-raising:

- Books that are being written anyway, whose authors give some or all of their royalties to the charity.
- Books that are dedicated to the charity.
- Books that are associated with the charity.
- Books about the appeal or charity itself.

In addition, there are occasionally gifts of royalties from work published prior to the appeal.

Appeal organizers may decide to take a book in the second, third or fourth categories and attempt to publish it themselves. This has the virtue of keeping costs down, but depends on having access to the requisite skills – researching, writing, editing, designing, printing, publishing and distributing. All these activities must be coordinated by an experienced professional who assumes responsibility for the key commercial decisions concerning technical specifications, pricing and the number of copies to be printed.

Demand for any book is far less predictable than for a stable commodity such as a toothbrush or a teapot. Books also have a very different sales and life cycle from other products. It can be as short as three months, in which case the book must be supported by a marketing blitz. Alternatively, they may generate steady sales over a considerably longer period. A strong title and a striking cover can make a huge difference, but only a publishing professional will have any idea of whether a book is a sleeper or a fizzer. That judgment will, in turn, have an impact on the number of copies to be held for stock and, therefore, the print ordering policy.

The alternative is to go through the publishing trade – in which case the expensive task of holding stock has to be divided between the publisher, the wholesaler, the bookseller and the charity itself. These matters are all open to negotiation. It is a far more complex business than most people realize, involving a major commitment of time and money. Compared with a special event, a book reaches the point of no return much more quickly, when it becomes more expensive to abandon it than to go on.

Any book which is intended to make its way in the open market must be accepted by W.H. Smith, which controls one-third of Britain's bookshops. No bookseller – let alone Smith's – will accept a book unless it has a Standard Book Number, registered with Whitaker's Booklisting Services of 12 Dyott Street, London WC1, and a bar code. Without these, a book cannot be processed through the warehouse. Then there is the matter of selling to specialist chains, such as Dillons or Waterstones. Beyond these, distribution rapidly becomes a question of persuading individual shops to take one or two copies apiece. There is no easy access to a system of national book distributors, so a publishing company may be inclined to suggest that the charity tries to distribute its books through its own network. All this argues, as with other commercial activities outlined in this book, for forming a publishing committee and recruiting a top-class publisher, bookseller and printer. They will understand the economics of book production, and will have a better chance than outsiders of negotiating concessions. From that point of view, it is worth bearing in mind the way in which the revenue from a book is normally split between the participants. In terms of percentages of the cover price, it may often work this way:

Author	9
Author's agent	1
Publisher	45
Bookseller	45

The cost of editing, production, printing and marketing comes out of the publisher's share. The bookseller, author and agent have costs, too. A charity may be able to bargain for as much as a 20 per cent allocation of the cover price – short of any outright donations.

One apparent way of increasing the appeal's income is simply to raise the cover price, but this comes back to the point that appeal-related books have to compete with other books for the buyer's custom. It may be possible to add, say, £1 and state explicitly on the cover that such a sum is being donated to an appeal, but there is usually very little more scope than that. On the contrary, if a book is being published by the charity itself, a better tactic may be to take advantage of the cost savings by charging a lower price. Once again, the non-professionals running a charity appeal very quickly come up against the need for shrewd advice from those in the trade. A more promising avenue may be to approach a book club, which will sell it through mail order, but that applies only to publishing ideas which will generate high sales.

Because publishing is such a competitive trade, a charity should examine ways of giving its books a unique quality which cannot easily be replicated. Assuming that the appeal's name and logo have been legally protected (see Chapter 8), an obvious ploy is to commission a book about the appeal or its underlying cause, preferably by an authoritative author. This can turn into something of a totem to be bought by as many as possible of the appeal's supporters, as a symbol of their commitment to the cause.

A closely related book is one written by one or more celebrities, assuming they will give their names and involvement for nothing. It shares the virtue of being harder for others to emulate, providing the publishing committee selects the right mix of theme and author. Those books are still competing within the general field of celebrity books – of which there are often quite a number, for the same commercial reasons as have attracted the charity to them. If the name is bankable, the book will be in demand, and the author is effectively contributing cast-iron royalty income to the appeal.

Sponsorship is, as in other commercial projects, a way for a charity to make the cost calculations more favourable. Remember, however, that this simply reduces the risk of loss: sponsorship does not guarantee a profit. A poor book will still sit on the shelves, and then be returned to the warehouse, unsold. Sponsorship should be handled separately through a wholly-owned trading company reflecting the commercial nature of the activity.

PITFALLS

Many appeals come unstuck producing a commemorative cookbook, where one or two people associated with the appeal decide that they will try their hands. They are an attractive idea in that cookbooks are an acceptable present for a wide range of people, they have a practical application and yet do not appear to require a high standard of narrative writing skill. A recipe can be described in a few paragraphs. Several successful cookbooks were published in conjunction with the Wishing Well Appeal. An apparently adequate manuscript can be produced by amateurs. The trouble really starts if the appeal organizers try to deal with commercial firms over production matters, such as typesetting, printing, binding, publishing and distribution to booksellers. Above all, they are likely to overestimate the demand for the book and, therefore, order too many copies. Professionals are not necessarily going to give a charity a free ride, and even if they do offer a concessionary rate, the book can still make a nasty loss. In that respect, it is just like any other commercial venture that a charity might undertake.

It is all too easy for a charity to imagine that, because their cause is so important to them, book distributors and retailers will carry it for nothing. This is a misconception. If W.H. Smith carried every charity book offered at no charge, its shops would have shelves and shelves displaying nothing else. Some charity organizers may believe that Smith's should, indeed, provide such a facility, but the fact is that they and the other leading booksellers are profit-making companies answerable to shareholders. It is unrealistic to expect them to admit every charity book for nothing. They may agree to accept a charity book at 20 per cent below cover price, instead of the normal 45 per cent or more discount, but free or even cheap distribution cannot be assumed. The publisher may be able to obtain special terms, but generally he will have to market it as a normal book. It must stand or fall on its attractiveness to the public. This applied to *Mutual Friends: Charles Dickens and Great Ormond Street Hospital* by Jules Kosky, the book published for Great Ormond Street, and several others published in connection with the Wishing Well Appeal. They had to compete for shelf space on equal terms with other books. The most valuable contribution a bookseller can make is to grant a charity book a prime display area in the shop.

Another common misconception is that the subject of an appeal-related book must be relevant to the appeal or its underlying cause. This may be helpful if the cause is deemed by the public to be sufficiently important, or if the book is sufficiently well written. It may, for example, portray an aspect of the cause in a new way or disclose previously unknown facts about the subject, but relevance is no guarantee of publishing success. Indeed, one might argue that relevance is irrelevant. It is certainly worth considering, but should be abandoned dispassionately if the indications are that there is little public demand for a book about the appeal. If the appeal is concerned with, say, an incurable disease, it may be expecting too much to ask the public to buy a book which dwells on that disease in distressing detail. They would probably rather put £5 in a collecting box than face such a harrowing ordeal.

What one can say is that the subjects of appeal-related books must not be unsuitable. Joke books are dangerous. Humour is subjective and can easily give offence in the most unexpected way. Such books must be edited with special care.

Nevertheless, joke books can be useful money-raisers – as long as you take care to avoid the pitfalls.

Histories of the relevant institution must be judged against the sales achieved by histories of comparable organizations. The publishing committee must guard against the book's becoming primarily a vehicle for listing the names of everyone associated with the appeal. While there is a strangely compelling fascination for people to see their own names in print, this exercise is more likely to devalue the appeal's publishing strategy, as further books may be assumed by the public to have similarly narcissistic appeal.

WISHING WELL EXPERIENCE

The decision to raise funds for the Wishing Appeal through publishing was taken more for historical reasons than because we thought it would be a serious money-spinner.

Charles Dickens's links with the Hospital for Sick Children are well known. Even before the Hospital was founded, he had done much to raise public awareness of the miserable lives led by so many London children and the lack of care which produced appalling rates of infant mortality, by depicting characters such as Tom Pinch and Tiny Tim in *A Christmas Carol* with a realism which stirred the public conscience. Dickens wrote two articles about the Hospital, one of which, *Drooping Buds*, describes six young patients he saw there. He also gave a reading of *A Christmas Carol* to raise funds for the Hospital. It was very successful, the 19th-century equivalent of today's dedicated television programme.

The association with Dickens was so strong that, until the 1920s, the Hospital incorporated short quotations from his works in the letterhead of its stationery. By that time the Hospital also had a strong tie with J.M. Barrie, the author of *Peter Pan*. In 1928 Barrie was thinking of giving the play to the Hospital. The following year, when he declined a request to serve on a committee in connection with a redevelopment plan, he made over all rights to the play. Barrie died in 1937 and the copyright would have automatically expired in 1988 but for some happy coincidences which put copyright on the public agenda. Interest had been aroused by the BBC's programme on the Wishing Well Appeal, *A Fighting Chance*. A new Copyright, Designs and Patents Bill was before Parliament. Lord Callaghan, the former Prime Minister, introduced an amendment to the Bill which means that the Hospital will retain the rights to the royalties from *Peter Pan* for as long as it exists.

So great was the emotional impact and the publicity associated with the Wishing Well Appeal, that those in the publishing trade agreed that it had a better chance than most of exploiting books as a means of raising revenue. Indeed, it did generate some £200,000, but this flowed from no fewer than 15 books, of which one – the Appeal's *Celebrity Cook Book* – accounted for £100,000, thanks to an extraordinarily generous contribution from everyone involved. *First and Always*, an anthology of poems edited by Lawrence Sail, produced another £50,000. This is not to belittle the sterling contributions from the other books published during the Appeal's life. In the case of *First and Always*, all concerned gave their work free: the poets, the paper suppliers, the printers and binders, the publishers and the book-sellers.

The Appeal's publishing strategy was to form a committee of key people in the publishing world. It was chaired by Peter Bagnall, a director of W.H. Smith, who was in a position to gain significant concessions from his company on behalf of the Appeal. A general publisher was Michael Haggiag of Aurum Press. David Grant, Managing Director of Hodder and Stoughton, covered children's books. Debbie Owen, wife of the politician Lord Owen, whose son had been a patient at Great Ormond Street, sat on the committee in her capacity as one of London's leading literary agents. Alan Kilkenny contributed public relations advice. The Chairman of the Appeal Trustees, the General Manager of the Hospital and the Dean of the Institute of Child Health completed the committee's membership.

Peter Bagnall's strategy paper specified that the committee should have five key roles.

The role of the Publishing Committee

1 To support the managements of the Hospital and Appeal in:
  (a) generation of ideas and projects
  (b) review of proposals for publications
  (c) review and supervision of standards
  (d) provision and vetting of contacts and introductions
2 To coordinate activity in the publishing field and maintain continuity
3 To develop a publishing philosophy in conjunction with the Hospital management
4 To establish the aims and methods of a publishing programme in conjunction with the Hospital management
5 To supervise the management of a publishing programme

Under Role 4, they laid down five aims.
1. To raise the profile of the Hospital and the Appeal through the association of its name with books published in the U.K. and elsewhere.
2. To raise funds for the Hospital's Development Appeal through the exploitation of material provided by the Hospital and from its endorsement of publications and publishing campaigns.
3. To maintain a continuous flow of revenue in the longer term.
4. To establish a long-term publishing programme for the Hospital on its own behalf in both professional and general fields.
5. To ensure that the quality of publications, materials and organizations associated with the Hospital were consistent with its reputation and aims.

We had many manuscripts sent to us during the Appeal and the authors had to be tactfully handled. In practice all offers were reviewed by our Marketing department and Peter Bagnall, who did an enormous amount to filter the material for us and to collect the views of other committee members where relevant.

CHECKLIST

- Ensure that publishing warrants your valuable time. Remember that many publishing ventures are not lucrative.
- Form a group of experts to advise on publishing deals and use their networks to help market the books
- Set up policy guidelines on
  - (a) the types of publishing partners and publication contacts your trustees would or would not countenance
  - (b) clearance procedures – literary and legal – and stipulate the minimum time you require to approve copy
  - (c) profit levels required by your charity
- Review your legal back-up
  - (a) ensure that your legal adviser is expert in intellectual property matters
  - (b) draw up a standard contract for general use
- Set up the correct financial arrangements:
  - (a) Income derived from royalties and other commercial deals in publicity must be handled by a trading company as VAT is incurred.
  - (b) Establish a system for investigating the financial viability of potential partners before entering into a contract (legal or financial advisers can help here).
  - (c) Ensure that you have clearly established, before signing a contract, how the financial returns from the joint venture can be monitored.

Chapter 28

COMPANY GIVING

We have already seen how company donations are solicited during the private phase of an appeal and how companies can enter into commercial partnerships with charities, such as joint promotions and sponsorship, etc., for mutual gain. Now we need to review the many other altruistic ways companies can help during the public phase – most of which give them a good return in terms of positive profile and improved relations with staff, shareholders, customers, suppliers, national and local government, opinion formers and all sectors of the community with whom they are in contact.

HOW TO APPROACH

It is essential to look for suitable links, such as children's product manufacturers for Great Ormond Street, pharmaceutical companies for medical research charities, or builders for housing associations. Having selected targets, learn as much

---

Subjects to investigate about companies

- Mission statement – has it devised one?
- Services or products – what are they?
- Customers – who are they?
- Headquarters and branches – where are they?
- Directors – who are they, and do they have links with the charity?
- Employees – how many?
- Shareholders – how many? It may be possible to obtain the shareholders' register as a ready-made mailing list.
- Marketing strategy – what is it?
- Community relations policy – what is it?
- History of charitable support – details?

about them as possible before approaching them to be sure of the best way to pitch your approach and which area of your work to ask them to support.

Some of the information that is required about companies can be obtained from their annual reports if they are registered at Companies House. Your first step is to obtain a copy of this document and the best way to do this is to approach the company itself. Most are delighted to help. Do not forget to monitor and act quickly on relevant information published in the marketing and specialist PR media.

The method of approach is the same – personal links wherever possible. Go to the top when you have a suitable contact, not forgetting that like approaches like for the best results: chairman to chairman, general manager to general manager, and so on. In the public phase, the chairman of an organization will often refer to a colleague before deciding. This may be the head of marketing to review a potential joint promotion, or the personnel director regarding Give As You Earn, the payroll deduction scheme. The ideal entrée can sometimes be a pincer movement – chairman to chairman at the volunteer level and staff member to the relevant company contact.

There is a wide selection of ways in which companies can help charities during a public appeal. The ways that they can help that are listed here (apart from methods of giving listed in Chapter 14) are just a few of the avenues open to companies that wish to support a charity. New ways are being invented all the time.

Ways companies can help a public appeal

- seconding staff
- adopting the charity – staff fund-raising
- matching staff fund-raising pound for pound
- staff training
- approaching their contacts on your behalf – suppliers, customers, shareholders
- Give As You Earn Scheme
- gifts in kind (office equipment and furniture, building materials, etc.)
- gifts in kind of company services, such as printing or design

---

EMPLOYEE FUND-RAISING

One of the new trends I saw growing apace during the Wishing Well Appeal was companies encouraging their staff to take on a 'charity of the year' and raising enormous sums in a wide range of imaginative ways. Wise companies are careful to ensure that they become involved only in a charity which has the backing of all staff – blue collar and white collar – and sometimes the funds raised by staff are matched, pound for pound, by the company. I believe that this is one of the most exciting new developments in fund-raising because of the immense benefit it brings to the employees, the dedicated people who do all the work – and I always like to see credit given where credit is due. Some outstanding examples of company involvement during the Wishing Well Appeal were Tesco, United Biscuits,

John Laing and Inchcape. All these companies had close links with the leadership of the Appeal, so they knew at the highest level what they were supporting.

Tesco

Tesco, the supermarket giant, raised a staggering £2 million for the Appeal – twice its target. The money came from a carefully planned and coordinated campaign to involve staff, customers and suppliers throughout the country.

It all started when Roy Walker, Secretary of Tesco Sports and Social Club, approached John Eastoe, then director of the company's charities and appeals activities, with the idea of a walk in aid of the Wishing Well Appeal. Sir Ian MacLaurin, Tesco Chairman and a member of the Wishing Well Appeal's Commerce and Industry Panel, endorsed Roy Walker's ideas and made the Wishing Well Tesco's top charity project for 1988, with a target of £1 million.

The campaign began at the start of 1988 with the sale of Great Ormond Street Hospital T-shirts, keyrings, badges and stickers to raise the money to finance events. Wishing Well Appeal collecting boxes were installed in the stores, posters were distributed and May 13 and 14 were designated National Days of Action. Meanwhile, the events got under way with a Pancake Race outside the group's Cheshunt head office, raising £5,000.

The centrepiece was Walker's Walk – a 1,000-mile march from John O'Groats to Land's End, led by Roy Walker and four other employees, beginning on 24 April and ending on 4 June. The marchers collected more than £1 million on the way, returning to head office to be greeted by Sir Ian, a brass band – and teeming rain!

Gold, Silver and Bronze commemorative certificates were awarded to all Tesco stores, depots and offices that took part, according to how much they raised against their targets.

When it was all over, the company produced a book, *GOSH – That Was the Year That Was,* as a fine memento of what Sir Ian rightly described as a truly magnificent achievement.

Tesco receives 30,000 letters a year asking the company to support charitable appeals. One in seven is successful. The policy is that the company's involvement is endorsed by the main board, and 20 per cent is added to all staff fund-raising. Sir Ian chairs the Charity Trustees and sits on the Save The Children Fund's Industry and Commerce Group. *I believe that it is the responsibility of top company people to show a lead in supporting the community, so that the boys and girls at floor level know where you are coming from,* he explained.

United Biscuits

United Biscuits' Chief Executive, Bob Clarke, and his successor, Eric Nicoli, headed the Marketing Panel of the Wishing Well Appeal, so we were delighted when they said they would see if their staff would run a special campaign for the Appeal. United Biscuits appointed David Parker as Appeal Coordinator to stimulate staff interest and fund-raising, but no pressure was applied and employees were free to support other children's hospitals if they so wished. Apart from an extraordinary range of imaginative staff fund-raising ideas, the company also set up joint promotions with the Appeal for two of its brands, Hula Hoops and Skips,

Employee fund-raising is seen as a potential growth area for charities. Above, promoting team spirit and fund-raising for the Wishing Well Appeal, British Telecom cyclists arrive in Brighton. Below, Tesco's staff toss the pancake – part of the outstanding achievement of their employees, customers and suppliers who raised an incredible £2 million for the Appeal. (Photograph: R. Hampson)

as well as sponsoring the Penguin Swimathon '88 – an event which netted £689,000 for the Appeal. Penguin Biscuits also provided the publicity for the Swimathon and I do not believe I have ever seen so many press cuttings for one event. I was aware that United Biscuits put the good of the cause first at all times and their own interests second, so I was glad to see that sponsoring the Swimathon had proved to be a real benefit to their business. The event was repeated the following year to benefit other children's charities, when once again many thousands of pounds were raised for deserving causes.

By the end of the Wishing Well Appeal, United Biscuits had contributed over £1 million, compared with their original target of £250,000. The help we received from the company through their staff was outstanding. The company donated £1 for every £1 raised by staff. It is sad that the public does not realize the immense contribution by companies to charity work through lending their most important resource – their staff. At the end, we invited a delegation from United Biscuits to Great Ormond Street, where cheques were presented and the staff met many patients, doctors and nurses. We did our best to convey to them that we appreciated their hard work on our behalf.

John Laing

Laing's staff raised funds for us throughout the country, thanks to the untiring efforts of Martin Laing, who was a member of the Appeal's Commerce and Industry Panel. They supported other children's hospitals at the same time, raising a total of £825,000. Of this, just over £500,000 was for the Wishing Well Appeal and the rest was spread among 19 other children's hospitals in the U.K. Laing's Charitable Trust contributed £200,000 towards the total. The staff embarked on a massive number of events, from sponsored slimming and keeping silent, to barbecues and car boot sales. Like Tesco, they went from Land's End to John O'Groats. David Bottom, Chairman of John Laing Construction, and Brian Morris, Area Director of Laing Homes West, cycled the distance in ten days, raising nearly £60,000. Laing's way of thanking their staff for such a marvellous effort was to lay on an elaborate dinner and floor show. The memorable evening was compèred by Angela Rippon and hosted by Martin Laing and his wife.

Inchcape

The late Sir George Turnbull, Chairman and Chief Executive of the Inchcape international services and marketing group, was a member of the Appeal's Commerce and Industry Panel. The company undertook two major initiatives.

In the first place, the Inchcape Charitable Trust committed itself to donating £60,000 over four years. The trust is funded almost equally by the company and by Inchcape Family Investments, representing Lord Inchcape's family interest. Secondly, Sir George went to major motor manufacturers in the U.K. and said: 'Give me a car and I will find ways of raising funds with it.' Inchcape, which owns the Toyota GB dealership, was given a Toyota Celica, a Renault 5, a Peugeot 405 and a special Teardrop edition of a Metro (which sported the Wishing Well Appeal logo). Three were raffled and the Renault was offered as a prize in a competition organized by the magazine *Woman's Realm*. Altogether, the four cars raised

Charities should feature high-profile events which are in tune with the character and purpose of their cause. Hence the Wishing Well Appeal staged many sports events which highlighted youth and healthy living. Above, Linford Christie and Fatima Whitbread joined Wellwishers in the Alliance & Leicester Cashplus Walk in 1988.

£71,500, more than twice their retail value. So they showed considerable imagination and ingenuity in dreaming up money-raising schemes which helped to promote their own activities, ensuring maximum benefit to both parties.

A further £73,500 was raised by Inchcape employees through a series of special events. They entered the London Marathon, held raffles, darts matches, concerts and many other occasions organized either by branches or through the Sports and Social Club.

GIVE AS YOU EARN

Since 1987 it has been possible for anyone who is receiving wages or a pension taxed through Pay As You Earn to make donations to charities deemed acceptable by the Inland Revenue through the Give As You Earn scheme. For many years, it was possible to have donations deducted by one's employer, but the advantage of the new scheme is in the arrangement for tax. If an employer agrees to operate a Give As You Earn scheme, people can make donations from their wages to charity, up to a maximum of £900 a year or £75 a month without paying tax on what they give. A donation of £75 actually costs the donor £56.25. The remaining £18.75 that goes to the charity is money the donor would have paid in tax. The advantage to the charity is that it does not have to go through the process of reclaiming tax as it does with a covenant.

An employer must agree to operate the scheme and pass the donations to an approved agency, such as the Charities Aid Foundation, which checks the acceptability of the recipient. The agency makes a small administrative charge. Even this can be circumvented if the employees form themselves into a Charity Committee which undertakes distribution of the donations via official vouchers (which look like cheques).

An employee can change his mind about the size of his donation and decide to leave the scheme at any time. He can nominate up to eight charities to receive his gift and keep their names confidential. Existing employee charity funds can be converted to Give As You Earn arrangements.

The Wishing Well Appeal was fortunate in that the Give As You Earn legislation was passed just before the Appeal went public. It attracted about 400 Give As You Earn donors who contributed about 0.1 per cent (£31,000) of the initial Appeal target. We wrote to them all after the Appeal to thank them for their support and to urge them to keep giving to Great Ormond Street. Nevertheless, Give As You Earn is not very appropriate to a one-off appeal. Give As You Earn donors are likely, through inertia, to stay with the same one or two charities. This means the one-off appeal must either find new Give As You Earn donors or try to wean away existing ones and run the risk of being accused of poaching.

British Telecom introduced payroll giving in 1987. The initial take-up among employees was poor but in 1988, after a decision to match employees' contributions pound for pound, the scheme grew rapidly. A further very effective way of encouraging involvement was the setting up of an employees' committee to run the scheme – people like self-management and the opportunity to choose who is to receive their donations. They also appreciate being approached face to face and not through a letter and the feeling, which British Telecom management cultivates, that they are under no pressure to participate.

British Telecom Give As You Earn 1988-93

	Employee donations	BT matching	Total donation to charity through Give As You Earn
	£'000	£'000	£'000
1988/89	112	112	224
1989/90	250	250	500
1990/91	400	400	800
1991/92	600	600	1200
1992/93 (budget)	800	800	1600

Key points to Give As You Earn

- Tax-efficient form of charitable giving
- Importance of company matching
- Plenty of room for growth
- Face to face/fun/no pressure
- Working with charities
- Employee choice
- Employee-led campaigns

COMPANY HOUSE JOURNALS

These provide a very useful mouthpiece which may be used to help charities by encouraging company employees to become involved. They can promote ideas for employee fund-raising and report on how the appeal is progressing. Pictures of staff presenting cheques and other related events stimulate interest. The whole enterprise is greatly enhanced if it is promoted by the company chairman or some similar figure. So it is a good idea to put the editors of these journals on your mailing list for press releases, so they can keep staff fully informed and maybe tempt them into becoming involved.

GIFTS IN KIND/SECONDEES

Part of the strategy of the Wishing Well Appeal was to raise as much as possible through gifts in kind and to bolster our skilled manpower with as many people as possible seconded to us from companies. As a result, we spent only half of our administration budget. It is sometimes easier for a company to give goods or services than straight donations. It can be more beneficial to them if the charity can be seen to be using their products in a high-profile manner – computers, carpets, furniture and hi-tech equipment. Tax relief is available to the donor of the gift.

Secondees have become very popular. At any one time, the not-for-profit organization Business in the Community has between 30 and 40 secondees on its books. When companies merge and there are more managers on the payroll than the combined group requires, this is an ideal way to continue to use their skills for the good of the community. This practice has been developed by the major clearing banks for many years and we had Midland Bank secondees during the Wishing Well Appeal. Initially, the Midland seconded a computer expert to set up our record systems. He was replaced by Jean Punter, who had been the Midland Chairman's secretary, to maintain those systems and be responsible for recording funds received by the Appeal. She did a marvellous job. While an employee is temporarily seconded to a charity, his employer may continue to bear the total expenditure attributable to his employment, including National Insurance, pension and other benefits (but rarely his out-of-pocket expenses). The secondment must be temporary, but any number of employees can be seconded.

OTHER TAXATION IMPLICATIONS

Charities should ensure that corporate donors realize that if a gift is forthcoming on the basis of a promised return, that constitutes a commercial return to the company and the charity could be seen to be trading (with all the attendant tax and charity law ramifications as discussed in Chapter 23). Therefore, charities should carefully consider any quid pro quo relationship where they are receiving a 'donation' in exchange for providing something – such as special publicity, etc. However, if no contractual obligation is entered into and if the charity is merely acknowledging a true donation, there should be no tax implication. It is particularly important to clarify this point with companies who cannot recover all their VAT, such as clearing banks and insurance companies.

CONCLUSION

It is hoped and expected that the involvement in charitable activities of this country's corporate sector will increase, as companies encounter a more professional attitude on the part of charities. Once they realize that charities understand the need for a partnership relationship, they should be more prepared to commit themselves for longer periods. That trend is led by the Per Cent Club, which was launched by the Prince of Wales in 1986. Its members are companies who are asked to contribute at least half of one per cent of their annual pre-tax profits. Some give one per cent, but the average still lags behind the organization's U.S. equivalent of 1.5 per cent. However, this situation may be affected by the different tax position. The British version of the club has several hundred members. Their community involvement includes financial assistance, secondment of staff, professional expertise, time given voluntarily by employees and the donation of goods, services, equipment and buildings, and the use of company facilities. Contributions are made to job creation and enterprise projects, education and training programmes, local economic development, inner city regeneration, the environment and the arts, as well as to charitable causes.

The more a charity keeps in touch with its donors and supporters, the more long-term loyalty it will earn. So it is vital to be seen to appreciate the hard work contributed by company employees. One of the most difficult things to do during a massive public appeal is to be sure that everyone receives due thanks in as personal a way as possible. To invite a group of employees to a special reception at the charity when a cheque is presented and to take them on a tour of the site – as we did at Great Ormond Street – was the least we could do to show our appreciation. It was also important not to forget the photographs for the house magazine and to keep continued contact with those concerned, telling them how their money had been used, possibly to name a specific room or item of equipment.

It is important to see a supporter's input to a charity as an investment; this applies especially to companies. They expect and deserve a good return on their money and/or time. It is in everyone's interests for the charity to see that the companies feel that the partnership is mutually beneficial.

Chapter 29

OTHER FUND-RAISING METHODS

There are masses of fund-raising methods – too many to cover in this book – and many which deserve a book in their own right, as can be seen in the Bibliography. Most of the fund-raising techniques crucial to a one-off appeal in the public phase have already been covered. However in this chapter I provide a short review of direct mail, telemarketing, public collections, lotteries and legacy generation.

A new era is dawning in the evolution of charity direct mail as practitioners develop ways of making this method of mass marketing more personal in order to forge closer relationships. Telemarketing has been tried by most major charities involved in volume direct mail and has reaped worthwhile returns. Public collections need special attention because of the new regulations introduced by the Charities Act 1992. Lotteries present a tangle of red tape and this is probably the area where most charities inadvertently break the law. Finally, generating legacies is the method which holds most scope for development and rewards in the future, as charities perfect the skill of targeting people who live longer – and have more to leave – and marketing reminds them to include charity bequests in their wills.

All these methods of fund-raising are important to most charities, if not during a one-off appeal, then certainly for their long-term prospects.

DIRECT MAIL

Direct mail is a completely different activity from mail order (selling through catalogues), although the two are sometimes confused. They are, however, similar in that they are both highly specialist activities.

An organization might have a number of motives for using direct mail, such as the building of awareness, communicating with existing supporters or trying to recruit new supporters.

Setting up an effective, profitable direct mail operation takes careful planning and a certain amount of investment. It is worth distinguishing between the direct mail which may be used by a national or local charity in communicating with supporters and potential supporters on a continuing basis, and 'one-off' direct mail which may be used in support of a specific project, such as a hospital or an emergency appeal.

Success factors

In both cases, success depends largely on two elements – the package and the list. Examination of any samples of good direct mail currently used by charities in this country will show that the preparation of direct mail packages is a highly skilled job which employs a number of very subtle marketing techniques.

Its purpose is to capture the attention of a donor or potential donor and persuade him to give generously and in the most effective way. Careful thought goes into suggested levels of giving, the packaging of the project or concept in the most attractive way and relating levels of giving to costs of the charity's operational work. Persuading donors to give tax-effectively – usually by deed of covenant or through Gift Aid – can make a very significant difference to direct mail results. Covenanted giving particularly can provide much higher levels of donations and higher donor loyalty.

Testing

One of the beauties of direct mail is that it can be – and should be – tested before large numbers of letters are sent out. Testing allows a charity to establish what levels of response and what levels of giving might be expected. It is those two statistics which determine the success or failure of the exercise. The figures will vary quite significantly depending on whether you are going to 'cold' potential donors or approaching your own list of supporters or potential supporters.

Lists

Lists may come from a number of sources. The most commonly used lists are those derived from electoral registers. These can now be categorized with considerable sophistication and it is possible to buy lists from electoral registers which have been profiled according to household type or buying patterns. There are also a number of agencies selling specialist lists, ranging from women investors through purchasers by mail order to the lists held by garden centres and nurseries. Costs range from £70 per 1,000 names and addresses upwards. Care should be taken with the probity of the lists (when they were last used, how accurate they are, how often they are used, whether they have been used by other charities and so on).

Finally, you may also decide to do a reciprocal mailing with another charity – effectively an exchange of lists, although safeguards should be written into the process and it should be handled with great care. The Institute of Charity Fund-raising Managers has a useful Code of Practice on reciprocal mailings.

Expected results

The question uppermost in people's minds is what results can you expect from direct mail? The answer is that they vary dramatically according to the package and the respondent. National charities may be getting response rates of between one and three per cent and average gifts of between £10-£30. For appropriate local projects, you might expect to see a response rate and average gift higher than these figures.

At the end of the day, the advice must be that you seek professional help and that you use direct mail with great care.

Golden rules

- Always test before using direct mail on a large scale.
- Have a clear, simple message and be tactful – people are rapid to react against unsolicited mail.
- Make it easy for donors to respond. What are you asking for?
- Keep reminding donors what their gifts will achieve.
- Keep refining the list.
- Direct mail is a highly specialist business – do take advice.
- Remember to say 'Thank you.'

Data protection

In October 1992, the European Commission published the second revised draft of a Directive on Data Protection which first appeared in September 1990. The Directive cannot be implemented until it has been approved by the Council of Ministers; this is expected in 1993/1994. Its final form will not be known for some time, but it will eventually put restrictions on the use of computerized personal data which will reduce the scope for direct mailing. Three main proposals are of concern:

1 Possible recipients may be entitled not just to 'opt out' of mailings; they may be unapproachable unless they 'opt in' by declaring their willingness to be written to. The seriousness of this is shown by research carried out by the NSPCC, which found that from a representative group 24 per cent would opt out, 76 per cent remain, while, if they had to opt in, only 4 per cent would do so.
2 Profiling – it would be in order to make a selection from the data of any desired grouping provided there was no danger of discriminating against any of the data subjects.
3 In order to transfer personal details from your list to another you would have to inform those affected what details you proposed to transfer and why.

Successful direct mail operations

The Wishing Well Appeal

The Wishing Well Appeal was the vehicle which brought the Hospital a list of not just warm but hot names – 80,000 of them during the Appeal. The Hospital continues to develop contact with these donors through direct mail. Great Ormond Street's most valuable list is parents of children who come to the Hospital. At the time of the Appeal, it treated 9,000 in-patients a year and handled 70,000 out-patient appointments. Establishing a direct mail campaign during the Appeal was a highly sensitive process. First, the list was not available to the Appeal Office because of the need for confidentiality over patient records. Second, great care had to be taken to ensure that the child of parents mailed had not died since treatment at the Hospital. In this case, the letter might have caused additional pain.

To overcome the confidentiality issue, the Hospital sent out letters which were individually signed by the relevant consultant. Parents were merely advised about the impending Appeal and told whom they should contact if they wished to help. No pressure was applied. Over 30 different versions of the letter were produced, so that consultants' letters could be individual. The letters were sent to parents just before the public launch of the Appeal. Although some viewed this exercise with trepidation, we had an excellent response. The process recruited not only donors but people who became active fund-raisers during the Appeal. Out of several thousand letters, only two or three replied in any adverse manner – although that was two or three too many. There was also considerable difficulty in coordinating lists of patients to eradicate duplications because patients had seen more than one consultant.

Additionally, towards the end of the private appeal, we produced a list of potential major donors (people or companies) where we had found no personal introductions. Soon after the public launch of the Appeal, backed, therefore, by considerable publicity, this group received a letter, personally signed by our Chairman, Lord Prior. This process produced a very positive response.

NSPCC

The NSPCC, unlike the Wishing Well Appeal, already had a sophisticated direct mail operation in existence before its special appeal. At this time it already received a significant proportion of its ongoing income from direct mail and used the technique in three areas during its 1985 centenary appeal.

The three areas mailed by the NSPCC

1 An appeal to all its 'warm donors', asking for an extra contribution in addition to their normal giving to the centenary appeal fund.

2 A massive 'cold' mailing to three million non-supporters, which used the publicity around the centenary appeal as a means of recruiting new donors and to enhance its ongoing income in future years.

3 A 'mop-up' mailing at the end of the centenary appeal to a carefully researched list of wealthy people who, for some reason, had fallen through the net of the private appeal and who had not yet given. A personalized letter, including a special version of the appeal brochure, asked up-front for a pledge of £1,000. This 'cold' mailing produced the expected response rate – but with an average pledge of £800!

TELEMARKETING

Telephone fund-raising ('telemarketing') consists of using telephone calls to raise the level of support among present or potential donors. The calls can be made by the appeal – which raises problems of extra volunteers and telephone lines – or by an agency.

Telemarketing began seriously in Britain about four years ago, but its use has declined over the last two. Typically, the total gross cost of outward calls is between £3 and £5 each and donation levels need to be high to justify the cost. There are non-quantifiable benefits – a chance to show existing donors that they are appreciated and to keep up their morale, or perhaps to keep them informed of progress and events. Supporters may provide useful feedback. Nevertheless, high costs, low levels of return and the risk of antagonizing people who receive the calls all indicate a very cautious approach to this form of fund-raising. Current experience suggests that it does best when linked to advertising in the press in aid of a specific, time-limited need.

If you decide to use your own volunteers for a telemarketing campaign you will need the telephone numbers of your known supporters which should be among your data. You will also need, vitally, to coach your volunteers in what to say and how to say it. Alternatively, you can employ an agency. The advantages of doing that are that it can run a trial on your behalf, it has experience, hardware, and trained personnel and it can train your volunteers. The disadvantage is that you lose control and cannot easily vet the quality of service provided.

There is an ICFM Code of Practice and The Direct Marketing Association is to operate a telephone preference service which will, through a central register, enable people to indicate that they do not wish to receive telephone calls from charities.

PUBLIC COLLECTIONS

Charities and voluntary organizations undertake a range of public collecting activities in support of their fund-raising. All of these activities are now regulated under the Charities Act 1992 (implemented in this respect from September 1993). A more detailed analysis of the major provisions of this Act is contained in Appendix 8.

There are hundreds of thousands of public collections taking place each year throughout the United Kingdom. Individual donations are low but, because their volume is high, public collections can be a very cost-effective way of raising considerable support for your appeal and in providing a very public face for the appeal from a public relations perspective. They offer a positive opportunity for the public to participate actively in supporting either a national or local appeal within their own community. They also provide useful feedback on the cause from its grassroots donors.

Preparation

First, and of critical importance, you need to ensure that you are aware of the regulations governing public collections and that you have obtained all the necessary consents. Since these requirements are covered in Appendix 8, I will not dwell on them here.

Certainly, at the busiest time of your appeal during the public phase, you might well be deluged with calls from the general public offering to undertake a collec-

---

Timing for public collections

- Plan well ahead.
- Avoid the periods when people are unlikely to be at home, such as summer holiday times. If you are collecting on a street, choose a day when there will be people about in the high street or shopping precinct.
- Try to link the collection with some other event the appeal is holding, for greater publicity.
- Try to obtain advance publicity via local press or radio.

---

tion on your behalf. Wherever possible, you need to try to anticipate this demand and establish clear guidelines. Identify how collections should be undertaken, prepare the relevant support documentation that volunteers require and provide clear guidance on how the income from the collection will be transmitted back to the appeal office. Failure to have any of this properly prepared is likely to lead to major disputes between collectors and the appeal office and, in any event, the demotivation of volunteers who want to help support the cause.

Collectors

Once you have decided where you want to collect, calculate how many collectors you need. The more collectors, the more money, so try all sources – supporters, national organizations, such as the Rotary Club, and local organizations, such as church groups and neighbourhood watch groups. After collection day some of the contacts may lead to fruitful community relationships.

From the perspective of any potential fund-raiser, public collections offer a major opportunity to engage a vast army of supporters in the actual process of helping your appeal reach its target. Because it involves the active participation of large numbers of volunteers who do not necessarily have the same degree of awareness and level of commitment to the cause as others more intimately connected with it, it is critically important that all the participants have the relevant information about the nature of the appeal, its purpose and progress to date. It is also necessary that they have sufficient information regarding both their legal responsibilities as collectors and the means by which the income from the collection will be transmitted back to the appeal office. Recruit carefully – it is the responsibility of the local appeal organizers to ensure collectors are of sufficient intelligence and integrity to perform their duties correctly.

Above all, always remember that volunteer collectors are ambassadors for your cause. If they are happy, well briefed and clear as to the purpose of the collection, not only will you raise money but you will also find an effective way of directly involving large numbers of the general public in supporting your appeal.

Techniques

There are so many charity collections. You must ensure that yours, however small, will be clearly branded with the appeal's logo and publicly available documentation. In addition, it is helpful to try to be different. Ask supporters who are collecting on your behalf if they would not mind dressing up in fancy dress. Provide small incentives, such as badges and pens with the logo of your organization printed clearly on them – people like to feel they are getting something, however small, in return for their support. Attempt to create a small interested crowd around the collecting area – success breeds success – and people will inevitably drift towards small gatherings of other people for no other reason than simple curiosity.

An attractive design for a collecting box is a practice developed many years ago. When we were planning the design of the box for the Wishing Well Appeal, a family friend coincidentally found in her attic a very attractive plaster collection box for the Great Ormond Street Hospital. It was modelled in the shape of a sick child in bed with nurse standing by. The design contrasted with that used for the more recent Appeal – a cardboard cut-out of a Wishing Well, equally imaginative and appealing.

There are many dangers to watch out for. I was told two salutary tales. The first involved a man who, on spotting an NSPCC staff member with his collecting box, was at great pains to avoid giving a donation. In averting his eyes, he fell over a nearby litter bin. So try not to stand near obvious obstacles. The second occurred when a male collector was approached by a lady with an exceptionally large bosom. She expected him to apply the sticker she was to receive following her donation. He was really rather spoiled for choice. As a result of his red-faced confusion, the sticker came to rest somewhere on the upper region of her shoulder. Moral: collectors of an unworldly disposition would do better to hand the lady the sticker and let her put it on herself!

Alexandra Rose Day Fund

Much of the work of organizing a public collection can be avoided by taking part in one organized by the Alexandra Rose Day Fund. Any 'people-caring' charity may apply to take part. Alexandra Rose Day will obtain the necessary permits, supply collecting boxes and, through its six regional offices, coordinate the various charities that will be taking part. The participating charities provide their own collectors and, at the end of the day, retain 80 per cent of what is in their boxes, sending the remainder to the Rose Day Fund. In June 1992, over 100 charities benefited from one of these flag days.

Static collection boxes

There are no regulations concerning unattended boxes that stand in homes or public premises. All you need is the owner's permission. Collection boxes can provide a steady and reliable flow of funds for a one-off appeal, although the amounts tend not to be large. Proceeds are enhanced if the box is imaginative and placed in a visible location where it will attract the eye of the potential donor.

It is also possible to use mechanical collecting boxes. This includes an element of fun when you part with your coins and is naturally very popular with children.

Remember, if boxes are not looked after regularly they will be vandalized or stolen. If they stand full for any length of time, the public may well become cynical about the appeal's need for money.

Servicing static collecting boxes

- Persuade the owner of the premises to be responsible and to telephone the collector when the box is nearly full.
- Alternatively, arrange for a collector to call regularly.
- I strongly advise that collection boxes should be provided sealed and only opened in the presence of a registered charity representative. This is to protect the charity and the collector.
- Remember that Part I of the Charities Act 1992 requires that you state on all collecting boxes that the funds are for a registered charity.

LOTTERIES

Lotteries are a way of distributing prizes by chance. The organizers of lotteries must recognize that they are bound strictly by regulations contained in the Lotteries and Amusements Act 1976 and in subsequent orders through statutory instrument pertinent to that Act which are issued from time to time by the Home Secretary. I recommend that first of all you seek the appropriate professional advice. The Institute of Charity Fundraising Managers has produced a Code of Practice on Lottery activity. You may also contact the Gaming Board, which is responsible for regulating lotteries with potential ticket sales in excess of £10,000, or the relevant local authority within whose boundaries you wish to undertake the lottery.

Some people and organizations find lotteries morally unacceptable. Any fund-raiser considering a lottery must, therefore, make sure that he is not unwittingly involving anyone (perhaps a trustee) who might hold such an opinion. Lotteries are, however, well suited to time-limited appeals and are often useful during a slack period between other events and fund-raising activities.

Legal and fiscal requirements

For the Inland Revenue lotteries are a form of trading and profits are therefore liable to tax. As with retail trading, there are exemptions:

- Small lotteries, raffles and draws held in the course of dances, bazaars or fêtes. These are regarded, like occasional trading, as incidental sources of income not in competition with commercial traders.
- A lottery organized by a specially constituted separate trading company, the profits of which are covenanted, or passed by Gift Aid to the charity.
- Where each lottery ticket carries a statement that a declared portion of the purchase price will be given to the stated charity, as long as the remainder is taken up in expenses. Then there are no profits to be taxed.
- A local authority lottery.

Types of lottery

The Lotteries and Amusement Act distinguishes between three main types of lottery.

1. Small lotteries, where the prizes total less than £50, which are run incidentally during an event or entertainment not counted as trading. The value of the prizes may exceed £50 if they have all been donated.

2. Larger, open, lotteries are known as society lotteries and are strictly regulated under the 1976 Act (but see the section on the National Lottery below). If the value of the total number of printed tickets does not exceed £10,000 (and/or the prizes are worth no more than £2,000), the lottery will be regulated by your local authority with whom you must register it. If the total value of tickets printed exceeds £10,000 (and/or the prizes are worth more than £2,000), you must register the lottery with the Gaming Board.

3. Private lotteries, where the sale of tickets is confined to members of a society or persons working in the same premises. All the proceeds must be donated to the society. If these conditions are met, it is not necessary to register with the Gaming Board.

The type of activity you select will be dependent on your appeal and the target audience. These factors will also help you choose your preferred prizes – for which you should seek donations. Try to ensure prizes are imaginative and appropriate to the appeal.

National Lottery

The government has now published the enabling legislation creating a new National State Lottery for the United Kingdom. This Bill (proceeding through Parliament at the time of going to press) establishes the broad structure and functions associated with the running, the regulating and the distribution of proceeds from the proposed National Lottery. It is itself the precursor to much more detailed legislation (that will be contained in future regulations) and directions to be made by the Secretary of State. These are unlikely to be developed before the end of 1993. The National Lottery itself is likely to begin operation in the summer of 1994 with the first proceeds available for distribution towards the end of 1994.

The government proposes that the National Lottery will be regulated by the Director General of a new body which will be known as OFLOT – the office of the National Lottery. The Director General will license and regulate commercial organizations wishing to promote National Lottery games. Charitable bodies already engaged in society lottery activity will be able to tender to become National Lottery promoters as well as retaining their right to undertake society lotteries. The Director General will be directly responsible to the Secretary of State and to Parliament (through an annual report laid before the House) for all aspects of the management of National Lottery games.

The Secretary of State for the National Heritage will be responsible for overseeing the distribution of proceeds from the National Lottery games to the beneficiary bodies. The Bill at present provides for five broad categories of beneficiary, each one receiving an equal share from the proceeds of the National Lottery. The beneficiary areas are: the arts (distributed through the Arts Council); the heritage (distributed through the National Heritage Board); sport (distributed through the Sports Council); charities and voluntary organizations (distributed through a new National Lotteries Charities Board established under this Act); and finally, the Millenium Fund (distributed by a Millenium Commission established again under this Act to celebrate the arrival of the next century). It is anticipated that charitable organizations whose objects enable them to apply for a grant under the aegis of heritage, sport or the arts will apply in the first instance to one of these bodies. The National Lottery Charities Board will therefore have broad powers to pick up those organizations who do not come under any of these categories as well as mainstream charity and voluntary organization activity.

In the case of each of the benefiting areas the government intends grant making to be independent of existing government policy and to provide funds which are additional to existing central and local government support. Each of the distributing bodies will provide grants weighted according to both national and regional variations of need. Precise guidelines for eligibility have as yet not been established and are unlikely to be until early 1994.

Amendments to existing legislation governing society lotteries

The same legislation will also provide a timely update of the 1976 Lotteries and Amusements Act which currently governs the operation of society lotteries undertaken by charities and voluntary organizations. The legislation provides a number of compensatory amendments designed to mitigate against the possible negative impact that the new National Lottery will have on existing lottery activities undertaken by charities and voluntary organizations.

It provides a relaxation in registration limits to the Gaming Board, an increase in the total acceptable turnover for lottery activity in any one year, a relaxation in expense expenditure by societies undertaking lotteries and an increase in prize levels. It is likely that these measures will be retained in the final version of the Act and will come into force in the autumn of 1993.

The legislation also creates additional regulation of society lotteries managed on behalf of charities by external commercial organizations. Under the legislation these individuals (and/or companies) are to be regarded in future as Lottery Managers. They will be subject to regulation by the Gaming Board to whom they will have to apply for a licence to operate society lotteries and will have to provide detailed accounts of all their activities, undertaken on behalf of charities and voluntary organizations. Failure to comply will lead to charges of criminal offences against the external commercial operators.

GENERATING LEGACIES

A legacy or bequest is any gift made under a will. It may be in the form of money, securities, property or the balance of an estate. Legacies are not an obvious source of income for a time-limited appeal. Marketing for legacies is very much a long-term investment and will see little real return within three or four years. However capital projects, such as those involving building work, do entail ongoing expenses over years and can benefit from pre-empted income. For some charities, legacies are the single largest source of income; the top 400 fund-raising charities received over £477 million in this way in 1991. Despite this, only 10 per cent of wills contain charitable bequests and one in four people dies without leaving a will.

Budgeting

One of the problems with legacies, from a budgeting point of view, is that this income source is very difficult to predict or control. An interesting way which has been developed for dealing with this is to establish a 'legacy equalization' account. This is a sub-account (discrete reserve) within your general accounts to which you send all legacies which accrue in any one year. Essentially, you agree to 'equalize out' a portion of that income each year and release it to the income and expenditure account. This technique enables fund-raisers to budget income levels for the unbudgetable!

Targeting

There is clearly scope for expanding this source of tax-free income. Marketing can be directed towards increasing the number of people making wills which contain bequests in your charity's favour. In the past, legacies have been treated as windfalls. The emphasis must now be on identifying those people most likely to make a bequest – mainly older ABC1 women – and approaching them appropriately. Any charity should be able to identify from its own records those supporters likely to be predisposed to making a will. Age is the most important factor, followed by affluence.

Methods of influencing testators

- by talking to/approaching major donors at a one-to-one personal level
- by advertising in newspapers and journals, especially women's and retirement magazines
- by direct mail – leaflets can give advice on making a will, explain that bequests are free from inheritance tax and give other information. A useful reminder for many people on small incomes is that they may have valuable assets, such as their houses
- by mentioning the opportunity of leaving a legacy in all fund-raising material and offering information on all tick-box coupons
- by writing to solicitors and banks who give advice on making wills, backed by advertisements in *The Banker, Law Society Gazette*, etc. Draw attention to the fact that no inheritance tax is payable on charitable legacies.
- by offering a trustee service. Charities can act as trust corporations, handling the estates of individuals and advising on related matters.

Another way of increasing legacy income is to seek discretionary bequests, those not directed at specific beneficiaries but left to the executors' discretion. The Wishing Well Appeal attracted one such bequest of £800,000. Firms, such as Smee & Ford, specialize in reading wills and, for a fee, in advising charities of the existence of discretionary bequests where a claim might be appropriate. For further information on this subject I suggest you refer to *Relationship Fund-raising* by Ken Burnett, included in the Bibliography, which has a useful section on legacy promotion.

CONCLUSION

There are many methods of raising funds in addition to those described here. People at the Wishing Well Appeal kept thinking up new ways and this process continues throughout the charitable field. The methods I have described are important for any appeal and any director should be sufficiently aware of them to understand each method, advise on them and give at least preliminary information to his volunteers. For additional advice, I recommend that you refer to the various Codes of Practice issued by the Institute of Charity Fundraising Managers and the specialist books listed in the Bibliography.

Chapter 30

ADMINISTRATION

An appeal office requires different administrative systems before and after the public launch. Before, all activities are usually planned and run by well-briefed staff and volunteers. After the public launch, it is very much more of a free-for-all. It can never be completely controlled but, if the public appeal has been accurately assessed at the planning stage, the management should be systematic and on top of the situation. If not, the appeal will receive bad publicity which could dissuade supporters from becoming involved.

It is also important to ensure that administrators are part of the decision-making appeal team from the start. They should be seen as part of the fund-raising effort and their thinking should be in tune with it. Even if they are not actually bringing in funds, they can encourage donors by suggesting more tax-effective ways of giving, by creating goodwill through contacts and generally giving an impression of a well-run, competent organization. It all helps to take the weight off the director's shoulders.

HANDLING ENQUIRIES

It is necessary to assess:

1. What types of response or enquiry are expected?
2. In what volume?
3. Who should handle fulfilment requirements and how?

1. Types of response or enquiry

These depend on the nature of your appeal and what you have set in motion: a huge special event, a massive advertising campaign, a full range of fund-raising triggered by a local group's structure or, perhaps, all of these, as was true of the Wishing Well Appeal.

> ### Possible range of responses and enquiries
>
> - Donations – cash, cheques, credit card payments, covenants, Gift Aid, Give As You Earn, legacies, gifts in kind.
> - Offers of help – for local groups, special events, to run a special event, to help with manning stands or street collections, etc.
> - Specifics – response to specific activities, such as buying tickets, advertisements, corporate hospitality packages, taking part in a national competition.
> - Trading – customers interested in buying from your catalogue or advertisements for products.
> - Joint promotions – companies interested in linking your charity's name with their products/services.
> - Publicity aids – local groups for the public appeal requesting publicity aids of varying kinds to boost their local fund-raising activity or requests for VIPs or charity representatives to collect cheques (see Chapter 22).
> - Press enquiries.

2. Assess the volume

If you know what the commonest queries are going to be and how many to expect, you can ensure that the appeal office has the manpower and training to respond correctly. It is difficult to gauge accurately the likely level of responses, but you can look at the responses received by similar appeals and adjust the numbers to allow for differences between your appeal's profile and the others'. Add to this the type and volume of specific promotions you have set in motion to happen at or soon after your launch, and you will come as near as possible to a useful estimate. However, the public never ceases to surprise even the best pundits.

The fact that you will be going for high impact to reach the widest audience may be good from a fund-raising point of view but problematic for administration. During the Wishing Well Appeal we staggered the advertisements placed in national newspapers so that we could handle the response from the administrative point of view. The most uncertain time is immediately after the launch. After that, it is easier to plan for peak activity times and to recruit more people to cope with specific events.

3. How to handle the fulfilment role

Having gauged the likely level of response, you should recruit sufficient staff or trained volunteers or arrange to divert response. The variety of responses listed in Section 1 above will have to be dealt with in person at your office, by telephone and through the post. The appeal representatives receiving a response in any of these ways need to know all the probable answers or to whom to pass queries. Make a list of which members of staff will deal with which types of query and which subjects. Remember that those dealing with postal, telephone or personal calls are frequently the public's first point of contact with your appeal. The impression they give is very important.

This activity will also link into the need to review constantly various supplies of stationery and promotional materials – such as collecting boxes, banners, posters, literature, etc. – to make sure re-ordering takes place in good time when stocks run low.

Personal response

Assess how much space will be needed for helpers who come into the appeal office, how many reception staff will be required, how cash will be handled safely and receipts issued (see the section on handling cash, later in this chapter). People need to come into a welcoming reception area and meet friendly staff who can deal efficiently with their enquiries. Most charities operate in restricted office space, so your publicity should encourage postal and telephone calls.

Postal response

At least two people should be present when mail is opened to validate cheques and other contents. A quick response is essential – it may sometimes be worth using coded reply paid envelopes to speed up the business of sorting the mail. The reply process can be accelerated with the support of an appropriate computer software system. The appeal office should have a set of standard replies that may be amended, while thank-you letters for gifts are issued automatically when the gift details are incorporated into the system.

Telephone response

You will have to decide how many telephone lines to install and who will man them. Make sure you have suitable hardware so calls get through without delay. It may be possible to direct all calls to a supporter's company which agrees to let you use its telephone lines during certain hours. However, this arrangement is usually made to deal with a specific activity, rather than the general response to an appeal. For one thing, it is not easy to prevail on the public to telephone only between the times you have agreed with the company. Regional offices of the appeal can be used to take calls and their people advised on how to develop an efficient, but friendly telephone manner and to use a standardized form to record the call.

Diverting response

It is best if the main appeal office handles general responses, with specials diverted to other units – either piggy-backing on other offices or arranging to set up offices to take responses to a special event. The Telethon does this well and similar banks of telephone lines are sometimes available to other high volume operations. British Telecom operates a Callstream 0898 service, which can be very effective in handling a large volume of activity. This service enables you to provide information services via the telephone (users dial a special access code) and to receive an income from calls. It has the advantage of enabling you to set up your own telephone-based information service with minimum cash outlay. The disadvantage is that you lose some control over the quality of service given. Further information on this service can be obtained from BT. Charities usually divert response received on trading activities by arranging for dedicated fulfilment houses to send out products or even promotional material, which should, therefore, carry a range of addresses and telephone numbers. Even in the appeal office it can help to give different telephone numbers for different queries, such as special events, local groups and the director's office. It may also be desirable to divert calls to public relations companies if specific enquiries need press information or, rarely, if there is bad publicity which produces too much response for the appeal office to handle satisfactorily. (Press queries are dealt with in Chapter 18.)

THE WISHING WELL APPEAL

Staffing

Wishing Well Appeal structure at October 1987
(at Public Launch)

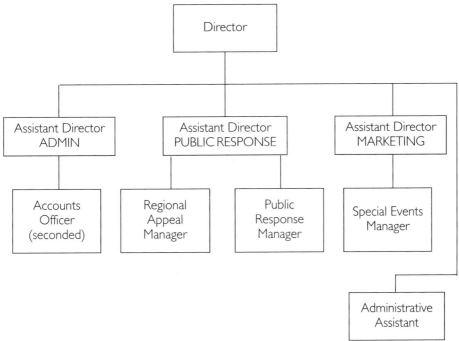

Total salaried: 12
Executives: 8
Secretaries: 4
Secondee: 1
Backed by 54 office volunteers
working a half day plus per week

As can be seen from the diagram of the staff structure in October 1987 at the beginning of the Wishing Well Appeal's public phase, we had three key staff groupings:

Administration   - All usual administrative matters, including computing and accounts

Marketing   - Developing and servicing all the activities of the Marketing Panel. This included public relations and commercial partnerships with companies.

Public Response   - The entire procedure of dealing with the public, including regional groups

It was Wishing Well Appeal policy to keep staff numbers low and I was concerned that the large response we anticipated as a result of our high-impact launch would find us inadequately staffed. The difficulty was to estimate from scratch how many people would be required. The problem was solved when Sir Kit McMahon,

Wishing Well Appeal Structure at October 1988
(when we were running at peak pressure)

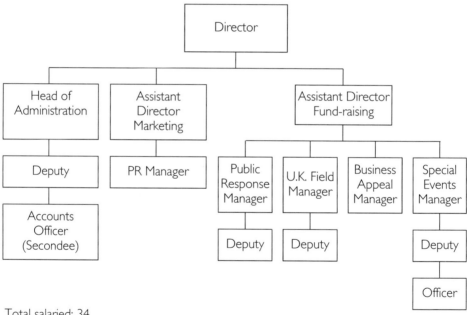

Total salaried: 34
Executives: 14
Admin assistants: 6
Secretaries: 14
(Secondee: 1)
Backed by 54 office volunteers
working a half day plus per week

the Appeal's Honorary Treasurer, arranged that for the first three months the staff of the Midland Bank would receive and handle all our mail. Their staff collected sackfuls of mail from 49 Great Ormond Street and acknowledged receipt of all gifts. The bank had previously installed a computer expert to start up our computer system and to handle our banking requirements.

At the same time, the management consultants Arthur Young (now Ernst & Young) made advisers available at cost only to review with me the likely future work flow and its implications for levels of both staff and volunteers, once we picked up the responsibilities directly. My own proposals for staff increases coincided with the recommendations of the advisers and our Executive Committee accepted that they were necessary and did not breach our policy on staffing. The main proposal was for a large increase in administrative assistants, in many cases those who had already proved themselves to be effective as volunteers, in order to deal with the general response from the public. Arthur Young also gave us invaluable advice on systems for processing the postal responses as well as VAT and accounting procedures.

As our staff grew, we were fortunate to take on David Williams as acting head of administration. Once again he was made available to the Appeal at cost by Arthur Young, but we had considerable additional voluntary input from his consultancy – this included advice on staff recruitment, computers, office facilities and layout.

Volunteers

In preparation for the public appeal we had manned our Appeal office with about 50 volunteers who had responded to a national newspaper advertisement. They were carefully interviewed and selected on the basis of their personal qualities as well as their experience and qualifications. They included retired people and students and nurses in the Hospital. They underwent training to teach them about the Hospital, the purpose of the Appeal, how the Appeal office worked, who did what and an in-depth study of their own planned role. As we had more volunteers than space, a rota was drawn up. All gave at least half a day per week – some considerably more.

During the public phase of the Appeal, the correct handling of volunteers was just as important as managing staff. They were crucial to our operation and helped us to keep our costs down. As some of them filled roles as important as some paid staff, it was a sensitive situation. There should be a clear distinction between the sorts of privileges accorded staff and volunteers, yet both must be part of the family. Research has shown the value of efficient management of volunteers and Sonia Millar, our staff member in charge of volunteers, handled her role most effectively. It is a question of providing the volunteers with appropriate tasks and duties – job descriptions in effect. Some were assigned a regular role; others, who needed more of a challenge, were given a variety of tasks – research has also illustrated the need for managers to be aware of the volunteers' different reasons for volunteering. The effectiveness of Sonia's role was demonstrated when we started to close down the Appeal office. Many of the volunteers said that they did not know how they would fill the void in their lives.

Initially, the Wishing Well Charity Shop – which at the height of the Appeal raised £2,000 a day – was staffed entirely by volunteers. Also, volunteers manned six telephone lines in the basement of 49 Great Ormond Street. One of them did nothing but receive letters for our In Memoriam scheme, an emotionally draining task because people were sending gifts to commemorate a death – in some cases, the deaths of children who had died at Great Ormond Street. Other letters were in memory of an elderly relative.

The volunteers generally sent standard replies, with handwritten postscripts personal to the donor. We thanked every donor, no matter how humble the gift because we were grateful – and because we were building the future donor base for the charity. We circulated the most moving letters. They were a great source of motivation to us. It is up to the charity to make sure that the work is rewarding rather than arduous for volunteers.

Apportioning credit

Another sensitive subject is making sure the right person or appeal unit receives due credit for a donation. What if the appeal receives a major gift from a donor who was dealt with by both the local group and by head office, or if the joint promotions and special events departments lay claim to the income from a special event sponsored by a large gift from a company? This can arise if both units are working hard-to-reach targets. The answer is to give credit to both of them but to make quite sure that the income is counted only once in the appeal's accounts!

Budgeting and accounts

The budget for the public appeal is much more complicated than the ones covering the earlier phases. The appeal director will have appointed staff to head different sections of his operations. Each of these, in consultation with the director, produces a mini-budget of income and expenditure expected for the coming year. It is then the departments' responsibility to stay within budget for all their activities. The overall budget is a summation of all these mini-budgets.

People used to dealing with budgets know that the important point is that they should contain no surprises. Most of us would be delighted if a charity generated more income or spent less than its budget. An accountant would say that the manager got his figures wrong, so you cannot win. Nevertheless, it is best to be cautious. Add every single cost you might incur – with the determined intention to keep costs down by actively looking for gifts in kind – and predict only income of which you are sure. As I am not an accountant, I suppose I am suggesting that you should make sure that every deviation from budget is good news. Above all, a charity can never afford to take risks in dealing with public funds.

Chapter 9 details the financial management, control and reporting needs of an appeal. During the public appeal, cash-flow is crucial to the successful financing of the appeal and reports should be presented regularly to the Trustees/Executive Panel which reveal the appeal's actual cash position against forecast. In addition the cash forecasts will require regular review and updating to assess the adequacy of funds for future operations. In the event of a predicted shortfall steps will need to be taken to facilitate the earlier collection of income or the deferment of payments. If these adjustments cannot be made, however, expenditure may need to be

pruned or bank finance negotiated. Additionally, sophisticated financial information can help appeal managers to build on success and to avoid failures in fund-
raising terms. If the appeal is on target or ahead of it, this information can be used
to raise the morale of staff and volunteers and to encourage wavering potential
donors to back success.

Information systems

The need for efficient information systems is discussed in more detail in Chapter
10. It is often very difficult to set up an efficient system for your public appeal
when you have an enormous flood of responses to input on to the donor database
and to respond to appropriately. In the Wishing Well Appeal, we put donor details
on computer to build up a file for future use. It recorded when and how much
people donated, their names, addresses and occupations, so that we could go back
to people and ask them if they would do something else. However, that sort of
exercise requires staff to key data into the computer. The Wishing Well was so
overwhelmed that initially we had a huge backlog. In the end we sent the records
to a Bristol firm which set up a database for us, for a fee. We could then interrogate
the database. It is quite useful to use external agencies, as the management can
become badly overstretched if an appeal tries to do everything in-house.

HANDLING CASH

The story does not end when the cash enters the building. For us, it was just the
beginning. Firemen would go to Euston Station in London, have a cash collection
and come in with buckets of coins. It was wonderful, but it had to be counted,
bagged and banked, a paying-in slip completed and the sum recorded in the
system.

It used to take two people all morning to add up the cheques and cash and prepare the piles of paper and coins for banking. At least two people are needed to
count the cash, to act as a check on one another. Similarly valuables must be
recorded and described before being taken to an expert for valuation. To reduce
your work load, you may be able to arrange with your bank for supporters to pay
donations straight into it, as the staff there are much more likely to be able to
handle the increased flow of funds correctly.

Security must not be underestimated or overlooked for staff and volunteers, as
well as for the cash, although that is all too easy to do in the goodwill atmosphere
of an appeal. Counting must take place behind a locked door. Cash and valuables
must be locked in a safe overnight if they cannot be banked during the day.
Delivery trips to the bank must be thought out. Vary the messengers, the route and
the time.

It is equally important to send receipts for cash. People opening the post should
write the amount of cash received on the accompanying letter. The letters can go
to another department to send 'thank you' letters, tailored appropriately. That is in
itself a good control. If someone sends £600 and receives a letter thanking them for
£20, the appeal will soon hear about it. The Institute of Charity Fundraising
Managers has published guidelines for the handling of cash donations by charities.

Programme of activities

All activities linked to the appeal should be notified to one central point, where a list can be created and mailed to the staff and the main voluntary supporters. In the Wishing Well Appeal, we produced a list which coordinated special events, media events, the principal regional events, joint promotions, even important staff meetings and regional meetings. It kept everyone in touch on a daily basis with what was going on. In addition, once the organization reached the necessary size, we also had a central information list to tell other staff members who was going to see which company. This was important, so that they could, if necessary, help out a colleague. Somebody might be going to see a company to interest it in a joint promotion. If that person also knew that a major event needed a sponsor and if the joint promotion was not suitable for that company, then the sponsorship idea might be.

LESSONS

The most important lesson from this part of the appeal is that it is better to recruit senior staff at an early stage, so that they have time to develop their areas of activity. To save costs in the Wishing Well Appeal, my role was to develop their operations initially and then take on suitable expertise to run and continue developing the activity. This was a false economy. Earlier recruitment would have been safer for the Appeal, too, in case I had fallen under the proverbial bus! Understandably, the Executive Committee was determined to keep administrative costs down. Another point – we could have done with more office space if it had been available.

------------------------------ *Chapter 31* ------------------------------

FINALE – ANNOUNCING THE
ACHIEVEMENT

You may think it's all over when you hit the appeal's target, but there is still much work to be done. Every appeal generates its own momentum, donations continue to come in and, no matter when you decide to bring it to an end, the appeal will roll on. It is not a simple matter to decide when to announce the end of an appeal. To be honest with potential donors, who are giving money for a specific cause, you should make a public announcement as soon as possible. Do you cry halt when you actually have the target sum in the bank? Do you make an announcement before that to take into account money not yet received from pledges and covenants and risk their not being fulfilled? This may happen through business failure, death, illness, or other reasons. Whatever the cause, it could lead to an embarrassing shortfall. Different circumstances mean that individual appeals will arrive at different decisions about their end-dates. Here, I describe what happened at the Wishing Well Appeal.

When we could see that the Appeal would effectively end a year ahead of schedule we agonized for some time over the problem of pledges. Eventually, we decided to put the public completely in the picture by announcing that the target had been reached – on the assumption that pledges would be met. If we had kept quiet about the £6.7 million of pledged funds, which brought us to our target, and carried on fund-raising, we would have been guilty of misleading the public and our Trustees could have been in breach of trust. Luckily, only one or two pledgers immediately contacted us and said that presumably we did not now need their promised donations. We had to tell them, tactfully, that if pledges were withdrawn we would fall short of our target. In all cases they accepted this statement and luckily there were no involuntary defections through business failure or death. On that basis, we hit the target in January 1989, although we had planned to raise funds for the rest of the year. Many people urged us to continue in order to make more provision for the Great Ormond Street Hospital, an argument which the Executive Committee of the Appeal had to balance against the needs of many other deserving charities.

The Executive Committee's decision to cease once the target was reached was taken to keep faith with donors and other charities which also desperately needed funds. We then had to decide precisely when to make the announcement. The Appeal was moving forward like an ocean liner and we would not be able to reverse the engines and effect anything like the equivalent of an emergency stop. As we were bringing in, on average, £2 million a month, we could predict with some accuracy when we would hit the magic figure. That gave us a few weeks in which to plan our announcement. As soon as the announcement was made, there would inevitably be an immediate and drastic reduction in the inflow of funds. So, if we were to hit the target on the predicted date, it was crucial that there was no leak. That created the problem that many people planning important events would feel hurt at not being told immediately we had made our decision. It was a dilemma. In the end, we held a special get-together of all the panel members and regional group chairmen the day before the press conference. We told them the good news, thanked them for what they had done, and told them of what we intended to say at the Victory press conference. In this way, we felt we were in effect telling the family first, before the rest of the world. It was the best we could do and likely to have been the most widely understood decision.

It is a good general principle, as soon as any policy decision is made, to inform all key staff so that they can talk to the outside world with one voice. Rumours are obviated. So we briefed the staff before holding the target-hitting press conference. They were given copies of the press release, so that they were fully aware of the exact facts and statements we would be distributing. A personal letter was sent by the Chairman of the Wishing Well Appeal to all the main donors and supporters.

PUBLIC ANNOUNCEMENT

Victory press conference

The objective of a press conference is to impart a message to the widest audience. That was certainly our aim at the end of the Wishing Well Appeal – to say that we had hit our target and to thank all supporters for making it possible. We also wanted to announce it to the media because we believed we had reached our target so quickly through their continuous help and assistance. We had launched the Appeal to them, relying on their generous coverage to give the public phase a flying start. It was only fair to give them the success story, too.

The press conference was held in the Institute of Child Health Lecture Theatre, the same place from which the Appeal had been launched. We had key speakers, including our chairman, Lord Prior, Sir Kit McMahon, Chairman of Midland Bank and Honorary Treasurer of the Appeal, Mrs. Caroline Bond, Chairman of the Board of Governors of Hospitals for Sick Children, Great Ormond Street, and Professor Martin Barratt, Chairman of the Medical Redevelopment Working Party.

We related the success story and explained that, from this date, no new fund-raising initiatives would be instigated by the Wishing Well Appeal Office, as sufficient funds had been raised and pledged for the new building. However, we said that we hoped all those involved with the numerous events planned for the coming year would continue them. It was explained that the Hospital's general charitable needs – for research, equipment and family support – would continue

There is quite an art in devising a picture which tells the whole story your appeal wishes to communicate. The Wishing Well Appeal sifted through many ideas for a picture story to conclude the Appeal. We decided on the above – which shows Appeal Chairman, Jim Prior, with eight-year-old Laura Samways-Marshall, peeling off the tear from the Appeal logo.

to need funds. We hoped, therefore, that the proceeds of these events would be shared between the Hospital's ongoing needs, other children's hospitals and other charities (provided the changed purpose of an event was made clear beforehand). While it is important for the motivation of volunteers and staff to celebrate success, care needs to be taken regarding what message is communicated to the outside world, particularly if the charity is going to be dependent on ongoing fund-raising. There is a real danger of people getting the message 'They're rich – they don't need my money any more.' We provided display panels, press packs, telephone facilities and all the usual paraphernalia for the press conference. We hoped to tell the fullest story and to thank everyone. We also gave careful thought to the photograph which we hoped would best illustrate the announcement.

We held a photocall for Jim Prior. He appeared with Laura Samways-Marshall, then aged eight, who approached a poster of our teardrop logo and peeled off the tear. Some thought it was a good idea, but others pointed out that the Hospital intended to continue using the teardrop logo for ongoing fund-raising – in which case the tear would have to reappear! On balance, though, the peeling-off seemed the most vivid symbol of the Appeal's success. The event was once again laid on by the Grayling Company, public relations consultants, at no cost to the Appeal. We received an extraordinary amount of press coverage for months afterwards.

Posters

Another method of publicizing our announcement and thanking everyone at the same time was to embark on a poster advertising campaign, again matching the campaign we held at the public launch. As before, the sites were provided throughout the country, at no cost to the Appeal, by Mills and Allen. These posters had the simple slogan 'Thank you for helping Great Ormond Street Get Better'. This exercise was broadly appreciated by our supporters. After many appeals, people do not feel properly thanked for what they have done – an omission that can do untold damage to future fund-raising projects and other appeals. It could be argued that these valuable spaces were being occupied by a charity that had achieved its target and did not need yet more publicity. This provided us with another dilemma but although we were sensitive about the point, we felt that it was more important to preserve the public's goodwill towards Great Ormond Street in particular and charities in general.

Abbey service

Once the Wishing Well Appeal had reached its target in 1989, it could not be allowed to pass without celebration. The Executive Committee decided that the best occasion would be an ecumenical thanksgiving service to which we would invite our Royal Patrons, the Prince and Princess of Wales. We went first to St. Paul's Cathedral, which all concerned (including those responsible for Westminster Abbey) believe is a better location for such occasions. It is a big, open church which enables the whole congregation to sit together. The Abbey is split by its famous choir screen, dividing those at the front from those at the back. However, St. Paul's could not offer a suitable date and the Abbey welcomed us in the warmest fashion.

Although it is not essential, it is advisable to find someone who has experience of Royal protocol to organize such an event on behalf of the appeal. We were fortunate in that our U.K. Field Manager, Paddy Vincent, had been stationed on HMS *Britannia*, The Royal Yacht, for two years and so was admirably placed to take on the detail of this exacting task. We arranged it in four months. Allow more time if possible. After obtaining advice from the Chaplain of Great Ormond Street, we put forward our proposals at a meeting with the Abbey's Dean and Assistant Receiver General (Protocol) – who was most helpful and is the person to turn to if your appeal team does not have anyone with suitable experience.

Next, we had to decide whom to invite and where they should be seated. The Prince and Princess of Wales graciously agreed to attend. We allocated half the tickets to the Appeal's specialist panels and major donors. The rest were given to the regional and national organizations, as well as individuals who had been responsible for spectacular regional events. The chief dignitaries were placed at the front of the Abbey, but we tried to divide most of the different categories of guests between front and rear to be as fair as possible. It is unwise to number different groups of people invited to a major event but, somehow, it slipped through on this occasion. The inevitable result was that some of the recipients – reasonably enough – read into the numbers a sort of pecking order. This was never our intention. The best arrangement is to give the groups names or colours to avoid such a misunderstanding. With our thanksgiving event, there was also the possibility of upsetting the thousands of people who had helped us but for whom there was simply not enough space in the Abbey. A decision was taken to ask groups to nominate representatives. We also decided not to give the event huge publicity, but just to let it receive the publicity inevitably generated by the presence of Their Royal Highnesses and the Appeal's newsworthiness.

We organized a Guard of Honour outside the West Door, consisting of representatives of the military and quasi-military organizations that had made a major contribution to the Appeal. There were Scouts, Guides, police, firemen, an airman, an airwoman, a female corporal and an army air corps soldier from Gatow in Germany, representing the whole community there. We had gunners from the Royal Artillery at Woolwich and sailors of the Royal Navy. And there were two nurses and four former patients from the Hospital.

Lord Prior gave a moving address during the Service. He said:

In visits to the Hospital one quickly becomes aware of the determination of everyone to give of their best, to enable children, often pathetically ill, to be nursed and treated so that they can experience a life which the vast majority of us take for granted. It is this that the famous teardrop logo so poignantly depicts. The quiet dignity of sick children calmly talking about their operations and disabilities, the innocence of pain to be borne, the anxious look of parents as they wait for news of their loved ones, touches a chord within us all, which is a part of that spirit that cannot be explained in any other way, than in a belief that there is a God who guides and comforts us. Thank goodness that an Appeal launched with all the razzmatazz and publicity required to alert the public and raise so vast a sum can end with spiritual thanksgiving and quiet dignity.

Ten of the leading figures in the Appeal, including the panel chairmen, were presented to Their Royal Highnesses before the service. Immediately after the service, in the Jerusalem Chamber next to the West Door, the Prince and Princess met some of the regional chairmen and leading Appeal staff and volunteers. A reception – or, strictly speaking, two – followed. The Abbey can contain 2,000 people, a large number to fit into one reception room. So those who were sitting behind the choir screen during the service went across the road to the Methodist Central Hall. Those in front of the choir screen were due to be entertained in a marquee that had been erected in College Garden, off the south side of the Abbey. This was far from ideal, but was all that could be done in the time available, as all other possible reception venues of suitable size were already booked. Such an important occasion would normally require a year's planning. Sadly, despite the service being held in midsummer, we were blighted with heavy rain and those scheduled to be in the marquee had to be entertained in the Cloisters. Nevertheless our photographer managed to take excellent shots.

For those who could not attend, I sent a letter enclosing a copy of the Order of Service, Lord Prior's address and a copy of a speech given at the reception by Jonathan Dimbleby, in the hope that it would give them the flavour of a most memorable day.

Souvenir brochure

It may also be appropriate to publish a final report or souvenir brochure at the end of the appeal. This can act as a 'thank you' to everyone involved, telling them how the money has been spent. By showing them that their contribution has really been appreciated, it is an effective way of encouraging them to remain involved in the longer term. However, like the appeal brochure, these publications are expensive and should not be undertaken lightly. It is a good vehicle for sponsorship, once again, and this is how we paid for ours.

CLOSING THE APPEAL OFFICE

One of the most difficult personnel problems I had at the Wishing Well Appeal was asking staff to leave almost a year earlier than they had expected because we had raised the necessary funds so far ahead of time. This was not something we could have insisted upon, as they all had contracts which would have had to be honoured. I had to thank staff and tell them that they had worked themselves out of a job. I spoke personally to small groups of staff and encouraged questions.

It came as something of a shock to some, while others had expected it. The task was not easy, but I believe that giving it a great deal of time helped to ensure that it passed off smoothly for the Hospital and for the individuals concerned. We also put in a considerable amount of work helping each staff member to find another post and providing introductions where relevant. All had two months' notice and some had more. A small group was asked to stay on to run the ongoing fundraising operation needed by the Hospital.

To thank the staff for doing a brilliant job with great dedication and for being cheerful about moving elsewhere, we held a special dinner at the Institute of Chartered Accountants in the City of London. We invited all staff members and their partners, as well as 50 or more volunteers without whom we could not have run the Appeal Office. As a mark of the Hospital's gratitude, a specially inscribed handpainted enamel box was given to each member of the team. They are encouraged to keep in touch. Some of our sterling volunteers still work with the Hospital and others asked me which charity they should help next. The individual panel chairmen also held dinners and get-togethers to thank their panel members for the work they had done. In some cases they made small personal presentations to each member.

REMEMBER TO SAY THANK YOU

All too often, fund-raisers concentrate all their efforts on developing sophisticated strategies and methods to extract the necessary funds, then fail to recognize the importance of constantly thanking supporters, keeping them involved and making them feel good for having taken part. By the time the appeal team – honorary and staff – reach the end of an appeal, they are usually tired out. They are in need of and deserve a real demonstration by the charity that it appreciates what they have done. This argues for a private celebration on a scale that recognizes the achievements and contribution of everyone concerned.

I have worked with several top industrialists who have moaned and groaned about the time they had to commit, with comments like 'never again', only to see them evincing regret when it was all over because it has left a gap in their lives. It is a gap left not only by the workload, but also through missing the new friends and colleagues whom they had come to know well and with whom it is likely they will lose contact. This is when the charity often says that, yes, it had asked them to take on only this specific appeal, but it would be highly desirable if they would stay involved – probably in a less onerous position – to help the future financial evolution of the charity. One way of doing this is to enrol willing benefactors in an informal association whose members can be kept informed and consulted on future plans and developments. Oxford University has done this and given its group the honorific of the Court of Benefactors. If that is indeed how the charity's trustees or governors feel about such voluntary helpers, then it is all the more important to show their appreciation for a valuable contribution to an achievement of which they can all be proud. This is not easy because every supporter should have been given special treatment to reflect their status if their work has been significant. However, it is difficult for a charity to distribute suitable recognition to everyone.

That is not to say that the trustees of the charity should not seriously consider whether the appeal's achievements merit one or more recommendations for official honours. It is open to anyone to make such a recommendation: the procedure is simple and informal, requiring only a letter to the Principal Private Secretary (Honours) to the Prime Minister, at 10 Downing Street, London SW1. The grounds on which the recommendation is based (achievement, length of service, etc.) should be stated in detail and supported by any distinguished people who know the circumstances. In the case of a hospital appeal, the chairman of the Board of Governors would also involve the Department of Health. There are many other ways of thanking supporters outside the appeal organization: specially signed letters or certificates, badges, brooches, medallions. Band Aid even awarded platinum discs to certain key volunteers.

At the Wishing Well Appeal, initially some of our advisers tried to convince us that it was not financially worthwhile to send 'thank-you' letters to people who gave less than £10. However we were looking to the Hospital's future and we know that today's small donors are likely to become ongoing supporters in the future – if they feel valued. So everyone received a letter which was personally addressed and signed, with a special postscript where appropriate.

It is important to keep donors in touch with the progress of the development or project which they have made possible. Major donors should be invited to future milestones. In the case of building appeals, these would include the laying of a foundation stone and the open day which should be held upon completion. By doing so, these valuable supporters will have a better understanding of the growth and evolution of the charity and will thereby be more likely to receive sympathetically any future calls on their time or money. In most cases, those involved with an appeal care deeply about its progress. It would be wrong to ignore them once the appeal hits its target.

Part V

SMALLER AND LOCAL APPEALS

Chapter 32

How They Differ From The Large-Scale Appeal

This chapter applies the principles explained in the preceding sections of this book to smaller and local appeals, which account for the majority of fund-raising projects. Many readers may have been saying to themselves, 'Why do I need to know about the mega appeal to understand how to approach my local appeal, which is minuscule by comparison?' or 'It's all very well explaining how to raise money for a really emotive cause like sick children, but what about the run-of-the-mill appeal, for a school or church – or even for an unpopular cause?' I appreciate that point of view, as I started by organizing local appeals before I became a national appeal director. However, in the main, the same principles apply whether an appeal is big or small, local or national. The differences lie in matters of emphasis and priority. Essentially, the small appeal is a microcosm of the large appeal. All appeals need to go through the same stages of preparation and execution.

Stages of an appeal

- making the case for an appeal
- defining appeal objectives
- researching potential sources of funds
- researching potential leadership
- deciding on strategy:
    - private and/or public appeal?
    - methods of giving and of fund-raising?
    - staff and/or volunteers?
- handling publicity
- preparing for success, failure and the aftermath

So it is not enough for a local appeal organizer simply to read this chapter. Virtually all the previous chapters can offer ideas and insight for those concerned with regional and smaller appeals. The main difference is one of scale.

Where, then, do the differences lie? To begin with, every appeal is different, no matter how similar they may seem. It is wise to approach each one with an open, inquiring mind, free from preconceived ideas. The framework I have outlined here indicates the areas to be taken into account: the answers, responses and treatment will vary infinitely.

MAKING THE CASE

First, you must make the case. Collect all facts about the charity, its past, present and plans as listed in the BROADSWORD mnemonic in Chapter 4. Your findings will be subject to close scrutiny by a local audience; some will want the facility for which funds are required, while others may not.

Pros and cons

- Establishing a new, combined hospital may involve closing others.
- Providing a sheltered house for psycho-geriatric residents may be badly needed, but potential neighbours may have other ideas about its effect on the balance of their locality.
- Restoring a 18th-century landscape park may enhance a national treasure, but the prospect of greatly increased traffic may antagonize nearby residents.

These sorts of dangers may seem very obvious, but it is surprising how many charities start to plan appeals without discovering the level of latent opposition. Similarly, many do not realize that their chances of receiving that vital planning permission for a building may not be as cut and dried as they imagine. Begin by ensuring that you have won over those in the affected area before taking your appeal plans any further. Even though your charity and the local authority may be aware of the need for the facility you are seeking to finance, you must collect as many details as possible to assist you in giving all concerned the most vivid and compelling presentation of the problem to be overcome.

Years ago, Help the Aged was trying to find sites and raise additional funds for sheltered housing schemes. It was not enough merely to state that more schemes were needed in any given area. We had to research how many elderly people were on the relevant housing waiting list and how long they could expect to wait, and relate these details to the particular locality.

APPEAL OBJECTIVES

Be clear about the objective of your appeal. Is it purely to raise a one-off sum of money or also intended to raise your charity's profile and so increase future giving? You may need to attract more volunteers to help run your project or care for the charity's beneficiaries. All the effort should deliver the maximum long-term benefit to the charity and its cause.

RESEARCHING POTENTIAL SOURCES OF FUNDS

There is no point in thinking about a target for an appeal until the likely catchment area or constituency for a cause or facility has been thoroughly investigated.

> **Questions to ask**
>
> What can be deduced from comparable previous appeals?
> Who cares or can be persuaded to care?
> What likely donors are within reach:
>   wealthy individuals?
>   companies?
>   grant-making trusts?
>   interested groups or associations?
>   statutory bodies?

When reviewing previous comparable appeals it is helpful to use the following six 'W's' checklist to make sure you cover all relevant aspects:

What   Name of charity, objectives, operational results so far.

Why   Why was the appeal needed – problems which were overcome, specific statistics which proved the need.

Where   Address and telephone number of HQ, offices, operational locations, planned areas of activity.

When   When was it started, timing information on project and fund-raising.

Who   Who started the charity, who chaired and led the appeal, who ran the operations, and what their qualifications were. Who gave/raised the funds. Big donors involved.

Ways   Methods used to raise the funds – ongoing fund-raising methods and results, special appeals and results.

It is important to consider whether your local project has national significance. A medical research project for a local organization may be a natural recipient of funds from one or more national grant-making trusts. If you are appealing on behalf of a school, the alumni will probably be spread nationally or even internationally. Your local appeal for the disabled may look to larger national charities in this field for support. As some national charities like to promote specific projects, you may find that they are willing to take on your appeal for you. Help the Aged runs appeals on behalf of local charities for the elderly through its Project FundRaising Department. It was set up in 1977 to provide local fund-raising committees with the specialist knowledge, expertise and assistance necessary, from the earliest planning stages to the final completion and beyond. Project FundRaising undertakes a feasibility study, installs a campaign director, if necessary, and recovers some of its costs which are added to the appeal target.

Most would say that the best way to raise funds is quickly and simply through a few large gifts without all the fuss and bother of a public appeal. A housing charity recently asked me for advice on how to raise £3 million. I was able to arrange for them to have an unofficial meeting with representatives of three government departments. At the end of this, they had effectively raised a large percentage of the funds they needed. I am sure this is the best strategy for charities that do not appeal significantly to the public – saving a great deal of time and money. Nevertheless, any charity choosing such a route misses the valuable publicity which might coat its cause for years to come, stimulating a steady income into the future.

RESEARCHING THE COMMUNITY

To ensure that you do not overlook any worthwhile sources of funds, you should find out about the local community in a variety of ways.

Wealthy individuals

Talk to everyone who might know about these often shy people. Ask councillors, magistrates, mayors' offices, other charities, local historians, businessmen, journalists, police, publicans and others who regularly come into contact with the public. Comb the electoral roll, especially sections dealing with exclusive neighbourhoods.

Companies

Obtain a list of local employers, names of directors or partners, and the size and profitability of the businesses. It may be worth asking at Companies House. (There are three branches – in London, Cardiff and Edinburgh. There are also satellite offices which can order the microfiche from the main centres.) A company's annual report often provides details of community involvement and marketing strategy which may give useful information relevant to your cause. Be on the look-out for businessmen who are keen to burnish their standing. The bigger businesses in any district may have staff associations which, though not charities, are very willing to undertake charitable work. Check all the reference books listed in Chapter 5, the Bibliography, and in the local town hall.

Local charities and grant-making trusts

The 1960 Charities Act requires the Charity Commission to send two copies of the listings of local charities on its index to the relevant county and district authorities. This information is publicly available on request. Keeping and providing the information is not given high priority by some authorities; it may require persistence to discover the responsible officer and extract it. Some authorities are very helpful to the extent of having charity information bureaux. Local knowledge and local contacts are invaluable in these tasks. Finding names of correspondents and trustees may require dogged detection work. When found, they should be cultivated. So, too, should trustees of charities which, though not local, are potential donors to your cause. Many local trusts will be confined to supporting causes within a closely defined catchment area.

   There are tens of thousands of grant-making trusts which are often not listed in the directories given in the Bibliography because of their localized range. Although total amounts held by these trusts may be small, their contribution to local and regional appeals can be very significant. Two little-used but useful ways of finding and researching little-known dormant trusts are parish records – local trusts are often linked to the church – and long-established solicitors' practices who act for the trusts. A little investigation and probing can be very rewarding. I was advised recently of a situation whereby a local fund-raiser raised £25,000 from a dormant trust – this amount represented 80 per cent of the appeal target!

Other bodies

The National Council for Voluntary Organizations (NCVO) aims to promote the common interests of voluntary organizations and to provide a range of resources that will increase their effectiveness. The National Association of Councils for Voluntary Service (NACVS) or Action with Communities in Rural England (ACRE) will be able to put you in contact with your local Council for Voluntary Service or Rural Community Council. They should be able to give you information on local voluntary organizations, clubs, associations and societies and how much they do to support the local community. Many produce their own guides giving local fund-raising advice and other useful information.

Public libraries often keep lists of local clubs. Bodies which help charities continually are schools, churches, police and the armed forces, fire services, residents' and tenants' associations, ladies' organizations and working men's clubs. Other local charities will usually help you, but will be more co-operative if they believe that you will operate in a way that will assist the community rather than becoming a rival.

Local press

It is usually worth cultivating the editor of the local newspaper and the journalists who have covered the district for some time. They can be a valuable source of knowledge and opinion. Scanning the local press is an excellent way of discovering the area and the identity of potential donors or volunteers.

Statutory bodies

Local authorities can fund activities relating to their own areas or residents. For example, a local authority could make a grant to a home for the elderly even though it was to be built outside its own territory, provided it catered for its own residents. It is worth getting to know the officers who advise the councillors with the power to decide grants. It can be a complex operation, for which the National Council for Voluntary Organizations provides useful advice.

Institute of Charity Fundraising Managers

The ICFM has a regional structure through which every member and the Institute itself can call on a vast array of experience and advice covering every aspect of fund-raising. Currently there are 11 ICFM Local Groups covering the whole of the U.K. Each one is, quite properly, distinctive in character, deciding very largely its own approach to its own business. The officers of the Institute meet Local Group representatives twice a year to aid communication.

LEADERSHIP

While you are researching the donor categories, bear in mind that any potential donor or donor organization may be or contain your ideal leader. Many of the qualities listed in Chapter 6 are required, but the scope of the smaller and local appeal is more limited and national leaders are not so readily available. Much depends on the type of locality where the appeal is based and who would have the best chance of galvanizing the community into activity. You may be lucky enough to have a national celebrity living locally, although he might be better employed as president or vice-president. This is another category of potential supporter to be diligently researched. Collect as many credible names as possible and check their suitability with other influential people. The first person consulted may respond that there is only one name worth considering – only to be contradicted by the next to be approached, who is equally adamant that the nominated leader would be nothing short of disastrous. That necessitates a consensus of at least another three or four wise souls to decide the matter. The second comment may have come from the nominee's arch enemy; in my experience, effective achievers always stimulate resentment somewhere. Your priority is not to run a popularity contest, but to find the leader most likely to maximize your appeal's success.

Every community has a hierarchy with which the appeal initiators must become familiar in order to find the keys to influencing the maximum number of targets. This is by no means as easy as it sounds. Time, thorough research and sensitivity are required to approach potential leaders effectively.

Leaders of some local appeals I have organized

Location	Charity	Leader
London Borough of Lambeth	Help the Aged (sheltered housing)	Mayor of Lambeth
Royal Borough of Kensington & Chelsea	Help the Aged (sheltered housing & geriatric day hospital)	The Earl Cadogan, major landowner
Royal Borough of Kensington & Chelsea	Guinness Trust (community centre for elderly)	Lord Farnham, merchant banker
London Borough of Newham	Guinness Trust (housing & day care for elderly)	Saxon Tate, Vice-chairman, Tate & Lyle, big local employer
Buckinghamshire	Help the Aged (housing for elderly)	John Paterson, industrialist & High Sheriff
London Borough of Hammersmith & Fulham	Charing Cross Medical Research Centre (its local appeal)	Sir Clifford Chetwood, Chairman of G. Wimpey, big local employer

STRATEGY

How thoroughly should you plan your local appeal? Does it depend on the amount to be raised? It certainly does not require an elaborate plan to raise a relatively small sum, say £10,000, in an affluent area. However, that same sum represents a formidable challenge in a poor district with high unemployment.

Nevertheless, careful planning gives a greater chance of improving every facet of an appeal. You will have to decide how you intend to raise the funds, once research has demonstrated that it is feasible to reach the required target. Should you split the appeal into a private and a public phase? Should you omit the public appeal? Your cause may touch only a few easily identified people.

Research will establish the target audience for the appeal – your potential donors. Then you must decide what strategy to use, how to market your appeal to each sector of your audience and what fund-raising techniques are appropriate. (See Appendix 4.)

Will statutory bodies contribute? This is a good place to start, as it gives confidence to potential donors to know that substantial organizations have given their tacit approval and such bodies like the partnership arrangement whereby donations trigger government input. That gives your appeal an immediate entrée into government departments. Can you tap wealthy individuals, successful businesses and grant-making trusts? If so, you would be wise to have a private appeal to such groups before you embark on a public campaign.

As explained in Chapter 5, you should work out the likely source of funds and produce a gifts schedule, possibly linking it to a shopping list so that donors can see what their money will buy. You may also encourage different organizations to take on a target amount, which will be enough to name a particular area in the scheme, or to fund a specific item on the shopping list. Such presentational points will stimulate morale and help to raise your fund-raisers' sights. You must not forget the importance of trying to secure several large lead gifts – large, that is, in proportion to your target. These will lift morale and add to your appeal's credibility as a project worth supporting.

Other strategic questions revolve around choosing the methods of fund-raising most appropriate to your donors, to suit their type, size of pocket or the time they can give as volunteers.

You will also need to decide how you intend to handle the appeal's administration – with paid staff or volunteers? Or will your appeal chairman's secretary act as appeal treasurer and secretary, as happened in the appeal for the Fieldhead home for elderly ladies, in Buckinghamshire. This will be determined by the scope of the appeal. Fund-raising techniques and human resources are discussed later.

If you are appealing to an area where there is a fair-sized community with few wealthy pockets, then you will use different techniques. All communities have leaders and opinion-formers; these are the people to identify. You should still split your catchment area and find a leader for each to assist the appeal. These people will tell you how best to approach their sectors and what types of fund-raising methods are likely to work best or have been successful. In such circumstances, you might encourage and stimulate every sector to run a series of events to cater for prevailing tastes in each. This policy relies on good publicity and administrative back-up. This technique might be appropriate if your cause is not regarded as emotive; people might prefer to get something for their money, such as a ticket to an event, rather than to make a straightforward donation. As usual, it is a question of trying to understand people before deciding how best to approach them. This is certainly one of the most important lessons in fund-raising.

Direct fund-raising

When appealing to a select few, such as for a school or church, some use a device known as direct fund-raising, although it is less common now. The fund-raiser makes a direct approach to the prospective donor, rather than invoking peer-group pressure. A school may draw up lists of potential donors, but the fund-raisers will go to see those people to make the case. A telephone call or letter may be invoked to support the fund-raiser.

I have never raised funds for a school or church, so I am not qualified to compare this technique with using like to approach like. However, were I to direct such an appeal, I am sure that I would try to invoke influence before falling back on direct fund-raising.

STRUCTURE

One of your first steps should be to decide on the type of legal entity to embody the appeal organization, as discussed in Chapter 9. Many local appeals run for existing charities use the same legal entity and operate under that banner. Money raised in that way has to be kept separately, with separate accounts. However, all appeals need a central management committee of chairman, secretary, treasurer and press officer, with the possible additions of patron, president, vice-president and vice-chairman. Beyond that, there are many different ways of structuring a local appeal – all related to cause, locality and size of the target.

Three examples are:

(1) A range of influential people – probably friends and contacts of a well-placed chairman.
(2) Having analyzed the area by sectors – industry, commerce, traders, councillors, magistrates, churches, arts societies, sports clubs, voluntary groups – find a leading member of each to join your appeal committee and be responsible for approaches to their own sector.
(3) Divide the vicinity into geographical areas and appoint an influential person to generate support in each area.

I have used all these structures and can vouch for each, as long as they are tailored to the characteristics of the cause and the area concerned. For further advice, I recommend the London Voluntary Service Council (LVSC) publication *Voluntary But Not Amateur* for additional details on legal structure, other legal requirements and fund-raising advice. Other useful publications are produced by the National Council for Voluntary Organizations who, on request, will send a free publications list.

Administration

The case histories on local appeals in Chapter 33 give an idea of the human resources required – paid and voluntary.

Most appeals for more than, say, £100,000 will require someone who can be relied on to be the appeal 'anchor', coordinating all activities from the centre. Whether this individual is full-time or part-time will depend on the target, relative to the resources of the catchment area. However, it is wise to make it a remunerated post to ensure that the incumbent takes full responsibility and allocates sufficient time.

The Appeal Secretary or Administrator, unless an experienced fund-raiser, which is unlikely, should have access to fund-raising expertise. Hence he may be directed by a staff fund-raiser or a consultant.

APPEAL SECRETARY'S KEY DUTIES

Servicing committees
Planning meetings with the various chairmen, producing agenda and minutes. Progress chasing and implementation of committee decisions where relevant.

Research database
Installing and developing a comprehensive database on past and potential donors and potential leadership. Recording who agrees to approach whom, chasing and recording the results.

Administration systems
Setting up the initial files and records on the Appeal. (Some will be computerized.)

Public relations
Organizing functions. Coordinating the production of literature/reports. Fielding press enquiries.

Finance
Keeping expenditure within an agreed budget.
Handling, banking and recording donations.

Appeal secretaries require analytical minds, a systematic approach and a capacity to pay attention to detail. They should be computer literate and be able to write well. Typing and shorthand skills are useful. A good memory for names is an asset and an ability to motivate and to cajole tactfully is essential.

Personal attributes of an appeal secretary

- Being well turned out, with excellent interpersonal skills and the confidence to deal with people at all levels.
- Resourceful, self-motivated and determined to achieve, plus an ability to work alone to some degree.
- Patience and a well-tuned sense of humour are also very helpful attributes.

This type of post often involves a short-term contract of perhaps, two years initially. Candidates with a secretarial or administrative background are often recruited. For a larger appeal, the appeal secretary may start the ball rolling in advance of a more expensive Appeal Director being appointed.

TIMING

The timing of the smaller, local appeal can vary enormously. If there are few potential donors you may be able to plan for a short time-frame (months rather than years). The more simplified operation required to approach effectively people well known to their local community can radically shorten the whole exercise. If, on the other hand, you intend to appeal to a larger constituency (such as a city) and your target is more substantial, you will need to include a variety of fund-raising methods in your strategy – so the process will take longer. Whether or not you have a part-time or full-time fund-raiser and how expert he is will also make a significant difference.

In very general terms, preparation can take three, six or nine months, depending on the size of target, scale and type of appeal, leadership quality and the constituency. Obtaining lead gifts could also involve a period of between three to nine months with a public appeal leading on from that. For example, a £1.5 million community-based appeal would usually take a time-scale of at least 18 months to two years – if it is run by an experienced campaign director. This would be correspondingly longer or shorter depending on the cause, leadership, target and catchment area. The case histories in the next chapter give varying examples of appeal calendars.

PUBLICITY

Decisions about publicity will be determined by the quality of the expertise you recruit. You may be able to call on the services of the public relations staff or agency of the appeal chairman's company, the local authority's PR officer or a local PR consultancy. I regard this aspect of an appeal as all-important – but I am an ex-PR manager, so I would say that. Another way to achieve wide local coverage is to involve the local newspaper in the structure of the appeal, including some ownership of it. At best, they might launch a campaign in the paper to raise the needed funds. At least, they should report positively on your cause, plans and activities. However, do not take it amiss if they decline to join your ranks, as they may wish to remain independent in order to cover your appeal's progress objectively. This may be even more valuable.

As explained in Chapter 8, you will want to use a corporate identity relevant to your organization and to make sure it is used as an identity stamp on all your literature, stationery and promotional material. Is your current one ideal? Can it be improved? Do you need to create a special theme, through a landmark anniversary or by crystallizing your cause in a vivid slogan, for example? Your image should be in keeping with the character of your organization. It should look professional. The correct dimensions and colour should be spelled out in a short house style guidance sheet. You will then need to produce the literature referred to in Part II:

- Preliminary Report making the case for an appeal
- strategic plan of action for the leaders you have recruited
- brochure to present to those capable of making larger gifts
- leaflet and other supporting literature for circulation to the public.

FUND-RAISING METHODS

Appendices 2 and 4 list the main methods of giving, fund-raising techniques and an example as to how these can be developed by different groups or panels.

Generally, during a public appeal, people like to dream up their own fund-raising ideas. The fund-raiser's job is to guide, advise and try to avoid disasters. The trouble is that you often hear about the latter only after the event! You need to encourage your supporters to keep you up to date about what they are planning and when, so that you can coordinate from the centre and ensure that two or more important events do not clash. Although you cannot control all the fund-raising methods once the public appeal has been launched, it is wise to try to influence them, both for the purpose of coordination and to encourage supporters to use tried and effective methods. When I was a local group's fund-raiser, my team would keep their eyes open for fund-raising events that worked well and raised large sums. We would try to get chapter and verse on these paragons and distil them into a data sheet which described how to emulate them. These sheets soon became our bible.

Big gift fund-raising is discussed in Part III, while other general fund-raising methods are covered in Part IV of this book. However, just as we issued every kind of advice note and fund-raising idea to the local groups in the Wishing Well Appeal, you will need to have the same sort of back-up material ready to support your fund-raisers in your locality. This might include a standard letter on the appeal asking for help, which can be angled to the recipient's particular needs. You might also circulate a paper listing some of the more lucrative events they could organize, with advice and instruction notes. You could produce a wide list of ideas to give more choice to fund-raisers desperate to do something different. If an event needs effective and tight administration to succeed and you do not have that facility at your fingertips, it is better to avoid it than to plunge on regardless. The damage could leave you worse off.

When I was at Help the Aged, we developed a method of fund-raising entitled 'The Flower Fund'. Although not a new idea, it was relevant to the local appeal which was particularly applicable to the elderly. People were asked to send donations instead of buying flowers in memory of a loved one who had died. What was different was that it did not just happen – it was planned. Leaflets explained the scheme: how the gifts would help elderly local people and bring comfort to the grieving family, and it included a form to be completed. Once all the gifts had been received by the charity, the donors' names were listed under a statement that they had kindly sent a donation to the Flower Fund set up in memory of the departed and this list was sent to the bereaved family. Thus, in a time of sorrow, they helped to bring a little happiness to some of the needy old people who still shared life with us.

Such a scheme needed very sensitive handling. It was advertised locally and literature was passed throughout the community – to churches, voluntary bodies and even undertakers. It was a novel method of channelling the way many people naturally respond at a time of bereavement and, tactfully presented, gave a lasting tribute to the deceased and support to the grieving family at their time of loss. I suppose the only people who suffered were the florists!

If one of its main supporters dies during an appeal or if a widely popular supporter dies even when there is no appeal, a charity can set up a special appeal in his memory. This happened in an appeal I ran on behalf of the Guinness Trust to build a community centre for the elderly in Chelsea. It was named in memory of Viscount Boyd of Merton, who was a tireless trustee, a much-loved politician and a member of the Guinness family. Undoubtedly the link between the cause and a special person's memory had a great deal to do with the success of the appeal.

Local appeals should not overlook the possibilities of a local joint promotion as a means of raising money. I learned of a garage in Beaconsfield, Buckinghamshire, which imported a highly sophisticated German car-wash machine. Their idea to promote the new machine was to contact two local charities and offer them £1 for every wash on a given day. The event was sponsored by the garage's petrol company and the washes were free to the motorists. The response was enormous, halting Beaconsfield's traffic for several hours. The charities received a large sum and the garage generated a gratifying amount of publicity. Some local residents and traders might have had other views, though!

A method available to smaller and local appeals, which is not relevant to a national campaign, is to raise funds under the banner of a 'big brother'. Local appeals or groups may take part in the Alexandra Rose Day, Britain's oldest flag day. It was founded by Queen Alexandra in 1912 to help organizations caring for the sick, the old, the young and the disabled. Working with Alexandra Rose Day, local voluntary organizations are permitted to retain 80 per cent of the funds they raise. The remaining 20 per cent covers the central costs and helps to finance the 'Charities in Crisis' Emergency Grants Fund for people-caring charities facing acute difficulties. For further information, contact the National Director, Alexandra Rose Day. Broadcast appeals can also take a local angle. For instance the ITV Telethon supports small, local charities as well as national ones. Its grant-making policy ensures that funds raised in a particular region stay in that region. Other opportunities for smaller charities to come under a larger umbrella include the big city marathon races which take place regularly round Britain and abroad.

Such involvement may not project the role of your own appeal to the same extent, but the return can amply justify the effort, as these are events in which many people like to participate.

People will be tempted to attend a local fund-raising event if it is held somewhere they do not otherwise have an opportunity to visit, such as an impressive country house. It can often be advantageous to plan an event around a venue, which, if not splendid, is unusual. It is very likely that the splendid place will have been used before, so you can gather useful advice from those who have organized events there.

PREPARING FOR FAILURE OR SUCCESS AND THE AFTERMATH

It is prudent to plan for the possibilities of not raising enough funds by your deadline or going over your appeal target.

Most appeals are tempted to go on and on in the hope that eventually they will hit the target. If inflation happens to be running high, the target may have to be adjusted more than once, leading to the possibility that it may recede farther into the distance. Going on might then become counterproductive, as it can have the effect of boring or even antagonizing those who have decided they have already given enough and resent being approached yet again – and again. Occasionally, appeals cut their losses and scale down the project. It is best to plan for this contingency at the outset. Then you will not be so likely to make decisions on the spur of the moment, when emotions may be running high. Draw up more than one level of shopping list, reducing the number of items or shaving their specifications.

There is also what some would regard as a most desirable problem – what to do if you go over target. This deserves equally careful planning. You may decide to earmark the extra funds for a second phase of the facility you are financing, such as a new building extension, or you may wish to give the money to related causes elsewhere in the country. Either way, such decisions are best taken before the problem arises. Naturally, this must be permissible in terms of the trust deed or legal entity of your charity. Also, it is very important that the initial publicity material explains clearly what is planned if the appeal exceeds its target, or the opposite, so that donors have fair warning of what may happen to their money. Neither they nor you should be caught unawares. (See Appendix 8 – Schemes.)

What about afterwards – the future? An experienced fund-raiser will always try to find reasons for keeping the supporters in touch after the appeal closes, rather than simply winding down and leaving. Can the charity use more help now the appeal has raised its profile? Even if volunteers 'joined up' originally for two or three years, they will almost inevitably have found great satisfaction in what they did and have many happy memories. In that case, they will welcome a chance to continue, perhaps with fewer duties, doing something similar and seeing the fruits of their work develop. A few public announcements, in the press perhaps, about the ongoing benefits of your donors' generosity will give substance to your thank-yous and remind them that what they did was worthwhile.

CONCLUSION

As smaller and local appeals vary so widely, it is instructive to examine five completely different examples. They are discussed in Chapter 33 and cover:

(a) A school appeal in Scotland
(b) A church appeal in the Midlands
(c) A housing scheme for the elderly in Bristol
(d) A hospice in Basingstoke
(e) A church development appeal in Highgate

The purpose of this book is to advise on the organization of appeals, no matter what type of cause or locality. I have tried to show how the basic principles can be adapted to any circumstances – and I hope that I have provided a little encouragement to anyone who is daunted by the task he has been persuaded to undertake. It is important to bear in mind that, usually, fund-raising is not the problem. The problem is making the case. If that can be done convincingly, then I find that the money always follows. This serves only to emphasize one of the recurrent themes of this book, that the most valuable work is the initial preparation: establishing the need, clarifying thoughts, deciding strategy, finding leaders. Get those factors right and the rest of the appeal, while it may not exactly be plain sailing, will generate a momentum which should see you through to a successful conclusion.

By devising a variety of imaginative ways to commemorate an appeal, a charity
can demonstrate its gratitude to those who have worked so hard to ensure its
success. One such gesture is illustrated above. Nurse Meike Okelnaan and
patient Joanne Schofield throw the first pennies into the Wishing Well Fountain,
donated to Great Ormond Street Hospital by the Drinking Fountain Association.
Sculpted by Catharine Marr-Johnson, it replaces the original fountain once situ-
ated in the garden behind the first hospital building (see page 85).

Chapter 33

CASE HISTORIES

The difference between theory and practice in running charity appeals can be compared to that between the parade ground and the battlefield. Although all the principles I have described in this book have been tested in real life, it has to be said that most appeals are unpredictable and require flexibility and adaptation. The reason is that, however glossy the wrapping, when you launch an appeal you are basically asking people to give without receiving any immediate or direct benefit in return, apart from a warm glow and the fact that they are making a long-term investment in their community. That calls for donations to be acts of faith and self-lessness – commodities which are in short supply at the best of times, and qualities which appeal leaders need in abundance. So I thought it would be helpful for you to compare my view of how local appeals should be run with the styles and strategies adopted by others. Although the examples which follow contain varying levels of success, each approach was valid in its own way, allowing for the circumstances with which each set of organizers was confronted.

The case histories were written by the individuals involved with each of the appeals and include their own assessments and lessons to be learned. It would be wrong for me to say what I would have done in their shoes, for it is too easy to be wise after the event. Readers can make their own judgment of the comparative success of each appeal and compare the lessons they learned with the principles and guidelines set down in this book. All set off down the road in good faith and all overcame the inevitable hurdles in their own way. I have selected only a very few smaller appeals from the hundreds which take place up and down the United Kingdom every year, but I hope that they provide a cross-section which will have some relevance to the next appeal with which you become involved.

GEORGE WATSON'S COLLEGE DEVELOPMENT PROJECT

This case history was supplied by Craigmyle and Company, fund-raising consultants.

Background

George Watson's College is a co-educational school in Edinburgh. It was founded in 1741 under the terms of the will of George Watson, the first accountant of the Bank of Scotland. Originally intended as a hospital for ten resident Foundationers, it has become one of the top academic and sporting schools in the U.K. In 1870 it became a fee-paying institution, preserving its broad social appeal by offering a proportion of Foundationer places. The following year George Watson's Ladies' College was opened.

In 1974 the schools combined to become one of the largest schools in Scotland with a roll of 2,400 pupils. The numbers were later limited to 2,100 -1,250 seniors and 850 juniors – from approximately 1,300 families. The school offers an exceptionally wide range of academic subjects and extra-curricular activities. It maintains a strong family atmosphere and close links with former pupils through the Watsonian Club.

Until 1985, the school's capital development was impeded by its grant-aided status. However, through private gifts, sale of land and careful management of resources, it was able to make many improvements to academic and boarding accommodation. In the decade to 1990, almost £1 million was invested.

Until 1989, the Merchant Company was directly responsible for governing George Watson's College. Then a new council was established to govern the school. It initiated a development programme to mark the 250th anniversary of 'George Watson's Hospital' and the 120th anniversary of the Ladies' College. An appeal was launched under the slogan 'Watson's 250'.

A major development programme

The council reviewed the school's objectives and the resources it had to meet those objectives. An ambitious development programme was drawn up which was planned to unfold over three phases.

Programmed phases of redevelopment

Phase One concentrated on science, technology, sport and drama. It included modernizing science laboratories, improving a design centre, constructing all-weather hockey pitches, resurfacing tennis courts and upgrading drama facilities.

Phase Two encompassed new music facilities and building a recreation room in a new boarding house.

Phase Three was to build a new theatre.

The total cost of the development programme was estimated to be £1.7 million. The appeal was intended to raise £1.2 million and pay for the first two phases. The new theatre was to be financed from any appeal revenue left over from Phases One and Two, topped up by the school's other resources. The appeal target was considered ambitious, but achievable if the basic principles of effective fund-raising were faithfully applied. Success would depend on the ability to obtain major gifts and significant support from the appeal constituency – parents of current and former pupils, Watsonians and grant-making trusts. Approaches were also made to companies.

The appeal timetable

The original timetable was:

Stage One	January-April 1990	Initial preparation and Advance Gifts One (major donors).
Stage Two	May-July 1990	Advance Gifts Two. Follow-up to Stage One.
Stage Three	September-November 1990	Main approach to parents (excluding special prospects) Follow-up to Stage Two.
Stage Four	December 1990-April 1991	Remaining approaches. Follow-up to Stage Three.

Since it was a school appeal and therefore had a very 'private' constituency, there was no need for public or high-profile events. Fund-raising was based largely on personal approaches, meetings and targeted direct mail.

Appeal leadership

The Rt. Hon. Malcolm Rifkind QC, MP, a Watsonian, agreed to be appeal president. The main thrust of the appeal was handled by a steering group of ten members, led by a chairman and vice-chairman. This committee included Watsonians, parents of former and current pupils and the principal, deputy principal and bursar of the college.

Results

The appeal closed on 31 March 1991. By then, £1.1 million had been received, including tax recovered on covenanted and other tax-assisted donations. The school confidently expected to reach its target after taking account of outstanding promises from individuals, companies and trusts.

The total cost of the appeal was just over 6 per cent of the sum raised.

Of the £1 million, 48 per cent came from Watsonians and parents of current and former pupils. Major gifts contributed 28 per cent, trusts and companies 6%, with the remaining 18 per cent from two support groups. By 1 March 1991 just over 30 per cent of parents of current pupils had contributed, with more indicating that they were considering doing so.

The detailed breakdown appears overleaf.

	No. in category	No. of donations	% response	Total £
Major gifts	49	31	63	282,562
Parents of current pupils	1340	405	30	236,776
Watsonians	4210	509	12	236,132
250 Group	106	85	80	121,828
Support group	69	52	75	64,298
Trusts, companies, other	-	55	-	58,609
Parents of former pupils	206	15	7	14,313
Totals	5980	1152		1,014,518

Analysis

The success of the campaign was based on:
1. Establishing a strong and attractive case.
2. A professionally defined financial need.
3. A clearly defined constituency.
4. Concentration on major gifts.
5. Strong, committed and effective appeal leadership.

Above all, the high morale and reputation of the school were the fundamental sources that fuelled the efforts of all concerned. That ensured that the strategy was meticulously executed. By the time of the appeal's public launch, a substantial sum had been raised through a combination of personal approaches and carefully targeted mailings. Because every effort was made to approach parents directly, the active involvement of a group of committed parents was of key importance.

ABINGTON PARISH CHURCH

This case history was supplied by Ronald Pearce Associates.

Background

In 1979, this Anglican church launched a Christian Giving campaign which increased regular income from direct giving from £8,000 to £20,000 a year. By 1989, this had risen to only £25,000, seriously lagging behind inflation, so a major professionally guided campaign was conceived.

It consisted of three phases: planning, preparation and activity. It was aimed at all members and prospective members of the church, a total of 250 families.

Leadership

A ten-member planning group was formed to guide the professional campaign director and be the authoritative body governing the campaign. This group selected and enlisted the active help of the leaders and members of four other committees, each of which took responsibility for one aspect of the project:

1. Publications – brochure, letterheads, and other printed materials.
2. Hostess – to deal with the social side of the campaign. A focal point was the weekly Parish Supper.
3. Arrangements – to draw up practical details of the Parish Supper, including time, menu, seating, public address system, parking, etc.
4. Fund-raising – briefings before the six suppers and report meetings afterwards.

This organization allowed busy people to fulfil particular tasks within a calendar of six weeks' concerted activity, without duplication. Prior to each supper, the hostess committee was briefed and members personally invited guests – of their own choice selected from Parish records – to the supper. A total of 222 people accepted invitations to these occasions, where they learned about the campaign's objectives through speeches by three committee members and the vicar.

Assessing the target

The campaign target for this type of appeal is determined by the financial needs of the parish, and by considering how much each section of the appeal's constituency is likely to yield. This involved analyzing existing standards and patterns of regular giving, covenanted or not, and discussing the question with individual church members and the campaign planning group. The aim is to encourage increased giving, through example and according to individuals' means. Hence a well-paid professional might be targeted to give £1,000 a year and a labourer £100 a year. Both are regarded as equally generous. On this basis, the 1990 Christian Giving Campaign aimed at a target of £40,000 a year gross, including tax rebates on covenanted giving.

Strategy

The fundamental principle of the campaign strategy was that all committee members had to declare their own support before approaching others to invite their participation. This achieved three important aims:

1. It established the standard and pattern of giving.
2. It encouraged other church members to take part.
3. It provided the campaign director with a valuable guide to the standards and pattern of response likely to be achieved and, therefore, an indication of how realistic the campaign target was.

Results

The campaign increased total pledged giving from £25,000 to £41,515 a year at the conclusion of the main active phase. But by then, the campaign committee's members had not completed their intended 20 visits each, owing to absence of possible participants on holiday or through illness.

Such outstanding approaches were dealt with by a post-campaign administration committee, which added several thousand pounds more to the total.

Analysis

Prior to the campaign, committed giving had ranged up to £10 a week. From the end of the campaign, top pledges were £25 weekly and the whole range of giving had improved substantially. The £5,285 pre-campaign level of tax rebates on covenants had increased to £9,053.

Of the church members participating, 66 per cent are giving weekly, 16 per cent monthly, 4 per cent quarterly and 14 per cent annually. This means that 48.5 per cent of regular church income will be received weekly, 30.25 per cent monthly, 4.25 per cent quarterly and 17 per cent yearly.

Individual Christian Giving Campaigns share some of the qualities of the one-off and the on-going appeal. They are designed in the light of the accumulated experience and knowledge of thousands of such campaigns over many years for various denominations in the U.K., Ireland, the United States, South Africa and other countries.

The Main Factors

- Detailed, businesslike advance planning of every essential step in a calendar of events and activities, which will be carried out in a logical sequence.
- Complete analysis of the situation at the start of the campaign.
- Planning everything to be cost-effective. The total cost of the campaign was £6,000 for an additional income of £16,500 per annum.
- Selecting and enlisting the voluntary help of the best financial leaders and committee members.
- Securing the financial commitment of all committee members before approaching other prospective donors.
- Careful, detailed briefing of all committee members before allowing them to take part in the active phase of the campaign.
- Ensuring that all prospective participants are fully informed about all aspects of the campaign before the visit of a committee member. This is done by letter, by the Parish Supper speeches, by Sunday announcements and by brochure.
- Acknowledging all pledges with a letter of thanks.
- Constant technical analysis and control of activity by the campaign director throughout the campaign.
- Effective office administration and communication, and providing necessary services and facilities required by committee members.
- An effective post-campaign administration system.

ABBEYFIELD BRISTOL SOCIETY
EXTRA CARE APPEAL

This case history was supplied by Mrs. S. M. Perry, Administrator, Abbeyfield Bristol Society.

Background

The Abbeyfield Bristol Society was founded in 1966 and opened its first house two years later. This Abbeyfield Society is the biggest such society in England and Wales, with 12 supportive care houses providing sheltered accommodation for independent, active, elderly residents in family-sized houses, each with a resident housekeeper.

In 1978 an Extra Care house was opened for the frail elderly in need of 24-hour care. The demand for places became more acute and we decided to buy an adjoining property in which to expand. This we eventually did in 1989. Plans were drawn up for ten additional bedsitting rooms, sluice facilities, additional bathrooms and toilets, better lounge and dining areas, and an office for the house matron. We estimated that the conversion work, equipment and furnishings would cost £400,000. We added another £100,000 to set up an endowment fund for residents with limited resources, making a total appeal of £500,000.

Appeal strategy

There was not much time to formulate a strategy, given a timetable that was effectively foisted on us by circumstances. We appointed an appeal chairman, who was already involved in Abbeyfield and had expressed interest in fund-raising for the Society. The next step was to approach potential members of the appeal committee. A committee of seven was formed, including the appeal chairman, the Society's chairman, treasurer and administrator, who acted as appeal secretary.

The constituency for the appeal had to be restricted to within the Bristol city boundary, as there are other Abbeyfield Societies nearby at Bath, Portishead, Keynsham and Chipping Sodbury. We wrote to a list of possible patrons, such as the Lord Bishop of Bristol, the Bishop of Clifton, our local MP, the Rt. Hon. William Waldegrave, the Lord Mayor of Bristol, the Vice Chancellor and Professor of Social Work at Bristol University and other leading figures in the community. Only two declined, due to pressure of other commitments, and one of these sent a generous donation.

After liaising with Abbeyfield's national public relations department, we wrote to The Prince of Wales, the National Society's Royal Patron, who had officially opened our Extra Care House in 1980. He kindly agreed to write a message of support for use in our appeal brochure. We produced a brochure that was designed to be easy to read and attractive to look at. Our appeal slogan was 'Abbeyfield Extra Care... Continuing the Caring'.

Appeal programme

We divided fund-raising into three categories: trusts and large companies, fund-raising events organized by or through the appeal committee, and small fund-raising activities encouraged directly or indirectly by Abbeyfield volunteers, residents, housekeepers, friends and supporters. We had an official appeal launch, aiming to obtain as much publicity as possible throughout the year. The Bishops of Bristol and Clifton sportingly donned hard hats and wielded sledgehammers to knock out the first bricks at the opening ceremony.

We approached a number of Bristol businesses in the hope of obtaining substantial donations which could be presented to the Bishops at the launch, but our efforts came to nothing. Instead, we arranged for the first two residents who had made donations to present their cheques to the Bishops. We were also fortunate in obtaining a gift of £20,000 from a trust with which our company secretary was connected.

We held three prestigious events during the appeal and about 100 other events, ranging from coffee mornings to cheese and wine evenings, sponsored activities, an 'As New' shop, and a Caribbean Evening at our Caribbean house. Several people arranged dinner parties for which they charged their guests. A resident in a supportive care house charged every visitor 20p, raising over £50, and we received gifts in memory of residents who had died.

The first of the major events was a reception in the magnificent setting of Bristol's Mansion House, the Lord Mayor's official residence. This is a very privileged setting to which we were very fortunate to gain access. The reception was hosted by the Lord Mayor and combined with an art sale organized by a local art gallery. The gallery owner gave a percentage of his profits and we solicited donations from those attending.

Through one of our appeal committee members, we were the beneficiaries of the annual concert staged by a Bristol amateur choir in St. Mary Redcliffe Church, regarded as Bristol's second Anglican 'cathedral'. HRH The Princess Royal graciously agreed to be our guest of honour. Music was provided by one of the County of Avon School Orchestras and sponsorship by a firm of stockbrokers paid for the reception afterwards.

The third event was an evening at Badminton House. The Duchess of Beaufort is President of Abbeyfield's Western Region. A very successful evening was arranged, with a cold buffet supper prepared by volunteers. A piano trio played in the ballroom, donating their services free.

Results

The appeal officially finished at the end of December 1991. By the start of 1992, it had raised £80,000. However, we continued to receive donations as a direct result of the appeal and, by the following July, the total raised was nearing £124,00 (net).

Although this figure is disappointingly short of our £500,000 target, it has to be seen in the context of a severely restricted catchment area and the fact that the appeal campaign was battling against a deep economic recession.

> ### Analysis
>
> - The bulk of the organization of the appeal was handled by the existing Abbeyfield office staff. One part-time staff member was employed in the run-up to the Christmas Concert in 1990. This meant that we could state in our literature that all money raised would go to the appeal. Administration cost virtually nothing: we even had many posters and tickets printed in-house at little cost.
> - We endeavoured to be meticulous in our planning, taking pains to ensure that everyone knew exactly what was expected of them, for how long and when.
> - Continuity is important. We chose a colour theme for our stationery which we followed through for our brochure, tickets, leaflets and programmes for major events.
> - We obtained very good press coverage – not easy in a city the size of Bristol.
> - We were careful not to overstretch ourselves.
> - We received many valuable gifts in kind: stationery, the sketch for our brochure cover, the professionally painted sign outside our Extra Care House, the readers for the Christmas Concert, many raffle prizes, and tireless hard work and unstinting enthusiasm of many friends and volunteers.
> - Raising money is VERY hard work!

Conclusions

1. With hindsight, we would not have launched our appeal at the start of a major recession, but it had to be launched then or forgone, because the optimum moment would have passed.
2. We considered using professional fund-raisers and investigated three. All required a substantial financial outlay and to find people who could be trained by them to do the necessary work with no guarantee of financial return. We felt that the likely cost of £15,000-20,000 might deter many from raising small sums if they felt that much of it was funding a professional fund-raiser.
3. Perhaps the burden on the Abbeyfield office could have been reduced if we had had a stronger appeal committee. But it is vital to have administrative continuity and a central point where there is at least one person who knows exactly what is going on across the whole spectrum.
4. The appeal committee might have been used as the nucleus of more concentrated networking, but those with experience, expertise and clout also have the most claims on their time. Some of our patrons were very supportive and generous, financially and with their time. Others seemed to feel that it was enough to lend their name and were not prepared to use their contacts as we had hoped.
5. Although we did not achieve our target, we had aimed deliberately high. The appeal has raised our public profile and united groups of friends, volunteers and residents in the common cause of raising money for Abbeyfield.
6. Above all, be professional, keep people informed and, very important, remember to say 'thank you' to everyone for everything!

ST. MICHAEL'S HOSPICE, BASINGSTOKE

This case study was contributed by Andrew de Mille of Andrew de Mille Fund-raising Consultants.

Background

In the 1980s a hospice care committee was established in Basingstoke, aiming to build a 15 bed hospice with day centre and home care service for terminally ill patients.

The chairman of the hospice committee in 1989 was a prominent local accountant. His analysis of the project had produced building costs estimated at £1.5 million, and projected running costs of £600,000 per year. Negotiations with the Health Authority were proceeding well for the transfer of a building site, although it had made it clear that it had no capital available for the project.

The fund-raising was not proceeding so well. In May that year the Mayor of Basingstoke publicly launched her personal dream – to see a hospice for terminally ill patients built in the town – and she was determined that it would now happen. The talking had gone on long enough, she said. The Mayor's appeal was launched alongside the hospice committee's efforts, seeking the support of the whole community in fund-raising. Wide publicity was generated and every week the Mayor's picture could be seen in local papers collecting cheques from local organizations. By October 1989, half way through the Mayoral year, £19,500 had been collected. It was reluctantly agreed by the committee that they should seek professional help.

The fund-raising consultant working at community level frequently finds situations like this one, where there are several initiatives already under way, where begging letters have indiscriminately been sent everywhere and where publicity has generated little more than wide public disbelief in the feasibility of a daunting target. So it was at Basingstoke when Andrew de Mille was appointed as consultant, initially to undertake a brief survey of fund-raising needs and sources and to advise on fund-raising strategy.

Initial planning

The main purpose of the initial survey was to assess the following important elements of the project:

1. The fund-raising case and statistical support for it.
2. Possible funding sources.
3. The strength of leadership (and potential leadership) available for fund-raising.
4. The most appropriate structure to enable new leaders to be brought in without apparently 'ousting' the originators of the project.

The planning study concluded that three strands of fund-raising activity should be developed, enlisting the help of energetic and influential people to supplement those already involved where necessary.

Three main strands of fund-raising

1. Basingstoke companies – major capital contributors.
2. 'Friends of the Hospice' – grass roots activity producing regular income over time and eventually meeting up to 30 per cent of running costs.
3. The 'Basil de Ferranti Memorial Appeal' – major capital contributions being sought from trusts, companies and individuals connected with the late Basil de Ferranti, former MEP for the area, who had died of cancer and whose widow became President of the Hospice.

Each of the main fund-raising areas had its own target, based on the number and perceived 'quality' of the prospects identified and on the consultant's experience of other hospice projects. The overall target, however, would be achieved only if some very substantial contributions could be obtained by the company and Basil de Ferranti appeals.

The organizing charity, SHARE (Support Help and Relief Extended), had been set up to provide home care only. The initial survey recommended the formation of a new charity, St. Michael's Hospice (North Hampshire), to own the building, provide a vehicle for involving new leaders and provide a broader range of charitable objects than SHARE, which would become a 'sister' charity within the overall structure.

The initial survey was completed in October 1989 and was followed by a more detailed planning stage in which the leadership needs of the proposed structure were tackled. In discussions between the committee chairman and consultant one major problem presented itself: the chairman felt he could not commit the time to encourage, enthuse and coordinate all the strands of fund-raising in addition to keeping his fragmenting committee together. Slow fund-raising performance had caused uncertainty and frustration, leading to heated discussions within the committee which generally divided into factions of 'carers', 'planners' and 'fund-raisers' – each with different but pressing priorities. Given the demands of a busy accountant's practice in addition to the hospice, the chairman decided to find a replacement for himself and the consultant privately drew up a specification for him which prompted him to suggest two prominent local businessmen.

A meeting was arranged shortly afterwards at which the first of these was sounded out as to his likely interest in becoming involved. Some days later the chairman announced that he was stepping down in favour of the 'newcomer' and so the *fait accompli* was effectively completed! The new chairman was ideally qualified in every way – a former Mayor of Basingstoke, a successful businessman, a prominent Rotarian and very well known in the area as someone who achieved his goals. Best of all, he had recently appointed a Managing Director to run his printing company and had time to devote to the cause.

Developing the fund-raising organization

Fund-raising depends on people. The new chairman's first task in January 1990 was to identify leaders for each of the fund-raising sectors. Several week's research and discussion were well rewarded – first the chief executive of a major local company agreed to help assemble the Basingstoke business group and host its first meetings. Then a member of the original hospice committee offered to chair the 'Friends' organization and to coordinate the process of setting up and motivating local support groups. A prominent merchant banker who lived in the area agreed to chair the Basil de Ferranti appeal. The campaign organization chart was thus beginning to come to life exactly as planned. By March 1990, good teams had been assembled to undertake the various fund-raising tasks, each with their own chairman or leader.

As a businessman, former Mayor and a Rotarian, the new chairman was able to use his local knowledge and influence to form a building committee consisting of a commercial architect, a local building contractor and other building professionals who all agreed that they would work free of charge or at cost. They radically re-examined the building design and recommended a design and building contract using a patented system, the product of the building company concerned. They estimated a building cost including all fees of less than £1.1 million – constituting a substantial saving on target figures. Effectively, this could be construed as the first major gift, since the savings implied amounted to £400,000!

Fund-raising development phase

The Mayoral year ended in May 1990. By then, the Mayor's appeal had raised £120,000, of which community activity had generated £80,000; a single donation of £40,000 was also received. Previous Mayor's appeals in Basingstoke had never produced more than £40,000 in total. The resounding success of the Mayor's tireless efforts had the additional lasting benefit of involving very many local people in fund-raising support groups – the future lifeblood of the hospice for its revenue fund-raising needs.

The chairman received the Mayor's cheque in May 1990 and used the occasion to launch the hospice appeal. This was an event dictated by circumstances, but one which drew even wider attention to what had become a community-wide venture. The chairman announced a two-stage target; firstly aiming to raise £1.1 million for building costs within the next 12 months, and secondly to have raised a year's running costs by the time the hospice opened in Spring 1992. There was over £600,000 committed on launch day – well over half of the declared building target.

During the early part of 1990 discussions with major local businesses produced increasing evidence of a factor no one had planned for – recession. Basingstoke was seeing its first unemployment for very many years; business orders were falling and confidence was declining. Company covenants were slow in coming and far below the levels projected. Two companies had contributed a total of £100,000 by May 1990, but others were slow in committing themselves and several months later the business total was little further progressed. With major business problems facing them, the business group members postponed meetings and were difficult to enthuse. It was decided to leave them until 'better times' and concentrate fire power in other directions. The £400,000 saving in building costs allowed a degree of flexibility which would not otherwise have existed.

The Basil de Ferranti Memorial appeal was fortunate in having good reason to appeal outside its catchment area. The Basil de Ferranti group met in London during 1990 and within four months had secured good leading gifts. By December

1990, its target had been achieved, largely underpinned by one contribution of £70,000, four of £50,000 one of £37,000, five of £35,000 and several of £10,000 and £5,000. Charitable trusts accounted for several of these major contributions. Small contributions amounted to over £20,000, and spurred on by their success, the group members started organizing 'up-market' social events which produced a further £30,000.

Problems of credibility

In spite of the progress in the major gift campaigns, grass roots fund-raisers still faced general disbelief in the community that the project could succeed. The chairman placed great emphasis on starting the building to create credibility for the project and overcame committee opposition to letting the building contract when cash available was still only equal to half the cost. The effect on local fund-raising was, with publicity, almost instantaneous – the credibility gap was at last bridged and community fund-raising took off.

Achieving the project

Building commenced in May 1991 and was completed in February 1992. When the hospice doors opened for day-care patients in March 1992, building costs were fully met and continuing fund-raising for running costs was meeting targets. The first in-patients were admitted in July 1992.

Analysis		
Gift table – major giving		
	£	£
1 ×	140,000	-	140,000
1 ×	70,000	-	70,000
1 ×	67,000	-	67,000
4 ×	50,000	-	200,000
1 ×	38,000	-	38,000
1 ×	30,000	-	30,000
2 ×	25,000	-	50,000
1 ×	20,000	-	20,000
1 ×	12,000	-	12,000
6 ×	10,000	-	60,000
13 ×	5,000	-	65,000
32 gifts/grants produced		£752,000

- half of the £1.5m fund was produced by 32 gifts.
- three-quarters of the £1.5m fund was produced by over 250 gifts.
- the full £1.5m fund was produced by immense community-wide effort involving thousands of people – at least 2,000 gifts and probably more. The need to build such wide community involvement was in order to have the infrastructure in place for further revenue fund-raising purposes.

Success in galvanizing the entire community around the fund-raising created a political climate in which the Health Authority had to be seen to be supporting the project. After negotiations over very many months, the Health Authority committed £140,000 from the sum put aside by central government for care-of-the-dying projects – the so-called Virginia Bottomley fund – towards working capital costs in starting the hospice. The Health Authority further committed itself to a substantial proportion of running costs. The community fund-raising organization would be required to raise £20,000 per month, at 1992 prices, far into the future. With careful management and motivation of volunteers through the community-wide fund-raising organization now in place, this target was being met month by month during 1992. A structured and targeted legacy programme was also introduced in 1990, which produced its first fruits the following year.

Fund-raising costs

The project was undertaken at extremely low cost. Almost all services were given free or at substantial discounts. The total cost of fund-raising consultancy, including all expenses, was some £30,000. The office, secretarial work, printing and other materials were all free of charge. Fund-raising consultancy was always limited to very few days per month and was no longer needed after July 1991 following the appointment of a paid fund-raising coordinator earlier in the year. The total fund-raising cost was therefore about 2.1 per cent of funds raised.

Conclusion

This case study underlines the immense importance of obtaining the right quality of leadership at each level of the fund-raising structure. The strength of the building committee was largely due to the quality of influence and leadership which assembled it, and its contribution to the project was enormous. The failure to achieve the companies' campaign target merely caused redoubled efforts in other directions, particularly in community fund-raising, bringing forward a legacy campaign originally planned for a later date, and in strengthening the case for Health Authority support, which eventually amounted to £140,000. The major gifts were almost all brought about by personal contact with the donors concerned.

If the project case is strongly argued and if appropriate structures and levels of leadership are applied, the ability of communities to meet the cost of real needs by fund-raising is almost unlimited.

ST. MICHAEL'S, HIGHGATE, DEVELOPMENT PROGRAMME

This case history was supplied by Richard Molineux of Molineux Fundraising.

St. Michael's is a substantial Anglican Victorian church in the middle of Highgate, North London. In 1986 the Parochial Church Council identified a £345,000 works programme, against available assets of £245,000. Therefore £100,000 was needed, and Molineux Fundraising, a professional firm, was asked to advise on how best to raise this sum.

> **Three main tasks**
>
> - To build up a group of committed volunteers willing to give and to generate funds in an organized way that would provide specific tasks for everyone.
> - To draw up a compelling statement of the case for carrying out the work now, that would be generally accepted and suitable for publishing in a range of printed and other forms.
> - To establish a timetable for action.

Campaign

The constituency would clearly include the church's own congregation, but should it also include the non-church-going population of Highgate? We decided to be as all-inclusive as possible. The role of Molineux at this time was to arrange for a thorough review of the nature of the work – whom it would serve and what benefits would flow from it – and encapsulate this in a programme that the Parochial Church Council would approve and promote.

Organization

People were being recruited into the fund-raising organization. The aim was not only to achieve the target – and a bit more in case early cost estimates were wrong – but also to involve as many people as possible to make it a true parish effort. The initial fund-raising planning phase was concerned with how to run the fund-raising campaign once it was launched. A separate building committee commissioned and monitored building work.

The original fund-raising planning team involved 12 people, including the vicar, architect, churchwardens, fund-raising consultant and a lay chairman who was a prominent and active member of the local community. He kept the whole structure moving forward and motivated. This team, guided by the consultant, decided on a fund-raising framework that would create a team or designate a person to be directly responsible for each of a range of key tasks. Some were direct fund-raising, others support or preparatory roles. The key features were:

- A group dedicated to raising large gifts from the small number able to make them.
- A group concerned with visiting the whole congregation on a person-to-person basis to ask for support, as donors themselves.
- A group dedicated solely to planning and implementing the launch.

Launch

Prior to the launch, the local press were invited to a personal briefing by the chairman, provided with a carefully prepared press pack and given an opportunity to discuss the plans. Publicity was good.

It was decided that the heart of the actual fund-raising campaign should be concentrated into the four weeks following the launch, during which everyone on the

Parochial Church Council electoral roll would be visited in their homes by one of a number of teams of visitors. A major effort was put into creating these teams. They had their own convener whose task was to hold weekly meetings of team leaders. They reported on progress, problems and issues to be tackled. This system created a powerful momentum.

The programme of visits was made effective because the launch was a significant, enjoyable, social event. The launch committee, chaired by a hotelier, planned a launch supper in a local school hall with a splendid meal cooked by members of the congregation. A very high percentage of the church turned out for the supper and were both inspired and prepared for the visits. At about the same time, the major gifts campaign was set up by a private presentation to selected people at the chairman's home, at which the architect gave an audio-visual presentation of the plans and answered questions. This led to the formation of the major gifts group.

Case statement

St. Michael's Parish Centre is the Parochial Church Council's response, after long deliberation and wide consultation, to the need for space dedicated to the educational and social aspects of parish life. It will also be of benefit to the whole community.

Our old Church Hall, inconvenient and remote, was sold in 1983. This provided the nucleus of a fund towards a package of improvements, including on-site provision of facilities for the purposes outlined in the Vicar's message, and the rebuilding of the organ, which was on the verge of collapse. That has evolved into the development programme now before you.

We are ready to embark on the Parish Centre, a handsome building designed by Melville Poole, a member of St. Michael's congregation, and approved by all the relevant planning, diocesan and historic buildings authorities. It will stand on the north side of the church. The upper floor will be a large assembly room with a magnificent view across Highgate Cemetery to London's skyline; below will be other, flexibly laid-out meeting rooms, kitchens, lavatories and storage space. The Centre will be linked to St. Michael's by a new door in the north aisle and will connect to the vestries. It will also have its own entrance via the newly paved north side, with easy access for wheelchairs and the disabled. The whole ensemble, to be built in the same brick as St. Michael's, will harmonize with the church and satisfy the eye as a building in its own right.

At the same time, on the south side, we plan to build a garden of remembrance, to be accessible from the church by a new door in the south aisle and associated with the recently-dedicated Book of Remembrance. Thus the environment of the church will be enhanced in a coherent architectural design.

Within the church, the sacristy behind the organ is to be redeveloped, thus completing the work associated with the organ. The organ itself has been entirely rebuilt, sounding splendid, but on borrowed money.

We expect the building work to start in January 1987, and plan to dedicate the Parish Centre the following Christmas.

Fund-raising pack

A special pack was produced to be taken to homes as the basis for discussing people's gifts. The pack contained:

- The case statement.
- Message from the vicar.
- Names of the development programme team.
- Schedule of costs.
- Explanation of tax-effective giving methods, such as covenants.
- Plan of the parish centre.
- Breakdown of the programme into component parts, individually costed so that people could designate the gift to a specific area like the east windows (£15,000) or the doors (£4,000).
- A sheet saying where the money had to come from.

Finally, the pack contained a simple form promising to make a gift. This was the form visitors took back to the office. The treasurer filled it in and had it returned for signature. This meant that, on visits, no one had to struggle with trying to get the forms filled correctly. All that was needed was the promise of a given sum and a signature. Easy to ask for, easy to do.

The pack was contained in a simple folder. On the cover was the campaign logo and the words 'St. Michael's Highgate Development Programme' superimposed on a half-tone map of Highgate with the church at its heart, picked out in bold.

Results

At the final progress meeting attended by the consultant in January 1987, the treasurer reported that £127,000 had been raised. The total rose to nearly £200,000 as earlier initiatives with trusts, companies and major potential donors bore fruit. Fund-raising consultancy fees and the cost of fund-raising publications came to about 5 per cent of the amount raised.

Analysis

1. The word 'appeal' was never used throughout the campaign. This was not a begging operation. It was presented for what it was, a serious contribution to the life of the area. Those who asked for money were themselves donors; this attitude was very important to success. If something is worth doing and will be of benefit to the donors, then a begging or appeal approach may be inappropriate.
2. No major fund-raising events were planned. They are time-consuming, unpredictable and may produce small donations from those who could make major donations. The time for special events is often after all possibilities for personal visits and discussion have been exhausted.
3. Some 70 per cent of the £200,000 raised came from about 30 gifts. The effort put into securing those gifts showed that, to achieve a serious gift, the potential donor must be treated seriously: given the chance to query, to investigate and to reflect before committing the gift.

4. Planning, planning and more planning is a major key to success – as is drafting, redrafting and redrafting public statements.

5. The final key to success is to involve as many people as possible in a purposeful way. Jobs and targets make fund-raising in a local community work. Uncertainty and ambiguity of purpose or result tend to bring all to nought. As was said at the launch: 'If the trumpet give an uncertain sound, who shall follow?'

Part VI

AFTERMATH

Chapter 34

REVIEWING RESULTS
AND FUTURE PLANNING

In this chapter I compare the results of the Wishing Well Appeal with two more recent successful appeals – the Royal Marsden Hospital Cancer Appeal and the Sick Kids appeal for the Royal Hospital for Sick Children in Edinburgh.

In the final part of the chapter I concentrate on the essential activities of planning the ongoing fund-raising role after an appeal.

REVIEWING RESULTS

Reviewing results at the end of an appeal is often overlooked. However, it is important for the charity and for the voluntary sector as a whole. The charity should learn from what happened in the appeal and see how its predictions matched up to the result. Above all, it should learn which sections of the community responded best, using a process of detailed donor profiling – vital information for future fund-raising. Also, you need to know which methods of fund-raising are worth building because they seemed to fit well with your cause and brought in more funds. Your results are important to the voluntary world as a case history from which other charities can learn. That is, indeed, the major reason for this book.

Analyze sources of funds

When analyzing an appeal, your first task should be to gather as much information as possible about the appeal results. Naturally, you will have plenty already, but there will be loose ends to tie. You will need to collate the data in a way that enables you to make sense of it. First you could review the number of major gifts you received.

THE WISHING WELL APPEAL

Help
Great Ormond Street
get better.

Big Gifts

An analysis of big gifts received by the Wishing Well Appeal was as follows:

Number	Amount (£'000)
1	4,000
1	3,000
1	2,000
4	1,000–1,500
7	500–1,000
5	250–500
4	150–250
11	100–150

At least £3.5 million was pledged during the preparatory stage – a great encouragement to other major donors during the private appeal.

When we announced the achievement of the target in January 1989, the split between banked and pledged funds was as follows:

cash in bank (including interest) £34.42 million; committed future payments £6.75 million and committed through covenants £1.1 million, to give a total of £42.27 million.

I have already pointed out that you need to be very sensitive as to when you announce publicly that your target has been reached if the total includes pledges and future commitments through covenants.

Here is a full analysis of how the above sum was raised:

Analysis

Category	At public launch £,000	%	Final £,000	%
Corporate	892	14.2	7,874	22.9
Trusts	3,632	57.9	7,314	21.3
Personal over £1,000	1,436	22.9	2,932	8.5
Personal £100–£1,000	8	0.1	10,893	31.7
Personal less than £100	1	–	3,161	9.2
Give As You Earn	–	–	31	0.1
Interest received	220	3.6	1,524	4.4
Investment income	83	1.3	659	1.9
Pledges	2,291	–	6,758	–
Covenants	947	–	1,124	–
TOTALS	9,510	100	42,270	100

The table opposite shows the results in January 1989 when the public appeal was closed. The final total for the appeal was £54 million. If government funding is included, a grand total of £84 million was raised.

Trends

You will see that a staggering 40 per cent-plus came from people giving or raising amounts of up to £1,000. This was most unusual and it confounds the normal rule of thumb for capital appeals that 60-80 per cent of the funds come from 10 per cent of the donors. The catalyst for the Wishing Well Appeal was its powerful emotive pull and our ability to convince the public that every little would help – as it triumphantly did. The average monthly cash inflow during the public phase of the Appeal was about £2 million.

Another new trend during the Appeal was the lead that several major companies gave their staff in fund-raising until the whole workforce had joined in to raise vast sums for the cause. In some cases, companies encouraged staff by matching the funds they raised with a pound-for-pound donation from central coffers. Others, including Tesco and United Biscuits, seconded a member of staff full time to stimulate employee fund-raising for the Wishing Well Appeal.

The regional groups formed an area of activity which sprang into action and became the backbone of the public phase of the Appeal. Setting up a network of regional groups from scratch is usually a laborious process taking many months. The urgency of the Wishing Well Appeal cut through that, kindling devotion, dedication and enthusiasm which lives on, rooting for the Hospital well after the Appeal ended.

Why such a wide response?

The starting point of the Wishing Well Appeal was the natural wish of many people to do something for sick children. The cause was the most emotive possible and it was enhanced by deep, widely-felt affection for Great Ormond Street. To that, however, the Appeal organization added detailed planning and sophisticated marketing techniques to communicate the Hospital's plight to both private and public potential donors. Great Ormond Street has a strong effect on those who have anything to do with it. Joy and tragedy are daily bread. Parents are chilled to realize that their child is ill enough to be referred there, but relieved to know that he will receive the best treatment.

This deep well of emotion had to be tapped; we could not afford to fail. If all the planning time is included, we spent just under four years preparing for and running the Appeal. It seemed an agonizingly long time – but it was worth it. The response was magnificent. I feel very privileged to have been part of the Wishing Well Appeal team.

Lessons

The Wishing Well Appeal broke new ground in so many ways that it inevitably provided many valuable lessons – these four in particular:

1. Our preoccupation with the need to keep overheads down led us to restrict staff numbers unduly. Without the timely and generous support of Midland Bank, we would have been seriously swamped by the size and extent of the public's response. We had to recruit the support of management consultants to persuade our Executive Committee that we should double staff numbers and appoint deputies to key positions. Quite correctly, the Executive Committee kept a tight rein on administrative expenditure. Equally, too little expenditure can prejudice results.

2. We discovered the problems of success. The response we triggered was resented by some other children's hospitals and by several charities. I can understand their point of view; they felt that the Wishing Well Appeal was encroaching on their ability to raise funds for their cherished causes. Nevertheless, many other charities applauded our good fortune, especially because they knew ours was a one-off Appeal. Consequently, the Hospital has been instrumental in forming a consortium, entitled Children in Hospital. This will raise funds for all children's hospitals in ways that individual institutions cannot.

3. We re-discovered the crucial importance of volunteers and the responsibilities that go with accepting their help. A one-off appeal has to set up an organization for a limited period and then wind it up. That, and the need to limit costs, restricts the numbers of paid staff you can involve and makes volunteer help essential. Volunteers are entitled to appropriate advice and training – and sometimes may need a consoling comment.

4. The Hospital learned what it meant to the British people and to many people beyond these shores. The response generated by the Appeal was a huge morale boost to the dedicated staff, who were working in very trying, unsatisfactory conditions.

THE ROYAL MARSDEN HOSPITAL CANCER APPEAL

It is interesting to review the results of the more recent highly successful £25 million cancer appeal for the Royal Marsden Hospital. This was the first building appeal in the hospital's history and the government provided matching funding for one of the three projects – to build and equip new facilities in Fulham Road, London, and Sutton.

Leadership

The hospital's Patron and President are Her Majesty, The Queen, and Her Royal Highness, The Princess of Wales, respectively. The leadership for the appeal was provided by Marmaduke Hussey, Chairman of the BBC, who recruited a top-level team.

Structure

The appeal structure was established by February 1990 and evolved somewhat after that. The key was to recruit and manage a number of high-powered specialists so that they were motivated and challenged to work together for the greatest

---

Strategy

- to raise the money, preferably in two years from the official launch (21 February, 1990)
- to keep normal overhead expenses to 5p in the pound by 'thinking free' as much as possible in terms of office furnishings, equipment and staff
- to achieve a national profile without spending significant monies on paid advertising
- to market a profile in keeping with that of the hospital while effectively branding the appeal in all public exposure, merchandise, etc.
- to delegate through functional committees as much of the fund-raising and sourcing as possible
- to avoid becoming directly embroiled in particular activities or events as far as possible.

---

good of the appeal. The specialists headed five committees – City & Industry, Treasury, Entertainments & Events, Marketing & Media and Sports

The appeal staff was headed by Richard Duncan. He was backed by 13-15 paid staff plus two secondees, occasional short-term contract people for particular projects and as many volunteers as possible.

Results

The appeal did not meet its two-year-from-launch deadline, largely for economic reasons. Overhead expenses were maintained at 5p in the pound, while other expenses equalled a further 5 per cent of funds raised. A breakdown of the percentages received from different sectors during the most active period of the appeal is show here.

Royal Marsden Appeal income breakdown

Category	£,000	% *
Corporate	2,621	15.4
Trusts	7,763	45.6
Personal over £1,000	1,752	10.3
Personal £100–£1,000	733	4.3
Personal less than £100	1,995	11.7
Give As You Earn	18	0.1
Interest received	2,150	12.6
Pledges	2,132	
Covenants	280	
TOTALS	19,444	100

* The donor category of pledges and covenants was not clarified. Therefore, percentages were based on cash total only.

Note: Funds raised before these dates have not been included as they were not broken down into categories of donor. If these earlier funds are included, the appeal had raised £24 million by the end of June 1992.

Trends

Certain trends emerged which could be categorized in one of two ways:

- Those which seem to have evolved naturally, encouraged by the publicity campaign and personal contacts, and resulted in:
  - company employee interest and commitment
  - interest from the local community for the new Children's Cancer Unit.
- Those clearly influenced by the economic environment.

The appeal spanned a period of reasonable economic activity in the United Kingdom followed by a longer, increasing and prolonged economic depression. This meant that fund-raising targets for the City & Industry Committee and the corporate sector in general were frequently reviewed and substantially reduced. In many cases, the response was negligible. However, company employees were often collectively most generous, setting an example for the corporate management to match or support.

Other trends included:

- Latterly the cancellation or reduction of events became a feature, fortunately not to any great extent or reduction in income.
- Reduction in flag day takings (in the City and local boroughs) in 1991and more so in 1992.
- Reduction in sales of advertising.
- Charity fatigue in general, and particularly among 'the great and the good', and to some extent with the media as the target was approached.

Comment

Commenting on the appeal, Richard Duncan said:

The most unusual result of the appeal would seem to be the number of large pro-file events which raised a sizeable proportion of the total target. However, this does not show up in the way the analysis figures have been recorded as this is based on the donor and not the method of collecting from the donor. This was part of the strategy to establish public awareness using the 'ripple' approach, i.e. a gradual but persistent build-up with the media ('advertorials', celebrities) and the general public (events and roadshows). In this context it is very helpful to have, as we did, a long list of committed celebrities including several who could be relied upon on a regular basis.

Problems faced included:

1. *The establishment of a regional fund-raising organization due to charity fatigue i.e. busy local people had been very involved in other charities' fund-raising already.*
2. *The establishment of product promotion opportunities – as cancer does not asso-ciate well with most popular products/vendors.*

If we collectively have done an effective job we will have left various 'legacies' behind, such as the overall public awareness of The Royal Marsden Hospital (which was by no means the case at the outset, even in our patient catchment area) which can be maintained and used. This includes the records and systems to follow up the above events and past donors and various events, one-offs or annuals, which will con-tinue to bring in money.

Anyone reading the above should notice a lot of similarities between our appeal structure and approach and that of Great Ormond Street's Wishing Well Appeal. We make no apology for this. We were most fortunate to follow close behind Great Ormond Street Hospital and to learn a lot from them. They, to my mind, did 'invent the wheel' and were kindly willing to share their experience and advice with us and many other charities. They showed us all what was possible then, and even in today's tough economic environment their strategy, structure and approach is still valid. I would, therefore, commend their 'wheel' to any new charitable appeals for close study if not downright plagiarism.

THE 'SICK KIDS APPEAL'

(The Royal Hospital for Sick Children, Edinburgh)

THE SICK KIDS

This £11m appeal is another excellent case history to review when comparing campaign results.

The purpose of the appeal was to provide facilities that could be housed only in a new wing and others that required extensive refurbishment – as identified by clinicians and parents – including four operating theatre suites, 24 surgical beds, 16 parent and child rooms, an intensive care area, a neonatal unit, a research unit for the Department of Child Life and Health and associated administrative units. The local Health Board had indicated that it was unable to provide the necessary funds until 'well into the next century' and a public appeal was seen as the only possible source of funding.

Strategy

The basic strategy was to establish a campaign that would touch every sector of the community in the East of Scotland, while ensuring that careful efforts were made to gain major support from trusts, foundations, companies and wealthy individuals. The Director's preference was to devise a precise strategy, clear it with the appeal committee and present it to the panels, which were asked to add new ideas or suggest ways of executing the strategy. The panels were all made up of top professionals working in critical areas of the life of the East of Scotland. Members were impressed and motivated by the professional approach of the campaign. The appeal strategy was designed and endorsed in December 1989. The private appeal, targeted at trusts, companies and professionals, took place from April 1990 until the launch of the public appeal in September 1991. This phase was 'officially' closed in April 1992.

Leadership

The hospital's Patron is Her Majesty Queen Elizabeth The Queen Mother. The Chairman of the appeal was James Miller, Chairman of The Miller Group Ltd. With roots deep in many aspects of life in Scotland and a high reputation as a well-liked, much-respected leader of the largest privately owned business in Scotland, James Miller was well placed to help with important contacts. His wholehearted commitment to the appeal and his generosity with time for meetings were a tremendous strength. He guided and inspired a high-powered committee and was unstinting in his availability to meet a wide variety of people who were important to the campaign. His company led the way with a substantial contribution to the appeal.

Structure

Reporting to the Appeal Director, James Tysoe, four Assistant Directors managed seven panels as follows:

Assistant Director	Panel(s)
1. Fund-raising Direct	– Commerce & Industry – International – Banking & Finance
2. Special Events	– Special Events
3. Marketing	– Marketing
4. Public Affairs	– Public Affairs – Media Advisory

The full complement was made up by four deputies to the Assistant Directors and 12 volunteers.

Activities

The range of activities was all encompassing and spread throughout the East of Scotland. It was critically important to achieve both urgency and intensity during the public phase because the appeal was restricted to the East of Scotland and, therefore, had a target population of less than 1.9 million. PR and advertising played a key role throughout the campaign. Massive media support was sought and sustained by virtue of producing stories encompassing so many differing areas of Scottish life and including local personalities. A compelling multi-media campaign covered TV, the press – with full-page launch advertisements and a series of imaginative, controversial smaller advertisements – as well as several hundred bus sides, radio advertisements and posters throughout the locality.

Over 3,000 local voluntary groups took part in nominating the Sick Kids campaign as their charity of the year or by running a one-off fund-raising activity. Some 700 schools participated, as many of the children knew someone who had been in the hospital. The special events panel organized several massive themed events during the public phase which raised money through sponsorship and registration. Promotional merchandise was sold at these events, as well as at a shop in central Edinburgh, for the four months leading up to Christmas 1991. Additionally a major direct sales campaign resulted in the sale of over 100,000 lapel logo badges. Only items of high quality were selected and this contributed to the high 51 per cent net profit margin on all merchandise.

A direct mail campaign was organized using very carefully profiled segments. Seven mailings were sent out using 5,000 names at a time. Special letters with videos were sent to secretaries of targeted companies, asking them to pass the details to their bosses. A relatively high 9 per cent response rate was achieved and an above-average level of gift from all mailings made this an important part of the intense personal approach campaign.

Results

The target was 'at least £10 million' although, after a few months, this had to be adjusted upwards to £11 million because VAT was no longer recoverable on new building work. The total raised was £11.6 million, at 8.89 per cent cost and donations were still coming in months after the official close. As illustrated here, the recession had a dampening effect on the efforts of the Commerce, Industry and Finance panels, judging by the relatively low proportion of company donations. A breakdown of contributions by sectors, in percentage terms, shows the following details.

Breakdown of contributions by sectors

Category	% of total
Trusts & Foundations	21
Companies	9
Individual donors	13
Events & Trading	21
HMG/Health Board	17
Sale of space to University	9
Interest income	10

International

It was decided to develop an international aspect to the appeal. The basis was the strong cultural links which exist because there are hundreds of Scottish clubs and associations around the world – St. Andrews, Caledonian, and Scottish Dance Clubs, Pipe Bands, etc. Also 20 of the major companies in Scotland are Japanese owned. The cultural links were exploited via a special mailing to all the individuals whose names and addresses could be found, the companies were contacted by a letter and a copy of the brochure (both translated into Japanese). The response from the first just covered its cost, the response from the second was zero. A great deal of work was put into researching EC funds but produced very little. A foundation was set up in America and received a few tens of thousands, although this might have improved if it had been pursued a little longer.

Comment

According to the Director, James Tysoe, *The insights and counsel given by Marion Allford enabled me to establish the parameters of a winning strategy for the Edinburgh Sick Kids Appeal by focusing only on those areas requiring the greatest time and effort. Whilst our campaign was essentially regional and had many special characteristics we owe a great debt to this. A well researched and professionally executed appeal can be successful – even in the midst of the worst recession in sixty years – if you take guidance from the principles outlined in this book. We've proved it!*

PLANNING FOR FUTURE INCOME

This book does not attempt to cover the principles of ongoing fund-raising. However, as the opportunities available to a charity's ongoing fund-raising are considerably enhanced by the increased donor base and heightened profile which an appeal generates, the two concepts must blend into one another. A smooth and carefully managed transition can make a tremendous difference to the charity's future.

All too often, there is little continuity after an appeal. The appeal staff go, and take many of their contacts with them. The remaining ongoing staff can become deflated and lack impetus. If the appeal's major donors then receive a cold letter addressed to 'Dear Friend', instead of the warm and lasting gratitude which is their due, the charity can cause serious offence. These are the people who will want to know not just that sufficient funds have been raised, but how the money is being spent at every stage. They should be invited back at regular intervals for such occasions as the laying of a foundation stone and, of course, the official opening if a building is being financed. There are parallel opportunities for other types of appeal, for the purchase of books or equipment or to expand an organization by taking on new or more highly qualified staff, for example. The important point is not to let the contact go stale; maintain interest by catering for it specifically. If there is no appropriate event to invite them to in one year, simply hold a social function for your valued supporters. They will appreciate the gesture and repay you several times over when next you have to call for funds. The most fundamental task to begin immediately after an appeal has finished – or even before it finishes, if you have time – is to draw up your plan for future fund-raising.

The main steps are:

- Research – profile supporters and identify the most successful fund-raising methods
- Make a new case for more fund-raising (if it is needed)
- Create a new business plan
- Create a new marketing and fund-raising strategy directed towards existing and potential donors
- Review your organizational structure and the roles of volunteers and staff
- Review fund-raising methods
- Produce a budget for income and expenditure
- Write a programme of activities
- Keep in touch as closely as possible with appeal donors, giving them special attention and trying to convert one-off supporters into ongoing contributors.

The consolidation of existing donors into future, regular donors is vital. The NSPCC started planning the consolidation phase halfway through its centenary year. They asked the important question 'How can we keep key supporters' and donors' involvement long-term?' Giles Pegram, Appeals Director, said, 'When our appeal target of £12 million was set, it seemed massive. Yet we always believed that, in the longer term, it would be the permanent effect of the centenary on our normal income that would be remembered. The centenary represented a turning point. By consolidating a relationship with donors and supporters effectively, we now raise £40 million a year.'

Research

There should be continuous research into the requirements of the beneficiaries of your charity and whether any other charities or agencies are generating similar provision. Market research should be commissioned at the end of your appeal to give a point of comparison with your findings at the start of the appeal. Has the public's perception of you changed? If so, how? There may be other specific questions, the answers to which may help the charity pinpoint its future direction.

It is essential to research your donor profile. You must understand who made major contributions to your appeal and why. What is the profile of public donors – age, sex, profession, geographical distribution, socio-economic ranking? This information will be extremely helpful in developing an ongoing direct-mail campaign. Your database must be brought up to date, ensuring that all donors are correctly logged and showing clearly which donors require special treatment. Those who have played a special part in the appeal should receive individual letters, personally signed.

Another important area for research is the type of fund-raising which worked best with your supporters. Maybe, like the Royal Marsden Appeal, special events proved to be the most popular way of supporting the Appeal. This information may affect your future fund-raising strategy so that you plan to have a range of regular high-profile events which become a fixture in your area's social calendar.

Make a new case for the need to raise funds

It is best if it is made clear during the appeal that you will continue to need funds after it has closed (if that, indeed, is so). The appeal meets a specific need; it is not the end of the story. Americans seem to be much better at this than the British, as they manage to create a reservoir of regular supporters who give set amounts each year. When an appeal is mounted, those supporters are asked to give extra in addition to their normal contributions. In Britain, many appeal supporters think that the particular charity has had its turn and now it is another appeal's turn. However, you can convert one-off donors into regulars if you have taken the time and trouble to educate them into that way of thinking.

Ideally, making the case should include the introduction of a partnership arrangement with a government department, showing that it is contributing. Such projects are always more popular with donors, who often feel that their gifts should generate government funds as a stamp of approval for the project. Never forget the appeal rule that donors respond more readily to a concrete shopping list of items to be funded – and possibly named – so produce an annual shopping list.

Create a new business plan

You should review the needs of the charity's beneficiaries, how much additional provision the charity intends to aim for, by what date. What will the cost be and how will the money be raised?

Having identified the outstanding need, like any other business, you must then work out how to generate the resources to meet that need. Apart from fund-raising, other business aspects should be reviewed, including your trading activities. Does the charity have a property portfolio? Is it being managed to the best advantage?

Having carried out a housekeeping review, you should, in effect, go back over the preparatory exercises undertaken before the one-off appeal. A fresh business plan will help you to focus on weaknesses and strengths.

Marketing and fund-raising strategy

It is often wise to have a slight publicity pause after an appeal. Let the high fund-raising profile created by your appeal subside a little. Make it clear that the appeal is over, the target has been met, the project has been financed and a line has been firmly drawn under it. During this period, concentrate publicity on the benefits produced by the charity or the development of the recently funded appeal project. Take time to develop a new case for fund-raising and to re-launch the need. You may do it through the media in a public manner, by communicating directly with known supporters or making fresh approaches to new potential donors.

How you communicate with supporters at this time is crucial. There is always a big dip in morale immediately after the euphoria of a successful appeal. It is essential to come up with new plans swiftly, so that your staff, volunteers and supporters know which way they are pointing. Make sure that they are brought into the thinking in preparation of the new plan. Following a short break after a successful conclusion to the appeal, you can afford to project a message which explains that the success of the appeal is not the end, but has led the charity to develop a new momentum which must be maintained if its gains are not to be dissipated. Close relationships will have to be maintained with the companies and their staff who have associated themselves with your cause and who may wish to continue their support. You should go to great lengths to understand why they had a positive experience and try to tailor future activities to a similar end. If a company has sponsored a major special event, you might try to turn it into an annual event with its sponsorship committed for, perhaps, three years or more. This becomes a positive relationship for both partners.

Another strategy is to find guardians or custodians of different parts of the charity's programme. This might be done to raise a regular amount, say, to fund a nurse at a hospice. This can have all sorts of benefits for both parties, as the nurse would have an incentive to keep in close touch with her sponsor, leading to such opportunities as articles in a sponsoring company's staff newspaper or personal appearances at the company's offices or factory.

Volunteers and staff structures

After an appeal, your staff numbers will almost certainly have to be reduced and the honorary panels revamped. Great care must be taken to handle departing staff fairly and thoughtfully. You should ensure that they have satisfactory warning that their employment with the appeal is coming to an end. Help them to find new appointments by networking with other charities and organizations in the voluntary sector. This was done to some effect after the Wishing Well Appeal.

I believe it is best to keep the chief executive who led the appeal while new plans are set in train. He is probably an entrepreneurial type who is happiest in a start-up situation. By staying on, he will have the opportunity to see that all the systems are running smoothly again after the hurly-burly of an appeal. After a year or so, he will probably feel the need for a new challenge. That is the time to recruit his replacement, who will have a new set of skills. In my view, the ongoing fund-raiser is a different type of professional manager, who will bring his own way of doing things and possibly add to the appeal team.

There then remains a considerable challenge to lift the morale of the remaining staff, who will naturally feel flat until they realize that a new and exciting pro-gramme is being planned for the charity's future. Take time to interview each of them, assess their roles and skills and find out how they see themselves devel-oping. Send them on training courses that will help them reach those goals.

Choosing fund-raising methods

It is always harder to raise money on a continual basis than it is with the momentum of an appeal to back you. It is not so easy to get gifts in kind. Companies give such gifts once, but rarely year after year. So this is the time to develop methods such as:

- Direct mail
- Trading – mail order, shops, character licensing, joint promotions
- Special events – turned into annual events with a new twist
- Legacy generation
- A regular appeal week, to focus effort through Local Groups via
  - lotteries
  - flag days
  - house-to-house collections
  - car boot sales

However, specific projects can still be put to major potential donors – especially wealthy individuals, trusts and companies.

Look ahead

You may say that it is wrong to try to hang on to people recruited purely on the basis of a one-off appeal. My view is 'nothing ventured, nothing gained'. At the outset, most people say that they can commit themselves only for the duration of the appeal, but are then reluctant to walk away after they have put so much of themselves into such an all-consuming endeavour. I always admired the National Society for the Prevention of Cruelty to Children, which evolved a Financial Development Board to keep close to some of their most influential supporters. I advised Great Ormond Street Hospital to do something similar.

You may really feel that you recruited a group to provide extra resources and that once that has been achieved, their job is over – but is it? Who is going to be managing those resources in the years ahead? Will they not need support, help and encouragement? Will donors not wish to take pleasure from the benefit which their contributions have given to the community? So, to my mind it never ends. An appeal's supporters are a wonderful source of energy and good will which should be nurtured for as long as possible for the benefit of your charity – and the com-munity as a whole.

EPILOGUE

This book is about how to run a one-off appeal. It presumes you want to do it to the best of your ability, learning from others so that you do not have to re-invent the wheel and aspiring to best professional standards. It assumes that you have already decided it is worth doing – an obvious but important assumption. I felt it would be fitting at the end of this book to remember that fund-raising is never an end in itself. However, as a fund-raiser, you are the enabler of a great endeavour. Without your determination and know-how, charity plans would remain unfulfilled dreams.

In the voluntary sector, talking about professionalism for its own sake is like comparing a mercenary with a member of Her Majesty's Forces. By campaigning for your cause as staff, volunteer or freelance fund-raiser, you have the chance to take positive action about something in which you believe. That is what drives us on – not the love of fund-raising for its own sake. So it seems incredible that there should be debate about whether professionalism is a good thing in the voluntary sector.

The aspect which seemed to interest journalists most about the Wishing Well Appeal was its businesslike approach. I did my best to point out that this was not new. It would be impossible for this country's top charities to raise hundreds of millions of pounds annually if they operated in any other way. Nevertheless, the press remained intrigued at the thought that fund-raisers could use market research, strategic planning and sophisticated marketing techniques. As for the public, the majority applauded what we were able to do. There were detractors, those that equated 'businesslike' with 'slick'. In 1992, the *Sunday Telegraph Magazine* published an article which stated: *The biggest* [charities] *are run with all the hard-nosed techniques of the most competitive free enterprise.* It went on to wonder whether this cut-throat efficiency alienated the very people who are most likely to give and asked: *Do we yearn for the homely image of the old-fashioned volunteer with the collecting box?*

The question was raised again by the Archbishop of Canterbury, Dr. George Carey, when he spoke to The Charity Directors' Network. This group had changed its name from The Moving Spirit, a change which Dr. Carey questioned. He wondered whether its members had come to believe that their original title was pretentious or embarrassingly spiritual in a secular world. To my mind The Moving Spirit is indeed a very special name, as it truly describes the impetus which leads those who are active in the voluntary sector – the spirit which has moved them to aspire to higher ideals, irrespective of religious beliefs. The Archbishop raised several questions; in particular he said:

> *I remember that William Waldegrave issued an apt warning as Health Minister to managers in the NHS. He told them in effect that the wholesale importation of language from the business world could give the public the impression that the distinctive caring ethos of the Health Service had been abandoned. As large charities draw – quite properly – on the skills and expertise of the business and government sectors, they may run similar risks. It is no doubt inevitable that in many larger charities the influence of paid staff is much greater in relation to volunteer management committees than it used to be. Of course, effective charities need to pursue value for money. They need to be efficient. They need to pursue their performance rigorously. They need some people who get their excitement from hitting membership and fund-raising targets. But how difficult it must be to ensure that the management and marketing techniques remain subordinate to the spirit of charity: the servants, not the masters! If a charity director is too eager to tell me about the size of the budget, the number of staff under management and the scale of the donor list, a warning light starts to flash in my mind!*

This seems to betray certain prejudices, reminiscent of the sort of attitude I encountered once when I interviewed a senior cleric to enlist his support for an appeal. I had gone to a meeting with one of our top supporters and was, I thought, well on my way to convincing him that he should help us. I had come from another meeting and had some professionally produced display panels about our appeal with me. So, to illustrate a point, I took them out of their folder and showed them to the small group. The cleric's face dropped immediately. *It all looks very professional*, he said. *Are you sure you really need our help?*

The lesson this taught me was that approaching potential supporters does not depend on being suave, hi-tech or polished. It requires the presentation of your case in the right way, to the right audience, at the right time. That is the truly professional approach. Nevertheless, it is worrying that the churchman responded in the way that he did. The display panels were not plush or expensive-looking. They were all about communication – a workmanlike approach intended to communicate a visual interpretation of a clear message.

Communications is where the revolution has taken place. In this century we have made enormous strides in mass communications. It has changed the world and people's concepts. It has also made many of us more compassionate because we have been brought face to face with misery on a horrifying scale. Modern communications methods are a vital, powerful and beneficial force to be used as a mouthpiece for a cause. To deploy the latest techniques is to be professional and doing the best for your cause.

Returning to the Archbishop's point, it should not be difficult to ensure that the management and marketing of a charity remain subordinate to its spirit. As I say in Chapter 10, keeping fund-raisers 'close to the rock face' is all-important.

Constantly reminding them why they do what they do – be it organizing a star-studded rock concert for their charity or the slog of researching company records ready for a private appeal. The belief in their cause is why most volunteers are involved. The same goes for staff members whose skills would, in most cases, earn them much more in the commercial world. To pursue a charitable objective, a higher ideal, is why most of them eschew a larger salary – an action some could not contemplate without the support and encouragement of their families. I say that in response to the implied criticism in the Archbishop's question – the necessary evil in this case being charity staff!

I am reminded of another story. A BBC Television reporter was interviewing workers on a building site. 'What is your role?', he asked a rather dishevelled individual standing nearby. 'Well, Guv,' the man replied, 'I have to move these bricks 'ere from this side of the site to the other.' Approaching another labourer with a cigarette lurking in the corner of his mouth, he asked the same question. 'Mine's a back-breaking job mate,' was the rejoinder. 'I got to hump them bricks into my hod and take 'em up to the first storey of the scaffolding.' On questioning the third man, our journalist received a more purposeful reply: 'I'm helping to build a cathedral.'

When the pros and cons of professionalism were debated at the 1992 Institute of Charity Fundraising Managers' Convention, Lord Judd acknowledged professionalism as a desired attribute but made a very strong plea for people to be led by the passion they feel for their cause. I could not agree more. It is very easy to tell if people have a true vocation – they infect their friends and contacts with the same zeal. William Waldegrave was right to wonder if this same drive could survive the implied passive state of being a 'service provider'.

I can honestly say that, with a cause like the Wishing Well Appeal, it was impossible to forget our mission. The children we met in hospital and the ethos of Great Ormond Street Hospital itself were constant reminders. We were just part of the long history of people who had gone before us, ensuring that sick children had the best care our society could provide.

Having shared with you the knowledge I have gained as a fund-raiser and particularly during the Wishing Well Appeal, I feel it is fitting to finish this Epilogue with some of the moving words spoken by Derek Bacon, Chaplain of Great Ormond Street Hospital. He preached a sermon at Guildford Cathedral immediately after the public phase of the Appeal. I share this excerpt with you because his words illustrate, so movingly, the spirit which inspired the vast army which was recruited to ensure such a special place has a future.

Tom was about five months old when he underwent surgery for a reconstruction of the skull. He lay, restless, between his parents, his mother leaning over occasionally to give him the breast. My part was to bring symbols of healing; oil, bread, wine. And in all the anxiety of those moments there was a sense of containment, of something only partly understood but bringing great peace.

It was at first anything but peaceful with Jane, a strident four-year-old leukaemic, who, in no uncertain terms, showed me the door of her cubicle.

It took a couple of days for me to regain my self-esteem; then when I risked going back I was received graciously and offered a fruit gum. It was in the week following as we shared a milkshake that I was invited to help her take her bath.

So it came to pass that with great dignity she allowed her dad and me to gently sponge her down, then, taking a towel, to caress her dry.

Some weeks later on a Sunday afternoon in the chapel with her beaming permission at every stage we said the prayers, poured the water, made the sign, lit the candle to acknowledge that in living or in dying this unforgettable child was Christ's and Christ was hers.

Unlike the daughter of Jairus Jane didn't make it. Tom didn't either. Nor do many, many others. And the immeasurable rending of hearts that fact represents is the aching, unfair reality beneath the familiar image of the institution within which I live and work. It is the shadow against which all the successes shine so brightly.

The sermon went on to talk of the young Doctor West, his concern at the lack of hospital care for children in London, his dream of a special hospital for them and the start of that dream, on St. Valentine's Day in 1852, when a house in Great Ormond Street with 10 beds was opened for the purpose.

He could not have imagined how his vision would fuse with that of figures like Dickens and Shaftesbury, would catch royal interest and concern, would touch the hearts of many who proved ready to raise further finance in 1858 and '65 to provide for necessary expansion. Nor could he have foreseen the scale of the enterprise now afoot, the range of the need and the strength of the response to today's Wishing Well Appeal to renew and rebuild for tomorrow.

From the ends of this country, from within and beyond these islands, people who know it by experience or by repute, patients and staff past and present, family circles and networks of friends, many and varied groupings have been bound together in concerned action for the plight of the hospital and for the children who now depend upon it and who will depend upon it.

Widow's mite, crumbs from rich tables, energy and imagination, all have come together in an undertaking which has had about it at times such a splendid and singular madness that, even for those who conceived and planned the appeal, the response has seemed nothing less than awesome. And it will continue to evoke, I am sure, the profoundest satisfaction and gratitude.

What might have been seen simply as a successful marketing operation has touched an altogether deeper vein. That spending of the self for others is, I believe, the spiritual centre of life. It is what the medicine of the gospel is about. It is close to what Christians call God. It is the pattern of Jesus. It is what I see ordinary men and women offer day in, day out in my work setting, as the best of them pursue a tradition of loving care.

So let's give glad thanks for all who walk the corridors of Great Ormond Street today, and those who make it what it is for so many; thanks too for our welcome to this cathedral, for the gifts, skills and value of each person here, reflecting the rich potential of a gathering like this to change the world for the good; for our share in the work of healing; our store of memories past telling of suffering, courage and inspiration; and our place, yours and mine, in the unfolding mystery of love.

Part VII

APPENDICES

Appendix 1

THE WISHING WELL APPEAL ORGANIZATION

Panel Structure

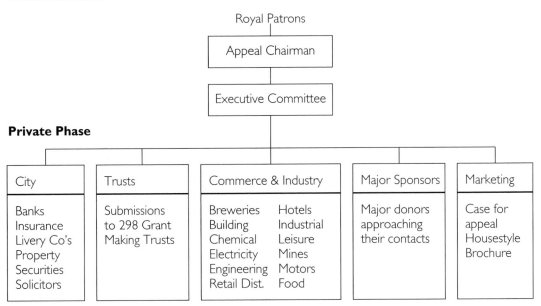

Royal Patrons

Appeal Chairman

Executive Committee

Private Phase

City	Trusts	Commerce & Industry		Major Sponsors	Marketing
Banks	Submissions	Breweries	Hotels	Major donors	Case for
Insurance	to 298 Grant	Building	Industrial	approaching	appeal
Livery Co's	Making Trusts	Chemical	Leisure	their contacts	Housestyle
Property		Electricity	Mines		Brochure
Securities		Engineering	Motors		
Solicitors		Retail Dist.	Food		

Public Phase (from end October 1987 until end 1989)

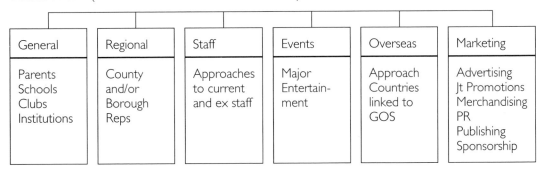

General	Regional	Staff	Events	Overseas	Marketing
Parents	County	Approaches	Major	Approach	Advertising
Schools	and/or	to current	Entertain-	Countries	Jt Promotions
Clubs	Borough	and ex staff	ment	linked to	Merchandising
Institutions	Reps			GOS	PR
					Publishing
					Sponsorship

USUAL METHODS OF GIVING

PRIVATE APPEAL

SOURCE	METHOD
Wealthy Individuals	Donations
	Covenants
	Gift Aid
	Loans
	Gifts in Kind
	Legacies
Companies	As above (excluding legacies)
	Secondees
Grant-making Trusts	Grants
Statutory Bodies	Grants
	Contractual Funding

PUBLIC APPEAL

SOURCE	METHOD
Individuals	Donations
	Covenants
	Gift Aid
	Loans
	Gifts in Kind
	Give As You Earn
	Fund-raising
	Legacies
Companies	As above (excluding legacies)
	Employee Fund-raising
	Secondees
	Commercial Partnerships
	Sponsorship
Smaller Grant-making Trusts	Grants

Note: The Index lists where most of the above are explained in the text.

TAX-EFFICIENT GIVING EXAMPLES

This clear example of tax-efficient methods of giving, produced for the Centenary Scholarship Appeal of The City of London School for Girls, is included with the kind permission of the Headmistress.

****

If donors take advantage of the various tax concessions available to them, then the government will add a least a third to their gifts, substantially increasing their value to us.

DEEDS OF COVENANT

As a taxpayer you can make covenanted payments to the City of London School for Girls out of your taxed income - monthly, quarterly or annually for a minimum of four years. The Deed of Covenant allows us to reclaim income tax at the basic rate (currently 25 per cent). Thus, for example, a gift of £1,500 net per annum over four years is worth £2,000 per annum to us, and a total of £8,000 over four years. Some examples:

Net Annual Gift to be Covenanted	Will Cost A basic rate Taxpayer	A 40% Taxpayer†	Gross Annual Value to the Appeal	Gross Total Value over 4 years
£10,000*	£10,000	£8,000	£13,333	£53,332
£ 7,500*	£ 7,500	£6,000	£10,000	£40,000
£ 5,000*	£ 5,000	£4,000	£ 6,667	£26,668
£ 2,500*	£ 2,500	£2,000	£ 3,334	£13,336
£ 1,000*	£ 1,000	£ 800	£ 1,333	£ 5,332

* The amount on the Covenant form
† A higher-rate taxpayer can claim back for himself the difference between base rate and higher rate tax on the gross value of his Covenant.

COMPANY GIFTS

Under a Deed of Covenant for four or more years, a limited company can deduct the gross amount of its annual covenanted gift from its profits before corporation tax is assessed. Some examples:

Annual Payment by Deed of Covenant over 4 years	Actual Annual Cost to a Company paying 33% corporation tax	Total Gross Value over 4 years
£11,250	£10,050	£60,000
£ 7,500	£ 6,700	£40,000
£ 5,625	£ 5,025	£30,000
£ 3,750	£ 1,675	£10,000
£ 938	£ 838	£ 5,000

Note: Close companies should consult their advisers before undertaking a Covenant or a payment under the Gift Aid scheme.

GIFT AID SCHEME

This enables the City of London School for Girls to recover basic rate tax on one-off donations of £250 or more. As with Covenants, the donor will get any higher-rate tax relief which is due direct from the Inland Revenue. This new scheme applies to gifts of £250 or more from both individuals and close companies. (There is no minimum figure for other companies.) Under it, people or companies wishing to make a substantial gift to charity in say, a successful year, can give a lump sum with the benefit of tax relief. The advantage to the charity is that the tax refund is made immediately. Some examples:

Gift Aid for (net)	Will give us (gross)	And cost a	
		40% taxpayer	Company paying 33% corporation tax
£6,000	£8,000	£4,800	£5,360
£4,500	£6,000	£3,600	£4,020
£1,500	£2,000	£1,200	£1,340
£1,400	£ 533	£ 320	£ 357

Note: As tax rates etc. change periodically, the latest position should be checked with the *Tax Pack for Charities* (from the Inland Revenue) or *The Guide to Charitable Giving and Taxation* (published by Craigmyle & Co.).

Appendix 3

GIFT GUIDE & GIFT OPPORTUNITIES

This is a useful example which shows how the Gift Guide for donors links in with gift opportunities. It is included with the kind permission of the National Autistic Care and Training Appeal.

****

The following Gift Guide shows how a £3 million target can be reached. The National ACT Appeal Committee invites you to study it carefully to help you to decide on the level at which you can best make a contribution. Please remember that every donation, be it large or small, takes us a step nearer to reaching our goal.

Gift guide for donors

SINGLE DONATIONS

Number of gifts	Value £	Total £
2 x	100,000	200,000
8 x	50,000	400,000
16 x	25,000	400,000
20 x	10,000	200,000
60 x	5,000	300,000
100 x	2,000	200,000

COVENANTED DONATIONS

Number of gifts	Annual payment £	Gross value £	Total value £
40 x	1,000	5,333	214,000
20 x	750	4,000	80,000
80 x	500	2,667	213,200
50 x	250	1,333	66,600
200 x	100	533	106,600
100 x	75	400	40,000
100 x	50	266	26,600

SPECIAL EVENTS AND OTHER GIFTS	553,000
Total	3,000,000

Note: Figures to the nearest £100
Covenants have been calculated on the basis of a 4-year deed @ 25% tax.

Gift opportunities

A gift of £100,000 would entitle you to associate your name closely with one of the Appeal projects. Detailed below are some of the specific needs within the various projects described in the Appeal brochure. We are also seeking sponsorship of salary and salary-related costs for posts within the Diagnostic and Assessment Centre and the Regional Service Development. If you would like further information, or are interested in making a gift in kind, the National ACT Appeal office would be happy to discuss this with you.

PROJECT SPONSORSHIP	£
Entrance Hall, Landing and Staircase	50,000
Bedroom	15,000
Bathroom	5,000
Sitting Room	10,000
Dining Room	8,000
Kitchen	10,000
Class Room	6,000
Crafts Room	7,000
Market Garden	35,000
Patio Recreation Area	20,000
Playground Safety Equipment	10,000
Computer for Diagnostic Information	8,000
Video and Sound Equipment	8,000
Two-Way Observation Mirror	2,000

POST SPONSORSHIP (Annual)	
Director of Diagnostic and Assessment Centre	25,000
Consultant Psychiatrist (Part-Time)	15,000
Speech Therapist	15,000
Social Worker	16,000
Regional Development Officer (x3)	20,000
Family Services Worker (x3)	15,000

The Trustees of ACT will be delighted to name any aspect of the Appeal projects as a sponsored or commemorative gift.

BASIC FUND-RAISING TECHNIQUES

THE PRIVATE APPEAL

SECTOR TO APPROACH	STRUCTURE	FUND-RAISING TECHNIQUES
Major donors generally	Marketing Panel	Helps to make the case for an appeal and to produce appeal brochure.
Companies	Business Panel(s)	Produce Gifts Guide to Donors of leading gifts required. Give targets to each panel and approach. Use peer-group fund-raising (personal approaches).
Wealthy individuals	Nil	Use personal contacts where possible. Ideally, major donor approaches major donor.
Grant-making trusts	Nil	Officer to officer approach. Lobby trustees where appropriate.
Statutory bodies	Nil	Charity approaches body, lobbied by influential supporters.

BASIC FUND-RAISING TECHNIQUES

THE PUBLIC APPEAL

SECTOR TO APPROACH	STRUCTURE	FUND-RAISING TECHNIQUES
General public	Marketing Panel	Decides the messages to project and methods of communication. Produces publicity campaign and promotional material. Direct Mail.
Companies	Business Panel(s)	Employee Fund-raising. Company matching employee fund-raising. Secondees. Gifts in Kind. Give as You Earn Joint Promotions with charity. Sponsorship.
National organizations, societies and clubs	Nil	Contact at national level initially.
'Society' circles, sports, arts, etc.	Special Events Panel	Develops 3/4 major events a year (smaller events handled by local groups).
Existing supporters, fund-raisers,	Local Groups	Guidance notes from Appeal office.
Traders, schools		Schools education pack and fund-raising ideas.
Churches, Clubs and Associations		Special Appeals week. Public collections. Events etc.
Purchasers of goods	Trading Company	Shops. Mail Order Catalogue. Logo/character licensing.

A Sample Calendar for a £10m Target

This type of programme sets target dates which usually change, to some extent, as the appeal plans progress.

YEARS:	1				2				3				4				5				*Targets
QUARTERS:	1	2	3	4	1	2	3	4	1	2	3	4	1	2	3	4	1	2	3	4	
1 *Project Development* — Selecting and costing the shopping list. Producing case statement. Moving on to defining a policy for the order in which funds raised are spent.		→																			
2 *Appeal Preparatory Phase* — Researching, reviewing feasibility, planning, budgeting, recruiting, producing house style, literature, forming panels for private phase and allocating approaches.	←			→																	
3 *Private Appeal Phase* — Pre-launch campaign aimed at large potential donors – wealthy people, companies, statutory bodies, trusts and foundations. Plan public appeal.					←		→														£6m
4 *Public Launch* — High-profile event to launch public appeal.					NO APPEAL PUBLICITY UNTIL THIS POINT					X											
5 *Public Appeal – Intensive Phase* — Advertising and PR campaign to support media and special events, local events, trading activities, joint promotions with companies, direct mail, Give As You Earn, legacy promotion, etc.										←		→									£3m
6 *'Topping-up' Phase*															◆						£1m
7 *Appeal Completion*																		X			£10m
8 *Enhance or Establish Ongoing Fund-raising* — New Business Plan developed for after the appeal, and new fund-raising strategy produced. Marketing strategy to follow.																		←			

* NOTE: The proportion raised before the public phase will vary according to the type of cause.

Appendix 6

SPECIAL EVENTS BUDGET SHEET

1 Brief Description of Event:
  - date
  - name of region (where applicable)
  - venue
  - event
  - closed audience
    or general public (please specify)
  - anticipated attendance
  - insurance arrangements

2 Event Organizer:
  - name
  - address
  - daytime tel. no
  - evening tel. no
  Co-organizer:
  - address
  - daytime tel. no
  - evening tel. no

3 Projected Income:	**£**	**£**
• ticket sales (number and price)	....	
• brochure sales	....	
• advertising revenue	....	
• sponsorship	....	
• donations	....	
• raffles	....	
• collecting tins	....	
• other (please specify)	....	
	_____	_____
TOTAL	_____	_____

4 Expected Expenditure:
- hire of venue ....
- catering ....
- decoration ....
- printing ....
- publicity/advertising ....
- postage ....
- telephone ....
- administration/staff ....
- insurance ....
- contingency ....
- other (please specify) ....

TOTAL _____ (_____)

5 Anticipated Net Income: _____

6 To Be Collected By (date):

7 Name of Bankers (if appropriate)

Signed .... (Event Organizer)

Date ....

Approved .... (Charity Representative's signature and title)

Date ....

Appendix 7

TAX IMPLICATIONS OF SPECIAL EVENTS

by Pesh Framjee

When organizing and running special events, it is important to comply with charity law and the regulations of the Inland Revenue and the Customs and Excise. A mass of legal requirements exists to ensure that charities do not obtain any advantage over commercial, 'for-profit' organizations which are running similar operations.

The need for care increases as charities extend their activities more and more into the marketing budgets of corporate donors, who are motivated partly by altruism and partly by enlightened self-interest. This has resulted in tit-for-tat operations where the charities receive money and the donor benefits in some less tangible way. Typical of this sort of fund-raising are commercial sponsorships and affinity card schemes which offer the commercial partner advertising and publicity. These activities are scrutinized closely by the authorities, alert to the implications for direct (income/corporation) and indirect (VAT) tax.

CORPORATION TAX

We have already seen that trading is allowed under both charity and tax law when it is carried out as part of the primary purpose of a charity or the work in connection with the trade is mainly carried out by the beneficiaries of the charity (see Chapter 23). The problem of what exactly is trading often arises. Our everyday understanding of the word 'trading' is considerably widened by section 832 of the Income and Corporation Taxes Act 1988 (ICTA 1988), which states that a trade includes 'every trade, manufacture, adventure, or concern in the nature of trade'. This definition is not particularly helpful and appears to be all encompassing. Consequently, on several occasions, the Courts have had to scrutinize activities to decide whether they fall within the definition of trade. As a result, more and more charities are being enmeshed in the trading net for activities that they thought were part of their normal fund-raising effort.

In addition to the statutory exemption for primary purpose trading, mentioned above, there is an important extra statutory concession. This is most likely to be used by fund-raisers when organizing events.

Extra statutory concession

In recognition of the fact that Section 832's unsatisfactory definition of trading would catch a number of activities which have traditionally been associated with charity fund-raising, the Inland Revenue published an Extra Statutory Concession, C4, which states:

> *Bazaars, jumble sales, gymkhanas, carnivals, fireworks displays and similar activities arranged by voluntary organizations or charities for the purpose of raising funds for charity may fall within the definition of 'trade' in ICTA 1988 Section 832, with the result that any profits would be liable to corporation tax. Tax is not, however, charged on such profits provided the following conditions are satisfied:*
> - *the organization or charity is not regularly carrying out these trading activities;*
> - *the trading is not in competition with other traders;*
> - *the activities are supported substantially because the public are aware that any profits will be devoted to charity; and*
> - *the profits are transferred to charities or otherwise applied for charitable purposes.*

If they are to qualify for the direct tax concessions, most fund-raising events will have to fall within that described above, but there are certain caveats. All the conditions of the concession must be met and there is no right of appeal if the Revenue refuses to grant the benefit of the concession. Doubt can be created by certain phrases in the concession and it is worth considering some of the contentious areas.

Similar activities

These can often be stumbling blocks. In particular, many charities hold large-scale fund-raising events and the Revenue's view is that these are not 'similar' to bazaars, jumble sales, gymkhanas, etc., which have a 'small beer' feel to them.

This issue is debatable and what may be a major event to one charity may be regarded as 'small beer' by another. However, it seems that the Revenue is increasingly taking the view that large events will usually fall outside the concession.

Regularly carrying out

The word 'regularly' is, perhaps, misleading. For example, once a year is regular but would usually be acceptable. The Revenue more often applies a frequency test. It may be the case that a charity carries out events both regularly and frequently when operating through fund-raising branches. For example, a charity with 400 local branches may hold one or more coffee mornings each weekend. However, the Revenue does not usually target small-scale events carried out by different branches.

Trade not in competition

This is a very important criterion and is increasingly under the spotlight. Many 'for profit' traders running jumble sales, car boot sales and so on believe that it is unfair that charities do not pay tax on trading profits. This is viewed with even greater concern as a result of the EC position on 'unfair competition'.

Reason for support

This is another grey area and difficult to establish. For example, a concert in aid of charity may be supported by some because they are sympathetic to the cause, while others may attend purely to hear the music. Most charities do not consider this to be trading, but the Revenue clearly does. If there are high-profile celebrities involved, the Revenue may question whether the event meets the criterion.

Ancillary income

Another area of confusion is whether other income, such as advertising income, is acceptable. In practice, the Revenue will accept this income as being part of the event if it is ancillary and incidental to the event. For example, income raised from advertising billboards at a gymkhana seems to be acceptable.

VAT AND 'ONE-OFF' FUND-RAISING EVENTS

The corporation tax concessions are similar but not identical to the VAT exemption. The VAT exemption, in fact deals with the matter of one-off fund-raising events. It is important to understand fully what constitutes a one-off fund-raising event and how it works.

From 1 April 1989 a new VAT exemption was introduced for charities. The exemption, which was included in the new group 12 to schedule 6 of the VAT Act 1983, makes it necessary to treat as an exempt activity the following:

1. The supply of goods and services by a charity in connection with a fund-raising event organized for charitable purposes by a charity or jointly by more than one charity.
2. The supply of goods and services by a qualifying body in connection with the fund-raising event organized exclusively for its own benefit. (All charities and most non-profit organizations are qualifying bodies.)

For the purpose of items 1 and 2, 'fund-raising event' means fête, ball, bazaar, gala show, performance or similar event, which is separate from and not forming any part of a series or regular run of like or similar events. For the purpose of item 1, 'charity' includes a body corporate which is wholly owned by a charity and whose profits (from whatever source) are payable to a charity by virtue of deed of covenant or trust or otherwise.

This exemption applies to all admission charges, the sale of commemorative brochures, the sale of advertising space in these brochures and sponsorship in connection with fund-raising events which are separate from and not forming any part of a series or regular run of like or similar events. This means that the charity does not have to charge VAT on its outputs (income) but cannot recover VAT on its inputs (costs).

This exemption is often called the 'one-off' fund-raising events exemption; to a certain extent this may be a misnomer. The 'one-off' criterion is designed to prevent fund-raising events by charities and other qualifying bodies having an unfair tax advantage over the activities of commercial organizations which are liable to VAT.

In respect of publicity material encompassing a number of events, it was thought that charities could not include various events on the same publicity material. This is, in fact, incorrect and such inclusion will not put them outside the terms of the exemption. Similarly, even if the event is regular, such as an annual carol concert, it would still qualify for the exemption as 'one-off' is not synonymous with 'once and for all'.

The basic rules

Much of the doubt is caused by certain terms in the legislation quoted above – 'similar event' and 'part of a series or regular run of like and similar events'. This is a grey area and the definition of a 'similar event' or a 'series' seems constantly to be changing. Nevertheless, the guidance and interpretations below are indications of the criteria that Customs may use.

Customs have intimated that if these events also involve the sale of trading goods, such as greeting cards and handicrafts, there may be a problem. The event should be able to stand alone if it is to qualify for the exemption. Events which require a season ticket or where a payment allows reduced admission to subsequent events will not qualify. There also appears to be a sort of size criterion, which, perhaps, is a reflection of the desire to prevent excessive distortion of competition. Thus, larger events held at the same venue as frequently as once a month will have to be excluded from the exemption but activities such as coffee mornings, jumble sales and other low-key occasions, can be held on the same premises at any level of frequency and still come within the exemption.

This is similar to and yet different from the Inland Revenue extra statutory concession (C4), since it appears to allow any level of frequency. A fête or disco held twice in the same month would qualify for the exemption if the venues were some distance apart. For this sort of local fund-raising event, some duplication, even within a five-mile radius, is considered tolerable. On the other hand, Customs believe that a play, concert or gala performance held twice in the same month in the same provincial city or the same part of London could give an unfair advantage to a charity over a commercial organization and, therefore, cannot be exempt from VAT.

Apart from the very low-key events referred to above, identical events held at the same venue on consecutive days or even several times in the same week will not qualify. However, this is not as restrictive as it seems since a gala ball is accepted as different from a dinner dance, and an opera performance is different from a concert and each of them qualifies if it is distinct from the others. So it is important to define the event appropriately!

Events extending over several dates

It was previously thought that an event that continued over several days could not be one-off. Customs has been generous and has indicated that a two- or three-day event for which there is a single admission charge comes within the terms of the exemption. However, if there is a separate admission charge for each day, the exemption will not be available.

Fund-raising committees

National campaigns carried out through the country will qualify so long as other criteria are met. For example, events carried out by fund-raising committees will qualify as long as the restrictions on locations are met. It is important that regional fund-raisers liaise with head office so that a regional event does not jeopardize a national event if it is seen to be held in the same geographic area and, therefore, threatens the one-off status of another event.

One-off fund-raising events held jointly by charities

The wording of the legislation is precise; the goods and services must be supplied by a charity (or its wholly-owned trading subsidiary if it transfers all its profits to the charity). Furthermore, item 2 states that the event must be organized exclusively for the benefit of the charity.

Charities may enter into joint ventures with other charities to run a fund-raising event. If such an agreement leads to the constitution of a separate legal entity, it will be unable to use the exemption unless it is a charity. However, if the agreement falls short of a formal partnership, each of the charities should qualify in its own right for the exemption.

Fund-raising events organized on behalf of charities

If another organization runs a one-off fund-raising event as agent for a charity, the income passed to the charity is covered by the exemption. In some cases, professional fund-raisers or the event's organizers may deduct an element of the gross receipts to cover their own expenses. If so, this cost will be treated as the consideration for agency services and would be subject to VAT. Consequently, the charity will have to bear this VAT as irrecoverable VAT just as it would have if it had made all the arrangements for the event itself.

Using a trading subsidiary

Many charities have found that where commercial sponsorship with an element of advertising was involved, the Inland Revenue often treated the activity as taxable unless it came within the extra statutory exemption (C4). Consequently, these events were run through the trading subsidiary.

Before 1 April 1991 such an event was not entitled to the VAT exemption. At that date legislation was amended to allow exemption from VAT for one-off fund-raising events organized by wholly owned charity subsidiaries whose profits from whatever source are payable to a charity. It should be noted, however, that the extension of the exemption is a double-edged sword, as it could result in a trading subsidiary, which was previously able to make a full recovery of input tax, becoming partly exempt for VAT purposes and, therefore, not entitled to recovery of all its input tax. In any case, any input tax incurred by the subsidiary on expenditure referable to the exempt fund-raising event would be irrecoverable exempt input tax.

Looking beyond the obvious

For the reasons mentioned above, many charities find that the exemption may be a poisoned chalice. The costs of not being able to recover input VAT can often exceed the benefit of not having to charge it. This is especially so when the 'person' being charged is able to recover the VAT – a corporate sponsor, for example.

Previously, a charity could almost choose whether it wanted to treat the event as standard rated by channelling it through a trading subsidiary. Now, it has no option and if the event is a qualifying event, it has to be treated as exempt if it meets the requirements.

This also means that, in principle, there is no entitlement to recover input VAT on standard-rated expenditure associated with the event. In certain circumstances – in particular, where the charity's customers are businesses which are able to recover the VAT that is charged to them – it would be advantageous for the event to fail to qualify for the exemption. This would allow the charity or its subsidiary company to recover the VAT on related costs and to add output VAT to the income payable by its customers.

The sale of donated goods is zero-rated for VAT and very often donated goods are auctioned or sold at fund-raising events. If the goods to be sold have been donated, the event could be treated either as exempt or zero-rated. In these circumstances, the law provides that zero rating takes precedence. Thus, by not treating the event as exempt, all input VAT could be recovered.

As a result, where previously charities looked for ways of qualifying for the exemption, they may now have to consider ways of falling outside it! Generally, a little planning will allow a charity to arrange the structure so that an event can qualify or fall outside the exemption according to which is more favourable.

Events which do not qualify for exemption

Where the event does not qualify for the exemption, a little planning can help. It is still possible for the charity to set a basic minimum charge, as a ticket price, for example, which will be standard-rated for VAT, and to invite those attending the event to make a voluntary donation. This voluntary donation will be outside the scope of VAT if all the following conditions are met:

- All publicity material, such as leaflets, tickets, etc., should state clearly that anyone paying only the minimum charge will be admitted without further payment.
- The additional voluntary donation should not secure any benefit. For example, there should be no special seats reserved for those making donations.
- While the charity can indicate a desired level of donation, the size of this donation should be left to the ticket purchaser.
- In the case of film, theatre performances, concerts, sporting fixtures, etc., the minimum ticket price should not be less than the usual price charged commercially for the same sort of event.

- In the case of dances, dinners and similar functions, the minimum total sum on which the charity has to account for VAT should not be less than the total costs incurred in arranging the event. That is, the basic ticket price should be such that the event is expected to break even.

CONCLUSION

I know of instances where Customs and the Inland Revenue have asked to see documentation, such as tickets, advertising and contracts, several years after the event. Therefore, it is a useful discipline to retain these. Attention must also be given to wording and descriptions in newsletters.

Finally, remember that although an event may be exempt from VAT, there may be other tax implications where sponsorship is involved. If your charity appears to be supplying something in exchange for the 'donation', beware. This is a complex area and, where possible, try to obtain clearance from the Inland Revenue and Customs and Excise.

Appendix 8

THE CHARITIES ACT 1992

This appendix concentrates on the sections of the Charities Act 1992 which will most affect appeal organizers and has been compiled mainly by three professionals in this field: Jonathan Burchfield who is Head of the Charity Group at solicitors Turner Kenneth Brown, Pesh Framjee who is the Partner in charge of the Charity Unit at BDO Binder Hamlyn, chartered accountants, and Stephen Lee, Director of the Institute of Charity Fundraising Managers (ICFM). Stephen played a major part in assisting the Home Office in the drafting of the fund-raising provisions of the Act as it progressed through Parliament and is, therefore, uniquely qualified to comment in this connection.

The first Part of this new Act is being consolidated with the 1960 Act and the Charitable Trustees Incorporation Act 1872 into one Act to be called the 'Consolidated Charities Act 1993'. However, all references in this Appendix are to the individual Acts, as these will be more familiar to readers. References in paragraph headings relate only to Sections of the 1992 Act. It is hoped this will be a convenience to readers.

The Charities Act received Royal Assent on 16 March 1992. It was touch and go for the first major piece of charity legislation in 30 years and there were fears that in the scramble on the last day of Parliament, it would somehow fail to reach the statute book. This would have been a great loss to the charitable sector, since the underlying purpose of the Act is to enhance public confidence in the charitable sector by ensuring that charities are seen to be suitably managed and properly regulated.

Part I of the Act seeks principally to enhance the existing powers of the Charity Commissioners to identify, investigate and remedy abuse, while Part II deals with fund-raising on behalf of charities and charitable institutions. Part III makes fresh provisions for the control of charitable collections. In particular, the Act focuses attention on controlling excessive sums which may be retained by professional fund-raisers and also the inability of charities in many cases to stop unauthorized fund-raisers using their names.

The Act (and regulations issued pursuant to it) is a complex piece of legislation, reflecting the fact that the world has changed enormously since the Charities Act 1960 and the charity world has been far from immune to those changes.

LEGAL STATUS AND CHARITY NAMES

(Sections 2-5)

From 1 January 1993, every registered charity (see Chapter 9, for when a charity has to register) with a gross income exceeding £5,000 in its last financial year has had to state the fact that it is a registered charity on all:

- notices, advertisements and other documents issued by or on behalf of the charity and soliciting money or other property for the benefit of the charity;
- bills of exchange, promissory notes, endorsements, cheques and orders for money or goods purporting to be signed on behalf of the charity; and
- bills rendered by the charity and invoices, receipts and letters of credit.

This is, therefore, a very wide provision; indeed, the inclusion of the words 'or on behalf of' in the first section above makes it even wider than it appears at first sight. It could be stretched to include letters issued by charities' trading subsidiaries and work undertaken on behalf of charities by outside agencies. At the time of writing, ICFM advice is to include the required statement on all published documents (including letterhead paper) of the charity and to use a suitable, general statement when raising funds through trading subsidiaries.

The contravention of this section is a criminal offence and is an offence of strict liability, that is, there can be no defence. The offence is committed, in the case of documents, by anyone actually issuing or authorizing the issue of the document; in the case of cheques and similar items, whoever signs them is liable.

If in doubt, therefore, display your registered status. This is most easily done by using such wording as 'charity registered no. 123456'. In the case of trading companies and any other items that could be regarded as being issued on behalf of a charity, the wording suggested by ICFM is 'XYZ Trading Limited raises funds on behalf of XYZ Charity, charity registration no. 123456. Profits from the trading company are passed by covenant [or Gift Aid] directly to the charity'.

As from 1 September 1992, the Charity Commissioners have, for the first time, been given the power to require that a charity's name be changed where it is the same or too like that of another charity, or where it is misleading or offensive. Obviously, a charity's name needs to be chosen with great care (the name of the Wishing Well Appeal was a very important factor in its success). All possible searches should be made at Companies House and the Charity Commission to ensure that the name you choose is available.

DISQUALIFICATION FROM BEING A CHARITY TRUSTEE

(Sections 45 and 46)

As mentioned in Chapter 9, remember the wide definition of the expression 'charity trustee'. The Act provides that anyone coming within the following categories shall automatically be disqualified from being a charity trustee or holding assets on behalf of a charity.

1. Anyone convicted of an offence at any time involving dishonesty or deception (unless the conviction is 'spent' under the Rehabilitation of Offenders Act 1974).
2. Anyone who has been made at any time either bankrupt or the subject of a sequestration order, without in either case having been discharged.
3. Anyone who has made at any time a composition or arrangement with creditors and has not been discharged.
4. Anyone who has been at any time removed by the Commissioners under their powers to act for a charity's protection or by the High Court on grounds of misconduct or mismanagement in the administration of a charity for which he or she was responsible (directly or indirectly) or whose conduct contributed to or facilitated the default.
5. Anyone who has been at any time removed under corresponding provisions of Scottish law relating to the management of charities.
6. Anyone who has been at any time subject to a disqualification under the Company Directors Disqualification Act 1986 or the Insolvency Act 1986.

The Commissioners have power to waive these grounds for disqualification, on application, for any individual either generally or in relation to a particular charity or class of charities. However, they cannot do so if the charity concerned is a company and the person in question is prohibited from acting as a director and leave has not been granted under the Company Directors Disqualification Act for the director to be a director of any other company.

If any person acts as a charity trustee or holds assets on behalf of a charity while disqualified, he is guilty of a criminal offence unless the charity concerned is a company and the person has been disqualified only on grounds of bankruptcy or under the Company Directors Disqualification Act. To prevent the impossible problems that would otherwise arise, it is made clear that any acts performed as a charity trustee or holding trustee for a charity by a person while disqualified will not be invalidated. However, the individuals concerned are given no protection – indeed, any sums received from the charity by way of remuneration or expenses may be ordered to be repaid to the charity.

Charities need, therefore, to ensure that none of their present charity trustees could be liable to disqualification. This potentially embarrassing, but necessary enquiry could be included in standard questionnaires supplied to prospective charity trustees before they are appointed and could be repeated at regular intervals.

ACCOUNTS

(Sections 19-27)

This part of the appendix concentrates on the new accounting, auditing and reporting regime. It is important to recognize that the detailed requirements are still to come in the form of regulations expected in late 1993. However, the accounting regulations in the main endorse the revised Statement of Recommended Practice on Accounting by Charities (SORP 2). It is important also to note that Sections 19-23 do not apply to:

• charities with income under £1,000 per annum

- exempt charities
- charitable companies – at present, but this may well change.

Accounting Requirements
(Section 19)

Section 19 deals with the duty to keep accounting records and extends the present requirements of Section 32 of the Charities Act 1960. The responsibility is squarely laid on the charity trustees to ensure that accounting records are kept which explain all the charity's transactions. This would, of course, encompass any special appeals run by the charity and also the individual constituent parts of the appeal – special events, for example. In particular, the results of fund-raising branches which raise funds in the name of the parent charity will usually have to be incorporated within the parent charity's accounts.

There was some concern that the requirements that accounting records should 'be able to disclose at any time with reasonable accuracy, the financial position of the charity at that time' would make difficult demands on very small charities. There were representations at the debate stage of the Bill which showed that some were reading the words 'disclose at any time', along with the requirement that 'the accounting records shall in particular contain entries showing from day to day all sums of money received and expended by the charity', to mean that charities would have to write up their books on a daily basis. In fact, this wording mirrors the requirements of Section 221 of the Companies Act 1985. It merely means that the records should be such that accounts could be drawn up to any day, even if this was done retrospectively. The accounts have to be kept for six years and if a charity ceases to exist, then the last trustees are responsible for continuing to preserve accounts for six years unless they obtain the Charity Commissioner's consent not to do so.

Much of the detail on the financial sections will be prescribed in the regulations to be made by the Secretary of State. Therefore, charities should continue to follow SORP 2 where applicable. SORP 2 has been revised and updated and it is expected that the regulations will, in the main, endorse the requirements of the revised SORP 2. The Act does state that the regulations may make provision regarding the methods and principles to be used when preparing accounts and may also specify any information to be provided by way of notes to the accounts. The regulations may also make provision for determining the financial year of a charity.

The Income Threshold
(Section 20)

The accounting requirements will be split according to the income of the charity. Originally, the Bill stated that charities with a gross income in any financial year of under £10,000 might elect to prepare a receipts and payments account and a statement of assets and liabilities, instead of a full statement of accounts.

There were numerous representations that this limit was too low, with the range of recommendations varying between £25,000 and £100,000 for a suitable income threshold. The government stated that statistics showed that most charities were, in fact, below the £10,000 threshold. They also made comments that a charity may have very large assets even though it may receive low income and that full accounts would be appropriate. It was explained that there was no real cause for concern as the minimum requirements for a statement of assets and liabilities would ensure that such charities would still be disclosing the assets they held. The Home Office was accommodating and the gross income limit has now been increased to £25,000.

Exempt charities and charitable companies are exempt from the requirements of Section 20. The former will, as a minimum, have to comply with the requirements of Section 32 of the Charities Act 1960 and, in practice, many exempt charities will have to comply with requirements prescribed under some other regime.

Charitable companies will of course have to follow the requirements of the Companies Act 1985 and best practice requires that they also comply with SORP 2.

The Audit Requirements

(Sections 21 and 22)

Contrary to popular misconception, prior to the Charities Act 1992 there was no legal requirement for all charities to be audited, although, of course, there could have been a requirement under other Acts, such as the Companies Act or the charity's own constitutional document. In addition, Section 8 of the Charities Act 1960 has always allowed the Charity Commissioners to call for a special audit and Section 22 of the Trustees Act 1925 also allows trustees to arrange for an audit if they require.

Section 21 of the Charities Act 1992 introduces the audit requirement. If the charity's gross income or total expenditure exceeds £100,000, it will require a professional audit by a person who is eligible to be a company auditor in accordance with Section 25 of the Companies Act 1989. This requirement will continue for three years. For example, if a charity's income exceeds £100,000 in year one it will have to be professionally audited in years one, two and three, even though its income or expenditure may not exceed the £100,000 threshold in years two or three.

There was concern that, as a result of the new registered auditor regime for company auditors which was introduced on 1 October 1991, many who previously could perform Companies Act audits may now be disallowed. This includes many qualified auditors who are not registered auditors under the new regime. Many chartered accountants who have been able to audit charitable companies, now cannot do so unless they are specifically registered auditors. This would now extend to unincorporated charities requiring an audit. Accordingly, a new subsection was included in the Charities Act which will allow the charity's audit to be performed by a person who is a member of a body specified in regulations and is under the rules of that body eligible for appointment as auditor of the charity. This may widen the net.

Independent examiner

Charities not reaching the £100,000 threshold and not opting for a full audit will require an independent examination by an independent examiner. This means that all registered charities with income over £1,000 must, at the very least, have such an independent examination.

The original definition of an independent examiner caused concern since it stated that the person had to 'be qualified by practical experience of the practice of accountancy'. It was thought that this wording might imply that even small charities had to be independently examined by professional accountants. In the Committee Stage, the government clarified the fact that this could be any suitable person, such as a bank manager or anybody else with the necessary financial acumen, and not necessarily a qualified auditor. Once again, the Home Office was helpful in changing the section, which now defines an independent examiner as 'an independent person who is reasonably believed by the trustees to have the requisite ability and practical experience to carry out a competent examination of the accounts'.

Powers of appointment

Where the charity does not appoint an auditor or independent examiner, the Commissioners may order that one is appointed. In such a case, expenses of any audit would be recoverable from the charity trustees, who would be jointly and severally personally liable for those expenses. If it is not practicable to recover the costs from them, then they could be recovered from the charity's funds.

Duties of the auditor

Section 22 states that the Secretary of State may, by regulations, make provisions with respect to the duties of the auditor. This is interesting – such regulations may require the auditor to consider important aspects of charity and trust law. At present, one rarely sees audit reports that refer to compliance with such law. It is expected that the new regulations will require the auditor to consider aspects of stewardship.

What is gross income or total expenditure?

Section 1 of the Act defines 'gross income' in relation to a charity as meaning 'its gross recorded income from all sources, including special trusts.

Problems could arise here and it is important that the regulations should be made more explicit. A charity may receive 'income' of a capital nature – for example, to be treated as a permanent endowment or used to build a hospital wing. The revised SORP 2 proposes that a statement should be prepared which would include all the resources entrusted to the charity.

'Total expenditure' is not defined in the Act and there may be difficulties where expenditure is perceived to be below the threshold but is pushed up by outstanding charges or other contingencies perhaps arising from branch or regional expenditure.

Annual Report

(Section 23)

SORP 2 has always recommended an annual report. This is a vital document and can be used to give useful qualitative information. Annual accounts may be successful at measuring inputs but say very little about outputs, or more importantly, outcomes, and the effect of the charity's performance on its stakeholders.

There is more to accountability than measuring effectiveness in pounds and pence: most readers of the accounts would like the objectives of the charity clearly explained.

Accounts are often an important fund-raising tool, but unfortunately many sets of accounts do not really explain developments and activities during the year. It is essential to have some commentary in the annual report which gives this information, along with a frank appraisal of the charity's achievements, how it has met its objectives and if it has not, why not. A discussion of important events and trends that affect the charity's work and a description of how it has and will respond to them would not go amiss. Similarly, the reason for holding funds, comments on the surplus or deficit, financial needs, future plans and a review of outstanding commitments and obligations would also be useful. Essentially, something to ensure that the numbers can be properly interpreted, for example: how are administrative and fund-raising costs treated?

Section 23 requires the trustees to prepare an annual report on the activities of the charity during the year and such other information relating to the charity or to its trustees or officers as may be prescribed by regulations made by the Secretary of State. Once again it is expected that the revised SORP 2 will be a good guideline of what to expect.

This report along with the annual accounts should be transmitted to the Commissioners within ten months of the year-end.

Public Inspection

(Section 25)

All annual reports and accounts held by the Commissioners shall be open to public inspection. In addition, charity trustees will be expected to send copies of the latest accounts within two months to anyone requesting them. A reasonable fee may be charged.

Fund-raisers must recognize the potential public relations impact of the report and accounts. While a charity must ensure that they comply with best practice and the law, the accounts must portray a message for the charity. They must be easily understood by the readers and clearly demonstrate how the trustees have fulfilled their duty of stewardship over the resources entrusted to the charity.

CHARITY INVESTMENTS

(Sections 38 and 39)

It was proposed at the Committee Stage of the Bill leading to the Act that three new clauses be inserted into the Bill to take charities' investment powers outside the

Trustee Investments Act 1961 and to replace such powers with more up-to-date regulations to be issued by the Secretary of State. Although the 1961 Act was, at the time, a liberalizing step enabling charity trustees to split a charity fund equally between, broadly, investments in U.K. shares ('wider-range investments') and gilts and money deposits ('narrower-range investments'), the recent economic climate in which shares have significantly out-performed gilts and in which international investments have an increased importance has made the Act outdated. It is claimed that it has lost charities millions of pounds of revenue and capital growth. Indeed, there is a general argument in favour of amending the Act to enable charity trustees to make whatever they consider to be the best investment decisions for charity money.

The provisions added at the Committee Stage could alter the position for charities, although the general law for non-charitable trusts remains the same. It was argued that charities should not be singled out for reform and that, instead, a general reform of trust law should be made. However, this argument did not win favour and, therefore, the position is changed only for the time being for charities. It should be noted that the governing instrument of a new charity that may be established for a capital appeal should invariably extend the investment powers of charity trustees.

Relaxation of Restriction on Wider-Range Investments

The 1961 Act prevents trustees from making or retaining any wider-range investments unless the trust fund is divided into two equal parts, with one part being invested in wider-range investments and the other part being invested in narrower-range investments. The Act enables the Secretary of State to vary this strict equal division as to such proportions as may be specified in future by an order made with the consent of the Treasury. Where trust funds have already been divided into the specified equal shares, the fund may, subsequent to such an order, be divided – but only once again – in pursuance of the order.

Extension of Powers of Investment

The Secretary of State now has the power to make regulations (again, subject to the consent of the Treasury) specifying further investments which are authorized investments for charities.

The indication that regulations will be forthcoming to relax the provisions of the Trustee Investments Act could be a very significant step for charities. Charity trustees may then have a greater degree of flexibility than other trustees. What is not yet known is when or to what extent the Trustee Investments Act provisions will be amended. Indeed, the requirement to obtain the consent of the Treasury may mean that change will be a long time in coming.

In the meantime, check your charity's governing instrument. If the investment powers are very narrow, discuss with your professional advisers whether they could or should be expanded by means of a suitable application to the Charity Commissioners.

Also consider whether the governing instrument includes a power to delegate investment decisions to investment managers. If it does not, again, it may be possible to vary the position by means of a suitable application to the Commissioners.

If you are setting up a new charity for a capital appeal, check that the investment powers are widely drawn and that power to delegate investment management is included.

SCHEMES

(Section 15)

When references are made to 'schemes' of the Charity Commission, they are not seeking to imply any devious thinking on the part of the Commissioners! These schemes are the formal arrangements by which the Commissioners make orders to vary existing structures and arrangements where they are deficient in practice or have become out-of-date or impracticable.

Retaining Unspent Appeal Money

Following the intentions of donors has always been a central principle of charity law and lies at the heart of the bond of trust established between fund-raisers and donors at each point that a donation is made.

Section 15 of the Charities Act 1992 clarifies further the responsibilities under which all fund-raisers operate when they seek to raise funds on behalf of the charity or voluntary organization.

Where a charity makes a public appeal soliciting money or other property for a specific project, such as the acquisition of particular equipment, the charity might find either that the outcome of this appeal is insufficient to purchase the equipment asked for or, alternatively, that funds are achieved over and above the amount the charity can possibly spend on this specific item.

If the appeal does not specify what will happen to any unspent money, Section 15 of the Act amends the procedures that apply when a charity has to try to return the money to the people who gave it. Where you can find donors and they do not want their gifts returned, they will have to sign a disclaimer to this effect in a form laid down by the Charity Commissioners before you can spend that donation on alternative activities. Where you cannot find or identify the donors, the charity is under a duty to advertise, again in a form established by the Commissioners, to enable donors to come forward and register whether they are happy for their donation to be spent on different charitable activities from those for which the original donation was given.

Failure to comply with these requirements could, under new and increased powers of investigation granted to the Charity Commissioners under the new Act, lead to the Commissioners initiating a public investigation of any charity not complying with this important principle of charity law.

In order to raise funds effectively and efficiently, it is advisable that wherever funds are being solicited for a particular project – and a one-off capital campaign is most definitely a particular project – to include within any appeal literature a statement to the effect that any additional funds raised from this particular appeal will be used to further the general charitable purposes of the organization. Such a clear, legible statement on each and every fund-raising notice absolves the charity (and the fund-raiser) of the need to inform donors subsequently of the intention to use their money in a manner that was not initially specified in the original appeal.

FUND-RAISING PRACTICE

(Sections 58-64)

Part II of the Charities Act provides entirely new law designed, in the first instance, to protect donors wherever they are approached to make a gift to a charity and to voluntary organizations.

The underlying principle behind Part II of the Charities Act is to ensure that wherever and whenever an individual or a company is receiving direct financial reward from fund-raising activities on behalf of a charity or voluntary organization, this fact will be made known to each and every potential donor. This is not to say that it is not highly appropriate for fund-raisers from commercial companies to receive a reward from certain types of fund-raising practice – the intention here is simply that when such reward is being obtained, the general public has a right to know so that they can make their donations based on this knowledge.

Under Part II of the Charities Act, 'professional fund-raisers', 'fund-raising businesses' and 'commercial participators' are defined as those individuals (corporate or otherwise) who might receive personal remuneration from fund-raising activities they undertake on behalf of charities and voluntary organizations. It is these individuals, and/or the companies within which they work, that are regulated under Part II of the Charities Act.

Where an individual and/or a company is receiving direct remuneration from fund-raising activities undertaken on behalf of charities and voluntary organizations, it is the responsibility of that individual/company to have a formal written contractual agreement with the charity or voluntary organization on behalf of which they are raising funds. This contract must be established in a form still to be developed in the regulations. If there is no contract or if the contract does not conform precisely to the prescribed form, the contract will be legally binding only if the individual/corporate fund-raiser can prove in a court of law that it should be sustainable. This new requirement provides considerable additional security to charities and voluntary organizations in their relationships with external fund-raisers and commercial companies.

Additionally, each and every time an external fund-raiser/commercial company solicits funds or property on behalf of a charity or voluntary organization and in the process of so doing receives individual reward, he/it will have to make a statement to the donor indicating the following points:

(a) The name of the charity or voluntary organization on whose behalf he is raising funds.
(b) If this is for more than one charity and voluntary organization, then he must specify each of them and indicate the proportion by which each will benefit from the fund-raising activity.
(c) In general terms, he must indicate the method by which he will receive his remuneration from this fund-raising activity.

Failure to comply with the requirement to make this statement at each and every point of potential donation will be a criminal offence on the part of the external fund-raiser/commercial company.

Additional requirements, supported by new potential criminal offences, are also established in relation to particular fund-raising practices. Any charity or voluntary organization employing external agencies to undertake television or radio advertising campaigns and telemarketing campaigns should be aware of these additional requirements contained within the Charities Act.

The Act also introduces broad-based opportunities for charities and voluntary organizations to control fund-raising activities undertaken in their name with which they would not wish to be associated. Under these new powers, charities and voluntary organizations can take out an injunction against any individual raising funds on their behalf in a manner with which they would not wish to be associated (subject to first writing to the fund-raiser and asking him to desist).

The Act also establishes a broad new criminal offence: to imply, in any way, that you are raising funds for a registered charity when in fact the organization is not a registered charity. This new regulation provides further security for the unique position granted to charitable status by the general public in this country but will mean that charity fund-raisers raising funds, for example, through charity trading subsidiaries, will need to be careful that they word their appeals so as not to contravene this new potential criminal offence.

PUBLIC CHARITABLE COLLECTIONS

(Sections 65 – 74)

Part III of the new Act regulates fund-raising activities undertaken by charities and voluntary organizations (either directly or on their behalf) in public places. The Act supersedes the existing legislation contained in the House to House Collections Act 1939 and the Police, Factories, Etc. (Miscellaneous Provisions) Act 1916, which currently govern street collecting activities. In addition the Act repeals the War Charities Act 1940.

The new legislation is much broader in its impact upon collecting activities undertaken by or on behalf of charities and voluntary organizations. In essence, any individual (operating either within or outside a charity or voluntary organization) who wishes to undertake a fund-raising activity on behalf of a charity or voluntary organization, must first satisfy himself with regard to three questions:

1. Will my fund-raising involve me in any form of collecting activity?
   * The collecting activity might be in the form of a straightforward donation into a collecting tin; the engagement in a trading activity resulting in my receipt of income; the collection of property (e.g. donated goods, old newspapers, etc.); or the collection of income (from sponsorships, etc.). The legislation is very broad on this point – if you are collecting, potentially you are regulated under the Act.

2. If my fund-raising involves me in any form of collecting activity, I must then ask: Does this collecting activity occur in what the Act calls a public place?

- For the purposes of the Act a 'public place' means any highway, and any other place to which, at any time when the appeal is made, members of the public have or are permitted to have, access and which is either not within a building, or if it is within a building, is within a public area such as a station, airport, shopping precinct or similar public area. This is a very broad definition of what constitutes a public place. There are, however, a number of exemptions:

   (a) If the place where you wish to collect is on private property and the public has permission to be there only if payment for a ticket is required as a condition of access, then you are not regarded as being in a public place.

   (b) If the place where you wish to collect enables the public to have permission to be in that place only by virtue of permission given by the owner specifically for the appeal to take place, then you are also not in a public place.

   (c) Further exemptions are granted for certain areas of church property, attendance at public meetings and the siting by charities of static collection boxes in shops, pubs, etc.

3. If my fund-raising involves me in a collecting activity which will take place in a 'public place' as identified above, the final question I must ask myself is: Am I, in the course of these activities, making an appeal on behalf of a charity or voluntary organization when any portion of the income from my activity will go to benefit a charity or voluntary organization?

- If the answer to this last question is in any way 'yes', then I am likely to be regulated in my collecting activity under Part III of the Act.

In most cases, the incidence of regulation on your particular fund-raising activity in this part of the Act will require you to register your intention to raise funds with your local authority and to obtain from them permission to undertake the collecting activity through the medium of a licence to collect. Failure to apply for a licence or to provide false information in any application for a licence leads to an immediate criminal offence. Failure to have the required permit for a collecting activity, regulated under Part III of the Charities Act, also leads to criminal offences against both the organizer of the collection and possibly, each and every collector participating in it.

Detailed regulations outlining the mechanism for application to local authorities, the conditions that may be placed on collecting activities by local authorities and the conditions on the management and recording of collecting activities by fund-raisers are still to be developed.

Exemption Order Permits

In certain circumstances registered charities will be able to receive a permit directly from the Charity Commissioners which will exempt them from making applications to each separate local authority for a national public collecting activity.

In order to be eligible for application for an exemption order permit, a registered charity will have to show that the collecting activity will be undertaken throughout a substantial part of England and Wales. The Charity Commissioners are granted very broad powers to refuse such applications and/or to place whatever conditions they may wish to upon the granting of any such application. Only those organizations with registered charitable status will be able to apply for those permits.

The public collections legislation contained in Part III of the Act is applicable only to England and Wales. Fund-raisers wishing to collect on behalf of charities and voluntary organizations in Scotland also have to comply with legislation contained in the Civic Government (Scotland) Act of 1982. Fund-raisers wishing to undertake public collecting activities in Northern Ireland must also comply with the specific regulations pertaining to the Province which are administered directly by the Royal Ulster Constabulary. In all cases, failure to comply with these regulations will constitute criminal offences being committed by the organizers – and possibly each collector – participating in a public charitable collection.

The Charities Act 1992 provides a major challenge to anyone wishing to raise funds in an efficient, effective and, above all, legal manner. All fund-raisers for charities and voluntary organizations should be aware of this important and far-reaching legislation and should abide by its requirements in full. Further information with regard to the implementation of this legislation and to the content of the specific regulations associated with it can be obtained either from the Home Office or from the Institute of Charity Fundraising Managers.

Appendix 9

BIBLIOGRAPHY

GENERAL

Administration of Appeal Funds R.W. Suddards (Sweet and Maxwell 1991)

Charities Administration (Institute of Chartered Secretaries & Administrators)

Insurance protection: a guide for voluntary organizations C. Ford and A. Silley (National Council for Voluntary Organizations Publications 1992)

Management of Voluntary Organizations (Croner Publications 1988) – updated annually and subscription includes update

Step by Step: A guide to Volunteer Fundraising (Institute of Charity Fundraising Managers, and Volunteer Centre 1992)

Voluntary but not Amateur Forbes, Hayes and Reason (London Voluntary Service Council)

Who Can Help Voluntary Organisations (NCVO Information Sheet 1992)

LEGAL

But Is It Legal? S. Capper (Bedford Square Press 1988)

Charitable Status A. Philips and K. Smith (Directory of Social Change 1993)

Charities: Law and Practice E. Cairns (Sweet & Maxwell 1988)

Charities – The New Law – The Charities Act 1992 Stephen Lloyd and Fiona Middleton of Bates, Wells & Braithwaite (Jordan's 1992)

Charity Fundraising & the Public Interest P. Luxton (Avebury 1990)

Gaming, Lotteries, Fundraising and the Law Jarlath Finney (Sweet and Maxwell)

Law of Betting, Gaming and Lotteries Colin Smith and Stephen Monkcom (Butterworth)

Law Relating to Charities D.G. Cracknell (Longman Professional)

Legacies: A Practical Guide for Charities M. Norton (Directory of Social Change 1983)

Responsibilites of Charity Trustees (Charity Commission)

Starting a Charity Charity Commissioners leaflet CC21

The Effective Trustee (Vol.1: *Roles and Responsibilities*, Vol. 2: *Aims and Resources*, Vol 3: *Getting the Work Done*) Kevin Ford (Directory of Social Change 1993)

TAXATION AND FINANCE

A Practical guide to VAT for Charities Kate Sayer (Directory of Social Change 1992)

A Guide to Gift Aid (Directory of Social Change 1992)

Charity Finance Director's Handbook (Charles Letts & Co. for The Charity Finance Directors Group – published annually)

Charity Commissioners: how they can help Charity Trustees (Charity Commission)

Charities H.M. Customs & Excise VAT leaflet 701/1/92

Gift Aid: A Guide for Donors and Charities Inland Revenue (IR 113)

Giving and Inheriting (Which? 1992)

Guide to Charitable Giving & Taxation (Craigmyle & Co.)

Investment of Charity Funds (Directory of Social Change and Charities Aid Foundation 1993)

Tax Aspects of Charities R. Vincent, L. Austin and J. Clarke (Chartac Books)

Tax-effective Giving: A Practical Guide for Charities M. Norton (Directory of Social Change 1992)

Tax Pack for Charities Inland Revenue (1992)

Tolley's Charities Manual N. Russel (Tolley Publishing Co. 1988)

MARKETING AND FUND-RAISING

A Basic PR Guide for Charities D. & A. McIntosh (Directory of Social Change 1985)

Advertising by Charities K. Burnett (Directory of Social Change 1986)

Charities Aid Foundation Guide to Charity Sponsorship 1990 A.C. Clay (Hobson's Publishing)

Charity Shops in the U.K. (Survey produced by The Corporate Intelligence Group)

Community Fundraising Guide Sandy Adirondack (ITV Telethon/Institute of Fundraising Managers)

Complete Fundraising Handbook Sam Clarke (Directory of Social Change/Institute of Charity Fundraising Managers 1993)

Complete Guide to Fundraising P.W. & P.F. Sterrett (Mercury Books 1988)

Fund-raising and Grant Aid for Voluntary Organizations S. Bates (Bedford Square Press 1986)

Fundraising Notes (Directory of Social Change) (12 leaflets)

High Street Giving S. Hamble (Directory of Social Change 1990)

Hollis Press and Public Relations Annual (Hollis Directories Ltd.)

How Voluntary Organizations Can Benefit from Business (National Council for Voluntary Organizations information sheet 1992)

Marketing for Charities D. & A. McIntosh (Directory of Social Change 1984)

PR Planner (PR Planner Ltd)

U.K. Media Directory (Pims U.K. Ltd) Published bi-monthly

Relationship Fundraising Ken Burnett (White Lion Press Ltd. 1992)

Selective Bibliography of Fundraising books and pamphlets (National Council for Voluntary Organizations Reading List 1992)

U.K. Media Directory (Two Ten Communications Ltd.) Published bi-monthly

INSTITUTE OF FUNDRAISING MANAGERS' CODES OF PRACTICE AND GUIDELINES

Codes of Practice:
  Schools
  Reciprocal Mailing
  Lotteries
  Recruitment of Public Collection Collectors by Telephone
  House to House Collections
Guidance Notes
  Management of Static Collection Boxes
  Chain Letters
  Appointment of Fundraising Consultants

OVERSEAS

Company Giving in Europe ed. B. Dabson (Directory of Social Change 1991)
European Social Fund: Information for Voluntary Organizations W. Seary (National Council for Voluntary Organizations 1988)
Finance from Europe: a Guide to Grants and Loans (European Community)
Grants from Europe (National Council for Voluntary Organizations 1992)
Guide to European Foundations (can be seen at Charities Aid Foundation, Tonbridge)
International Giving and Volunteering (Charities Aid Foundation)
U.S. Foundation Support in Europe K. Robinson (ed.) (Directory of Social Change 1991)

CENTRAL AND LOCAL GOVERNMENT

Central Government Grants Guide A.-M. Doulton (Directory of Social Change 1993)
Getting in on the Act: a Guide to Local Authorities' Power to Fund Voluntary Organizations C. Grace and R. Gutch (National Council for Voluntary Organizations 1987)
Getting Ready for Contracts S. Adirondack and R. MacFarlane (Directory of Social Change 1991)
Government Grants: a Guide for Voluntary Organizations M. Jones (Bedford Square Press 1992)
Municipal Year Book (Municipal Journal Ltd.)

REFERENCE

The Sunday Times Book of the Rich Philip Beresford (Penguin Books)
Charity Trends (Charities Aid Foundation)
City of London Directory & Livery Companies' Guide (City Press)
Corporate Donors' Guide (Directory of Social Change 1988)
Corporate Register[1] (Hemmington Scott)
Crawfords Directory of City Connections (Economist Publications)
Debrett's Distinguished People of Today (Sterling Publications)
Directory of Charitable Organizations in Northern Ireland (Northern Ireland Council for Voluntary Service)
Directory of Directors (Reed Information Services)
Directory of Grant-Making Trusts[1] (Charities Aid Foundation)
Guide to Company Giving (Directory of Social Change 1993)
Guide to the Major Trusts L. Fitzherbert and M. Eastwood (Directory of Social Change 1993)
Hambro Company Guide[2] (Hemmington Scott)
Henderson Top 1000 Charities 1993 (Hemmington Scott)
Individual Giving and Volunteering Survey 1992 (Charities Aid Foundation)
Jordan's Survey of Private Companies (Jordan's)
    Volume I - *The Top 2000*
    Volume II - *The Second 2000*
Key British Enterprises (Dun & Bradstreet)
Major Companies and Their Charitable Giving (Directory of Social Change 1991)
Market Research Society Yearbook (Market Research Society)
Times 1000 (Times Books)
Who Owns Whom (Dun & Bradstreet)
Who's Who (A. & C. Black)

TECHNICAL JOURNALS

Charity (Charities Aid Foundation)
Update (Institute of Charity Fundraising Managers)
Professional Fundraising (Brainstorm Publishing Ltd.)
NCVO News (National Council for Voluntary Organisations)
NGO Finance (Plaza Publishing Ltd)
Third SECTOR (Third Sector Publications)

---

[1] Biennial
[2] Quarterly

Appendix 10

USEFUL ADDRESSES

Action with Communities in Rural England (ACRE)

Somerford Court,
Somerford Road,
Cirencester,
Gloucestershire GL7 1TW.
Tel: 0285 653477

Action Resource Centre

102 Village Park East,
London NW1 3SP.
Tel: 071 383 2200

Alexandra Rose Day

1 Castelnau,
London SW13 9RP.
Tel: 081 748 4824

Association of Fundraising Consultants

The Grove,
Harpenden,
Hertfordshire AL5 1AH.
Tel: 0582 762441

BBC Appeals Advisory Committee

BBC White City,
201 Wood Lane,
London W12 7TS.
Tel: 081 752 5252

BBC Children in Need Trust

Room 3262,
BBC White City,
201 Wood Lane,
London W12 7TS.
Tel: 081 752 4694

Broadcasting Support Services

252 Western Avenue,
London W3 6XJ.
Tel: 081 992 5522

Business in the Community

227a City Road,
London EC1V 1LX.
Tel: 071 253 3716

Central Appeals Advisory Committee (CAAC)

Room 5555,
White City,
201 Wood Lane,
London W12 7TS.
Tel: 081 752 5836

Charities Aid Foundation

48 Pembury Road,
Tonbridge,
Kent TN9 2JD.
Tel: 0732 771333

114-118 Southampton Row,
London WC1B 5AA.
Tel: 071 831 7798

Charity Christmas Card Council

49 Lamb's Conduit Street,
London WC1N 3NG.
Tel: 071 242 0546

Charity Commission

St. Alban's House,
57-60 Haymarket,
London SW1Y 2QX.
Tel: 071 210 3000
Central register: 071 210 4405.

Graeme House,
Derby Square,
Liverpool L2 7SB.
Tel: 051 227 3191

The Deane,
Tangier,
Taunton,
Somerset TA1 4AY.
Tel: 0832 322169

Comic Relief/Charity Projects

74 New Oxford Street,
London WC1A 1EF.
Tel: 071 436 1122

Customs & Excise Department, HM (VAT Administration)

King's Beam House,
Mark Lane,
London EC3R 7HE.
Tel: 071 626 1515

Data Protection Registrar

Springfield House,
Water Lane,
Wilmslow,
Cheshire SK9 5AX.
Tel: 0625 535777

Direct Marketing Association (U.K.) Ltd.

1st floor,
199 Knightsbridge,
London SW7 1YN.
Tel: 071 321 2525

Directory of Social Change

Radius Works,
Back Lane,
London NW3 1HL.
Tel: 071 435 8171
(Charities Advisory Trust:
071 794 9835)

FunderFinder

11 Upper York Street,
Wakefield, WF1 3LQ.
Tel: 0924 382120

Gaming Board for Great Britain

Berkshire House,
168/173 High Holborn,
London WC1V 7AA.
Tel: 071 240 0821

Give As You Earn

Foundation House,
Coach & Horses Passage,
The Pantiles,
Tunbridge Wells,
Kent TN2 5TZ.
Tel: 0892 540040

Home Office Voluntary Service Unit

50 Queen Anne's Gate,
London SW1H 9AT.
Tel: 071 273 2146

Independent Television Commission

70 Brompton Road,
London SW3 1EY.
Tel: 071 584 7011

Inland Revenue

Somerset House,
Strand,
London WC2R 1LB.
Tel: 071 438 6420

Charity Division,
St. John's House,
Merton Road,
Bootle,
Merseyside L69 4EJ.
Tel: 051 922 6363

Institute of Charity Fundraising Managers

5th floor,
Market Towers,
1 Nine Elms Lane,
London SW8 5NQ.
Tel: 071 627 3436

ITV Telethon

2nd Floor,
12 Lancelot Place,
London SW7 1DR.
Tel: 071 584 9977

London Voluntary Service Council

68 Chalton Street,
London NW1 1JR.
Tel: 071 388 0241

Lotteries Council

81 Mansel Street,
Swansea, SA1 5TT.
Tel: 0795 462845

National Association of Volunteer Bureaux

St. Peter's College,
College Road,
Saltley,
Birmingham B8 3TE.
Tel: 021 327 0265

National Association for Councils for Voluntary Service

3rd Floor, Arundel Court,
177 Arundel Street,
Sheffield, S1 2NU.
Tel: 0742 786636

National Council for Voluntary Organizations

Regent's Wharf,
8 All Saints' Street,
London N1 9RL.
Tel: 071 713 6161

National Society of Fund Raising Executives (ICFM sister body in U.S.A.)

635 West Seventh Street,
Cincinnati, Ohio, USA.
Tel: 0101 513 241 6778

Northern Ireland Council for Voluntary Action

2 Annadale Road,
Belfast BT7 3JH.
Tel: 0232 640011

Retired Executives' Clearing House (REACH)

89 Southwark Street,
London SE1 0HD.
Tel: 071 928 9452

Scottish Council for Voluntary Organizations

18-19 Claremont Crescent,
Edinburgh EH7 4QD.
Tel: 031 556 3882

Volunteer Centre U.K.

29 Lower King's Road,
Berkhamsted,
Hertfordshire HP4 2AB.
Tel: 0442 873311

Wales Council for Voluntary Action

Crescent Road,
Caerphilly,
Mid-Glamorgan CF8 1XL.
Tel: 0222 869224

INDEX

Indexer's note: the emphasis of the index is on general appeals, but issues pertaining to particular appeals will be found under those named appeals. Where there are several references of which one is more significant than the rest, this reference is denoted by page numbers in **bold**. Page numbers in *italic* refer to captions to black and white illustrations. The insert of colour illustrations is denoted by *col. insert*.

AAC *see* BBC Appeals Advisory Committee
AAFRC *see* American Association of Fund-Raising Counsel Inc.
Abbeyfield Bristol Society Extra Care Appeal 351-3
Abington Parish Church
  Christian Giving campaign 348-50
Accounting Standards Committee 101
accounts and accounting 134, **318-19**, **408-11**
  administrative costs 25
  records 120-1
  software 113-14;
  see also budgeting *and* tax and taxation
achievement announcement *see* results of appeal
ACRE *see* Action with Communities in Rural England
Action Research for the Crippled Child 209, 274, 280
Action Resource Centre 110, 423
Action with Communities in Rural England (ACRE) 335, 423
addresses, useful 423-6
Adjutant General 211
administration 158-61, 312-20, 338-40
  costs 24-5
  skills 62;
  see also accounts and accounting; computer systems; insurance; offices *and* staff
The Administration of Appeal Funds 94, 419
advertising 177, **191-9**, 270, 272
  outdoor 80, 198, **324**
  writing copy 195
Advertising Standards Authority Code 199
advertorials 185
affinity cards 249-50
affinity marketing 236, **248-9**
aftermath of appeals 342-3, **365-78**
Albert Edward, Prince of Wales, son of Queen Victoria 9
Alexandra, Princess of Wales, wife of Albert Edward, Prince of Wales 9
Alexandra Rose Day 306, 342, 423
Allders 12-13, 241

Allford, Marion xvi, *374*
American Association of Fund-Raising Counsel Inc. (AAFRC) 226
Andrew de Mille Fundraising Consultants 354
animal appeals 216
Anne, Princess Royal, daughter of Queen Elizabeth II 352
announcement of appeal achievement *see* results of appeal
annual reports 134
appeal weeks 377
appeals *see* business appeals; charities; failed appeals; international appeals; local appeals; private appeals; public appeals; smaller appeals *and under general terms and named appeals*
approach lists 158-9
armed forces 12, 73, 210, **213**, 325, 335
Arthur Young 232, 317
Associated British Foods 147
Association of Fundraising Consultants 57, 423
Association of Professional Computer Consultants 111
associations, clubs and societies 73, 213, 215
Astor, Viscount 48
auctions *see* Classic Car Auction, Brocket Hall
audio visuals 186-7
Aurum Press 288
Australia
  Melbourne Children's Hospital 225
Automotive and Financial Group Limited xiv
Aylard, Commander Richard xv

Bacon, Derek 381
Bagnall, Peter xv, 80, 288
Band Aid 4, 176, 256, 258, 327
Bank of England 278
Bank of Scotland 249, 346
banking decisions 99-100
Barchard, Betty 12
Barratt, Martin 12, 322

Barrie, J.M. 9, 10, 11, 13, 287
bars, public 264
Basil de Ferranti Memorial Appeal 355, 356-7
Baxter, Tony xv
BBC 80, 261, 262
    documentaries 13, 181, 184, 202, 287
BBC Appeals Advisory Committee (AAC) 181, 183, 423
BBC Children in Need 4, 142, 181-2, 193, 269, 423
BBC World Service 227
BDO Binder Hamlyn xv, 406
Becker, Boris 15, 256
Beecham 278
Bence Jones, Dr Henry 8
Benson, Graham 256
bequests see legacies
bicycle rides, sponsored 293
Bird, Lady 38
BITC see Business in the Community
'blocked funds' 222
Bond, Caroline 12, 52, 322
books, reference 419-22
books, writing see publishing
Bottom, David 294
Boy George 13, 14
Boy Scouts 12, 90, 210, 211, 243-4, 325, col. insert
Boyd, Alan 256
Boyd, Lord, Viscount Boyd of Merton 342
Boy's Brigade 210
BP 152, 154
Bramall, Lord 202
Brignull, Tony 131, 196
British Airways 278
British Deaf Association 209
British Diplomatic Spouses Association see Diplomatic Service Wives Association
British Forces Broadcasting Service 211
British Market Research Bureau 42
British Petroleum see BP
British Red Cross 94
British Telecom see BT
Broadcasting Support Services 423
BROADSWORD mnemonic 31, 78, 332
brochures 131-4
    souvenir 270, 272, 275, 326
Bruno, Frank 208
BT xiv, 152, 154, 293, 296-7, 314
budgeting 97-8, 318-19, 397-8; see also accounts and accounting and forecasting
Buffaloes 213
buildings
    insurance 122
    planning permission 28, 33;
    see also naming opportunities and shops
Burchfield, Jonathan xv, 406
business appeals 148-57
Business in the Community (BITC) xiii, 297, 423

business people 65-6, 72, 137;
    see also companies
business plans 29-31
business rates 96

CAAC see Central Appeals Advisory Committee (CAAC) 424
Cadbury Schweppes 278
cadet forces 210
Cadogan, Dr 8
Cadogan, Lord xiv, 47, 160, 166, 336
CAF see Charities Aid Foundation
Callaghan, Lord 11, 287
Calling the Falklands (radio programme) 213
Capital Radio 183
car-boot sales 265
Carey, Dr George 379-80
Carnegie Foundation 222
cars, vintage see Classic Car Auction, Brocket Hall
case histories of appeals 345-62
Cash, Pat 15
cash flow projections 98
cash handling 120, 319
catalogues see Christmas and mail order
celebrities
    involvement in events 256-7, 258-9
    see also under named celebrities
Celebrity Cook Book 287
Central Appeals Advisory Committee (CAAC) 424
Centre for International Briefing 221
chairmen of appeals 52-5
Channel Islands charity registrations 94
character licensing 245-6
Charing Cross Medical Research Centre Appeal 23, 41, 66, 75, 80, 103, 109, 121, 133, 336
Chariots of Fire run 15, 217, 279, 280
Charitable Status 88
charities
    accounts 92, 101, 408-12
    administrative costs 24-5
    annual reports 92, 101, 412
    audit requirements 410-11
    covenants 95
    'customers' 77
    definitions 90
    fund-raising practices 415-16
    image research 81
    investments 95, 100, 412-16
    joint promotions with companies 238-45
    management information 97
    names 407
    organizational structure 91-2
    protection of reputation 275
    registration 90-1
    setting up 92-3
    taxation 95-7
    trading 228-35

trustees 407-8
VAT 95-6, 401-5;
see also local *and* smaller charities
Charities Act 1992 xviii, 36, 59, 84, 88, 91, 92,
    100, 101, 114, 133, 204, 233, 237-8, 265, 270,
    272, 300, **406-18**
Charities Aid Foundation (CAF) xiv, 41, 42,
    121, 145, 152, 188-9, 224, 296, 424
'Charities in Crisis' Emergency Grants Fund
    342
Charities: Law and Practice 88
Charity Appointments (agency) 107
charity balls 273
Charity Christmas Card Council 424
Charity Commission 24-5, 36, 44, 84, 90, 93,
    101, 122, 230, 424
Charity Directors' Network 379
Charity People (agency) 107
Charity Recruitment (agency) 107
Charity Trends 42, 43
Charles, Prince of Wales ix, 6, 13, 17, 23, 71,
    156, *184*, 188, 207, 211, 227, 262, 264, *271*,
    272, 276, 298, 324, 325, 326
Chartered Institute of Marketing 106
Chatham House (Royal Institute for
    International Affairs) 220
checklists
    administration and personnel 123
    advertising 196, 199
    commercial partnerships 250
    events 268
    publishing 289
    special events agencies 252
    strategy 76
Chetwood, Sir Clifford 23-4, 336
Chief of the Air Staff 211
Children in Hospital 368
Children in Need *see* BBC Children in Need
Chinn, Sir Trevor 147
Christie, Linford *295*
Christie's 276
Christmas card sales 95; *see also* Charity
    Christmas Card Council
Christmas catalogues 234
Christ's Hospital School 7
churches 211, 217, 335, 348-50, 358-62
Cinemas Act 1985 265
City of London School for Girls Centenary
    Scholarship Appeal 388-9
Civic Government (Scotland) Act 1982 418
Clark, Nigel 80, 196
Clark, Sir Robert 66, 80
Clarke, Sir Bob 80, 171, 292
Clarke, William 70
Classic Car Auction, Brocket Hall 276, *277*
Clemance, Lora and Amy 15
Clore Foundation 147
clubs *see* associations, clubs and societies
Cluley, Bridget xv
Coe, Sebastian 15, *279*, 280

Cole, George 260
collection boxes 306-7, *col. insert*
collections, public 304-7, **416-18**
Collett Dickenson Pearce and Partners 80, 83,
    134, 191, 194, 196, 197, *198*, 276, 278
Comfort Fabric Softener 15, 244
Comic Relief 4, 176, 182, 269-70, 424
commercial partnerships 236-51
Commercial Union Insurance 266
Community Fundraising Guide 176
companies
    approaches to **153-5**, 158
    foreign companies 22, 421
    fund-raising by employees 291-6
    giving to appeals 152, **290-9**
    joint promotions with charities 238-45
    researching **44-5**, 290, 334
    secondments **110**, 153, 297-8
    tax-efficient giving 152-3;
    see also business *and under named companies*
Companies House 84, 291
Company Directors Disqualification Act 1986 408
Company of the Year Quiz 276, 278
competition between charities 31
computer records
    security 118;
    see also data protection *and* databases
computer systems
    hardware 110-12
    software **113-17**, 209;
    see also consultants
concerts 273
Connelly, Ken xiv
'Consolidated Charities Act 1993' 406
constituencies of appeals **42-6**, 165
consultants
    computer 111
    fund-raising **55-61**, 354, 358
    public relations 179
Consumer Credit Act 250
contracts
    commercial partnerships 237-8
Coram, Thomas 8
corporation tax 229-30, 237, **399-401**
council tax 96-7
covenants 119, 121, **144-5**, 153, 229, 248, 301,
    307, **388-9**
Craigmyle, Lord 56
Craigmyle and Company 345
Cram, Steve 15, *279*, 280
credit cards *see* affinity cards
Cross, Ben 280
Crown Paints 243
Crowther, Leslie 13
Customs and Excise 424; *see also* VAT
Cy-pres 36

Dahl, Roald 208
Daniel J. Edelman (agency) 205
Daniels, Paul 208

data protection 302; *see also* computer records
Data Protection Act 1984 113, **117-18**
Data Protection Registrar 424
databases 113, 114
    donor records 45, **117-20**, 206, 319, 339
    events 258
    on-line information 115
    postcodes 117;
    see also computer records
De Beers 278
de Mille, Andrew 354
Debenhams 12, 241
Defries, Stuart xv
DeLuca, Nicholas xv
desk-top publishing 114
Diana, Princess of Wales 6, 13, 15, 17, 23, 71,
    104, 114, 156, *184*, 188, 207, 208, 211, 227,
    245, 257, 262, 264, *271*, 272, 274, 278, 324,
    325, 326, 369, *col. insert*
diary systems 114-15
Dickens, Charles 8, 9, *10*, 286, 287, 382
Dimbleby, Jonathan 6-7, 12, 188, 261, 278, 326
Diplomatic Service Wives Association 227
direct mail **300-3**, 373, 378
Direct Marketing Association 304, 424
directors of appeals 55-6, 61-4
Directory of Grant-Making Trusts 43
Directory of Social Change 43, 106, 222, 424
Disaster Appeal Scheme 94
disaster funds 94, 101, 138
display panels 187
documents, appeal 86-7; *see also* accounts;
    annual reports; brochures; business plans;
    marketing documents; preliminary reports
    and progress reports
donations *see* gifts
donor records 45, **117-20**, 206, 319, 339
donors
    approaches to 138, **140-1**
    major donors 136-47
    motivation 192-3
    researching 42, **220-2**;
    see also supporters *and* wealthy individuals
Dougall (horse) *214*
Drinking Fountain Association *344*
Driscoll, James *247*
Drucker, Dr Henry xv
Duchess of Beaufort 352
Duffield, Vivien 138, 147
Duncan, Richard 369, 371

Eagle Star 278
Eastoe, John 292
economic situation *see* recession
Edberg, Stefan 15, 256
Edward, Prince, son of Queen Elizabeth II 280
Edward, Prince of Wales, son of King George
    V 48, 71
Edward, son of Queen Victoria *see* Albert
    Edward, Prince of Wales

*Efficiency Scrutiny Review of Government
    Support to the Voluntary Sector* 45
electronic mail 114-15
Eli Lilly 272, 276
Elizabeth, Queen, wife of King George VI 11
    as Queen Mother 372
Elizabeth II, Queen 71, 369
embassies, foreign 221
employee fund-raising 291-6
*Employers Liability (Compulsory Insurance) Act
    1969* 121
enquiry handling 312-15
entertainment (legalities) 264
equipment donations 39
Ernst & Young *see* Arthur Young
European Commission
    approaches to 144
events 252-82
    and appeal closures 167-8
    annual events 377
    brochures **270, 272**, 275
    budget sheets 397-8
    calendars 189
    codes of practice 273
    financial vetting 257-8
    insurance 122, 266
    legal factors 264-5
    mailing lists 267
    management 115
    press rota 263-4
    schedules 320
    sponsorship 260-2
    tax implications 399-405
    timing 174
    VAT 266, **401-5**
Execucare (agency) 107
exemption order permits 417-18
expatriates 220, 221, 227

failed appeals 101
Falklands garrison 213
Farnham, Lord 336
Farrell, John xv, 80, 84, 196, 240
Fat Cats' Diet 15
fax software 115
feasibility of appeals 47-50
Federation of Army Wives 12
A Fighting Chance (BBC documentary) 13, 181,
    184, 202, 287
film libraries 186
film premieres 17, 272, 273-4, 276, *279*
film shows 265
financial management *see* accounts and
    accounting; banking decisions; budgeting;
    cash flow; cash handling; forecasting;
    results; targets *and* tax and taxation
fire services 12, 211, 213, 325, 335, *col. insert*
First and Always (anthology of poems) 287
Ford Foundation 222
forecasting 98-9

foreign *see* international
Fosters Classic tennis evening 15, **256-7**, 274, 276, *col. insert*
foundations 43-4
Foundling Hospital, Coram's Fields 8
Framjee, Pesh xv, 399, 406
France
  L'Hôpital des Enfants Malades, Paris 8
Free Foresters 213
Freemasons 213
Friendly Societies 213
Frizzel Group 249
Frost, David 15
Funderfinder 44, 424
fund-raisers
  experience 22
  professionalism xi, xviii, 57, 106, 251, 379, 381
  training 57, **105-6**, 155;
  see also consultants; staff *and* volunteers
fund-raising 420
  case histories 5, 345-62
  coordination 74-5
  direct 338
  in schools 215-17
  management 37
  other methods **300-11**, 392-3; *see also* commercial partnerships; events; publishing *and* trading
fund-raising, ongoing *see* future planning
future planning 375-8

Gaming Board for Great Britain 307, 308, 309, 424
Gatward, Isobel 13
Gatward, James 13, 256, 261
GEC 209
General Synod of the Church of England 217
geo-demographic coding systems 115
George V, King 11
  as Prince of Wales 71
George Watson's College Development Project 345-8
Gift Aid 119, 121, 145, 152, 229, 248, 301, 307, **388-9**
gift schedules 38, 137-8, 146-7, 390-1
gifts
  assets 145
gifts in kind 98, 119, 153, 297
  drawbacks 39-40
  requirement lists 35-6
Girl Guides 12, 90, 210, 211, 325
Give As You Earn 291, **296-7**, 425
giving, methods of 79, **386-7**, 421
  tax-efficient 144-5, 152-3, 388-9
Godfrey, Neil 83, **196**
Goodwood 274
GOSH - That Was the Year That Was 292
government 421
  contributions to appeals 29

approaches to 143-4
researching 45-6
Grant, David 288
grants 45-6; *see also* trusts, grant-making
Grayling Company 80, 188, 324
Great Ormond Street Children's Hospital 5, 21, *34*, 381-2
  1875 illustration *col. insert*
  1930s appeal 48
  boilerhouse 36, 38, 146
  chapel *col. insert*
  early Royal patrons and supporters 9, 11
  founding and history 7-12
  fountains 85, *344*
  model of new building *col. insert*
  newspaper campaign offers 169
  Nurses League 215
  objectives 9
  problem to be met by appeal 33, 35
  staircase *139*, 140
  wishing well fountain *85*, 344
  see also Wishing Well Appeal
Guide to the Major Trusts 44
Guildford Cathedral
  sermon 381-2
Guinness 278
Guinness Book of Records 274
Guinness Trust 336, 342
GUS 245
Guthrie, Bill 256

Haggiag, Michael 288
Haines, Gay 278
Hanway, Jonas 8
Hardy, Robert 13
Harry, Prince, son of Charles, Prince of Wales 13, 15
Haswell, Charles 256
Heath, Len 80
Help a London Child (radio appeal) 183
Help the Aged 47, 83, 106, 199, 332, 336
  Flower Fund 341
  Project FundRaising 333
Hill Samuel Group 66, 103, 109, 121
Hodder and Stoughton 288
Holliday, Sue xv, 80, 196
The Hollis Press and Public Relations Annual 179
Home Office Voluntary Service Unit 425
honours recommendations 327
Hooker, Dr Michael 56
House of Commons 278
House of Lords 278
house styles 82, 173
How to Sleep at Night: Checklist for Events 253
Hula Hoops 15, 216, 292
Hussey, Marmaduke 369

IBTT *see* Independent Broadcasting Telethon Trust

ICFM *see* Institute of Charity Fund-raising Managers
Imagination (design and special events company) 80
In Memoriam schemes 318, 341
Inchcape 294, 296
income tax 237; *see also* Inland Revenue
Independent Broadcasting Telethon Trust (IBTT) 182
Independent newspaper 278
Independent Television Commission 194, 425
Individual Giving and Volunteering 41
inflation allowances 28
inheritance tax 310
Inland Revenue 121, 425; *see also* tax and taxation
Inner Wheel 210
Insolvency Act 1986 408
Institute of Charity Fundraising Managers (ICFM) xv, 22, 106, 111, 253, **335**, 381, 406, 418
  codes of practice and guidelines 57, 215, 273, 301, 304, 307, 319, 421
Institute of Child Health 9, 11, 21, 37, 146, 187, 224, 272, 322, 425
insurance 121-2
  events 266
intellectual property 246, 289
international appeals 219-27
The International Giving and Volunteering Survey 224
International Marketing Promotions 80, 83, 244
investments 95, 100, 412-16
Irwin, Jane 280
ISBNs *see* Standard Book Numbers
Isle of Man
  charity registrations 94
ITV 13, 262
ITV Telethon xiv, 4, 142, 176, 182, 193, 269-70, 314, 342, 425

Jackson, Godfrey xv
Jackson, Michael 15, 276, *col. insert*
James Capel 280
Jenkins, Peter xv
Jersey Lions Club 208
Jingle Bears 13, 213, **241**, *242*
John Laing 208, **294**
journals, reference 422
Judd, Lord 381

Kaufman, Jane xv
Kay, William xiv
Kayes 245
Kelly, Helen 109-10
Kennedy, Grace 13, *14*
Kilkenny, Alan 80, 179, 288
Kilkenny, Melinda xv
Kingshott, Dennis xv

Kleinwort Benson 149
Kodak 243
Kosky, Jules xv, 71, 84, 286

ladies organizations 335
Laing, John 208
Laing, Martin 294
Land's End to John O' Groats journeys 282, 292, 294
Langford, Bonnie 13
Latham, Bill 274-5
launching appeals 187-9
Leadenhall Ball 276
leadership 23, 46-7, **51-66**, 150-1, 171-2, 201-3, 225, 335-6
Leconte, Henri 15, 256
Lee, Stephen xv, 406
Leeds Permanent Building Society 249
legacies 119, 145-6, **309-11**, 377
legal bibliography 419-20
Lendl, Ivan 256
Leng, Virginia 280, *281*
Lewis, Katy 213
Lewis, Martyn 13, 186, *259*, 261
Lex Service xiv, 147, 154
Lions Club International 12
Live Aid 256
livery companies 143, 158
Lloyd, David 256
Lloyd's of London 276
loans, interest-free 153
local appeals 331-44; *see also* smaller appeals
local authorities 335
  approaches to 144
local charities 143, 334
logos 82-3, **173**, **174**, 234, 237
  legal protection 86
  licensing 245-6
London Fire Service 12, 213
London Marathon *184*, 241, 276, 278, *col. insert*
London Voluntary Service Council (LVSC) 338, 425
London Youth Games 274
London Zoo 12
Lord Lieutenant of Greater London 71, 73
Lord Mayor of London 71
Lord Mayor's Show 280, *281*
Lord Treloar Trust 280
lotteries 307-9
Lotteries and Amusements Act 1976 307, 308, 309
Lotteries Council 425
Lubar, Charles xv
Lulu *214*
Lundberg, Josephine 172
LVSC *see* London Voluntary Service Council
Lynn, Dame Vera 260

MacLaurin, Sir Ian 292
mail *see also* direct mail

mail order 115-16, 233-4
mailing lists 209, 217, 267
mailings, bulk 116
mailsort 116
marathons *see* London Marathon
Margaret, Princess, sister of Queen Elizabeth II 172
market research 41-2, 81-2
marketing 77-87, 131-5, 169-75, 420
   documents 86-7, 170-4
   panels 72-3, 79
   skills 62
   strategy 77-87, 170-4
   structure 79-81
Marks, Alfred 13
Mars 15, 241; *see also* London Marathon
Mary, Princess of Wales, wife of George, Prince of Wales 71
Mary, Princess Royal, sister of King George V 11
Masefield, John 11
Maxwell, Robert 86
Mayor of Lambeth 336
McCarthy, Brian 99
McMahon, Sir Kit 99, 100, 316, 322
McVitie's 244
Mead, Dr 9
Meaney, Sir Patrick 149
media
   announcements to 167
   enquiries from 135
   targeting 179-83;
   see also press, radio *and* television
merchandise 231
Metropolitan Police 12, *212*, 213
Midland Bank xiv, 12, 13, 80, 99, 109, 110, 121, 197, 206, 225, 298, 317, 368
Millar, Sonia 317
Millenium Fund 309
Miller, James 372
Mills Allen 80, 197, 324
Mitty, Roger xv
mnemonics *see* BROADSWORD
Molineux, Richard 358
Molineux Fundraising 358
Mooney, Bel 182
Morris, Brian 294
Moving Spirit *see* Charity Directors' Network
Mr Wishing Well (character)188, *212*, 245-6, *281*
Mr Wishing Well (horse) *col. insert*
Municipal Handbook 201
Murphy, Rev. Denis 217
music and dancing 265
Mutual Friends: Charles Dickens and Great Ormond Street Hospital 286

NACVS *see* National Association of Councils for Voluntary Service

names of appeals
   legal protection 86
   uniqueness checking 83-4
naming opportunities **38-9**, 40, 137-8, 140, 159, 204, 213, 243
National Association of Councils for Voluntary Service (NACVS) 335
National Association of Volunteer Bureaux 109, 425
National Autistic Care and Training Appeal 390-1
National Council for Voluntary Organizations (NCVO) 45, 57, 106, 144, 335, 338, 425
National Health Service 11
national organizations 210-18
National Society for the Prevention of Cruelty to Children (NSPCC) xv, 22, 26, 194, 234, 249, 302, 303, 378
   Centenary Appeal 49, 52, 59, 172, 182, 201, 203, 375
National Society of Fundraising Executives (NSFRE) 226, 426
National Trust 249
National Westminster Bank 152
NCVO *see* National Council for Voluntary Organizations
newsletters, appeal 189
newspapers *see* press *and under named newspapers*
Nicholas, Paul 13
Nichols, Geoffrey 225
Nicol, Sylvia 52
Nicoli, Éric 80, 240, 292
Non-profit Organizations Course 106
Norden, Joyce xv
Norman, Matthew 15
Northern Ireland
   charity enquiries 44
   charity registrations 94
   public collections legislation 418
Northern Ireland Council for Voluntary Action 426
NSFRE *see* National Society of Fundraising Executives
NSPCC *see* National Society for the Prevention of Cruelty to Children
Nuffield Hospital 42
nurses *16, 34, 281, 325, 344*

O'Connor, Hazel 13, *14*
offices, appeal 103-4, 162
   closing 326-7;
   see also administration
Ogilvy-Mather Direct 199
Older, Sarah 15
Open University 106
Operation Jingle Bear 213, 241, *242*
O'Reilly, Terence 13
Osborne, Doreen xv

overheads *see* administration costs
overseas *see* international
Owen, Debbie 288
Oxfam 231
Oxford University 21, 327

Page, Jacqueline xv
Palliser, Sir Michael 224, 225, 226
Palumbo, Lord 60
pancake tossing *293*
parachute jumps *16*, 273
Parker, David 292
Pasteur, Louis 8
Paterson, John 167, 336
patronage *see* Royal Family
Payne, Diana xiv
payroll 121
    software 116
Pearce, Frank 80
Pegram, Giles xv, 22, 26, 59, 375
Penguin Swimathon 13, **244, 245, 274**, 276,
    294
Penny, Jo 15
Per Cent Club 152, 298
Perry, Mrs S.M. 351
personal contact management software 116
personnel
    policies 107-8
    records software 116;
    see also staff
phases of appeals *see* research; launching;
    private appeals; public appeals *and*
    aftermath
photocalls 183
photograph libraries 186
Pims UK Ltd 179
planning *see* buildings; future planning;
    strategy *and* timing
plaques *see* naming opportunities
plays 265
police 12, 73, 213, 325, 335
Post Office 116
    PAF ROM compact disk 117
postal responses 314
postcodes 115, 116, 117
posters 80, 197, **324**
PR Planner 179; *see also* public relations
preliminary reports 31-40
preparation for appeals 21-123
press
    conferences 183, 187, 322
    coverage 166, 177
    local press 335
    releases 183, 185
    rota 263-4
    scanning 43, 45, 160
Priestley, J.B. 11, 48
Princes and Princesses of Wales *see under*
    Christian names
Prince's Youth Business Trust 15, 73, 149

Prior, Lord xii, 12, 15, *16*, 17, 23, 63, 64, 69, 71,
    72, 94, 144, 189, 201, 207, 209, 211, 225, 303,
    322, *323*, 324
private appeals 60, 69, **127-162**
    administration and personnel 158-62
    business appeals 148-57
    fund-raising techniques 392
    major donors 136-47
    marketing 131-5
product sponsorship 246, 248
professional advice *see* consultants *and* project
    advisors
Professional Fundraising (magazine) 5
professionalism xi, xviii, 57, 106, 251, 379, 381
progress reports 134
project advisors 74
project management 37
    software 117
public appeals 165-328
    administration 312-20
    advertising 191-9
    announcement of achievement 321-8
    commercial partnerships 236-51
    company giving 290-9
    events 252-82
    international appeals 219-27
    marketing 169-75
    national organizations 210-18
    other fund-raising methods **300-11**, 393
    publicity planning 176-90
    publishing 283-9
    regional groups 200-9
    trading 228-35
public relations 183-6, 189; *see also* consultants
publicity 176-90
    adverse 189
    local appeals 340
    timing 60, 69, 134-5
    vetting 74;
    see also advertising; press; radio *and* televi-
    sion coverage
publishing 283-9
Punch illustration *10*
Punter, Jean 99, 298

Queen Elizabeth Foundation for the Disabled
    42
Queen Elizabeth Hospital for Children 11-12
questions from donors 28-9
quizzes *see* Company of the Year Quiz

radio
    coverage 182-3, 213;
    see also under named radio stations
Raising Money from Trusts 44
Ram, Ed 80
Rank Hovis McDougall 154
Rank Organization 149, 194
REACH *see* Retired Executives' Clearing
    House

Read, Isobel xiv
recession 4, 47
recruitment *see* staff appointment *and under named recruitment agencies*
Red Nose Days 182
regional fund-raising (integration) 120
regional groups 167, 200-9
Relationship Fundraising 77, 311
Report on Volunteering 65
research 41-50
  companies 44-5, 290
  donors 42, 220-2
  government and statutory bodies 45-6
  international appeals 219-22
  preliminary 27-40
  smaller appeals 332-5
residents' associations 335
results of appeal
  announcement 321-8
  reviewing 365-8
Retired Executives' Clearing House (REACH) 109, 426
Reynolds, Sir Peter 154
Richard, Cliff 15, 17, **274-5**, 276
Rifkind, Malcolm 347
Rippon, Angela 294
Robertson, Liz 241
Rockefeller Foundation 222
Rockley, Lord 149
Ronald Pearce Associates 348
Rotary clubs 12, 211, 305
Round Table 211
Rowe, Sir Thomas 7
Royal Air Force Gatow 213, 325
Royal Ascot 274
Royal Family
  Palace procedures 262-4
  patronage of appeals 9, 11, 71
  see also members of Royal Family by Christian name
Royal Gala Variety Performance 276, 278
Royal Hospital for Sick Children, Edinburgh 5, 149, 371-4; *see also* Sick Kids Appeal
Royal Institute for International Affairs *see* Chatham House
Royal Marsden Hospital Cancer Appeal 5, 149, **369-71**
  logo *368*
Royal National Lifeboat Institute 249
Royal Opera House, Covent Garden 272, 274
Royal Society for Nature Conservation (RSNC) Wildlife Trusts 249
Royal Society for the Prevention of Cruelty to Animals (RSPCA) 194
runs, sponsored *see Chariots of Fire* run *and* London Marathon
Russell, Sally xiv
Rusted, Philip xv, 256

Sackville-West, Vita 11
Sadler, Philip xv
Sail, Lawrence 287
Sainsbury, Jean 147
Sala, George Augustus 148
Salmon, John xv, 80, **82, 83**, 196
Samaritans 25
Samuel Montagu 225
Samuels, Reg 206
Samuelson, Michael 146-7, 256
Samuelson Lighting 256
Samways-Marshall, Laura *323*, 324
Save the Children Fund 83, 209, 240, 274, 292
Savile, Sir Jimmy 52
scanner appeals 21
Scarlet, Iain 57
School of Nursing 9, 11
schools 73, 210, 335
  fund-raising in 215-17;
  see also City of London School for Girls *and* George Watson's College
Scicon 110
Scotland
  charity enquiries 44
  charity registrations 94
  public collections legislation 418;
  see also Bank of Scotland; George Watson's College *and* Royal Hospital for Sick Children, Edinburgh
Scottish clubs 373
Scottish Council for Voluntary Organizations 426
Second Sea Lord 211
secondees and secondments **110**, 153, 297-8
seed money 24, 88, 98, 255
Servite Houses Charitable Trust xiv
Shaftesbury, Lord 9, 382
SHARE *see* Support Help and Relief Extended
shops 230-3
  insurance 122
Sick Kids Appeal 5, 179, **372-4**
  logo *372*;
  see also Royal Hospital for Sick Children, Edinburgh
Skips 15, 292
Sky Sites 80
slims, sponsored 15
slogans 83
smaller appeals 331-44
  case histories 345-62
  computer systems 111
  fund-raising methods 341-2
  leadership 335-6
  publicity 340
  research 332-5
  strategy 336-8
  structure 338
  timing 340
smaller charities 249
Smee & Ford 311

societies *see* associations, clubs and societies
Soldier (magazine) 211
SORP2 *see* Statement of Recommended
    Practice on Accounting by Charities
Southwood, Lord 11
spacing between appeals 48
Spastics Society 272
special events *see* events
speech notes 186-7
sponsorship of events 260-2
Sport Aid 269
sporting contests 265
Spratt, Sir Greville 280
St Bartholomew's Medical Research Centre
    Appeal 41
St John Ambulance Brigade 83
St Mary Abbots Geriatric Day Hospital,
    Kensington 38, 166
St Michael's, Highgate, Development
    Programme 358-62
St Michael's Hospice, Basingstoke 354-8
St Thomas's Hospital 274
staff **104-10**, 161
    appointment 55, 63, 64-5, 107
    management 232
    meetings 107
    motivation 106
    payroll 116, 121
    termination of employment 377
    training **105-6**, 113;
    see also fund-raisers; personnel; secondees
        and volunteers
Standard Book Numbers 284
Statement of Recommended Practice on
    Accounting by Charities (SORP2) 101-2,
    408, 411, 412
steering groups 26, 51
Stewart, Alison xv
Stoke Mandeville Hospital Appeal 52
Stone, Jessica *16*, 273
Stoy Hayward 256
strategy of appeals 22, **67-87**, 128, 136-8, 148,
    166-8, 170-4, 176-9, 200-1, 336-7
streakers 17
Street, Nicola 15
structure of appeals 70-3
    legal and fiscal aspects of organization 88-
    102
Sumption, Harold 199
Sun newspaper
    'Dash for Cash' 13, 243
Support Help and Relief Extended (SHARE)
    355
supporters of appeals
    key 33
    known 37;
    see also donors
swims, sponsored 270; *see also* Penguin
    Swimathon
symbols *see* logos

Tadworth Court 12
Tan, Melvyn 208
Tarbuck, Jimmy 13, 188, 278, *col. insert*
Target Group Index 42
targets, appeal 35-7
    exceeded 343, **414-15**
    increased 15, 49
    un-met 36, 90, **414-15**
targets, company 151-2
Tate, Saxon 336
Tate & Lyle 336
Taussig, Debbie *214*
tax and taxation **95-7**, 420
    company donations 298
    lotteries 307
    repayment claims 121;
    see also corporation tax; council tax;
        Customs and Excise; income tax;
        inheritance tax; Inland Revenue *and*
        VAT
tax-efficient giving 144-5, 152-3
telemarketing 303-4
telephones
    Callstream 0898 service 314
    preference services 304
    responses 314
telethons 176, 181-2; *see also* ITV Telethon
television
    coverage 181, 261-2;
    see also under named television companies
tenants' associations 335
tennis matches, sponsored *see* Foster's Classic
    tennis evening
territories of appeals 209
Tesco xiv, **292**, *293*, 367
Thames TV 80
'thank yous' 24, 60, 156, 267, 298-9, 319, 324,
    326, **327-8**
Theatres Act 1968 265
thermometers, appeal 167
Thomas, Andrew xv
timing
    appeals 69-70
    calendar for £10m appeal 395
    events 174
    local appeals 340
    publicity 60, 69, **134-5**
    regional appeals 200-1
Tippet, Sir Anthony xv, 12, 18, 64
townswomen's guilds 210
trademarks *see* logos
Trades Union Congress 211
trading 228-35
training 57, **105-6**, 113, 155, 304
treasurers of appeals 65
Trethowan, Sir Ian 80
Tropical Child Health Unit 224
Trustee Investments Act 1961 100
trustees
    bibliography 420

disqualification 407-8
    insurance 122
trusts, grant-making **43-4**, 136, 158, 222, 421
    approaches to **141-3**
    dormant trusts 334
    researching 334
Tumbletots 210
Turnbull, Sir George 294
Turner Kenneth Brown xv, 86, 88, 232, 237,
    406
Turpin, Dick 280, 282
TVS 13, 256, 261, 274, 278
Two-Ten Communications Ltd 179
Tysoe, James xv, 372, 374

United Biscuits xiv, 80, 208-9, 240, 244, 274,
    292, 294, 367; *see also* Penguin Swimathon
United States of America
    fund-raising 225-6
    hospital support 75
universities 217

'vaccination effect' 60, 69, 127, 130
Variety Club of Great Britain 12, 13, 146, 209,
    241, *271, 272*
VAT 95-6, 114, 230, 237, 248, **401-5**
    special events 266, 401-5;
    see also Customs and Excise
vehicles
    insurance 122
Victoria, Queen 9, 71
videos 186-7
Vincent, Paddy xv, 201, 204, 213, 325
Voluntary But Not Amateur 338
voluntary organizations *see* National Council
    for Voluntary Organizations
Volunteer Centre UK 65, 109, 426
volunteers **108-9**, 232, 305
    management 65
    motivation 381
    thanking 156
    training 155, 304
Volvo 15, 241, 243, *col. insert*

Waldegrave, Jane xv, 253, 267
Waldegrave, William 380, 381
Wales
    charity registrations 94
    public collections legislation 418
Wales Council for Voluntary Action 426
Walker, Roy 292
Waterman, Dennis 260
wealthy individuals 43, 158, 221
    approaches to 141
    researching 334
Weatherill, Lord 203
Webb, Peter 194
Webb Ivory Group 233
The Week's Good Cause (radio appeal) 182-3
Wells, Colonel Lewis 56

Wendy Wools 13, *247*
West, Dr Charles 7, 8, 382
Westminster, Duke of 52
Westminster Abbey 6, 17, 275
Weston, Garry 147
W.H. Smith 15, 80, 284, 288
Whitbread, Fatima *293*
Whyke, Alex and Daniel 15, 17
Wildish, Nigel 88
Williams, David xv, 317
Willow (film) 17, *271*, **272**, 276
wills *see* legacies
Wimpey 336
Wimpy International 243-4
windsurfing *col. insert*
Wisdom, Norman 213
Wishing Well Appeal **6-18**, 381, 382
    achievement announcements 321-6
    administrative costs 25
    advertising 196-8
    Advisory Council 64-5
    Appeal Office 12, 103-4, 326-7
    Appeal Trustees 70-1
    banking 99-100
    bequests 311
    brochures 133
    Business Panels 72, 149
    charitable status 94
    charity shops 317-18
    Cheque Clinics 260
    closure 3, 321-8
    commercial partnerships 240-5
    commercial sponsorship 15
    company employee fund-raising 291-6
    computer systems 110
    corporate gifts 154-5
    covenants 121
    direct mail 302-3
    Director's role 22
    events 254, 275-82
    film premieres 17, *271*, **272**, 276
    fund-raising ideas 208
    gifts in kind 25
    government contribution 15, 146
    house style 82
    In Memoriam scheme 318
    insurance 266-7
    international appeal 17, 223-7
    investment decisions 100
    Kensington Palace receptions 156, 211, 227
    launch 4-5, 6, 187-8, 264
    local groups 341
    logo 12, 13, 15, **82-3**, *85*, 86, 176, **196**, 240,
        247, 323, 324, 325, *366*
    major gifts 146-7, 157, 366
    Marketing Panel 171-2
    media relations 189-90
    medical advisors 74
    merchandise 246, *247*
    name, origin of 84, *85*

objectives 5, 67
organization 38
payroll servicing 121
President 71-2
press queries 189
publicity 178, 179, 180, 181, **196-8**
publishing 286-8
regional appeal 200-9
regional groups 73
relationship with Great Ormond Street
    Hospital 64, 74
results 3, 129-30, 366-8
Royal patronage 71, 262; *see also members of*
    Royal Family by Christian name
slogan 83, *85*
Special Events Panel 73, 256-7
staff 12, 63, 109, 161, 205, **315-17**, *col. insert*
strategy 68, 128
structure 149, 385
success factors 26
support from children and young people
    15, 210

support from national organizations 210-18
    passim
target 15, 36-7, 49
'thank you's' 324, 328, *col. insert*
Thanksgiving Service 6-7, 17-18, 275, **324-6**
trading 232-3
volunteers 12, 317-18, 368
Wishing Well Ball 276
Wolfson Centre 11
Woman's Realm 17, 294
women's institutes 12, 211
Women's Royal Naval Service (WRNS) 12,
    212, 213, 241, 242
word-processing 113
working men's clubs 210, 335
World Wide Fund for Nature 234, 240
WRNS *see* Women's Royal Naval Service

yacht races 282
Young Men's Christian Association (YMCA)
    83
youth clubs 12, 210, 239